Tokyo

West Tokyo & Around p128

Shinjuku & Northwest Tokyo p142

Ueno & Yanesen p170

Kōrakuen & Akihabara p158

Asakusa & Sumida River p184

Marunouchi & Nihombashi p54

Harajuku & Aoyama p116

Shibuya & Setagaya p100

Roppongi & Around p78

Ginza & Tsukiji p66

Ebisu, Meguro & Around p90

Odaiba & Tokyo Bay p198

Rob Goss, Cherise Fong, Todd Fong, Melinda Joe, Kim Kahan, Louise George Kittaka, Manami Okazaki, Winnie Tan

Cherry blossoms, Ueno Park (p172)

CONTENTS

Souvenirs (p73), kokeshi dolls

Yanaka Ginza (p180)

TOKYO
THE JOURNEY BEGINS HERE

If 20-plus years in Tokyo has taught me anything, it's that my adopted home is a city that refuses to fit a simple description. It might look uniform from afar – with its stereotypical crowds and concrete sprawl – but like a *nō* actor Japan's capital wears many masks. On the one hand, traditions endure, yet the city also loves reinvention and modern redevelopment. It can be arty, creative and avant-garde, or stubbornly stuck in its ways. It's hectic but with pockets of calm. In Shinjuku district alone, a short stroll can take you from skyscrapers to ramshackle drinking streets and tranquil gardens to heaving department stores. Two people's Tokyo experience might be entirely different, yet each can be unforgettable. All that makes it both a great place to live and to visit.

Rob Goss

Instagram @robgosswriter

Rob is a multi-award-winning writer from Dartmoor in the UK but has called the east side of Tokyo home for some 20 years. He updated the Harajuku & Aoyama, Ueno & Yanesen and Odaiba & Tokyo Bay chapters.

My favourite experience has always been going for a city walk. Whether it's the retro backstreets of Yanaka or fashionable Omotesandō, it doesn't matter. Tokyo reveals itself more deeply when you slowly take it in on foot – even more so if you are happy to get lost.

One of my passions is exploring waterfalls – and the **Tama** (p140) area of Tokyo is teeming with them. I am particularly fortunate to have easy access to the tranquil, waterfall-filled forests around the village of **Hinohara** (p140; pictured) in Okutama. I can hike to multiple stunning cascades in a day – and still be home in time for supper in my West Tokyo commuter town.

Louise George Kittaka

Instagram @louisegeorgekittaka

Louise is a bilingual writer, university lecturer and cross-cultural consultant. She updated the West Tokyo & Around and Shinjuku & Northwest Tokyo chapters.

Despite being just two hours from Tokyo, **Nikkō** (p214) is a different world – and one I just can't get enough of. You'll want to come with your camera fully charged to capture all of Nikkō's natural beauty, but the majesty of its natural and historical sights is what ends up capturing you – from the roar of Kegon falls, to the awesome beauty of **Tōshō-gū** (pictured).

Winnie Tan

Instagram @weeniemon

Winnie lived in Japan for eight years and has authored Lonely Planet guides on Japan, Tokyo and her hometown, Kuala Lumpur. Winnie updated the Day Trips chapter.

SUSHI, RAMEN & MORE

Kickstart your morning at one of Tokyo's superb independent cafes; warm up on a cold afternoon with a hearty bowl of ramen; or live it up with Buddhist-inspired haute cuisine at some of the world's finest *kaiseki* restaurants: a never-ending array of culinary experiences awaits you. And whatever your budget, you won't struggle to eat and drink well, so work up an appetite and loosen your belt a notch – it's time to eat.

Ramen Like a Local

When it comes to ramen, it's okay to slurp. It helps cool the noodles but also enhances the flavour and aroma.

Culinary Capital

With some 180 Michelin-starred restaurants around the city, you don't have to stray far to try some of the world's best food.

Time for Dessert

Got a sweet tooth? Tokyo's scrumptious desserts, many of which are light, fluffy and buttery, look good and taste even better.

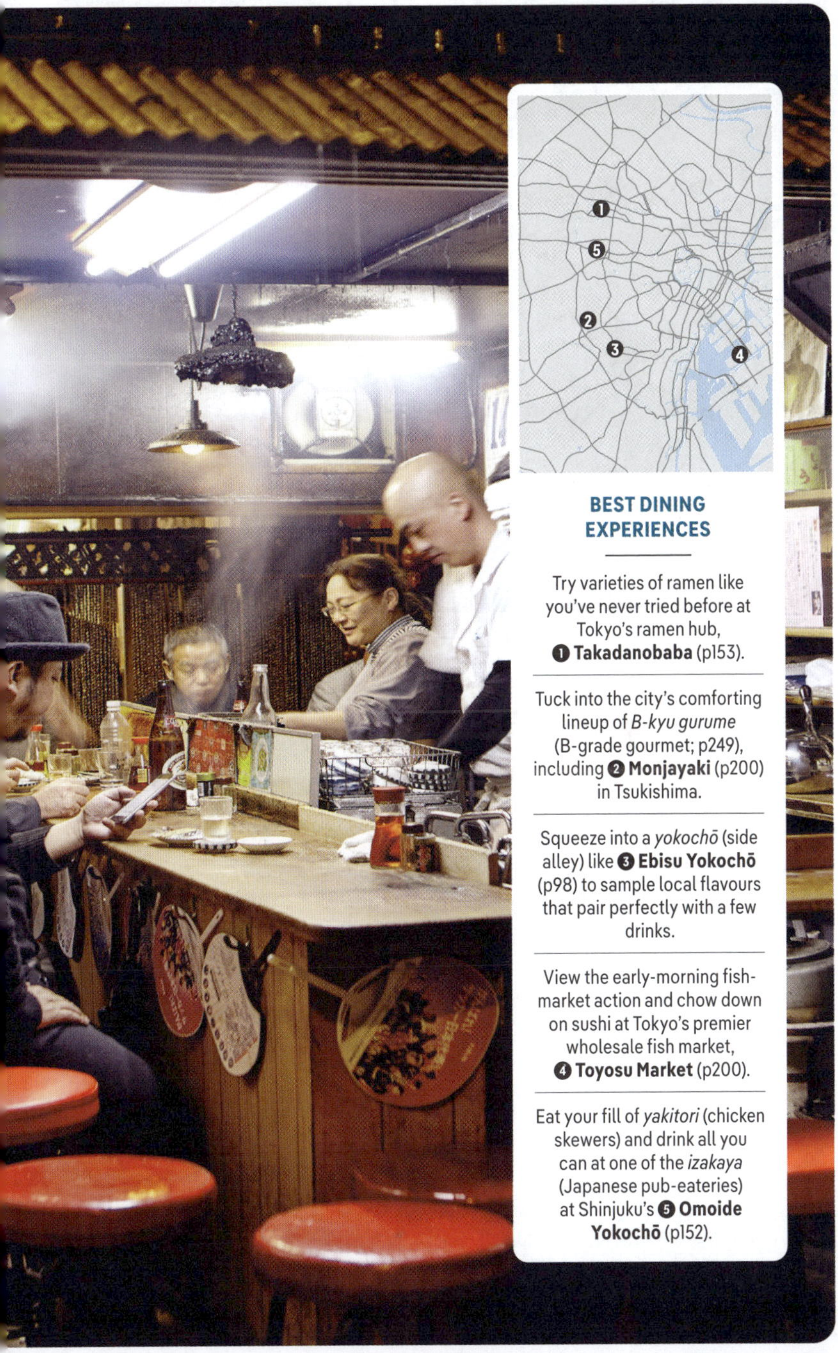

BEST DINING EXPERIENCES

Try varieties of ramen like you've never tried before at Tokyo's ramen hub, ❶ **Takadanobaba** (p153).

Tuck into the city's comforting lineup of *B-kyu gurume* (B-grade gourmet; p249), including ❷ **Monjayaki** (p200) in Tsukishima.

Squeeze into a *yokochō* (side alley) like ❸ **Ebisu Yokochō** (p98) to sample local flavours that pair perfectly with a few drinks.

View the early-morning fish-market action and chow down on sushi at Tokyo's premier wholesale fish market, ❹ **Toyosu Market** (p200).

Eat your fill of *yakitori* (chicken skewers) and drink all you can at one of the *izakaya* (Japanese pub-eateries) at Shinjuku's ❺ **Omoide Yokochō** (p152).

Tokyu Plaza Omotesando Harajuku (p118)

GET INSPIRED

With world-class architecture, immersive art installations and sleek museums dotted around the city, Tokyo is a feast for not just the eyes, but for all the senses. Get lost in the striking urban surroundings, spend quiet afternoons discovering everything from traditional arts and crafts to groundbreaking modern art, and let the city be your muse.

Planning Ahead

Tickets to popular exhibits such as those by teamLab have timed entries and always sell out quickly. Purchase tickets online whenever possible.

Boutiques & Art

Some boutiques around Ginza and Omotesandō, such as Maison Hermés and Espace Louis Vuitton, also house small galleries.

BEST INSPIRING EXPERIENCES

Witness the fusion of traditional and modern art, and beautiful species of goldfish you've never seen before, at ❶ **Art Aquarium** (p75).

Spend an afternoon admiring architecture and visiting the quiet galleries of ❷ **Harajuku and Aoyama** (p116), with exhibits from *ukiyo-e* (woodblock prints) to avant-garde sculpture.

Take a crash course in Japanese traditional art, beginning from the prehistoric period, at the ❸ **Tokyo National Museum** (p176) in Ueno.

Embark on an in-depth, engaging journey at ❹ **teamLab Planets** in Toyosu (p203).

Go off the beaten path and explore lesser-known galleries like ❺ **SCAI the Bathhouse** (p181) in the charming neighbourhoods of Yanesen.

THRIFT & LUXURY

From over-the-top Harajuku fashion and cutting-edge designer brands to beautifully crafted knives and lacquerware in traditional motifs, it's undeniable that Tokyo has impeccable style. Whether you are after luxury goods or that special piece with a storied past, chances are high you'll find it here.

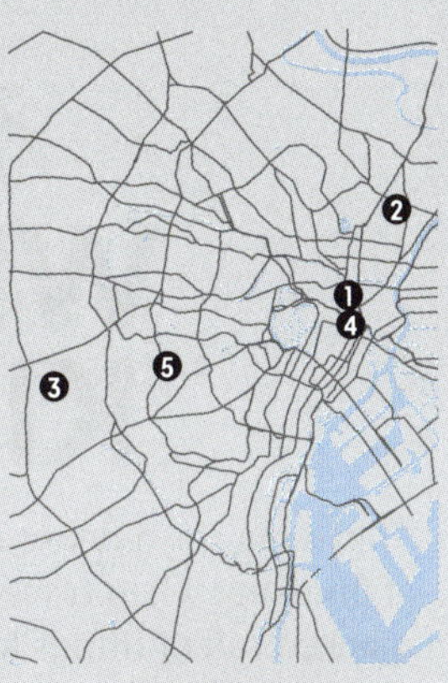

Thrifting Tip

Prices at many curated Tokyo thrift shops are comparable to buying new. For a real bargain, try sifting the shelves at no-frills thrift chain Tanpopo House.

Extra Packaging

Shop attendants will often ask if you need a bag or extra packaging. To refuse them, say *fukuro wa daijoubu desu*.

Shopping Light & Easy

Coin lockers are available at stations to stash purchases you don't want to carry around; they tend to fill up later in the day.

BEST SHOPPING EXPERIENCES

Walk Tokyo's most stylish boulevard and shop for the season's latest luxury styles on Ginza's ❶ **Chūo-dori avenue** (p72).

Try out a handcrafted knife and stock your kitchen with quality cooking tools and gadgets of every kind on ❷ **Kappabashi Street** (p190).

Check out the indie vibe at bohemian boutiques and vinyl stores in hipster hangout ❸ **Shimo-Kitazawa** (p111).

Step into Japan's first department store and enjoy shopping for elegant, handcrafted souvenirs at ❹ **Nihombashi Mitsukoshi** (p63) department store.

Embrace your sense of adventure and get lost among the cool boutiques and stylish cafes in the backstreets of ❺ **Harajuku** (p118).

WITH KIDS

Tokyo may be a dense metropolis that takes a bit of finessing when travelling with children, but it's packed full of things kids can get excited about. Around town, a cute mascot or pop-culture icon is never far away, and there are fun entertainment spaces that offer something for everyone in the family; plus, you'll find abundant food options that will appeal to little ones.

Family Dining

Budget-friendly, and with a universally appealing menu, family restaurants like Saizeriya or Denny's are popular options for larger groups. Many chain restaurants have kids' menus.

Baby Amenities

Restrooms around Tokyo can get cramped – head to department stores for more spacious cubicles. Many are equipped with baby seats, changing tables and other amenities.

Rent a Stroller

Many theme parks and department stores offer rental buggies. Some are free, others may charge a small fee. Ask for a 'baby car' (ベビーカー).

BEST EXPERIENCES FOR KIDS

Snap pictures of Pokémon and check out Tokyo's largest Pokémon Centre at Ikebukuro's ❶ **Sunshine City** (p157).

Hop on fun rides at the indoor/outdoor theme park in ❷ **Tokyo Dome City** (p160).

Check out the aquarium, merchandise shops and other kid-friendly attractions at ❸ **Tokyo Solamachi** (p188), following a trip up Tokyo Skytree.

Take older children and teenagers to arcades for an exciting bout of games, and try out *purikura* photo booths in ❹ **Akihabara** (p164).

Stand under the shadow of the giant Unicorn Gundam statue, then shop and play at ❺ **DiverCity** (p203), a mall and entertainment complex in Odaiba.

TRADITION, SHRINES & SUMO

Despite a reputation for being one of the most high-tech cities in the world, Tokyo's traditional roots run deep. Historic temples and shrines stand exactly where they have for centuries, while *kabuki* (Japanese theatre) and sumo tournaments offer a glimpse into the Edo period, when the shogun still reigned.

Temple or Shrine?

Temples gates are typically more ornate, covered by a sloping roof. Shrines are marked by *torii* entrance gates, which are almost pi-shaped and often red.

Edo Culture

Many of the most recognisable aspects of traditional Japanese culture date from the Edo period (1603–1868). Sumo, *kabuki* and kimono all gained popularity during this time.

Glimpse into the Past

The best places to experience traditional culture are the neighbourhoods surrounding the Sumida River, the locale for Tokyo's oldest temple and sumo wrestling tournaments.

BEST TRADITIONAL EXPERIENCES

Step through the iconic temple gates of Kaminari-mon and visit ❶ **Sensō-ji** (p192), Tokyo's oldest temple, in Asakusa.

Snag tickets to see a highly stylised *kabuki* performance at the city's prime *kabuki* theatre, ❷ **Kabuki-za** (p69), in Ginza.

Take a breather from the crowds of Harajuku and enjoy a stroll to the beautiful shrine of ❸ **Meiji-jingū** (p126).

Travel back in time and see what the city looked like generations ago at the ❹ **Edo-Tokyo Open Air Architectural Museum** (p133).

Witness the strength of the hulking *rikishi* (sumo wrestlers) as they compete at ❺ **Ryōgoku Kokugikan** (p186) in January, May and September.

Golden Gai (p148)

TOKYO BY NIGHT

The scent of charcoal-grilled skewers wafts through narrow alleyways as beer mugs clink, signalling the start of a lively evening. Elsewhere, revellers squeeze into tiny bars under neon lights while the hip young crowd works up a buzz before ducking into nightclubs. This is Tokyo at night – vibrant, fun, unforgettable.

Say Cheers!

You'll hear this wherever you go drinking; so do as the locals and say 'Kanpai!' – it's the Japanese word for 'cheers'.

Staying Safe

Tokyo is one of the safest cities in the world, but stay alert. Be wary of bars with touts – these often overcharge – and take safety precautions as you would at home.

BEST NIGHTLIFE EXPERIENCES

Slip into one of the tiny, themed bars at Shinjuku's ❶ **Golden Gai** (p148).

Let loose at your club of choice in Roppongi, like ❷ **1Oak** or ❷ **Cube** (p89), or chill with a late-night smoke at a shisha parlour.

Have a relaxing night out trying local fare, then visit some of the stylish cocktail bars and speakeasies in Ebisu, such as ❸ **Bar Trench** (p92).

Hop on a traditional ❹ **yakatabune** boat (p202) for a dinner cruise with a side serving of bayside night views.

Embrace your inner diva with an evening belting out songs at a ❺ **karaoke** joint (p43).

POP-CULTURE SENSATIONS

If you love pop culture, Japan's capital is your playground. Pose in front of a giant Gundam statue, collect your favourite Pokémon or come face-to-face with Totoro – you'll spot the characters you know and love all around the city. And if you don't have a favourite yet, the city will soon help you find one.

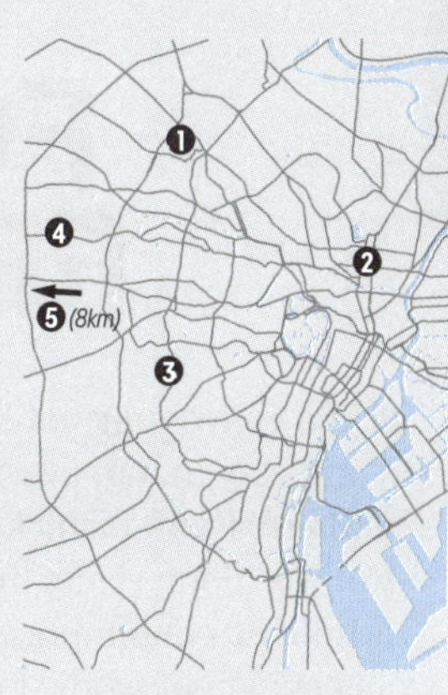

Cuteness Overload

Japan has a mascot for everything, and that's not an exaggeration. Everywhere from prefectures down to neighbourhoods have their own mascot, called *yurukyara*.

Getting the Goods

Most shops selling anime and manga merchandise are in Akihabara (p165; pictured) and Ikebukuro (p157). An outlier is Nakano Broadway, with its mish-mash of comics and merchandise.

Where Anime Comes to Life

The birthplace of Japanese anime is actually in Nerima City (p130), in the West Tokyo suburbs, where many animation studios are still located.

BEST POP-CULTURE EXPERIENCES

Find anime and manga products, and encounter your favourite Pokémon, in kid-friendly ❶ **Ikebukuro** (p157).

Try your luck (and claw-machine skills) at the arcades, and get immersed in the world of anime in ❷ **Akihabara** (p165).

See what new, vibrant styles the Harajuku youths are wearing on ❸ **Takeshita-dori** (p118), and maybe even do some experimenting yourself.

Sift through the cool collectible shops of ❹ **Nakano Broadway** (p130) for vintage memorabilia, old manga and so much more.

Learn all about the history and makings of anime at the ❺ **Ghibli Museum** (p134) in West Tokyo.

FOR FREE

While Tokyo may not be the cheapest city to travel to and stay in, not everything is expensive once you get here. From picnicking in lush public parks and strolling along rivers lined with cherry blossoms, to admiring contemporary art at indie galleries and checking out iconic locations, there are plenty of activities that won't cost you a single yen.

Art for Free

Many galleries don't charge a fee, including **Design Festa** (p123) in Harajuku and **Shiseido Gallery** (p74; pictured) in Ginza.

Neighbourhood Parks

Historical gardens generally cost a small entry fee (¥300 to ¥500), but many of the major parks are free, including **Yoyogi** (p125), **Inokashira** (p134; pictured) and **Ueno** (p170).

City Views

Get a bird's-eye view of the city from free observation decks. The Shinjuku Metropolitan Government Building deck is open daily from 9.30am to 10pm.

BEST FREE EXPERIENCES

Explore the sprawling grounds of ❶ **Ueno Park** (p172) and check out the shrines, sculptures and seasonal sights dotted around the area.

Enjoy a slow stroll along the ❷ **Meguro Riverside** (p97), and maybe sneak in some window shopping.

Sign up for a ❸ **free guided tour** run by English-speaking volunteers. The Japan National Tourism Organization (JNTO) has an online list of tours (p33).

Peek at gem stones, taxidermy, plant and animal specimens, and more, at ❹ **Intermediatheque** (p63).

Join the numerous lively festivals that take place throughout the year at Tokyo's largest and oldest temple, ❺ **Sensō-ji** (p192).

UNDER THE RADAR

One of the first things you'll notice about central Tokyo is the endlessly bustling crowds, seemingly at all hours of the day and night. Major hubs and tourist sites, like Shibuya and Asakusa, get plenty of traffic from both locals and visitors, but head just a short distance away and you'll stumble upon charming neighbourhoods that may not have the same glitzy or lively allure, but will have plenty to offer the discerning tourist.

Off the Beaten Track

Tokyo's dense, sprawling nature means there are plenty of hidden backstreet spots to be explored, even in areas like Harajuku (p116).

Everyday Tokyo

Witness slices of everyday life by going neighbourhood-hopping on the Sōbu line, west of Shinjuku – each neighbourhood has its own distinct character.

Walk the City

Opt to walk from one neighbourhood to another instead of taking the train, and see what wonders you discover along the way.

BEST UNDER THE RADAR EXPERIENCES

Wander the maze-like streets of ❶ **Shimo-Kitazawa** (p111) for atmospheric cafes and artistic hideaways.

Escape the shadow of skyscrapers and go trawling for old and secondhand books in ❷ **Jimbōchō** (p166).

Go on an exciting treasure hunt for artisanal crafts and coffee in ❸ **Kuramae** (p195).

Step into peaceful temples and wander the meandering backstreets in the charming suburbs of ❹ **Yanesen** (p170).

Ride one of Tokyo's last trams to explore the suburbs of ❺ **Setagaya** (p100), and add in a cafe stop or two.

URBAN OASES

Forget Tokyo's reputation for being just a vast urban sprawl – even in the city centre you'll find time-honoured gardens, rambling parks and picturesque spots for a picnic. Out west, you can go hiking in the wilds or try activities like white-water rafting, and then there are all the scenic day trip destinations just beyond the city. Yes, Tokyo is a modern metropolis, but natural respite is never far away.

Seasonal Sights

Some parts of the capital come into their own as the seasons change, including the autumnal colours at **Rikugi-en** (p183) and the spring cherry blossoms of **Ueno Park** (p172; pictured).

Go West

With mountains, forests and rivers, the **Tama** (p140; pictured) region is a great place get close to nature – it's only an hour from the centre.

Park Life

Unwind in **Yoyogi Park** (p125), **Inokashira Park** (p134) or one of the many other green spaces in the city. They're great for people-watching too.

BEST URBAN ESCAPES

Take in the spring cherry blossoms, or get some year-round respite from the urban sprawl, at ❶ **Shinjuku Gyoen** (p144)

Stroll the landscaped grounds of ❷ **Koishikawa Kōrakuen** (p160), a 400-year-old garden.

Stop for tea and sweets at ❸ **Hama-Rikyū**'s teahouse (p68), then enjoy the contrast of traditional landscaping against a backdrop of skyscrapers.

Escape the hustle and bustle of the city and go hiking up scenic ❹ **Takao-san** (p140) on the outskirts of Tokyo.

Have a night away from the city with a visit to ❺ **Hakone** (p208) for up-close Mt Fuji views and soothing hot springs.

Perfect Days

To see the very best of Tokyo's many sights, sounds and smells, we've created some itineraries that will have you hitting the ground running.

Kaminari-mon, Sensō-ji (p192)

RINTARO KANEMOTO/FOR LONELY PLANET

DAY 1

Asakusa & Sumida River

☀ Start your day in Asakusa at **Sensō-ji** (p192) – step through the iconic Kaminari-mon and proceed to the temple's grand Kannon-dō to pay respects at the altar and draw a quick *omikuji* (paper fortune). Afterwards, walk over to **Kappabashi** (p190) to pick up something for your kitchen – in the stores here you'll find everything from handcrafted knives to kitchen gadgets.

Lunch Back in Asakusa, get a bowl of *ten-don* (rice topped with tempura shrimp and vegetables) at **Dote no Iseya** (p186).

Ueno & Yanesen

☀ Head over to Ueno for a spot of museum-hopping in **Ueno Park** (p172). With a vast collection of Japanese art and artefacts, **Tokyo National Museum** (p176) is the standout of the park's museums, although the **Shitamachi Museum** (p172) is also worth a look for insights into the capital's past.

Dinner Fill up on *tonkatsu* (breaded, deep-fried pork cutlet) at **Isen Honten** (p173).

Ueno & Yanesen

☾ Check out the park's shrines and temples (p173), then have a stroll along **Ameya-yokochō** (p179) for end-of-day deals. Finish with a drink at **Cocktail Works** (p180) or **Bar Bookshelff** (p180).

DAY 2

Harajuku & Aoyama

☀ Begin your morning the mellow way with a stroll through the peaceful grounds of **Meiji-jingū** shrine (p126), and then enjoy some people-watching in **Yoyogi Park** (p125). If you need a mid-morning caffeine fix, stop by **Little Nap Coffee Stand** (p123).

Lunch Close to Harajuku Station, slurp up a bowl of ramen at **Kyūshū Jangara** (p119), which serves up thin noodles in a rich *tonkotsu* broth, but also offers a vegan ramen.

Harajuku & Aoyama

☀ Browse cool shops and art galleries like **Design Festa** (p123) and **Space Banksia** (p125) in the backstreets of Harajuku, before checking out the fashion houses and architecture along **Omotesandō-dōri** (p118). Afterwards, head into Aoyama for art at the vibrant **Nezu Museum** (p119) or the **Taro Okamoto Memorial Museum** (p122).

Dinner Cook up your own savoury *okonomiyaki* pancakes at art-covered **Sakura-tei** (p119).

Shibuya & Setagaya

☾ To end your day, head into Shibuya for all sorts of nightlife options. For a few drinks, go bar-hunting in **Nonbei Yokochō** (p102), then find a karaoke bar to embrace your inner diva or dance until sunrise at **Womb** (p102).

DAY 3

Marunouchi & Nihombashi

☀ Take a morning walk as part of the **Imperial Palace Tour** (p60) and venture into exclusive areas of the royal compound. If open, proceed to the **East Gardens** (p60) after the tour for a serene meander around the ruins of the former Edo castle.

Lunch Try one of the area's long-established restaurants, such as **Momijigawa** (p62) for soba noodles or **Janoichi** (p62) for sushi.

Kōrakuen & Akihabara

☀ Rummage through shelves of old books at **Jimbōchō** (p166), a neighbourhood known for its secondhand bookstores. Then sidle into a *kissaten* (coffee shop) for a bitter brew or cream soda (melon soda topped with a scoop of ice cream).

Dinner Dig into a hearty plate of Japanese curry at **Bondy** (p169).

Kōrakuen & Akihabara

☾ Explore Tokyo's *otaku* (geek) haven, starting with **Akihabara Radio Kaikan** (p165) for all things anime and hobby-related; then proceed to **Mandarake Complex** (p165) to browse the vintage manga selection. Stop by some **arcades** (p164) for a bit of fun in between, before ending the night with a drink and some retro gaming at **Game Bar A-Button** (p162).

WHEN TO GO

Tokyo is most beautiful in spring and autumn, while summer and winter are best for experiencing seasonal events.

Japan's capital is almost always packed, but certain times of the year can see crowds grow to epic proportions. Peak travel season is between late March and early April, when travellers from across the globe come to see the cherry blossoms, and booking accommodation months in advance is required. In summer, the many festivals make excellent highlights on any trip, but avoid August, when Tokyo's notorious heat and humidity make even short outdoor activities near-unbearable. As autumn rolls around, cool weather and fewer tourists make it the perfect time for long walks and city explorations. Winter is ushered in with dreamy fairy lights strung all around, and while Christmas is not a major holiday, there's plenty to do in the days leading up to New Year's Eve, when everything quietens down as Tokyoites leave for their hometowns.

⊛ I LIVE HERE

TOKYO FLAVOURS

Riley Masunaga is a Japanese–American working in Tokyo who likes to host events in his free time. @rileymasu

Something I always look forward to with the changing seasons is for the bakeries and *konbini* (convenience stores) in Tokyo to drop their seasonal treats, from sweet honeydew frappuccinos in summer to earthy chestnut crepes in autumn. As the leaves start to change and fall, these treats go out of rotation; so go all out and indulge while you're here – stop at every *konbini*, bakery or creamery that strikes your fancy.

GOLDEN WEEK

The week-long period lasting from late April to early May is marked by public holidays – known as Golden Week, this is peak travel season for locals. Expect inflated prices for flights and accommodation.

FROM LEFT: DOCTOR EGG/GETTY IMAGES, TANG YAN SONG/SHUTTERSTOCK

Sakura trees in Spring, Meguro Riverside (p97)

Weather through the Year

	JANUARY	FEBRUARY	MARCH	APRIL	MAY	JUNE
Avg. daytime max:	**12°C**	**12°C**	**16°C**	**21°C**	**24°C**	**28°C**
Days of rainfall:	**3**	**5**	**8**	**9**	**8**	**11**

STAYING DRY

Tokyo experiences sporadic rain showers from late May to late July, so it's a good idea to pack a small umbrella. Typhoons commonly occur in September and can disrupt public transport – heed weather warnings and stay inside.

Classic Festivals

For **Tanabata** (p197), bamboo sprigs adorned with bits of paper pop up around the city and colourful streamers line Kappabashi Street to celebrate the annual meeting of deities Orihime and Hikoboshi. **July**

Setsubun (p197) celebrates the coming of spring and ushers in good luck while banishing demons with a bean-throwing *mamemaki* ceremony. Witness this at Asakusa's Sensō-ji, or try an *ehōmaki* – a *maki* roll eaten while facing the year's 'lucky' direction. **February**

Platforms pop up around squares in summer for **Obon**, a festival which honours the ancestors. Join *yukata*-clad dancers in a traditional dance accompanied by drums and song. **August**

Snag a *kumade* – a decorative rake that symbolises 'raking in' luck and fortune – during **Tori no Ichi**. The festivities held at Sensō-ji in Asakusa are the largest. **November**

CITY STROLLS

Laura Pollacco is a British–Maltese photo-journalist and actor living in Tokyo. @laurapollacco

Tokyo is the kind of city you can just wander around and take joy in both the big and the small. In Shinjuku, just staring up at all the tall buildings with lights and screens brings a smile to my face, so too do the quieter suburban streets where kids play outside or elderly residents tend to their plants. There is something oddly nostalgic about this city, despite not having grown up here; like there's a story to be told around every corner.

Sanja Matsuri (p197)

Tokyo's Spirit

Join the fun at **Tokyo Pride** – the country's largest LGBTIQ+ festival, taking place around Yoyogi Park, with a parade that makes its way around Harajuku and Shibuya. **June**

The streets of Ikebukuro come alive with spirited performers putting on a show of folk dances at **Tokyo Yosakoi** – expect colourful outfits, energetic chanting and rhythmic dancing that will have you itching to join. **October**

The **Sanja Matsuri** (p197) is a boisterous affair, with volunteers and crowds moving through the streets of Asakusa with a portable shrine, called a *mikoshi*, hoisted upon their shoulders. **May**

Tokyo's summers might sizzle, but it doesn't stop festival-goers from flocking to the hottest music festivals. Local and international artists share the stages at **Summer Sonic** and **Ultra Japan**. **August, September**

SURVIVING SUMMER

Temperatures can approach 40°C (104°F) in summer, and the heat is only worsened by the humidity. Heatstroke is a common hazard, but luckily in Tokyo, air-conditioning and a cold isotonic drink are often within reach.

	JULY	AUGUST	SEPTEMBER	OCTOBER	NOVEMBER	DECEMBER
Avg. daytime max:	**34°C**	**34°C**	**31°C**	**25°C**	**18°C**	**13°C**
Days of rainfall:	**10**	**8**	**12**	**8**	**6**	**3**

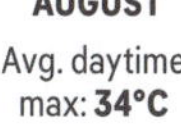

Summer in Tokyo

GET PREPARED FOR TOKYO

Useful things to load in your bag, your ears and your brain

Clothes

Jackets & scarves You'll want to have a selection of outerwear that you can layer up during spring and autumn – it's nice and temperate during the day, but temperatures can dip at night. For winter, have a windbreaker handy and bring a down jacket that's not too bulky. It rarely snows in Tokyo, but winds can bring a biting chill, so it's best to layer up.

Sweat-wicking clothing Expect to sweat a lot in summer, and know that the sweat will stick due to Tokyo's high humidity. Bring light, sweat-wicking clothes and have a pocket fan stashed in your bag, too, in case the heat gets unbearable.

Manners

Keep voices low when on public transport and know that talking on the phone in public is generally frowned upon.

Ride the escalator on the left and leave the right side open for people who might want to keep moving.

Hold on to your litter, general waste bins are rare; recycling bins can often be found next to vending machines or inside convenience stores.

Hats Covering your head is essential when out and about in summer – heatstroke is a real threat, especially in July and August.

📖 READ

Norwegian Wood (Haruki Murakami; 1987) Visit 1960s' Tokyo in this coming-of-age story that was Murakami's first novel to garner international recognition.

I Am a Cat (Natsume Sōseki; 1906) See Tokyo society in the Meiji era through a cat's eyes in this long-enduring work.

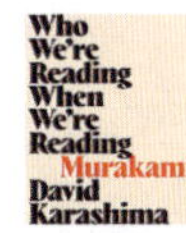

Who We're Reading When We're Reading Murakami (David Karashima; 2020) Discover those involved in bringing Murakami's novels to the international market.

Breasts and Eggs (Mieko Kawakami; 2008) Kawakami's work explores the relationship between women and their bodies in contemporary Japan.

Words

Konnichiwa means 'Hello'.
Arigatō gozaimasu is the most polite way to say 'Thank you'. There are shorter variants of the expression, such as *'dōmo'* or *'arigatō'*, but these are considered less polite.
Onegai shimasu can be useful when asking for something, the same way you would use 'Please'. For example, if you'd like a spoon, say *'Supūn, onegai shimasu'* (A spoon, please).
Sumimasen is used interchangeably as 'Sorry' or 'Excuse me', and can be used to get someone's attention.
Okaikei, onegai shimasu is how you ask for the bill when dining at a restaurant.
Betsu-betsu de means to split the bill. Some restaurants, but not all, will allow each customer in a group to pay separately.

Tennai de is what you say when you'd like to dine in – useful at fast-food restaurants.
Mochikaeri de is to take away.
Ōmori means a larger portion, and you can often use this phrase at ramen restaurants to ask for extra noodles.
Namimori means a small (or regular) portion, also used at ramen restaurants for when you just want a standard serving.
Nama bīru or **nama** is a word you'll hear a lot at an *izakaya* (Japanese pub-eatery) and means 'freshly poured beer'.
Eigo hanasemasu ka? is used if you require assistance in English and want to know if the other party speaks the language. In a pinch, sometimes 'Eigo?' will suffice.

🎬 WATCH

Suzume (Makoto Shinkai; 2022; pictured) This anime follows Suzume as she travels across Japan in a quest to stop the next big disaster.

From Up on Poppy Hill (Gorō Miyazaki; 2011) 1960s' Yokohama depicted in signature Studio Ghibli fashion in this coming-of-age film.

Naked Director (Masaharu Take; 2019) Semi-biographical TV series depicting the life of adult video director Toru Muranishi.

Drive My Car (Ryusuke Hamaguchi; 2021) A Golden Globe–winning film based on the short story by Haruki Murakami.

Midnight Diner (Joji Matsuoka; 2009) Sidle into this cosy eatery with an eclectic cast, all with their own unique stories.

🎧 LISTEN

Love All Serve All (Fujii Kaze; 2022) An album full of catchy tunes to dance to by a talented singer-songwriter.

E-Side 3 (Yoasobi; 2024) Japan's biggest J-Pop duo sing English versions of their own Japanese hits.

Cycle Hit 1991–1997 (Spitz; 2006) A compilation of classics from the 1990s from one of Japan's most prominent pop bands.

Abroad in Japan Hear about current events, travel experiences and all things Japan on this comprehensive podcast.

Haneda Airport

GETTING THERE

Tokyo is an incredibly well-connected city. Narita Airport, 70km east of the centre, operates more than 100 international routes, and more than 50 serve Haneda Airport, 20km south of the capital. From both, there are frequent bus and rail connections (some requiring a transfer) to central Tokyo locations.

Visas

Tourists and business travellers from 71 countries, including Australia, Canada, New Zealand, the UK and the US, can receive a free 90-day Temporary Visitor Visa upon arrival. Other nationalities need to arrange visas beforehand. For more information, check the website of the Ministry of Foreign Affairs of Japan *(mofa.go.jp)*.

Luggage

Trains and buses from Narita Airport and buses from Haneda Airport have good storage spaces for luggage, but if you'd rather not drag cases around, you could also have your luggage forwarded. The companies JAL-ABC *(jalabc.com/en)* and Yamato *(kuronekoyamato.co.jp/ytc/en)* offer luggage-forwarding services and storage at Narita and Haneda airports. Same-day delivery is often possible to hotels in Tokyo.

Currency

International terminals at Narita and Haneda airports have multiple currency-exchange counters. There are also ATMs that accept international cards, with Seven Bank being one of them.

Wi-Fi & SIM

Free wi-fi is available at Narita and Haneda. At both airports, you can also rent mobile wi-fi routers and buy SIM cards for your time in Japan. Another option is to set up an e-SIM service before travelling and then just activate it upon arrival.

FROM AIRPORTS TO THE CITY CENTRE

From Haneda Airport

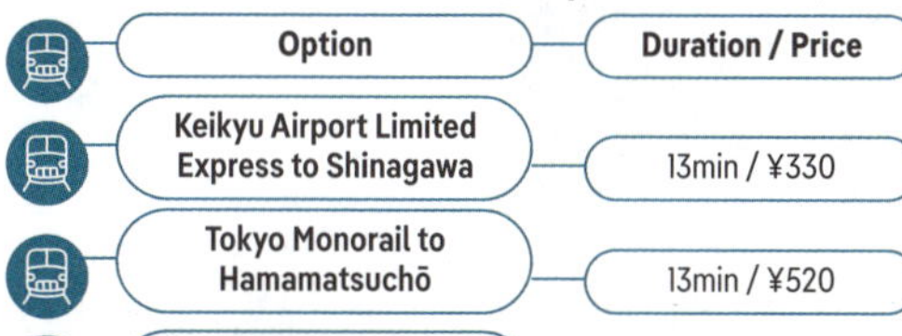

Option	Duration / Price
Keikyu Airport Limited Express to Shinagawa	13min / ¥330
Tokyo Monorail to Hamamatsuchō	13min / ¥520
Limousine Bus to Shinjuku, Shibuya	from 50min / from ¥1300

From Narita Airport

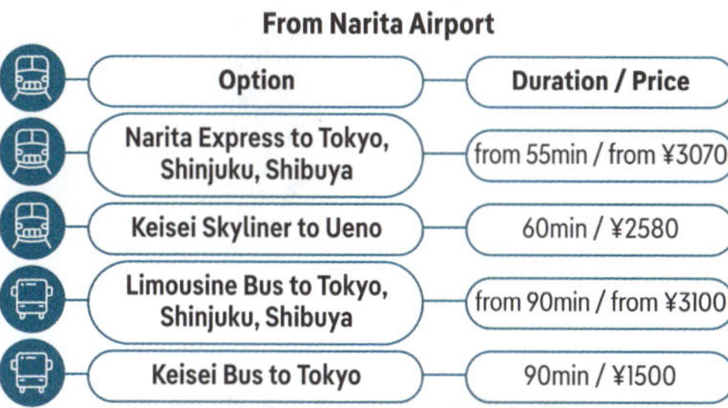

Option	Duration / Price
Narita Express to Tokyo, Shinjuku, Shibuya	from 55min / from ¥3070
Keisei Skyliner to Ueno	60min / ¥2580
Limousine Bus to Tokyo, Shinjuku, Shibuya	from 90min / from ¥3100
Keisei Bus to Tokyo	90min / ¥1500

700 Series Shinkansen bullet train

TIP

From Haneda Airport, the rail options go to Shinagawa or Hamamatsuchō stations. At both, you can transfer to the Yamanote loop line, which serves Tokyo, Shinjuku, Shibuya, Ueno and other major stations. Just be aware that it gets busy and isn't easy during peak hours with large luggage.

OTHER POINTS OF ENTRY

Rail

High-speed shinkansen (bullet trains) connect Tokyo to many other major cities, including Osaka, Kyoto and Hiroshima to the west, Kanazawa on the Sea of Japan coast, and Sendai, Morioka and Aomori in Tōhoku. If you are travelling extensively outside Tokyo, look into national and regional rail passes. JR East lists a selection at *jreast.co.jp*.

Bus

If time isn't an issue, long-distance buses are a cheaper way of getting between Tokyo and other parts of the country – whether a night bus from Kyoto or an early-morning departure to Mt Fuji – and there are numerous services from Tokyo Station, Shinjuku and Shibuya. Two useful websites for routes and tickets are *highway-buses.jp* and *willer-travel.com/en*.

Domestic Flights

Both Haneda and Narita airports offer numerous domestic flights that fan out across the country, from Hokkaido up north to Okinawa down south. Prices tend to be on the high side, but some routes now have low-cost carriers, such as Air Do, Jetstar Japan, Peach and Solaseed, offering great deals.

Shibuya station

GETTING AROUND

Tokyo may be one of the biggest and busiest cities on the planet, but with a far-ranging, efficient and clean public transportation network, the capital and its surrounds are easy to explore.

Subway

Operating from roughly 5.30am to midnight, the Tokyo Metro's nine subway lines have most of the capital's centre covered. The Ginza line is an especially handy option, with stops including Shibuya, Omotesandō, Ginza, Ueno and Asakusa. Another you might find yourself using a lot is the Marunouchi line, which runs through Ikebukuro, Shinjuku, Tokyo and Ginza, among other places. Complementing the Metro are several Toei subway lines, run by a different organisation but frequently connecting to the numerous Metro stations.

Train

Like the Metro, the five major Japan Railway (JR) lines in central Tokyo run from around 5.30am to midnight – they can be a crush in the morning and evening rush hours. The most useful is the JR Yamanote loop, which stops at Shinjuku, Shibuya, Ueno and Tokyo. To make using the train (and subway) easier to navigate, use a rechargeable Pasmo or Suica IC pass. They work on all train and subway lines in the city, as well as many buses, and they can also be used for shopping in convenience stores and supermarkets. Just tap them on the ticket scanners

TIP

Try and plan your day to avoid the rush-hour crush. 7.30am to 9.30am is especially busy on trains and subways, and getting on a packed commuter train with luggage can be extremely difficult.

to use. You can buy a Pasmo or Suica IC at Narita and Haneda airports, as well as ticket counters in stations.

Walking

Tokyo is a relatively safe city to explore on foot. If you like walking, it's easy to combine neighbourhoods like Yanaka, Ueno and Asakusa, or Tsukiji, Ginza and Nihombashi to make a good city saunter. Should you get lost, you are rarely far from a station or a *koban* (police box), where you can get directions. For insights from a local as you wander, check out the Japan National Tourism Organization *(japan.travel/en/plan/list-of-volunteer-guides)*, which has an online list of free guided walks led by English-speaking volunteers.

TIP

Pack good shoes for walking. Many people find themselves walking a lot more than normal when exploring Tokyo – the city is so good for exploring on foot.

Buses

For navigating the city centre, it's best to forget about buses. They can get bogged down in traffic and routes aren't always clear in English. JR and Tokyo Metro are far easier to use and much more efficient. On side trips to places like Hakone, Nikkō or Kamakura, however, buses can be crucial. Services from Narita and Haneda airports are also convenient ways

---

PUBLIC TRANSPORT ESSENTIALS

Money-Saving Passes

The **Tokyo Metro Pass** offers 24-, 48- or 72-hour unlimited use of the Tokyo Metro and Toei subway lines for ¥800 to ¥1500. The **Hakone Freepass** *(adult/child from ¥6100/ 1100)* covers train fares between Shinjuku and Hakone, plus two or three days of unlimited rides on all key forms of transport in Hakone, and discounts at some attractions. The **Tokyo Wide Pass** *(adult/child ¥15,000/7500)* is another option for excursions beyond the capital, giving three consecutive days of unlimited rail use in and around Tokyo, including express trains to Nikkō and the bullet train for ski trips to Echigo Yuzawa.

Manners

On trains, the metro and buses, there are clearly labelled priority seats for the elderly, disabled, expectant mothers and parents with small children. While it's not uncommon to see locals who don't fall into any of those categories using these seats, you really ought to leave them open. Other public transport manners to keep in mind include keeping your voice down and being mindful of your luggage – take your backpack off or hold it in front of you, so you don't knock anyone with it. Don't eat anything or try drinking a piping hot coffee on commuter trains and the metro, but feel free to get stuck into a *bentō* and a beer on longer distance trains like the shinkansen or the express service to Nikkō – if your seat comes with a tray, it's all good.

Women-Only Carriages

In response to the number of sexual harassment and abuse cases of women on trains, most JR trains and Tokyo Metro subways have women-only carriages for much of the morning commute. The exact timings vary by line, but the carriages and the timings are very clearly marked by signs on the platform and in the carriage windows. Children can also use these carriages.

Japan Travel by Navitime

The useful Navitime app has an excellent public transport route-planner, and features sightseeing activities and guides to such things as how to exchange money or rent a car. There's a paid premium version that includes functions like a six-hour rain radar, but the free version is good enough.

Scan the QR code for the Japan Travel by Navitime app

TRAVEL COSTS

Tokyo Metro ticket
From ¥180

JR ticket
From ¥150

Taxi ride
From ¥500

Taxis, Shibuya

to get into central Tokyo. Many buses will accept Pasmo or Suica IC cards, but for cash-only vehicles, you'll need coins and small notes (¥1000) – bus payment machines can't break ¥5000 or ¥10,000 notes for change.

Driving

Like buses, driving in central Tokyo is best avoided. As roads are congested, navigating without an English GPS can be a trial, and the costs are so much higher than using the far more efficient public transport options. If you really want to drive, you'll need to be at least 18 and have an International Driving Permit. You can book rental cars online in English from Nippon Rent-a-Car, Nissan Rent-a-Car and JR Rent-a-Car. Remember that Japan drives on the left.

Taxi

You'll find taxis at ranks beside most stations and in busy areas, or you can just flag them down. A reddish-orange sign (空車) on the dashboard means the taxi is vacant. A green sign (賃走) indicates it's occupied. You can also call a cab with apps such as Go *(go .goinc.jp/lp/inbound)*. Rates vary, but average around ¥500 for the first kilometre and then ¥100 for each subsequent 250m. Between 10pm and 5am, you'll pay 20% more. When taking a taxi, don't open the doors yourself – the driver opens them remotely.

ACCESSIBILITY

While most train and subway stations are fully accessible, station staff need to manually place a ramp for wheelchair users to board and alight the carriages. The situation is similar with buses. Most taxis don't have space for a wheelchair, with the exception being those that look like London black cabs. For travellers with visual impairments, streets and stations have yellow tactile paving to indicate directions and hazards. For more detailed information, see the Accessible Travel section on p232.

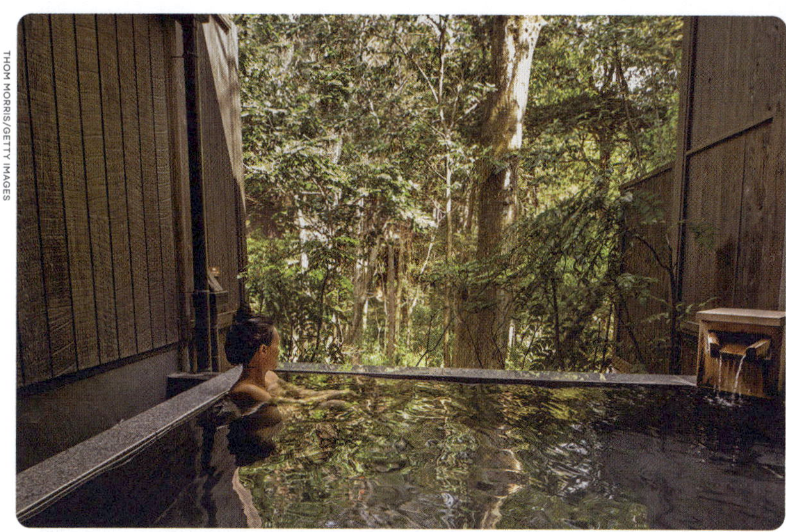

Onsen, Hakone (p208)

TRIP PLANNER

THE BLISS OF JAPANESE ONSEN

Most visitors to Japan have seen onsen (温泉) in brochures or online – those magical pools of hot water, many of them overlooking a river or bamboo forest, some even with Mt Fuji in the distance. They evoke tranquillity and calm, and for many visitors, they're a mesmerising item on the must-do list.

Where to Find Onsen in Tokyo

Tokyo has a number of authentic onsen experiences – although you'll find more on side trips to places like Hakone (p208) and Nikkō (p214) – but it's helpful to understand the difference between true onsen water and that of a typical *sentō* (public bath).

Most *sentō* just use heated tap water that's relaxing and therapeutic, but onsen baths always use natural hot-spring water sourced from deep within the earth. All public bathhouses and ryokan with onsen are required to have a sign displaying the quality of the water, and while said sign is nearly always in Japanese, online translation tools aren't bad at turning it into English.

How to Use Onsen

Most onsen have instructions in several languages, along with illustrated instructions. Thankfully, the process is fairly simple.

UNDRESS COMPLETELY

First, remove your clothes in the changing room and place them in the baskets provided. If you have valuables, use a locker.

WASH WELL

Next, carrying only a small towel (provided for free or purchased at check-in), head to the washing area, where there are small stools and individual taps, usually with soap and shampoo. Scrub-a-dub carefully,

35

Daikoku-yu
A bathhouse near Tokyo Skytree with outdoor and indoor baths, nice sauna, real onsen water and a local crowd. *daikokuyu.com*

Kogane-yu
A *sentō* in Kinshicho that shows how a bathhouse can adapt to the modern day. It has a bar, permanent DJ booth and a hipster vibe. *koganeyu.com*

Spa LaQua
This family-friendly super *sentō* by Tokyo Dome features multiple indoor and outdoor baths, saunas, massage salons and restaurants. *laqua.jp/spa*

Shimizu-yu
A local *sentō* in trendy Aoyama, ideal for a soak between all the fancy cafes and boutiques. *shimizuyu.jp*

rinsing all the soap off, and then, and only then, head over to the bath.

SOAK & RELAX

Ease into the bath slowly. Be sure to not let the towel touch the bathwater. If you want to look like a pro, fold it several times and balance it on your head. Alternatively, you can place it carefully next to you on the lip of the bath. The only thing that should touch the water is your skin. If you have long hair, tie it up.

Soak for as long as you like. Some need out after a minute or two; others stay for an hour. Some get out, rest on the bath's edge for a while, and then soak again. If you're visiting the onsen with someone of the opposite sex, note that different genders bathe separately, so it's a good idea to arrange a meeting-time beforehand – this will avoid one person being left twiddling their thumbs in the hall.

DRY UP

When you're done, collect your towel and head to the changing area. Dry your skin with the towel, wringing it carefully into the gutter rather than just onto the floor. This will mean you're not dripping water all over the changing area.

OTHER ONSEN TITBITS

- If you have tattoos, especially large ones, or sleeves, be mindful that many onsen and *sentō* prohibit bathing with tattoos. The reasons for this are complicated: tattoos were once reserved only for members of the Japanese mafia, the *yakuza*. By prohibiting tattoos, bath owners could make their establishments safer without targeting specific individuals. Times they are a-changing, but Japanese attitudes often remain.
- Many hotels, ryokan and onsen bathhouses have both indoor and outdoor baths. The latter, known as *rotenburo* (露天風呂), have the advantage of being exposed to the air. Sometimes you'll find a spectacular view, so it's worth looking for a door with a *rotenburo* sign and checking it out.
- You can take as much time as you like in the changing room. Often, you'll find razors, lotions, colognes and perfumes, cotton swabs and hair dryers, as well as sinks and mirrors.
- In the washing area, walk slowly and watch your step, as the floors can sometimes be very slippy.
- In the lobby, you can usually find a cooler of ice water or a vending machine with drinks. It's a good idea to replenish your liquids, as the baths can be dehydrating.

Bathing, onsen

Rotenburo (open-air bath), Hakone (p208)

Is Nudity Compulsory?

In a word, yes. But for anyone averse to bathing nude among strangers, there are two options: one is *kazokuburo* (家族風呂), which means 'family bath'. It's a private bath reserved for families, and because it's locked, you'll only be bathing with yourself and whomever else you bring in with you. Higher-end ryokan have a similar private bath, called a *kashikiriburo* (貸切風呂). These can usually be reserved for 30 minutes or an hour at check-in and are a great option for the modest or those with big tattoos. Since you're bathing in private, your tattoos won't upset other patrons.

A Simple Sentō

The humble neighbourhood bathhouse, aka the *sentō* (銭湯), is something of a dying breed in Tokyo – there are roughly 450 of them around the city, down from close to 2500 in the 1960s. After all, with homes and apartments all having their own plumbing nowadays, people are far less likely to head outside for a wash. That said, *sentō* still play an important role, especially for older Tokyoites, as a place to meet and chat, and to do so for a much smaller fee than visiting a plush onsen. As a visitor, a *sentō* is a great way to experience local community. The same basic bathing rules as an onsen apply, but unlike in the latter, many locals turn up to *sentō* with their own towels, soap and shampoo, so all they need do is pay a bathing fee.

The Super Sentō

Quite different to the neighbourhood *sentō* is the super *sentō* – a bathing complex that typically features multiple indoor and outdoor baths, saunas and chill-out spaces – maybe restaurants and massages too. Very often, super *sentō* use onsen water, although in place of the fully traditional onsen vibe you are more likely to find something geared towards families and fun.

HEALING WATERS

For as long as the Japanese have been bathing in onsen, it's been said that these mineral-rich waters bring health benefits – historic tales abound of wounded samurai and injured animals miraculously healing after a soak.

Onsen facilities today still tend to list their benefits, from improved circulation and muscle relaxation to the promotion of a deeper sleep and pain relief. A common claim is that the waters will help beautify the skin. One thing that can't be denied is that a good immersion in an onsen or *sentō* can be extremely relaxing.

Sushi restaurant, Tokyo

DINING OUT

You only need to step outside the door to find good food in Tokyo, which is chock-full of top-notch dining experiences.

When in Tokyo, it's not so much a matter of *what* to eat, but *how* to eat it all. The sheer variety of restaurants in this city of 14 million residents is staggering enough, and that's not even counting the well-stocked *konbini* (convenience stores) – a busy Tokyoite's go-to for a snack or lunch on the go.

A culinary tour involves slurping on flavour-packed ramen and savouring the day's freshest catch, indulging at Michelin-starred restaurants and dropping into cramped *izakaya* (pub-style eateries) for sticks of smoky *yakitori* (chicken skewers). And then there's the desserts, or just snacks – the fish-shaped *taiyaki* cakes stuffed with sweet red-bean paste, the skewers of *dango* (soft rice-flour balls) slathered in a sweet soy sauce glaze, and the calorie-packed fruit parfait. Whatever ends up on your plate, eating in the Japanese capital is equal parts about the delicious food and the unique experience.

Time to Eat

'Itadakimasu' is a phrase you'll often hear locals say, palms meeting briefly in a prayer-like gesture, before digging into a meal. The term, literally translating to 'I will receive', is an expression of gratitude for the dish one is about to eat. It's a custom many still practise, especially when dining in a group. When the meal is finished, *'gochisousama deshita'* is uttered to express thanks once again for the food and hospitality received. Customers often say this to the chef or waitstaff upon paying.

	RAMEN	**TSUKEMEN**	**TEMPURA**	**MONJAYAKI**
Best Tokyo Dishes	Tasty bowls of warm, soupy noodles jam-packed with umami.	Thick noodles for dipping, served alongside a bowl of rich broth.	Seafood and vegetables, lightly battered and fried. An Asakusa staple.	A runnier version of *okonomiyaki*, a savoury pancake cooked on a tabletop griddle.

If you're eating with a local host, this is also how you can thank them for the meal. Even at simple ramen joints, you'll hear locals say this aloud as they leave.

Etiquette

Dining in certain restaurants in Japan can feel intimidating, but there's no need to fret – places are often ready to accommodate, as long as you can get beyond any language barrier.

If you're keen to look like a local, here are a few things to keep in mind. When it comes to sushi, use either your hands or chopsticks, even at high-end establishments; dip the sushi in soy sauce (fish-first) and pop the whole thing in your mouth – it's meant to be eaten in one bite. If you're going to eat sushi, don't wear any perfumes or strongly scented deodorants, as that can interfere with the delicate flavours – in fact, it's never a bad idea to go light on aromas at any restaurant.

Chopsticks are the universal utensil at all Japanese restaurants – rarely will you find spoons, meaning miso soup can be enjoyed straight from the bowl, as you would drink from a cup; use chopsticks however you're comfortable with using them, just don't stick them upright in your rice bowl or use them to receive food from another person's chopsticks, as both gestures are only performed as part of funeral rites.

Vegan, Halal & Beyond

Tokyo is a diverse city, and that diversity applies to food as well, to a certain extent. Vegan cuisine is considered trendy, and you're likely to find places serving Western vegan fare in trendy neighbourhoods like Omotesandō or Ebisu, but these restaurants aren't as common elsewhere.

A great option for vegetarians is *shōjin ryōri*, a traditional Buddhist form of cooking typically enjoyed by monks; the style is meat-free and utilises seasonal ingredients while avoiding strong aromatics like garlic and onion. Though *shōjin ryōri* restaurants aren't as plentiful around town, Komaki Shokudō near Akihabara Station is a popular spot to go and give it a try. For more vegan and vegetarian options, the Happy Cow has an up-to-date list (*happycow.net/asia/japan/tokyo/*).

Tokyo Ramen Festa

FOOD & WINE FESTIVALS

Kanda Curry Grand Prix The city's best Japanese curry restaurants compete to see who's crowned the year's winner (November).

Furusato Matsuri Japan's best regional produce is gathered at Tokyo Dome in this epic food fest (January).

Tokyo Ramen Festa For two weeks, try up to 36 different ramen from across the country, all in one convenient location (October–November).

Mochitsuki Taikai i A *mochi* (sticky rice cakes) ceremony that's custom for ushering in the new year. Held at shrines or community centres (December–January).

Sakana & Japan Festival Cooked or raw, get all kinds of seafood any way you like at Tokyo's largest seafood festival (February).

NIGIRI SUSHI

Also called Edomae sushi, this is sushi with pieces of fish on top.

TAIYAKI

Sweet and slightly crispy pastry filled with red bean paste, shaped like tai (sea bream).

SOUFFLÉ PANCAKES

Light and airy, these are all the rage on social media. The taste lives up to the hype.

MELON CREAM SODA

Bright-green soda float with a cherry on top, this is a retro *kissaten* (coffee shop) staple.

Meat *yakitori*

Find information on Japan's soul food on p249.

KNOW YOUR MEAT

The names for different cuts of meat don't always get translated properly on English menus – here's a handy guide to understanding what you're getting at a Japanese restaurant or *izakaya*.

Bara Beef or pork belly.

Hire Lean pork or beef tenderloin, meaty and slightly tough.

Karubi Beef short ribs, tender and juicy. Best when barbecued.

Kawa Chicken skin. At *izakaya*, small pieces are served on a skewer.

Momo Chicken thigh.

Motsu/horumon Offal, typically beef intestines.

Mune Chicken breast.

Nankotsu Chicken cartilage.

Rōsu Pork loin with generous bits of fat.

Sasami Chicken tenders.

Sunagimo Gizzard. A *yakitori* staple that's tough and chewy.

Tan Beef tongue. Satisfying texture that's chewy yet tender.

More restaurants in Tokyo are beginning to offer a halal menu to cater to Muslim tourists – including ramen and *yakiniku* (barbecued meat) choices. Packaged food like those from the *konbini* or souvenir shops may not be halal, however. For resources, see *halal injapan.com* or the Japan National Tourism Organization's official Muslim guide (*muslimguide.jnto.go.jp/*).

In terms of gluten-free options, the good news is that rice is still the staple carb in Japan, but it's hard to find gluten-free alternatives to noodles and breads. The best bet are vegan or speciality restaurants, while popular ramen chain Afuri does a good gluten-free version using konjac noodles.

Most eateries are often good with adapting to those with allergies, and allergens are clearly marked on packaged foods, albeit in Japanese. For some basic Japanese words to help with that, see p228.

Meals on the Go

The quick pace of a city like Tokyo means that plenty of food options need to be cheap, quick and easy. Enter the *konbini*, where everything from *onigiri* (rice-ball snacks) to *bentō* (boxed meals) to steamed chicken breasts are available to grab.

A staple of students and commuters for quick lunches or late-night dinners due to their ubiquity and affordable prices, *gyudon* (beef rice bowl) restaurants like Matsuya or Yoshinoya can be found in just about any neighbourhood and are often open until the wee hours. But among the Japanese fast-food options, the most interesting of them all is probably the *tachigui* restaurant, where customers suck up some soba or swallow down pieces

---

FOOD WEBSITES

BYFOOD.COM

Listings of restaurants in Tokyo and around Japan, plus info on culinary tours and experiences.

HAPPYCOW.NET

The place to find vegan and vegetarian options in the city.

BEERTENGOKU.COM

Everything you need to know about Japanese craft beer, including bar reviews.

Variety of cakes and desserts, Tokyo

of sushi, all while standing at the counter – in these destinations, there's not a single stool in sight. They're often open early to accommodate the breakfast crowd, and though small and compact, things move quickly and prices are kept low, ensuring a constant rotation of customers.

Despite how popular quick meals are, however, it's still generally frowned upon to eat while one is on the move – though there are no rules against it, locals don't eat while walking or on the train.

Always Room for Dessert

Whether you're looking for gourmet cakes and confectioneries from world-class pastry chefs or well-loved Japanese sweets made from time-tested recipes, Tokyo has endless options on offer. Though instead of dense and decadent, traditional sweets here tend to be light and airy, or at least served in small portions – so even when you're stuffed, there's still just a little more room left to fit in some dessert. That said, you'll also find plenty of indulgent parfait and cream-filled crepes to fill what the Japanese call their *betsubara* – a separate stomach just for their favourite treats.

THE YEAR IN FOOD

WINTER

Strawberries begin to ripen and make an appearance in stores, lasting until spring. January and February are when the berries are the sweetest, so expect lots of enticing strawberry desserts and sweets all around town.

SPRING

Sakuramochi sweets are pink (like the cherry blossom, *sakura*, they're named after) and wrapped in an edible leaf that's been pickled in salt These are typically enjoyed during Hinamatsuri (3 March).

SUMMER

Food synonymous with Japanese summers include watermelon and *kakigori* (shaved ice). Watermelon is sometimes enjoyed with a sprinkle of salt, and *kakigori* is traditionally served in three colours – some suspect that all three might actually be the same flavour.

AUTUMN

Sweet potatoes, chestnuts and persimmons come into season. Look out for fragrant, freshly baked and warmed sweet potatoes at supermarkets or grab some from the speciality trucks driving around at night.

Hanbey (p149)

BAR OPEN

From intimate cocktail bars to lively *izakaya* and all-night karaoke, Tokyo's nightlife offers a diverse range of options.

Spend a quiet night sipping cocktails at a cosy bar, or belt out some tunes with strangers until dawn; it doesn't matter what your idea of fun is – Tokyo does it all. The city's vibrant, multi-faceted night-life must be experienced at least once – but with cheap alcohol, cool concept bars and some of Asia's hottest clubs, you might feel like one night isn't enough.

What's on offer often varies by neigh-bourhood. **Shinjuku** (p142) welcomes the thirsty and hungry at its many *iza-kaya* (Japanese pub-eateries), followed by a night of bar-hopping and bouts of kara-oke. If you're looking to dance and par-ty, make for the luxe clubs in **Shibuya** (p100) and **Roppongi** (p78), but head to the bars in nearby **Ebisu** (p90) first for some exquisite cocktails. Or for a quintes-sential night out, try eating and drinking at *yokochō* – lantern-lit side alleys with a collection of *izakaya* and bars; you'll find them in many of the capital's major neighbourhoods.

The Drinking Scene

The *izakaya* is where Tokyoites frequent-ly begin the night's activities, frothy jug of beer in hand and plates of edamame, fried chicken and *yakitori* skewers laid out on the table. They're one of the easi-est and cheapest places to drink in, with

Top Nighttime & Karaoke Spots

TWO ROOMS

Grab a cocktail and head to the terrace of this trendy bar for Aoyama views.

RAINBOW KARAOKE

Clean, family-friendly and reasonably priced karaoke inside Shibuya MODI.

WOMB

Famous Shibuya club with a bigger emphasis on music than partying. (p102)

DEATH MATCH IN HELL

This classic horror- and death-metal-themed bar is a Golden Gai institution. (p149)

a seemingly endless list of beverages and nibbles to choose from. Besides beer, fruity *chūhai* cocktails made from *shōchū* (strong distilled alcohol often made from potatoes) are go-to *izakaya* staples, as is *nihonshū* (sake), which you could order chilled, room temperature or even warmed.

A feature at many *izakaya* is *nomi-hōdai*, where for about ¥2000 per person, customers get all-you-can-drink alcohol for 90 minutes or two hours. The only caveat is that every person at the table must opt in.

For more alcohol on the cheap, head to *konbini* (convenience stores) for a few cans of *chūhai* – when the night gets going, you might spot partygoers taking swigs right out on the curb (just be sure to take your empty cans back to the *konbini*).

Karaoke

Any time is a good time for karaoke, but it's only at night that you'll hear the power ballads and rock anthems streaming out of the bars with a raucous crowd singing along. Join in on the fun at the venues in Shinjuku's **Golden Gai** (p148) and **Kabukicho** (p151), where karaoke is sometimes free or costs pocket change per song; you might have to wait a little while for your song to come on, though.

If the idea of singing in front of strangers sounds daunting, or if you prefer a bit more comfort and privacy, try a karaoke box instead. They're easily found around town and tend to open from late morning till the early hours. They also often offer all-you-can-drink deals, if you need something to help relax your singing muscles.

Major karaoke box chains, such as Big Echo and Karaokekan, have a large selection of new and classic English-language songs to choose from. For the best rates, look out for morning and afternoon discounts, where you can spend an hour singing and snacking for under ¥1500 per person.

Find out more about how to order sake on p229.

Taxi in Tokyo

NEED TO KNOW

Cover Charges

Many bars take a cover charge of between ¥500 and ¥1000; staff will generally inform customers of this beforehand. At *izakaya*, the amount is tacked onto your bill as an appetiser, known as *otōshi*. Clubs charge between ¥1000 and ¥4000.

Cash and Tipping

Though Tokyo is going increasingly cashless, many bars still take cash only, particularly around Shinjuku. There is no need to tip.

When to Go

Get dinner and drinks at an *izakaya* from 7pm. Bars typically don't start filling up until after 9pm, and clubs after 11pm. If you're out past midnight, prepare to stay out all night until the trains resume, or shell out for a taxi. Clubs stay open until 4am or 5am, as do most bars.

BEN FIDDICH

Unique cocktails in Shinjuku, crafted with ingredients from the owner's farm.

AIIRO CAFE

The place to start your night at the LGBTIQ+ Nichōme district. (p149)

HANBEY

Izakaya chain in Shinjuku and Shibuya with retro Showa-era aesthetics. (p151)

SAKURAI JAPANESE TEA EXPERIENCE

Start an Aoyama night out with a tea-infused martini or negroni at this intimate salon. (p122)

Kabuki-za theatre (p69)

SHOWTIME

When it comes to shows and events, Japan's capital delivers everything from traditional kabuki and centuries-old festivals to contemporary theatre in English.

As one would expect from a metropolis of Tokyo's scale, the entertainment offerings here are vast. Something is always happening somewhere, and across all artistic genres. But be sure to also leave yourself open to serendipity: if you hear something interesting wafting out of a random venue, take a chance and wander inside – that's where Tokyo's quintessential magic lies.

Performance Halls

Ginza's **Kabuki-za Theatre** (p69) showcases the elaborate visual storytelling practice of kabuki, a carnival-esque art form from the early 1600s, where dramatic song and dance performances are enhanced by special effects such as rotating stages and hidden lifts. Meanwhile, the National Nō Theatre in Sendagaya puts on *nō* – Japan's oldest surviving form of theatre performance – whose minimalist style is invoked through dramatic plot twists and subtle nuances. *Nō* is often performed with interludes featuring the comical art of *kyōgen*; the Suigian in Nihombashi holds nightly performances of these art forms along with sumptuous dinners.

Tokyo also boasts many venues for world-class performances of opera, ballet, and orchestral and chamber music, including

Top Choices – Live Jazz	A-TRAIN	BLUE NOTE	G'S BAR	HYPHEN
	Tiny New York–style jazz bar in Gakugei Daigaku serving quality diner food. (p99)	Legendary venue in Aoyama attracting major international artists. (p99)	Intimate Akasaka bar with live jazz every night. (p89)	Old-fashioned jazz club in Jiyugaoka for acoustic gigs. (p99)

Suntory Hall (Akasaka), Orchard Hall (Shibuya), Tokyo Bunka Kaikan (Ueno), New National Theatre (Shibuya), Tokyo Opera City (Hatsudai) and Tokyo Metropolitan Theatre (Ikebukuro). For top-notch jazz, R&B, pop and rock, local favourites include **Blue Note Tokyo** (p99; Aoyama), Cotton Club (Marunouchi) and **JZ Brat** (p107; Shibuya).

Festivals

There's always a festival (or three) taking place – with many clustered around summertime. Noteworthy celebrations include the portable shrine parades of the Kanda Matsuri (May); Tokyo Pride, the country's largest celebration of diversity (June); the exuberant **Sumida River Fireworks Festival** (p197), which dates to the Edo era (late July); the Fukagawa Hachiman Matsuri, a joyful water-spraying event popular since the Edo era (mid-Aug); and the vibrant Kōenji Awa Odori Festival (end of August).

Autumn brings the Tokyo International Film Festival (end of October or beginning of November) and the Kanda Used Book Festival (end of Oct or beginning of November).

Outdoor Art Installations

Outdoor art installations comprise a wonderful way to indulge in creative exploration. The Marunouchi Street Gallery features pieces rotated in collaboration with the Hakone Open-Air Museum, while the canal-side streets of Tennozu Isle are enhanced with murals.

Outdoor art events also take place regularly throughout the city, with annual initiatives including 'Have A Nice Day!' (HAND!), featuring art and music venues along the Yamanote line in February and March, and the Sumi-Yume Art Project, which sees creative works along the Sumida River from September to December.

English-Language Performances

Enjoying live performances in Tokyo can be challenging due to linguistic barriers, but some venues do offer English-language productions, including the Tokyu Theatre Orb in Shibuya Hikarie, whose lineup often includes international musicals.

In addition, some artistic troupes – comprised largely of locally-based international residents – regularly hold performances in English. These include nightly stand-up acts at the **Tokyo Comedy Bar** (p107) in Shibuya, and monthly bilingual improv shows from the Pirates of Tokyo Bay at What the Dickens pub in Ebisu. The Tokyo International Players and Sheepdog Theatre troupes also perform in various venues around town (check the troupes' websites for details).

Sumida River Fireworks Festival (p197)

Top Choices – Vinyl Bars & Cafes	**BAR LUTHER** Cocktails, whisky and a mix of old soul, rock and blues on the turntable. (p80)	**LION** A *kissaten* (coffee shop) for classical music fans that's been in business for a century. (p103)	**MASAKO** This retro cafe in Shimokitazawa plays a wide variety of jazz records. (p103)

ENTERTAINMENT BY NEIGHBOURHOOD

Marunouchi & Nihombashi	Catch jazz or R&B at the Cotton Club, or a dinner show set to *nō* and *kyōgen* at Suigian.
Ginza & Tsukiji	Watch the ancient drama of kabuki at Kabuki-za theatre (p69).
Roppongi & Around	Dance at one of Roppongi's hotspots, then chill at the otherworldly Shisha Bar Rakuen (p80).
Ebisu, Meguro & Around	Hang out in indie jazz cafes and vinyl bars, or catch a show at Liquidroom.
Shibuya & Setagaya	Experience Tokyo's live music scene at venues including Heaven's Door and Club Que.
Harajuku & Aoyama	Visit the National Nō Theatre, or see world-famous musicians at Blue Note Tokyo (p124).
West Tokyo & Around	Check indie venues such as Jirokichi and Gamuso.
Shinjuku & Northwest Tokyo	See live music in Kabukicho (p151), or visit the clubs and bars of the Nichōme gaybourhood (p149).
Ueno & Yanesen	Gaze at springtime blossoms at the Ueno Sakura Matsuri (p179).
Asakusa & Sumida River	Summer events include the Sumida River Fireworks Festival (p197).
Kōrakuen & Akihabara	Catch gigs by major Japanese and international performers at Tokyo Dome (p160).
Odaiba & Tokyo Bay	Events include the summer Odaiba Lantern Festival and spring Tennoz Canal Fes.

Springtime blossoms (p179), Ueno Sakura Matsuri

Yanaka Ginza (p180)

SHOP

When it comes to retail therapy, Tokyo has it all – from the finest traditional goods to the most vibrant youth fashions.

Maybe it shouldn't be a surprise that one of the world's biggest and busiest cities has you covered for any possible shopping needs you may have – and then some. From high fashion to streetwear, geeky gadgetry to intricate crafts, urban shopping complexes to tiny mom-and-pop stores, the capital won't let you down.

With Japan's legendary *konbini* (convenience stores), you're never far away from a late-night snack, cheap lunch or a quick caffeine fix. There are also vending machines on almost every street corner, reliably shocking first-time visitors with the sheer number of options – not just drinks, hot and cold, but scattered around the metropolis is also the occasional vending machine selling frozen *gyoza*, rice, coffee beans and plenty of other options. There are so many opportunities to shop, you might need to buy an extra case for the journey home. So save up your coins: you're in for a shopping extravaganza.

Depachika

A feature of Japanese retail culture that you'll find in spades around the metropolis is *depachika* – the basement level floors of department stores, which are typically dominated by food halls. In these havens of local culinary culture, you'll find freshly prepared *yakitori* (chicken skewers), pay-by-the-weight salads, *bentō*, deli goods, seasonal desserts and all manner of packaged sweets that make for fantastic *o-miyage* (take-home souvenirs). Popular *depachika* include Shibuya Tokyu Foodshow, Mitsukoshi and – the largest – Ikebukuro Tobu.

As for the term itself, it's a portmanteau (something Japan is very fond of) of *depāto* (department store) and *chika* (underground or basement).

Speciality Stores

Have a niche shopping need? Keen on browsing multiple floors of paraphernalia until you spot that perfect find? If yes, head to one of the numerous speciality shops, each featuring their own unique style. Tokyu Hands and LOFT stock everything from backpacks to stationery to cosmetics, and oh so much more. Needing no introduction is Daiso, which offers an eclectic collection of items for ¥100; shell out two more ¥100 coins at the slightly fancier 3Coins stores.

For electronics, head to Bic Camera. And for the quirkiest shopping experience, cruise the aisles at Don Quijote – known locally as 'Donki' – which will ensure hours (or minutes, depending on your taste) of wandering amid costumery, snacks and even sex toys. Then, of course, there are speciality areas – like the kitchenware stores of Kappabashi-dōri (p190), the bookshops of Jimbōchō (p166) and the musical instrument stores of Ochanomizu.

Flea Markets

A great way to get up close and personal with local life is through its flea markets, where you can find antique wares, books and endless household goods. While hard bargaining is not part of market culture here, you may be able to nudge your way towards a small discount; feel free to test the waters, but don't push too hard.

The schedules of flea markets often vary, so be sure to verify before heading out. The numerous venues include the earth-friendly Mottainai (Nakano and Gotanda; dates vary), Nogi Shrine (every fourth Sunday except in November), Oedo Antique Market (Tokyo International Forum; every first and third Sunday) and Yoyogi Park Earth Garden (once per season).

Konbini

The late Anthony Bourdain, who cited Tokyo as his favourite culinary city, was particularly fond of *konbini* (convenience store) egg sandwiches from Lawson, describing them as 'unnaturally fluffy, insanely delicious, and incongruously addictive'. The *tamago sando*, however, is just the tip of the *konbini*'s tasty iceberg.

Whether you find your way into a 7-Eleven, Family Mart, Mini Stop or Lawson, you'll be met with hundreds of drinking and snacking options. For a sweet tooth, you could hit the aisle full of chocolates, sweets and crisps for some Pocky chocolate-coated biscuit sticks. On a hot day, dig into the ice-cream freezer. Want something warm? Head to the glass display case at the register and ask for some fried chicken and steamed *nikuman* buns, or order a hot coffee for pocket change. And if you need something stronger than coffee, there'll be single-serve cup sakes and a fridge full of potent *chūhai* – a type of alcopop that comes in various fruity flavours and can weigh in at 9% ABV.

Local Shōtengai

Despite all of Tokyo's malls, shopping centres and urban complexes, the humble *shōtengai* (商店街) is still an important part of many neighbourhoods. Typically featuring a dated charm, these local shopping streets are where you'll find non-chain stores selling groceries and everyday items, but also clinics, restaurants and other neighbourhood essentials.

Lucky cat figurines, Tokyo flea market

Best Independent Shops

DAIKANYAMA TSUTAYA BOOKS Three buildings of books and magazines on lifestyle, travel, cooking and more. (p97)

ITOYA This mammoth 12-storey store in Ginza is a stationery-lover's dream. (p77)

KAKIMORI Create your own personalised notebook at this sweet Kuramae stationery shop. (p195)

OZU WASHI A 370-year-old *washi* (traditional paper) shop where you can also take a *washi* paper-making workshop (p63)

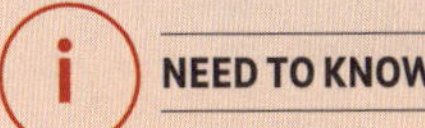

NEED TO KNOW

Cashless or card
You'll be able to pay with credit card or local cashless services at most stores in Tokyo, but always keep some cash handy, especially for smaller restaurants and stores.

Shop local
Want some snacks or sake to take home? Get it from a local supermarket or grocery store, instead of paying a premium at tourist-focused shops.

Take a bag
You'll be offered plastic and paper bags at every store – for a fee – but it all adds up to a lot of waste. Pack a reusable bag instead.

SHOPPING BY NEIGHBOURHOOD

Marunouchi & Nihombashi	Plush urban complexes and long-established shops specialising in traditional goods.
Ginza & Tsukiji	Glitzy retailers galore, including luxury boutiques, venerable department stores and swanky shopping malls such as Ginza Six.
Roppongi & Around	One-stop shopping for luxury items and everyday goods at mega-complexes Roppongi Hills and Tokyo Midtown.
Ebisu, Meguro & Around	Furniture and antique venues line Meguro-dōri, while boutique shops flank the stroll-worthy Meguro River.
Shibuya & Setagaya	The numerous outlets and shopping complexes of Shibuya feature the very latest in fashion.
Harajuku & Aoyama	The district of Harajuku teems with streetwear and boutique clothing choices; don't miss the shops along Cat Street.
West Tokyo & Around	Flavours of past eras abound, including vintage clothes in Kōenji, traditional crafts in Asagaya and antiques in Nishi-Ogikubo.
Shinjuku & Northwest Tokyo	Choose from numerous major department stores clustered on all sides of Shinjuku train station – the world's busiest.
Kōrakuen & Akihabara	All roads lead to Akihabara for electronics, manga and anime.
Ueno & Yanesen	Ameya-yokochō is one of the city's liveliest street markets, while seniors flock to Jizo-dōri (aka granny's Harajuku).
Asakusa & Sumida River	Plentiful souvenirs, and kitchenware along Kappabashi-dōri.
Odaiba & Tokyo Bay	Family-focused shopping malls with a mix of fashions, interior goods and stores for kids.

Whether you visit Sugamo's **Jizo-dōri** (p183) – affectionally known as 'granny's Harajuku' because of its elderly shoppers – or soak up the retro charm of **Yanaka Ginza** (p180), a stroll along a *shōtengai* will give you a different perspective on Tokyo life.

FLASH DISC RANCH
Used vinyl store in Shimokitazawa with music across all genres. (p111)

ORIENTAL BAZAAR
Longstanding Omotesandō shop offering *o-miyage*, including *ukiyo-e* (woodblock prints) and kimono. (p118)

GOOD DESIGN STORE TOKYO BY NOHARA
Stocks close to 1000 lifestyle items that have been awarded Japan's Good Design Award. (p63)

ONOYA
In business since 1868, this small store sells a selection of traditional textiles and fashion items like *tabi* footwear. (p73)

仲見世
浅
見世
KADO
MONKADO

THE GUIDE

Chapters in this section are organised by neighbourhood, each defined by its own identity. Within our neighbourhoods coverage you'll find unique experiences, local insights, insider tips and expert recommendations.

Nakamise-dōri (p192), Asakusa
RINTARO KANEMOTO/FOR LONELY PLANET

NEIGHBOURHOODS AT A GLANCE

Find the neighbourhoods that tick all your boxes.

Shinjuku & Northwest Tokyo (p142)

With its skyscrapers, shopping malls, nightlife and spacious parks, there's always something new to discover – day or night – in bustling Shinjuku.

West Tokyo & Around (p128)

Discover some of the city's most intriguing neighbourhoods, plus the Tama region's colourful temples, unique museums and natural wonders.

Shibuya & Setagaya (p100)

A mix of youthful energy, artistic expression and endless options for a great night out.

Harajuku & Aoyama (p116)

A centre of fashion and style – from streetwear and youth trends to haute couture and cutting-edge art and architecture.

Ebisu, Meguro & Around (p90)

Stylish shops and cafes, plus an arty, design-focused vibe make this a great place to get a feel for Tokyo's creative side.

Kōrakuen & Akihabara (p158)

Come for the *otaku* and anime stores, stay for the home electronics and a host of entertainment options.

Ueno & Yanesen (p170)

These east-side neighbourhoods offer top museums, green spaces and opportunities to experience traditional ways.

Asakusa & Sumida River (p184)

Visit the city's most vibrant temple, head up Tokyo Skytree for sweeping views, or time your trip for a sumo tournament.

Marunouchi & Nihombashi (p54)

The new and old commercial hearts of Tokyo are home to numerous remnants of the past, from the Imperial Palace to historic retailers and restaurants.

Ginza & Tsukiji (p66)

The place to go for luxury shopping and the finest cuisine, or to check out the lively stalls of Tsukiji Outer Market.

Odaiba & Tokyo Bay (p198)

Head to the bayside for family-friendly theme parks, a thriving fish market, hot-spring baths, visionary digital-art installations and canal-side galleries.

Roppongi & Around (p78)

A nightlife district teeming with bars and clubs, but also a vibrant contemporary art scene and sleek urban complexes.

Researched by Todd Fong

MARUNOUCHI & NIHOMBASHI

WHERE TOKYO BEGAN

Nihombashi (日本橋) and Marunouchi (丸の内) represent Tokyo's past and present gateways to the rest of the nation. The historical sites here still reveal the foundations of Tokyo's greatness.

The centre of Nihonbashi Bridge is marked with a zero-kilometre marker; from where all distances from Tokyo are measured. In the 17th century, all roads leading to Tokyo eventually ended here, such was the importance of Nihombashi, hub of Japanese trade and commerce for centuries. While the area has modernised, it has done so at a slower pace, with many historical businesses dating from the Edo period. Note that some attractions and place names use the alternative Nihonbashi spelling. The heart of the area is Tokyo Station with its two faces: the historic brick facade Marunouchi side, facing the Imperial Palace to the west, and the modern glass-and-steel Yaesu side, facing the skyscrapers of Yaesu on the east. Marunouchi's classic beauty augments the attractive boutiques and cafes lining its streets.

TIP

The Imperial Palace has several gates. Kikyō-mon is where the palace tour sets out from, and the three gates to the East Gardens are Ōte-mon, Hirakawa-mon and Kitahanebashi-mon, with Ōte-mon being the most easily accessible from Tokyo Station. All gates are marked on Google Maps.

Tokyo Station (p57)

See page 218 for places to stay in Marunouchi & Nihombashi

⭐ Highlights

❶ Tokyo Station
Not just for trainspotting: discover the station's endless variety of eateries, bars and shops. **p57**

❷ Imperial Palace
Tour the palace grounds and elegant gardens of Japan's royal family. **p60**

▼ ❸ Chidori-ga-fuchi
Enjoy a scenic boat ride on the Imperial Palace moat, beautiful in every season. **p61**

❹ KITTE
Explore this spacious former main post office turned trendy shopping centre, complete with a museum. **p63**

❺ Marunouchi Winter Illuminations
See the streets of Marunouchi transformed by a wonderful light show. **p56**

🚶 Getting Around

Train

Trains arrive at and depart from 28 platforms at Tokyo Station, heading to every corner of the nation. The circular and very useful Yamanote line train stops at the station.

Subway

Only the Marunouchi line serves Tokyo Station, but nearby stations like Ōtemachi and Nihonbashi are served by the Ginza, Asakusa, Tōzai, Chiyoda, Hanzomon and Mita lines.

Walking

Exploring on foot is your best option, but only one corridor connects the two sides of Tokyo Station internally, so you may want to walk around the station rather than through it.

O-MIYAGE: THE CULTURE OF GIFTING

For many Japanese travellers, picking up an *o-miyage* at the end of any trip, whether business or personal, is a social convention that's an absolute must.

O-miyage is a broad term that translates to 'souvenir', but it also denotes something bought specifically for others. The most common *o-miyage* are the packaged *mochi* (rice cakes) seen at places like Tokyo Station. Boxes of snacks like cookies or small cakes come in various sizes because they are meant to be shared with groups of friends or colleagues.

Because each region of Japan tends to have a dish or produce associated with it, *o-miyage* is a great way for travellers to share the region with friends and family.

A Million Points of Light
Stroll the seasonal Marunouchi illuminations

Between the months of November and February, hundreds of trees along Marunouchi Naka-dori and a few other selected side streets are strung up with 1.2 million **fairy lights**, giving the city a warm, cosy glow. It's the perfect setting for a stroll, and for part of that period (usually leading up to Christmas Day), you might find other seasonal events in the evenings like a Christmas Market or ice-skating rink. On top of that, the low-energy LED lights run from naturally produced energy sources: solar and wind power. Marunouchi Naka-dori runs parallel to Tokyo Station on the Marunouchi (West) side, and the illuminations are strung on the trees all the way to the area next to Yūrakuchō Station, which is a perfect distance for a wander, ending at a major train station.

The Beginning & End of Japan
Appreciating the Nihonbashi bridge

All roads to Tokyo once started and ended at this stately **bridge**, which before the 1964 Olympics did not need to endure the humiliation of being obscured by an unsightly overhead expressway. Though harder to imagine now, the regal sculptures of the mythical *kirin* (part deer, bull and dragon) that flank its centre posts demonstrate the prosperity of Tokyo while the *komainu* lion-dogs set at each corner offer it protection. Its current stone and steel form was completed in 1911, but for three centuries before that, Nihonbashi was a beautiful wooden bridge, often featured in the *ukiyo-e* woodblock prints made by the masters of their times.

The wrong that was done to the bridge with the construction of the expressway will finally be undone, albeit in a slow removal process that is scheduled to take until 2041. For now, try to imagine it in its splendour, made a little easier in spring when cherry blossoms bloom at both ends.

The Gateway to the Nation
Exploring the vast Tokyo Station

A symbol of the city right at the heart of Marunouchi, Tokyo Station's Marunouchi Building is a Renaissance-style red-brick structure that has a grand and instantly recognisable facade. Construction was completed in 1914, though it has undergone significant renovations and restorations over the years. Air

DRINKING IN MARUNOUCHI & NIHOMBASHI: PERK-UP SPOTS

Bongen Coffee Nihonbashi: A strong cup of coffee in one of the most zen cafes you've ever seen. *10am-5pm*

Good Coffee Farms Cafe: Single origin, farm-to-cup coffee and a selection of sweets in a no-frills coffee shop. *8am-5pm*

Aroma Coffee Yaesu: *Kissaten*-style coffee shop with reasonably priced morning set. Underground in the Yaechika mall. *7am-9.30pm Mon-Fri, to 9pm Sat, 7.30am-9pm Sun*

Bridge Coffee & Ice Cream: Great single origin hand drip in an iconic Nihombashi building. *8am-5.30pm Mon-Fri, from 9am Sat & Sun*

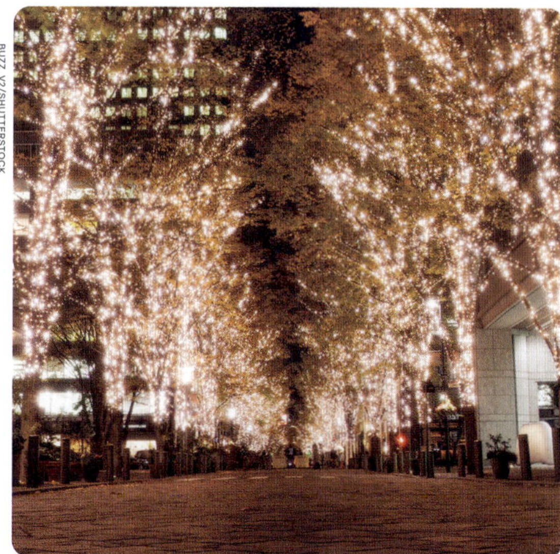

Fairy lights, Marunouchi Naka-dori Street

raids and bombings during WWII significantly damaged the roof, and after extensive work, the building was finally restored to its original state in 2012.

While the original **Tokyo Station** (*tokyostationcity.com*) was the Marunouchi Building, the transport hub has far expanded beyond the framework of the original edifice today, now containing 28 platforms and a 230m steel-and-glass roofline on the Yaesu side created to resemble a 'sail of light'. The views of Tokyo Station are now very distinct, with the traditional brick-faced Marunouchi Building facing the Imperial Palace grounds and the sleek Yaesu side of the station facing the equally modern Midtown Yaesu skyscraper to the east.

The station is where you'll go to board shinkansen – the bullet trains that shuttle passengers across the country, from Hokkaido to Kyūshū, at lightning speeds of up to 320km/h, with dozens of departures per hour during peak times. Even watching the trains arrive and depart is an attraction unto itself, best viewed from the rooftop garden of the KITTE building or a restaurant seat in the Midtown Yaesu building.

SECRETS OF TOKYO STATION

Unlike most major stations, the east and west sides of the stations are not identified by direction, but by name, the east called Yaesu and the west Marunouchi.

Complicating matters, there is only a single passageway through the station connecting the two sides that does not require you to pass through the ticket gates. Otherwise, you'll need to purchase an 'admission ticket' that will allow you to enter and exit the ticket gates without boarding a train.

Nevertheless, an endless network of underground passages link different parts of the station, surrounding buildings and various subway stations as distant as Ginza. It takes some keen navigation skills to avoid getting lost underground, but on bad weather days, at least you don't need to get drenched in rain or sweat.

EATING & DRINKING IN MARUNOUCHI & NIHOMBASHI: SWEET TREATS

Sembikiya Fruit Parlour: Historical fruit cafe in Nihombashi, now dealing in luxury produce. Its musk melon is available year-round. *11am-9pm* ¥¥

Usagiya Nihonbashi: No-frills traditional sweets store selling delicious *dorayaki* (red bean pancakes). *9.30am-6pm Mon-Fri* ¥

Ippuku & Matcha: Matcha drinks and dessert to eat on the terrace. A difficult-to-book secret tearoom is also available. *11am-8pm*

Coco Gelato: Tiny shop near Fukutoku Shrine selling regionally inspired flavours of gelato. *11-8pm* ¥

MARUNOUCHI & NIHOMBASHI

⭐ HIGHLIGHTS
1 Imperial Palace
2 National Museum of Modern Art (MOMAT)
3 Tokyo Station

⭐ SIGHTS
4 Bank of Japan Head Office
5 Fukutoku-jinja
6 Imperial Palace East Garden
7 Intermediatheque
8 Marunouchi Ekimae Square
9 Mitsui Memorial Museum
10 Mitsukoshi
11 Nihonbashi
12 Otemachi Forest
13 Seikado Bunko Art Museum
14 Tokyo International Forum
15 Zero Milestone in Japan Marker

🔴 ACTIVITIES, COURSES & TOURS
16 Nihombashi Cruise

⚫ SLEEPING
17 Hoshinoya Tokyo
18 Hotel Monte Hermana Tokyo
19 Hotel Ryumeikan Tokyo
20 Palace Hotel Tokyo

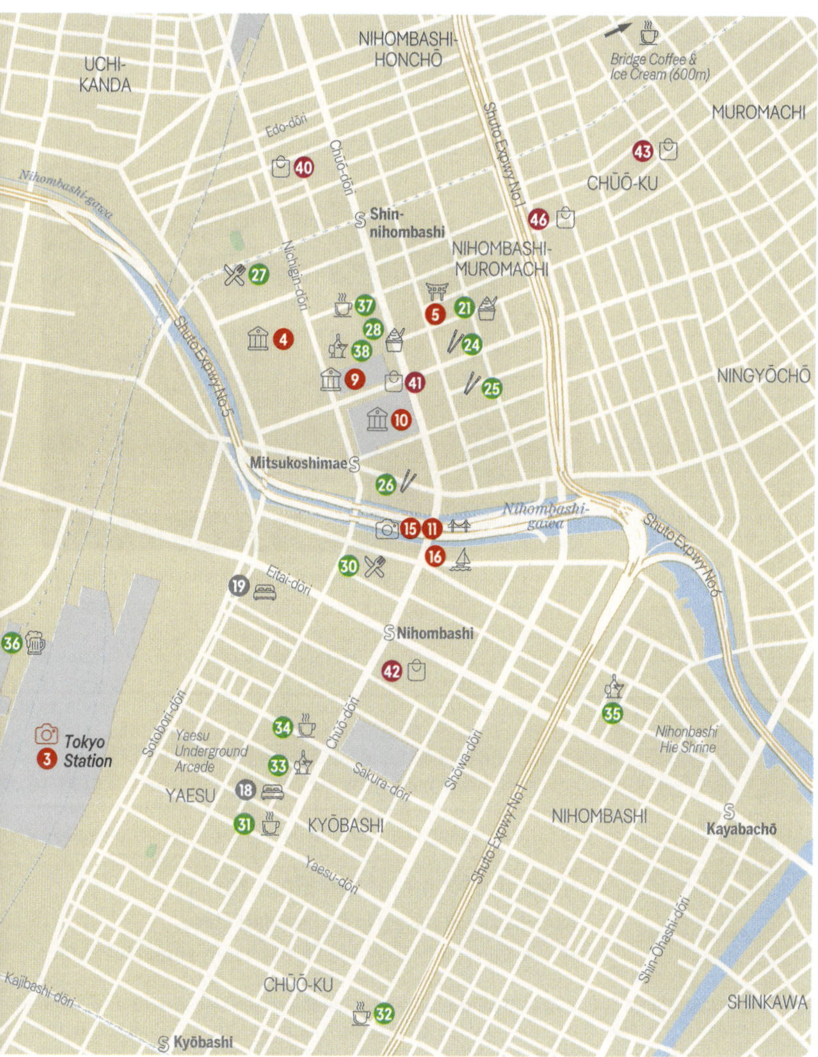

● EATING

21 Coco Gelato
22 est
23 Grill Ukai
24 Gyukatsu Motomura Coredo Muromachi
25 Janoichi Honten
26 Momijigawa
27 Nihombashi Izumoya
28 Sembikiya Fruit Parlour
29 The Cafe by AMAN
30 Usagiya Nihonbashi

● DRINKING & NIGHTLIFE

31 Aroma Coffee Yaesu
32 Bongen Coffee Nihonbashi
33 Cocktail Works Tokyo
34 Good Coffee Farms Cafe
35 Heiwa Doburoku Kabutocho Brewery
36 Hitachino Brewing
37 Ippuku & Matcha
38 Mandarin Bar
39 VIRTÙ

● SHOPPING

40 Cohana
41 Coredo Muromachi
42 Haibara
43 Hario Lampwork Factory
44 KITTE
45 Ōedo Antique Market
46 Ozu Washi

THE EAST GARDENS

Part of the Imperial Palace grounds, the **East Gardens** are open to the public and free to visit. You'll have three scenic areas to explore once you step through the garden gates – the Honmaru area is where the original foundations of the former Edo Castle still stand (and on which you can climb), while the Ninomaru and Sannomaru areas feature a lovely Japanese garden and a museum housing the Imperial Collection, respectively. The pond in the Ninomaru area is inhabited by koi carp bred by the Emperor Akihito.

The gardens are most beautiful in the spring with their cherry blossoms, but also the most crowded.

The East Gardens are closed on Mondays and Fridays, and from 8 December to 3 January.

Tsutsumi Yagura (guardhouse) of the Imperial Palace grounds

The array of shopping and dining options at Tokyo Station is staggering, contained in sprawling underground areas: Gransta and Yaechika. These include some of Tokyo's well-known retail and eating destinations: Ramen St for a selection of branches of the best ramen shops; Character St for products featuring famous figures from Japanese anime and television shows; and Okashi Land for an enormous variety of souvenir snacks to bring home. Tokyo Station contains such a diverse range of shopping, it is possible to spend an entire day exploring the area, not a bad idea on particularly hot or rainy days.

Visit the Home of the Emperor

As close as you can get to the Imperial Palace

Where Edo Castle once stood is the stately **Imperial Palace** (*sankan.kunaicho.go.jp/guide/koukyo.html; free*), where the emperor and empress of Japan reside. Originally built and occupied by the Tokugawa shogunate, the castle became the official residence of the imperial family when the shogunate was overthrown in 1868 and the capital and emperor moved from Kyoto to Tokyo. The palace sits on top of the foundation

EATING & DRINKING IN MARUNOUCHI & NIHOMBASHI: OUR PICKS

The Cafe by AMAN: Perfect for a casual date or a bite to eat, hidden in a little forest outside the AMAN Hotel. *lunch 11am-2.30pm, dessert 1-4pm, dinner 5-9pm* ¥¥¥

Mandarin Bar: Plush sofas and panoramic views from the 37th floor complement a wide range of unique cocktails. *3pm-midnight Sun-Thu, to 1am Fri & Sat* ¥¥

est: Japanese ingredients, French contemporary inspired, and exquisitely designed desserts at this Michelin-starred location *noon-3pm & 6-10pm Tue-Sun* ¥¥¥

Grill Ukai: Generously portioned and delicious dishes overlooking the plaza of the Mitsubishi Ichigokan Museum. *11.30am-3pm & 5.30-9.30pm Thu-Tue* ¥¥¥

of the aforementioned castle grounds, surrounded by its original moat. The buildings within the palace's vast compound are relatively new, having been rebuilt in the 1960s following WWII air raids that destroyed many of them. The only remaining structures from the Edo period are the two watchtowers and the imposing stone walls along the perimeter.

Not much of what's contained within those walls can be seen from the outside, so the best way to experience the palace is to join an official tour, which will take you through parts of the inner compound. You get to see the outside of the Kyūden – a somewhat understated, modern building where the throne room is located – the two historical watchtowers and several statehouses, and you get to walk on the ornate steel Nijūbashi bridge on the roughly 90-minute walking tour. No visitors are allowed inside any of the palace buildings, however, so you'll have to rely on your tour guide's description of what the interiors might contain.

These free tours are now given in multiple languages by local bilingual guides who have plenty of anecdotes and fun facts to share. Advance reservations (up to a month prior) are highly recommended, especially for larger groups, as only two tours are held each day, at 10am and 1.30pm, and places can fill up quickly. There is an option to arrive early and register on the spot, but space is not guaranteed. In the height of summer, from late July to the end of August, only the morning tour is available.

Drift Along the Palace Moat

Stunning views from a row boat at Chidori-ga-fuchi

There's no better way to experience the beauty of the Edo Castle moat and Tokyo's lush greenery than from the water at **Chidori-ga-fuchi**. Rowboats are available for rent from spring to autumn (*¥500-800 for 30 minutes*), with the period from late March to early April being especially breathtaking as you gently paddle through a pink river of *sakura* petals that drift slowly from the cherry blossom trees. Demand is naturally high during this period, and if there are no reservations available (*visit-chiyoda.tokyo/en/sakura/spot/boat.php*), your best bet is to arrive early to queue for a ticket, which comes with a designated time-slot.

For two evenings in summer, the moat is filled with floating lanterns that bob alongside the rowboats. These lanterns are inscribed with the wishes of those who set them afloat, and because only so many people (and lanterns) are allowed at once, you need to enter and win a special lottery

OTHER GREAT CHERRY BLOSSOM VIEWING SPOTS

Chidori-ga-fuchi (p61) on the north side of the Imperial Palace is one of Tokyo's top cherry blossom viewing locations, but not the only one in this area. Here are a few more recommendations to enjoy Japan's favourite season.

Nihombashi bridge (p56) is flanked with beautiful single trees that seem to glow against the darkened backdrop of the historic bridge.

Edozakura-dori runs between the historic **Bank of Japan Head Office** (p64), **Mitsukoshi Department Store** (p63), and the more modern **Coredo Muromachi** (p64) shopping and dining complexes. Both sides of the street are lined with cherry trees that create a long blossom tunnel during peak season.

Fukutoku Shrine (p64) has a few of the coveted weeping cherry trees; it also hosts *sakura*-inspired food and drink stalls in the plaza near the shrine during blossom season.

DRINKING WITH FRIENDS: OUR PICKS

Hitachino Brewing: A spacious bar to enjoy a few rounds of Hitachino's craft beers from Ibaraki Prefecture. *10am-10pm Mon-Sat, to 9pm Sun*	**VIRTÙ:** Classy but not snobby, this 39th-floor bar of the Four Seasons Hotel provides excellent service and an elegant atmosphere. *5pm-midnight Sun-Wed to 12.30am Thu-Sat*	**Heiwa Doburoku Kabu-tocho:** Once considered Japan's 'moonshine', fizzy cloudy *doburoku* gets a polish at this bar. *1-10.30pm Mon-Fri, from noon Sat, noon-9pm Sun*	**Cocktail Works Tokyo:** Old-school bar with friendly staff concocting refreshingly fruity cocktails. *6pm-2am Mon-Sat*

NIHOMBASHI'S BEST CULTURAL EVENTS

As an area important for preserving Edo culture, Nihombashi hosts several cultural events throughout the year.

The **Tokyo Kimono Show** is one of the world's largest annual kimono shows. Thousands flock to the main venues in Nihombashi for a few days each spring.

While the biennial **Sanno Matsuri** is a Tokyo-wide event, this important festival (held mid-June in even-numbered years) featuring a colourful parade of costumed participants carrying portable *mikoshi* shrines stops at **Nihombashi Hie Shrine** before continuing on to Ginza.

The **Nihombashi-Kyobashi Matsuri Parade** in late October celebrates the founding of the Nihombashi highway. A parade of 2000 representing all of Japan and food stalls are the highlights.

(*visit-chiyoda.tokyo/en/floating.lantern*) for the opportunity to row and buy a lantern of your own. The scene is still lovely to watch from anywhere along the 700m path that snakes around the moat. This path is also one of the best places for all-day *hanami* (cherry-blossom viewing) in spring, when the fully bloomed *sakura* trees are lit up as evening falls. Though it's often hard to grab a spot on a rowboat during peak periods, Chidori-ga-fuchi is often quiet at other times of the year.

Art & Culture in Marunouchi & Nihombashi

Enjoying the areas fascinating art museums

Many of the major historical buildings in the Marunouchi and Nihombashi neighbourhoods were built as offices and shops for some of Japan's most prominent companies. These family-run businesses amassed incredible wealth, a considerable sum of which was used to purchase works of art.

Two of Japan's largest family-run companies now display the collections of family members to the public. The **Mitsui Memorial Museum** (*mitsui-museum.jp; adult/student ¥1200/700, special exhibition fees vary*) displays pieces collected by the Mitsui family, founders of Mitsukoshi, the country's first department store. About half of the objects are tea ceremony utensils, six of which are designated as National Treasures of Japan. Given the Mitsui's samurai roots and business success starting in the Edo era, there are also several rare swords on display.

The **Seikado Bunko Art Museum** (*seikado.or.jp; adult/student ¥1500/1000*) was collected by two generations of the Iwasaki family, the founders of Mitsubishi. The huge collection focuses on Asian art, particularly classical works from China and Japan. Seikado began as a library, so the museum's strength is in books and printed materials, including occasional exhibitions of beautiful examples of *ukiyo-e* woodblock prints.

Since its establishment in 1952, Japan's first **National Museum of Modern Art** (MOMAT; *momat.go.jp; adult/student ¥500/250, special exhibition fees vary*) has amassed an immense collection of 13,000 works by Japanese and international artists, beginning from the 19th century. Floors 2 to 4 house the rotating displays, while special limited exhibitions are held on the 1st floor. Don't miss 'A Room with a View' – the lounge with large windows overlooking the Imperial Palace – and the beautiful *nihon-ga* (Japanese-style painting) room.

EATING IN MARUNOUCHI & NIHOMBASHI: EDO-TOKYO CUISINE

Nihombashi Izumoya: Serving *unagi* (eel) since the 1940s and run by the original owner's grandson; meals are presented in lacquer boxes. *11am-2pm & 5-9.30pm Mon-Sat* ¥¥¥

Janoichi Honten: Established in the late 1800s and still preparing classic Edomae sushi. Come for good priced lunches. *11.30am-2pm & 4.30-10pm Tue-Sat* ¥¥

Momijigawa: From when Tokyo Bay was swampland filled with wild ducks, this noodle shop serves traditional duck soba. *11am-2.30pm & 5-8.30pm Mon-Fri, 11am-3pm Sat & Sun* ¥¥

Gyukatsu Motomura Coredo Muromachi: Deep-fried breaded beef cutlets popular since just after the Edo period. The Nihombashi branch isn't as busy as others. *11am-9pm* ¥

Mitsukoshi

Designed & Made in Japan
Discovering the best Japan-created goods

Marunouchi and Nihombashi have been the home of the best goods manufactured in Japan for centuries, so it should be no surprise that an abundance of shops featuring Japanese designed and made goods still exist here. The famous **Mitsukoshi** department store *(cp.mistore.jp/global/en/nihombashi.html)* began life as a humble kimono shop in the early Edo period and many other shops established in the same era continue to do business in some modern form. While some continue to sell products that hearken back to the area's roots in commerce, others showcase a new generation of innovation and quality by modern artisans from across the nation.

One of the former is **Ozu Washi** *(ozuwashi.net)*, a wholesale paper seller which has operated in the same location of Nihombashi since 1653. Not only does Ozu carry a huge selection of beautiful handmade papers, but you can also participate in a workshop to make your own (p65). **Haibara** *(haibara.co.jp)* is another *washi* shop with a 220-year history in Nihonbashi and an elegant selection of curated paper-related goods.

For over 100 years, **Hario Lampwork Factory** *(hario-lwf. com)* has been crafting household goods from glass by hand at its main factory in Nihombashi and others around Japan. Drop by to watch the artisans at work and purchase some beautiful glass jewellery pieces.

Cohana *(cohana.style/en/store)* is a small shop selling products created for those who love handicrafts, particularly sewing. Unique sewing pins, pin cushions and sewing scissors are not only aesthetically gorgeous but highly functional in design.

For vintage Japanese goods, browse the scores of stalls of the **Oedo Antique Market** *(antique-market.jp/english)*, which

KITTE'S BEST SHOPS

The renovated former main post office, **KITTE**, is chock full of great shopping (and a fantastic free museum, **Intermediatheque**). Here are the best of its unique outlets for souvenirs and gifts.

Nakagawa Masashichi is a shop from Nara featuring modern Japanese-designed clothing, housewares and accessories. It's particularly known for its hand-woven linen products.

Snow Peak sells high-quality outdoor and camping goods designed and made in Japan with a lifetime repair warranty on all of its products.

Good Design Store Tokyo by Nohara carries nearly 1000 lifestyle items that have been awarded Japan's Good Design Award.

Hacoa offers unique items made from forest-rich Fukui Prefecture wood. Hacoa, transforming everyday items like USB drives and business card holders into works of art that can be engraved on site.

MARUNOUCHI & NIHOMBASHI ARCHITECTURE TOUR

Journey from Nihombashi to Marunouchi and take in the eclectic architecture on this stroll around the city centre.

START	END	LENGTH
Nihonbashi bridge	Tokyo International Forum	2.9km; 1½hr

Begin at precisely the centre of Tokyo: the historic ❶ **Zero Milestone in Japan marker** at Nihonbashi bridge (p56), then head to Japan's first department store, the ornate ❷ **Mitsukoshi** (p63) – both are built in a Western style and are important historical landmarks of the area.

Across the road are shopping complexes ❸ **Coredo Muromachi 1 and 2**. Walk down the lanterned street between the two buildings to see how tradition meets modern architecture. At the junction, you'll see a *torii* (entrance gate) that is the entry to ❹ **Fukutoku-jinja**, a small but elegant traditional shrine situated beneath a modern skyscraper. Continue to the green-roofed ❺ **Bank of Japan Head Office**, a classic Western-style building designed by Kingo

Tatsuno, who also designed Tokyo Station, our next stop. Along the way, stroll through the ❻ **Otemachi Forest**, a small nature reserve in the heart of Marunouchi preserving the landscape as it was before the area was developed. The best place to see Tokyo Station in all its grandeur is the plaza in front of it – ❼ **Marunouchi Ekimae Square**.

Continue along the length of the red-brick building and towards ❽ **KITTE** (p63) to check out the impressive interior or stop by the museum, Intermediatheque. Last is ❾ **Tokyo International Forum**. This architectural marvel by Rafael Viñoly features a glass boat-shaped building, and houses auditoriums, exhibition halls and the Mitsuo Aida Museum.

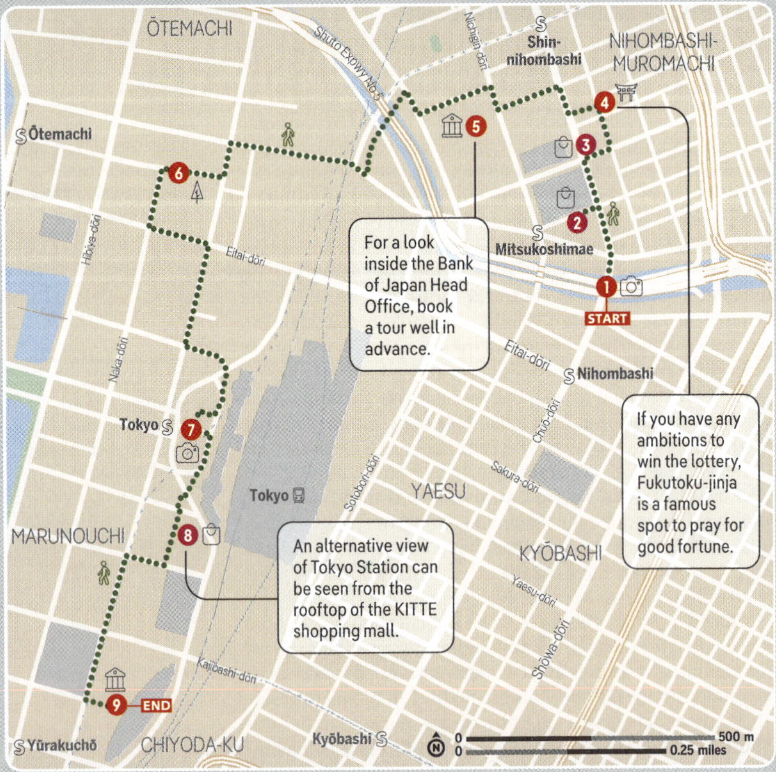

takes place twice a month from 9am to 4pm on irregular weekend dates. Antique ceramics, kimono and even tin toys are sold by reputable dealers at this popular event on the plaza of **Tokyo International Forum**.

Floating On Nihombashi's Ancient Rivers

Guided boat tours along Tokyo's original waterways

When Edo became the capital of Japan during the reign of the shogunate, the rivers and tributaries were the highways delivering food and commercial goods to the quickly growing city and beyond. But in the haste of the preparation for the 1964 Tokyo Olympic Games, many of these waterways were covered by overhead expressways to facilitate the anticipated vehicular traffic. The view of Nihonbashi bridge (p56) was one of the major casualties of hasty progress, but many of the once-beautiful rivers suffered the same fate of being hidden beneath unsightly expressways.

Still, a tour by boat provides a unique view of the city from a historical perspective. **Nihonbashi Cruise** (*nihonbashi-cruise.jp*) departs from a pier next to Nihonbashi Bridge, offering trips ranging from 45 to 90 minutes along the major waterways. You'll see landmarks like Tokyo Skytree and the moat of the Imperial Palace from a different angle and hear about how the rivers contributed to the growth of Tokyo over the centuries. You'll also pass under several iconic bridges, some so low that you feel you need to duck as you glide under them. There are several seasonal tours (excluding winter) including a panoramic port cruise, a romantic sunset cruise and a night cruise to enjoy the glow of the evening Tokyo Bay skyline.

Learn a Craft at a 370-Year-Old Shop

Traditional paper-making at Ozu Washi

The ancient roads from Nihombashi to the rest of Japan brought the founder of **Ozu Washi** (p63) to Edo in 1653, where he established a paper wholesaler. The location and products haven't changed much since then, and Ozu continues the tradition of making and selling handmade paper. Visitors are invited to join in the fun at Ozu's workshop, and experience making a sheet of *washi* using mulberry fibre and a sugeta paper mould. Participants choose from a standard smooth sheet of *washi* paper of A4 size or a lace *washi*, where the paper is covered by a mould and thinned using a spray of water to create intricate patterns. Some sessions also offer a 'design *washi*' experience where you can add coloured papers, pressed flowers and other materials to create a sheet of paper of your own design. Prices for workshops vary from ¥1000 to ¥1500.

While walk-ins are welcome if there is space, there's a good chance the workshop will be fully booked weeks in advance, so it's better to make an online reservation on Ozu Washi's website before visiting. The experience takes about an hour, but allow time to explore the shop's free history museum. It has a fascinating collection of ancient documents, tools and displays using traditional *washi* on the upper floor of the shop.

NIHOMBASHI IN UKIYO-E PRINTS

During the late Edo period, the majority of Japanese travelled vicariously through artists specialising in *ukiyo-e*, prints that could be mass produced from the carvings of wood blocks, stamped layer upon layer to add colour and texture to images.

While early *ukiyo-e* artists focused on portraits of beautiful women and kabuki actors, the later history of *ukiyo-e* moved on to landscapes, especially those seen along the major highways leading to Edo's Nihombashi.

Artists like Hokusai and Hiroshige produced images including *Thirty-six Views of Mt Fuji* and *The Fifty-three Stations of the Tōkaidō*, both of which feature scenes of Edo-era Nihombashi. But as the symbolic centre of Japan, Nihombashi was the subject of countless prints by other artists as well.

Researched by Todd Fong

GINZA & TSUKIJI

STYLISH, SUAVE AND SWANKY

The double lures of luxury shopping and the finest cuisine are still irresistible after all these years.

Ginza's (銀座) reputation as Tokyo's most exclusive neighbourhood is well earned. Home to designer boutiques and stylish cafes, it's a destination for Tokyoites looking to splurge. By day, the district is about shopping, art galleries and afternoon tea; by night, swanky cocktail bars and fine restaurants attract an even more refined crowd. A 10-minute walk from Ginza is Tsukiji (築地), once home to the capital's largest wholesale seafood market before it relocated to Toyosu in 2018. Many visitors prefer the raw authenticity of Tsukiji's outer market, however, so it still attracts a crowd wanting to enjoy sashimi rice bowls, Kobe beef and a mouthwatering array of street food. Nearby Hama-rikyū Gardens is an oasis on the bay built by past shoguns for pleasure.

TIP

A few train lines on the Tokyo Metro lead to the neighbourhood of Ginza, with most of the neighbourhood stations within walking distance of each other. The stations are Ginza, Ginza Itchōme and Higashi Ginza. The JR Yūrakuchō station is also relatively close by, as is Shinbashi Station.

Chuo-dori street, Ginza (p72)

See page 218 for places to stay in Ginza & Tsukij

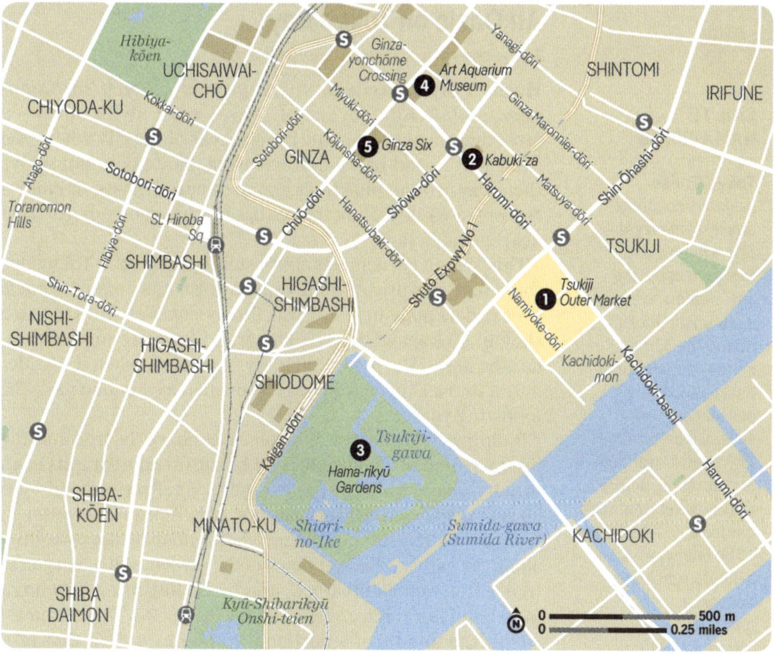

⭐ Highlights

① Tsukiji Outer Market

Still Tokyo's gourmet destination for fresh seafood and street food. **p75**

② Kabuki-za

Witness the dramatic theatrical art of kabuki at this famous Ginza theatre. **p69**

③ Hama-rikyū Gardens

Feel the breeze coming off Tokyo Bay as you stroll this Japanese garden. **p68**

④ Art Aquarium Museum

Goldfish become art in this fascinating exhibition of design. **p75**

⑤ Ginza Six

High-end shopping mall featuring an eclectic mix of art and fashion. **p72**

🚶 Getting Around

Subway
The Ginza, Marunouchi, Hibiya, Yūrakuchō and Oedo lines have stations in this area.

Train
The Yamanote line stations of Yūrakuchō and Shinbashi are also within walking distance.

Walking
Walking is the most enjoyable way to experience Ginza and Tsukiji's many side streets. On weekends and holidays the broad Chūō-dōri is closed to motorised traffic, creating a lovely destination for a stroll.

SAIL TO HAMA-RIKYŪ

Tokyo Cruise (suijobus.co.jp/en/cruise/hamarikyu) offers journeys to the gardens via the city's waterways in its futuristic-looking boats. The 35-minute journey departs from Asakusa and takes passengers under several iconic bridges that stretch over the Sumida River, before arriving directly at the gardens.

The one-way ¥1180 fare includes admission to the gardens.

You can't return to Asakusa by boat, but there are several nearby train and subway stations you can walk to from the garden. Alternatively, Hama-rikyū is a walkable distance from the Tsukiji Outer Market and even Ginza, so you can stretch your visit to Hama-rikyū into an full day excursion.

Only a limited number of departures stop at Hama-rikyū Gardens, so buy your tickets early to avoid disappointment.

An Oasis on Tokyo Bay

Enjoy the refined Hama-rikyū Gardens

Hama-rikyū Gardens (*tokyo-park.or.jp/teien/en/hama-rikyu; adult ¥300*) is one of Tokyo's most idyllic spots – a green haven away from the busier areas of the city where you can easily spend half a day exploring. Park-goers can weave their way around pine trees and manicured lawns, or enjoy a cup of tea while feeling the sea breeze that gently drifts from nearby Tokyo Bay.

This scenic garden was first established by the Tokugawa shogunate as a private family space, with improvements made over generations before it was finally completed by the 11th shogun, Tokugawa Ienari. The grand garden remained under the use of the imperial family until 1945, when it was donated to the City of Tokyo and reopened as a public park the following year.

Buildings from nearby Shiodome rise above the tree line, the juxtaposition of which makes for beautiful photographs of an urban oasis. Within the park are several reflective ponds, the largest being tidal **Shiori-no-ike**, which draws seawater in from Tokyo Bay. It could take over an hour of slow strolling along the paths to see every inch of the garden, and when you're in need of a quick breather, stop by **Nakajima-no-ochaya** for a bit of tea and *wagashi* (Japanese sweets). This teahouse sits in the middle of Shiori-no-ike and has a deck that provides an unobstructed view of the gardens from the water.

Add Drama To Your Day

Watch a Kabuki-za theatre performance

Everything about a kabuki show is truly a spectacle. From the actors' dramatic make-up, elaborate costumes and exaggerated movements in tune with the live music to the impeccable stagecraft, it's easy to see how it's managed to captivate audiences for centuries. This art form traces its origins to 17th-century Kyoto, where a female shrine attendant and her troupe of female performers first gained popularity for their distinct style of dance. A concern for morals at the time led to female performers being banned in 1652, eventually resulting in men taking over their roles. Kabuki retains an all-male cast today, and actors who play female roles are known as *onnagata* (which literally translates to 'female role').

A typical kabuki show comprises three to four acts, each lasting about an hour. Shows often depict dramatised events

EATING IN GINZA: SWEET TREATS

Ginza Kikunoya: An 1890 established shop selling lovely tins of sweets that pair perfectly with tea. *9.30am-6pm Mon, Tue, Thu & Fri, to 5.30pm Sat & Sun ¥*

Shiseido Parlour Salon de Café: Amazing parfaits in the restaurant, or tins of exquisite cookies from its shop. *11am-9pm Tue-Sat, to 8pm Sun ¥¥*

Louange Tokyo Le Musée: You'll likely need a reservation for the extraordinary afternoon tea in this stylish cafe. *11am-9pm ¥¥*

L'ibisco: A dozen flavours of authentic Italian gelato in this little 2nd-floor shop. *11am-7pm ¥*

Hamarikyū Gardens

from history, the most famous of which is the *Chūshingura*, which tells the tale of the 47 Rōnin, a group of lordless samurai who avenge the death of their master. A day at **Kabuki-za** *(kabuki-za.co.jp)*, Tokyo's premier theatre for kabuki, is a half-day affair with intermissions in between for audiences to dine on *bentō* (boxed meals). These meals are sold at the theatre common areas, and audiences can dine directly at their seats.

There are two performances daily, 25 days out of the month. English captioning devices are available to rent that provides essential, not comprehensive, translations of dialogue and lyrics. For just a quick taste of kabuki at a reasonable price *(from around ¥3000)*, 90 reserved single-act seats are available for purchase online the day before the performance, and 20 non-reserved seats are for sale on the day itself. About 20 reserved tickets are upgraded seating on the 2nd level while the others are on the 4th level, furthest from the stage and with a partially blocked view.

GINBURA IN GINZA

Now something of an old-fashioned term, **ginbura** is a combination of the words Ginza and *bura*, which means to wander aimlessly. To loiter, or *ginbura*, around Ginza was an activity that appeared to be all the rage beginning from the 1910s, when the neighbourhood, with its shophouses and bazaars, emerged as a hip hangout for Tokyoites.

Though the term is not often used now, the actual practice of *ginbura* is still very much alive, a testament to the lasting allure of this legendary Tokyo district.

You don't have to break your bank account to enjoy *ginbura*; it can be enjoyed by window shopping, popping into fashionable cafes or visiting the many free art galleries scattered around the district.

DRINKING IN GINZA: COOL CAFES

Yonemoto Coffee: Friendly staff and delicious coffee drinks and light fare on the outskirts of Tsukiji Outer Market. *7.30am-3.30pm Sun-Fri, to 4pm Sat*

Turret Coffee: Known for its double shot latte, one of Tokyo's best espresso drinks. *7am-5pm Mon, Tue, Fri & Sat, to 3pm Thu, 8am-4pm Sun*

Cafe de l'Ambre: Founded by coffee innovator Ichiro Sekiguchi; come for the perfect cup and nothing more. *11am-8pm Tue-Sat, to 6pm Sun*

Cafe Paulista: Tokyo's first cafe, founded in 1911, maintains its sophisticated air and strong brews. *9am-8pm Mon-Fri, to 7:30pm Sat, 11.30am-7pm Sun*

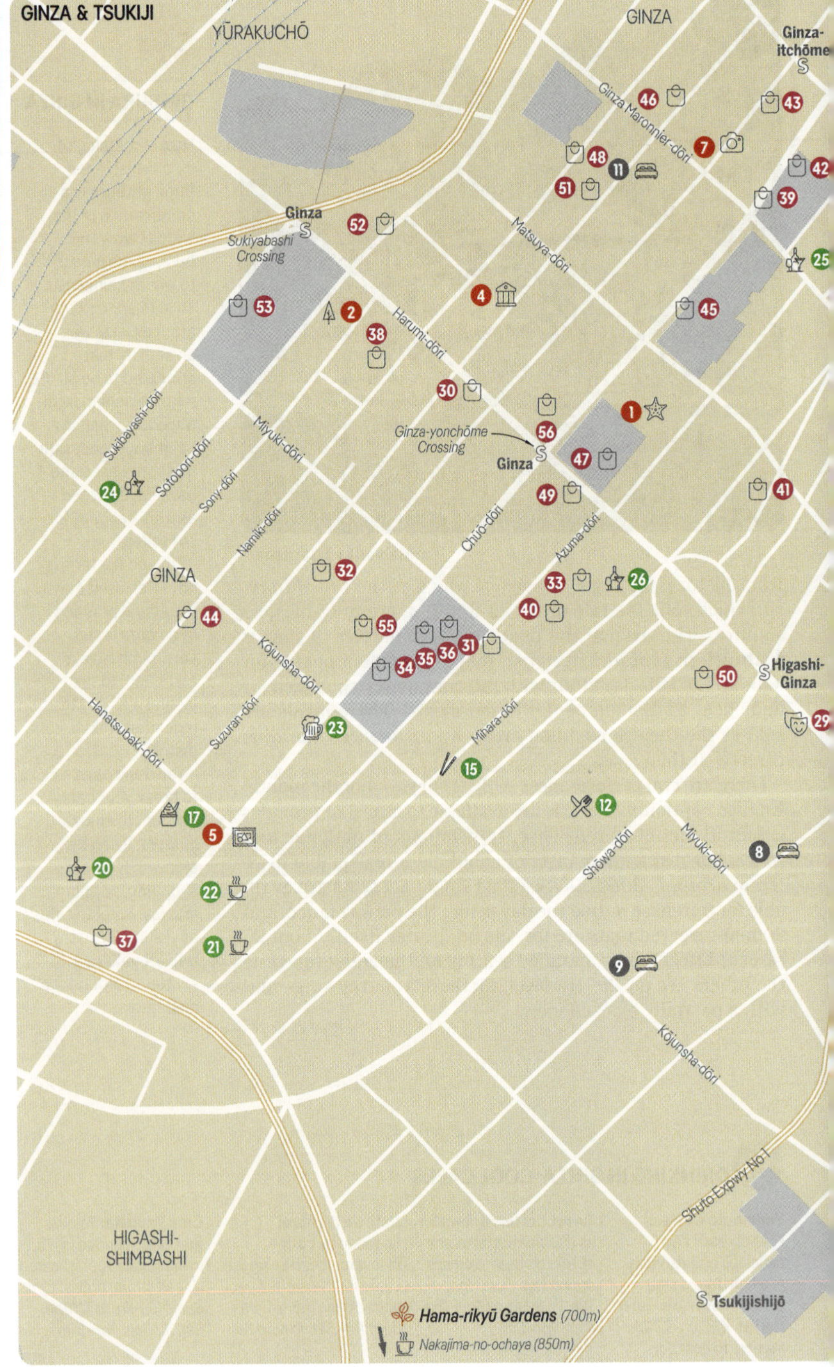
GINZA & TSUKIJI
YŪRAKUCHŌ
GINZA
Ginza-itchōme
Ginza Maronnier-dōri
Ginza
Sukiyabashi Crossing
Matsuya-dōri
Sukibayashi-dōri
Sotobori-dōri
Sony-dōri
Miyuki-dōri
Namiki-dōri
Harumi-dōri
Ginza-yonchōme Crossing
Ginza
Chuō-dōri
Azuma-dōri
GINZA
Kōjunsha-dōri
Suzuran-dōri
Hanatsubaki-dōri
Mihara-dōri
Higashi-Ginza
Shōwa-dōri
Miyuki-dōri
Kōjunsha-dōri
Shuto Expwy No.1
HIGASHI-SHIMBASHI
Tsukijishijō
Hama-rikyū Gardens (700m)
Nakajima-no-ochaya (850m)

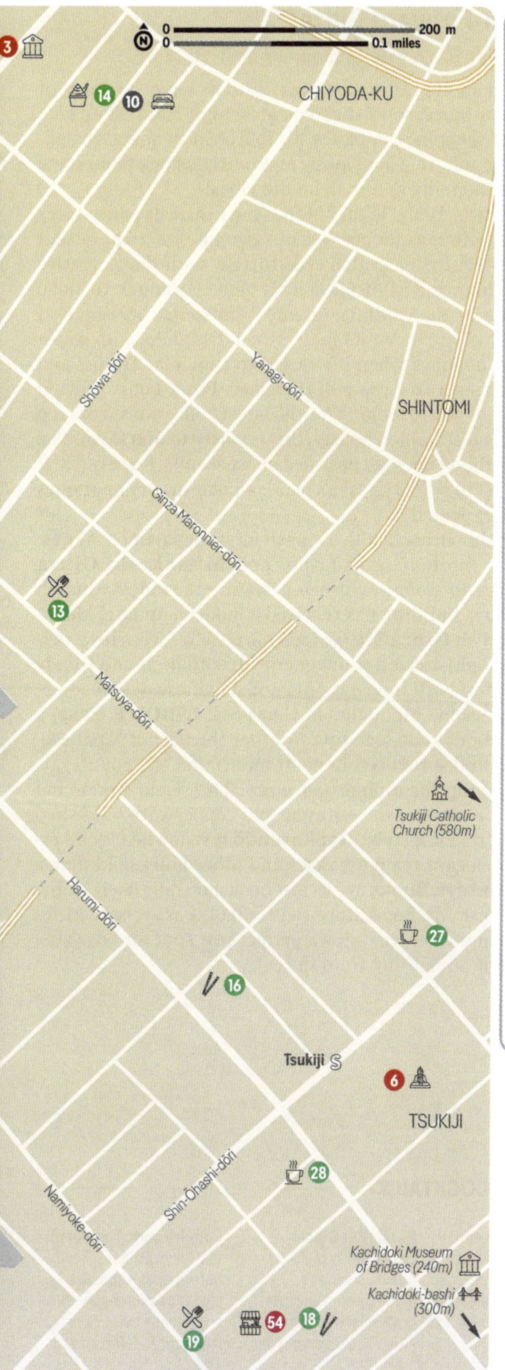

200 m
0.1 miles
CHIYODA-KU
Shōwa-dōri
Yanagi-dōri
SHINTOMI
Ginza Maronnier-dōri
Matsuya-dōri
Harumi-dōri
Tsukiji Catholic Church (580m)
Tsukiji
TSUKIJI
Namiyoke-dōri
Shin-Ōhashi-dōri
Kachidoki Museum of Bridges (240m)
Kachidoki-bashi (300m)

★ SIGHTS
1 Art Aquarium Museum
2 Ginza Sony Park
3 Pola Museum Annex
4 Seiko Museum
5 Shiseido Gallery
6 Tsukiji Hongwan-ji
7 V88 Building

● SLEEPING
8 Agora Tokyo Ginza
9 Dormy Inn Premium Ginza
10 Hotel Monterey La Soeur
11 Muji Hotel Ginza

● EATING
12 Kushiyaki Bistro Fukumimi
13 L'ibisco
14 Louange Tokyo Le Musée
15 Mugi to Olive
16 Nunotsune Sarashina
17 Shiseido Parlour Salon de Café
18 Sushi Sei
19 Yamachō

● DRINKING & NIGHTLIFE
20 Bar Butler Ginza
21 Cafe de l'Ambre
22 Cafe Paulista
23 Ginza Lion
24 Little Smith
25 Punch Room
26 Tír na nÓg
27 Turret Coffee
28 Yonemoto Coffee

● ENTERTAINMENT
29 Kabuki-za

● SHOPPING
30 Bottega Veneta Ginza Flagship Store
31 CIBONE Case
32 Dover Street Market Ginza
33 Ginza Kikunoya
34 Ginza Six
35 Ginza Tsutaya Books
36 Gyokusendō
37 Hakuhinkan
38 Hermès Ginza
39 Itōya
40 Kindal Ginza
41 Koju Ginza
42 Komehyo
43 Kurashi-no-Kaori
44 Louis Vuitton Ginza Namiki-dōri
45 Matsuya
46 Mikimoto Ginza 2
47 Mitsukoshi Ginza
48 MUJI Ginza
49 Nissan Crossing
50 Ōnoya
51 rt Ginza
52 Sanrio Nishiginza
53 Tokyu Plaza Ginza
54 Tsukiji Outer Market
55 UNIQLO Ginza
56 Wako

STOCK UP YOUR WARDROBE

Despite its luxury reputation, Ginza has fashion shops for every budget.

The **UNIQLO** flagship shop and **MUJI Ginza** both sell stylishly designed products at reasonable prices. The 12-storey UNIQLO stocks seasonal items year-round.

If you don't mind secondhand luxury, shops like **Komehyo**, **rt Ginza** and **Kindal** sell high-quality, brand-name items that could be mistaken for new. You'll also sometimes find rare vintage pieces.

Dover Street Market, connected to the UNIQLO flagship shop, has several floors selling the creations and collaborations of cutting-edge designers. Even if you wouldn't dream of wearing anything sold here, it's worth the time to browse, or admire the staff members' bold fashion choices.

Fashion-Forward Ginza

Navigate Tokyo's favourite shopping district

There's an air of prestige to Ginza. With its streets lined with luxury boutiques, sophisticated cafes, high-end restaurants and grand shopping complexes, it's Tokyo's most upscale neighbourhood, and it's where locals and tourists flock to do some weekend shopping and soak up the vibes.

Many international luxury brands have their flagship stores here; the buildings themselves are examples of great design and architecture – elevated even further with their creative and enticing window displays. This alone is enough to make Ginza one of the capital's foremost hotspots, but the real treat is strolling down its main street, Chūō-dori, on weekends and holidays when it's closed to vehicular traffic, and pedestrians get free roam of the place. From Louis Vuitton to Cartier, if you're looking for the latest collections from the world's biggest fashion houses, this is where to find them. The neighbourhood does get crowded on weekends, however, and queues just to enter the area's more popular luxury boutiques are to be expected.

The neighbourhood is also known for its department stores: **Matsuya** (*matsuyaginza.com*) and **Mitsukoshi Ginza** (*cp.mistore.jp/global/en/ginza.html*) are the oldest, though the Matsuya building has received a modern update. Meanwhile, stylish **Ginza Six** (*ginza6.tokyo*) is a favourite hangout for a sophisticated younger crowd, with high-end trendy brands from both international and Japanese designers.

Here are some highlights of Ginza Six. **CIBONE Case**, a lifestyle goods shop bringing together the best of Japanese-designed and -produced items from around the country, is a perfect stop for unique souvenirs. The sleek, wood-clad Ginza showroom of the 400-year-old copperware workshop from Niigata Prefecture, **Gyokusendō** is renowned for its exquisitely elegant tea pots, vases and other household items. **Ginza Tsutaya Books** modernist bookshop bills itself as 'the World's Best Art Book Store', with 60,000 art-related titles from around the planet. It's a perfect rest spot for browsing or enjoying something from the cafe.

DRINKING IN GINZA: BEST COCKTAILS

Tír na nÓg: Basement bar that can only be described as otherworldly. Lots of inventive drinks and cocktails. *cafe 11am-5pm, bar 5pm-4am*

Little Smith: No menu here – just ask for what you crave and the talented bartenders will make it for you. *6pm-3am Mon-Fri, to 1am Sat*

Bar Butler Ginza: Consistently high-quality cocktails made by consummate professionals. *5pm-2am Mon-Fri, to midnight Sat*

Punch Room: This bar at the Tokyo Edition, Ginza hotel makes a splash with signature punches with a Japanese twist. *6pm-midnight Tue-Thu, to 2am Fri & Sat*

Cafe de l'ambre (p74)

Ginza's Retro Cafes

Experience historic *kissaten*

Japan's *kissaten* have a reputation similar to that of Parisian cafes of the past – as a hub where writers, artists and intellectuals would gather to talk, work and smoke. Though the word *kissaten* directly translates to 'tea-drinking shop', these cosy establishments specialise in coffee and have a distinct, retro style that sets them apart from modern cafes. In the late Meiji (1868–1912) and Taisho (1912–26) periods, when *kissaten* became popular, many were centred around the trendy Ginza neighbourhood. These coffee shops often have warm, wooden interiors featuring velvet chairs and ornate lamps that dangle dimly from the ceiling in the Japanese-infused Western style that was so popular at the time.

The quintessential *kissaten* experience involves dropping into one of these cosy establishments and getting a cuppa along with some signature Western-style food. Staple dishes you'll find include *omurice,* a runny, fluffy omelette on top of tomato rice; and spaghetti Neapolitan, a slightly sweet, ketchup-based pasta. For dessert, you'll always be able to find a smooth

GINZA'S UNIQUE SOUVENIRS

Tasteful souvenirs with connections to Japanese culture, both modern and traditional, are easy to find in this diverse district.

Itōya: Stationery shop with 10 floors of fashionable items. Look for the red paperclip out the front. (p77)

Kurashi-no-Kaori: Minimalist living and personal care products, with fragrances inspired by the seasons and traditions of Japan.

Ōnoya: Small shop with a huge selection of traditional textiles, *tabi* footwear and personal goods, in business since 1868.

Koju Ginza: An array of products using the delicate fragrances of incense for both modern and traditional uses.

Sanrio Nishiginza: At the flagship Sanrio store you'll find an enormous array of Hello Kitty and friends, including occasional collaborations with traditional artisans.

EATING IN GINZA AND TSUKIJI: TOP SPOTS

Nunotsune Sarashina: This historic fresh soba noodle shop fills up fast – it's worth the wait for its richly flavoured broth. *11.30am-2pm Tue-Sat, plus 5-8pm Tue-Fri* ¥¥

Sushi Sei: Reasonably priced sashimi bowls and sushi for Tsukiji Outer Market, with friendly, helpful staff. *11am-3pm & 5.30-9.30pm Mon-Fri, 11am-9.30pm Sat & Sun* ¥¥

Kushiyaki Bistro Fukumimi: This *yakitori* restaurant got so popular they opened another location a few blocks away. *4-11.25pm, closed holidays* ¥¥

Mugi to Olive: Modest ramen shop that frequently wins awards for the rich flavours of its chicken-clam broth and firm noodles. *11am-3.30pm & 5.30-9.30pm Thu-Tue* ¥

FREE ART IN GINZA

Art is part of Ginza's DNA and free displays can be found all over the neighbourhood.

Pola Museum Annex: Not the Pola Museum of Art (which is not free), this annex of the museum offers small exhibitions that change regularly.

Shiseido Gallery: The sleek basement gallery of the Japanese cosmetic company displays the work of contemporary artists.

Seiko Museum: This surprisingly comprehensive museum features the art and beauty of Seiko timepieces over the history of the company.

Ginza Six Atrium: You can often find contemporary art suspended over and in the rest areas surrounding the large multistorey atrium of this chic shopping mall. (p72)

Ginza Sony Park: This brutalist public space donated by Sony often hosts free exhibitions.

Bottega Veneta

custard pudding *(purin)* with a bitter caramel top, and a melon cream-soda float. Many of the more traditional *kissaten* still allow smoking indoors.

Ginza's **Cafe Paulista** (p69) is regarded as Japan's original *kissaten*, though coffee purists who skip the food find **Cafe de l'ambre** to be top dog.

Skyline of Sculptures

An architectural walking tour

A stroll through Ginza is a lesson in the power of branding. Before you even peek into the display windows of flagship shops, luxury brands are grabbing your attention with buildings designed by famous architects in an array of materials. Take a walking tour around Ginza to discover a few of its most interesting pieces of modern architecture.

Ginza's **Bottega Veneta** flagship store combines angular metallic panels over a sleek Japanese-Italian-inspired interior, designed to represent Tokyo's futuristic spirit. The texture of the outer panels is meant to evoke the leather used in the brand's handbags. The **V88 building** was originally built for De Beers and based on the concept of curving streams of light. Its undulating stainless steel facade stands out all the more between its upright neighbours.

Toyo Ito's **Mikimoto Ginza 2** building grabs attention with its irregularly shaped windows positioned around a shiny white facade, practically begging passersby to look inside. On the contrary, **Hermès Ginza**, designed by Renzo Piano, is made from translucent glass blocks, making the interior of the store a bit of a mystery. Next door, the recently completed **Ginza Sony Park** is a brutalist structure with slanting floors, created as a public space and art exhibition venue on the site of the original Sony headquarters. The fact that Sony has dedicated a plot of land for public use in an area with one of the world's highest real estate prices is remarkable in itself.

Towering over Sukiyabashi Crossing, Ginza's answer to Shibuya's more chaotic Shibuya Crossing, **Tokyu Plaza Ginza** is a steel-and-glass cathedral of a mall. While its selection of shops has seen better days, the building still offers a viewpoint down on the multi-directional street crossing from several floors through floor-to-ceiling windows.

The Art of Goldfish

Edo aesthetics meets modern design

Despite what its name might suggest, there's only one type of fish at **Art Aquarium Museum** (*artaquarium.jp; adult/student ¥2500/2200*) – the goldfish. A popular temporary exhibit that was initially open only in summertime, Art Aquarium has moved to a permanent location in Ginza, where it can now present the beauty of what we might consider 'household pets' in ways never seen before, all year round. The aquarium is located inside **Mitsukoshi Ginza** (p72), on the 9th floor. As you step from the brightly lit shop floors into the darkened exhibition space, you'll be met with tanks of elegantly drifting goldfish that glisten in the light. The aquarium has a variety of these fish, ranging from common species to rare breeds, and all are presented beautifully in unique tanks and installations. Proceed through and you'll also encounter art pieces that evoke traditional Japanese design, from *ukiyo-e* (woodblock prints) to Edo *kiriko* (cut glass) motifs.

The presentation of it all is, however, distinctly modern – brightly coloured lights and mirrors imbue the space with a beautiful, futuristic and otherworldly vibe – reminiscent of the popular exhibits by creative company teamLab (p87) – and create an experience that's sure to leave a lasting impression.

Everyone's Favourite Fish Market

Tsukiji Outer Market still draws the crowds

Big waves were made when Tsukiji's famous tuna auction and wholesale market relocated to Toyosu; but aside from the opportunity to witness the auction firsthand, everything else that Tsukiji Market is known for is alive and well. **Tsukiji Outer Market** (*tsukiji.or.jp*) remains the ultimate spot to grab a bite of freshly caught seafood, munch on snacks or look for produce and kitchenware. Many sushi and *kaisendon* (assorted raw seafood on rice) shops are here, while street stalls also draw crowds with freshly grilled scallops and more. It's very much a tourist hotspot, but the market is still an important place for many restaurants in the city, whose staff come here to source ingredients. Most wholesale activities take place before 9am, when tourists aren't allowed in.

Prices for many restaurants and street vendors do tend to be elevated for the tourist crowds, but you can find more reasonably priced foods if you search around. The renowned

GINZA: JAPAN'S WINDOW ON THE WEST

Ginza's transformation into the area it is today began in 1872, when the area was constructed to be a 'fire-resistant city' of Western-style brick buildings.

While the architectural form wasn't enthusiastically embraced by the Japanese of the era, the curiosity with Western culture took root here, especially in the arts and fashion. In the early 20th century, Tokyo's *'moga'*, modern girls who embraced the social and fashion standards of the West, were the trendsetters of their day, frequenting Ginza's fashion boutiques, art galleries and cafes.

The district became a magnet for international artists, writers and musicians, whose reputations were magnified by the awe the rest of the country held for this influential neighbourhood.

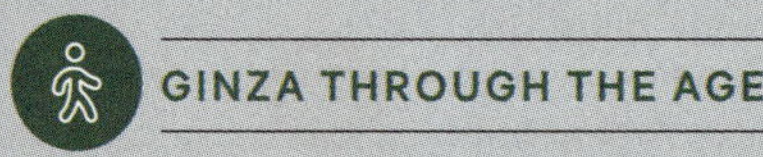

GINZA THROUGH THE AGES

From historic landmarks to chic new stores and cool architecture, this walk through Ginza will show you the neighbourhood's most iconic spots.

START	END	LENGTH
Kabuki-za	Hakuhinkan Toy Park	1.6km; 1hr

Begin your journey at **1 Kabuki-za** (p69), Tokyo's foremost theatre for kabuki. Then, turn right and continue up the road – next stop is **2 Mitsukoshi Ginza** (p72), one of Ginza's oldest department stores, and home to the Art Aquarium (p75). Just across the road from here is **3 Wako**, with its iconic clock, which is a department store specialising in timepieces, jewellery and accessories. Across the intersection is **4 Nissan Crossing**, a showroom for the eponymous car manufacturer featuring both classic and concept vehicles. Proceed down the avenue to the next major intersection, where you'll see **5 Hermès Ginza** (p74) and its cool glass-block facade. Turn left and then right onto Namiki-dōri, where many of Ginza's luxury boutiques are located. The architecture here is amazing, with the shining, iridescent and jellyfish-like **6 Louis Vuitton** store being particularly eye-catching.

Turn left at the intersection just outside the store and continue straight to the **7 Ginza Lion building**, Japan's oldest beer hall, looking the same as when it was built in 1934. Next door is the high-end mall, **8 Ginza Six** (p74). the neighbourhood's first cafe, **9 Cafe Paulista** (p69) is also on the same Chūō-dōri avenue. For young travellers or the young at heart, check out **10 Hakuhinkan Toy Park**, Ginza's favourite toy store since 1899.

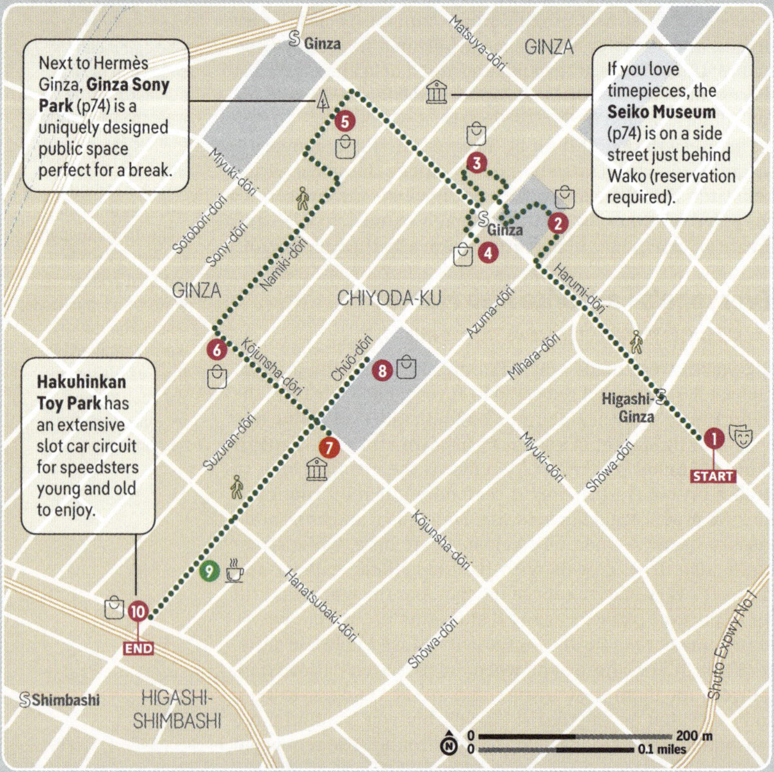

Yamachō stall, selling grilled *tamago-yaki* (rolled omelette), is the same bargain it has been for decades, for example.

Though official opening hours are from 9am to 2pm, some vendors might close earlier. A few things to take note of here: no bargaining is allowed; some stalls do not allow photography; and eating must be done in the vicinity of the stall the item was purchased from, or in designated areas.

Tsukiji Beyond the Fish

A stroll around the Tsukiji area

The Tsukiji area isn't only about the fish market, although that famous location has dominated the bucket lists of visitors to Tokyo for decades. Tsukiji's history began centuries before, when the earth removed for the construction of Edo Castle's formidable moats was brought here to solidify the marshlands along the Sumida River delta. The name Tsukiji literally translates to 'created land'. One of the structures built here in the 17th century was **Tsukiji Hongwan-ji** *(tsukiji hongwanji.jp)*, relocated from Asakusa after the 1657 Great Fire of Meireki, which destroyed two-thirds of the city. The temple's current iteration is a uniquely designed structure built in 1934 by the famous architect Chuta Ito. Ito's travels around the world influenced many design elements of this temple: the Indian Bodhi tree styled centre roof, the carvings of Chinese zodiac animals in temple decor, and the colourful stained-glass windows over the entrance that would look at home in a Catholic cathedral.

In the 1860s Japan opened its doors to the world after 270 years of isolation, and Tsukiji became the designed foreign settlement area for the newly renamed Tokyo. While a handful of small monuments mark former important sites, only a few actual structures from this period remain, including the **Tsukiji Catholic Church**, the third oldest in Japan.

Kachidoki-bashi is a historic drawbridge that was instrumental in the development of the area around Tsukiji for Japan's post-war boom period. The low-slung crossing has an elegant form that is most beautiful when lit up in the evening, reflected in the water below. The small **Kachidoki Museum of Bridges** on the Tsukiji-side displays the history and mechanical workings of the bridge.

You can walk to Hama-rikyū Gardens (p68) from the market area in about 10 minutes via the lovely Otemon Bridge, once made of wood but reconstructed in stone after the 1923 Great Kantō Earthquake.

Researched by Kim Kahan

ROPPONGI & AROUND

SKYSCRAPERS, ART AND HISTORICAL SHRINES

Roppongi is famed as a high-rise nightlife district teeming with bars and clubs, but dig deeper and you'll find contemporary art, shrines and tech that impress.

The Roppongi (六本木) area exemplifies 'metropolis', its main intersection sitting beneath a busy overpass, surrounded by gleaming skyscrapers. Yet it was once forested terrain – its name means 'six trees' – dotted with temples and mansions that became the embassies of today. Its reputation as a party town came when the US occupation forces were stationed here post-WWII. This image shifted when the sprawling Roppongi Hills complex was built at the turn of the millennium, followed by multi-use development Tokyo Midtown, then the National Art Center. The Azabudai Hills (home to teamLab Borderless) and Toranomon Hills complexes were completed in 2023, cementing Roppongi as a culture and tech powerhouse.

TIP

While crime rates in Roppongi have relaxed, stay aware and take precautions. Temptations here can be rife, but combined with the country's no-tolerance drug policies, it bears repeating: don't risk it.

LEFT: IVANGAR_FOTOGRAFIA/SHUTTERSTOCK; RIGHT: ZORAZHUANG/GETTY IMAGES

Roppongi streetscape

See page 218 for places to stay in Roppongi

⭐ Highlights

▼❶ Zōjō-ji
Go through the lovely gate to learn about ancient scrolls at this Edo-era shrine built for shogun Tokugawa Ieyasu. **p83**

❷ Aoyama Cemetery
Stroll along tranquil forested paths amid the graves of historic figures from Japan and abroad. **p82**

❸ Art Triangle Roppongi
Discover new and old works at three major art museums, plus countless smaller galleries. **p80**

❹ Toranomon Yokochō
Feast and drink with the after-work crowd at this popular and lively hangout. **p87**

❺ teamLab Borderless
Immerse yourself in mind-boggling digital art installations at teamLab in Azabudai Hills. **p87**

🚶 Getting Around

Subway
Roppongi and around is well-connected to Tokyo Metro. Roppongi Station is served by Oedo and Hibiya lines, and Akasaka/Akasaka-Mitsuke Stations join to the Chiyoda and Ginza, Marunouchi lines.

Walking
This is a hilly but very walkable neighbourhood. It's around 25 to 30 minutes from Roppongi to either Akasaka or Toranomon.

Bicycle
Cycle-sharing apps like Hello Cycling (credit card required) are easy to use around Roppongi's tarmacked roads. You might hit foot traffic in built-up areas, so be warned.

A FESTIVAL FULL OF ART

A much-anticipated annual event is **Roppongi Art Night** (*roppongiartnight.com; price varies*), a three-day festival that includes installations, exhibitions, artist talks and video screenings – many of which happen overnight – throughout the district.

As well as galleries, the streets are also host to Roppongi Art Night.

Past performances include Aoi Yamada's expressionist dance performance through the Roppongi Hills complex; the fantastical artistry of Dundu (luminous 5m-tall puppets from Stuttgart, Germany); and a blissful dawn concert by the Japan Philharmonic Orchestra. Make sure to pay a visit to **Complex 665**, a gallery housing art greats Ishii Taka and Koyama Tomio.

The event takes place in spring or autumn each year – check the website before making the trip.

Art Museums Galore

MAPS P81 & P84

A trio of creative offerings

The **Art Triangle Roppongi** (六本木アートトライアングル) is **Mori Art Museum** (森美術館; *mori.art.museum; adult/child ¥2300/free*), **Suntory Museum of Art** (サントリー美術館; *suntory.com/sma; adult/child ¥1700/free*) and **National Art Center** (国立新美術館; *nact.jp; varies*). Save your ticket stub from one to get reduced-price admission to the remaining two.

The Mori Art Museum is located in one of the area's two mega-complexes, **Roppongi Hills** (六本木ヒルズ), and features rotating contemporary exhibitions from both international and domestic artists, with past retrospectives from greats such as Shiota Chiharu and Takashi Murakami. There are also numerous on-site installations, including Louise Bourgeois' towering 9m spider, *Maman*, and street art along Keyakizaka-dori.

Roppongi's other mega-complex, **Tokyo Midtown** (東京ミッドタウン), holds the Suntory Museum of Art. Designed by renowned Japanese architect Kengo Kuma, its features include flooring that incorporates oak from recycled (Suntory, of course) whisky barrels. Mostly housing antiques, it also hosts collections on subjects from insect art to the artistry of the Ryūkyū Kingdom, and offers tea ceremonies on Thursday afternoons. Art is incorporated throughout all of Tokyo Midtown – pick up the *Art Handbook* pamphlet for details (and the *Bird Handbook* for depictions of the two-dozen-plus feathered species nesting there).

Nearby, the expansive National Art Center presents rotating exhibitions that have included 'My Eternal Soul', a retrospective on avant-garde artist Yayoi Kusama including her iconic dots, pumpkins and existentialist ruminations.

Tranquillity in a Concrete Jungle

MAP P84

Explore an ancient garden

Hotel New Otani Japanese Garden (ホテルニューオータニ日本庭園; *newotani.co.jp/en/tokyo/garden; free*) is a 400-year-old, 4-hectare garden in Akasaka, within the stately Hotel New Otani, that was built in preparation for the 1964 Olympics. The garden's unique features include enormous red-tinged stones, a koi (carp) pond traversed by a vermillion-red bridge, a traditional garden of sand and pebble, and numerous antique stone lanterns. There is also a teahouse and waterfall, and illuminations lasting from sunset to midnight.

DRINKING IN ROPPONGI: AFTER DARK

MAPS P81 & P84

Bar Luther: Drink whisky and gin while the bartender mixes old soul, rock and blues all night long at this popular analogue hideaway. *7pm-3.30am Mon-Sat*

Orchid: Live it up in the sophisticated, copper interior of Orchid. Whisky galore, and cocktails ranging from classics to new concoctions. *3pm-midnight*

Wall_Alternative: Sip Japanese natural wine and munch on bar snacks like *wagyū* on toast at this bar inside an art gallery. *6pm-midnight Mon-Sat*

Shisha Bar Rakuen Nishi-azabu: Ultra-cool, late-night spot you'll only find in Tokyo: shisha, lasers and Japanese gin in a red-lit room, plus high-quality cigars. *8pm-5am*

HIGHLIGHTS
1 Roppongi Hills

SIGHTS
2 Art Silo
3 Calm & Punk
4 Complex 665
5 Keyakizaka
6 Miaki Gallery
7 Mohri Garden
8 Mori Art Museum
9 Myōkyō-ji

10 National Art Center Tokyo
11 Ōyokochōzaka
12 Senshō-ji
13 SNOW Contemporary
14 Suntory Museum of Art
15 The Wall
16 Tokyo City View

SLEEPING
17 Hotel and Residence Roppongi

EATING
18 Bricolage Bread & Co
19 Common
20 Gonpachi Nishi-Azabu
21 Lilyan
22 Yelo

DRINKING & NIGHTLIFE
23 Reino
24 Shisha Bar Rakuen Nishi-azabu

25 These
see 15 Wall_Alternative
26 Wasachi

ENTERTAINMENT
27 Electrik Jinja
28 Roppongi Art Night

SHOPPING
29 Tokyo Midtown

Don't forget to try the homemade apple tart!

DRINKING AROUND ROPPONGI: COFFEE, MATCHA & MORE — MAPS P81 & P84

Wasachi: Get your matcha fix down an unassuming side street. Choose ceremonial-grade matcha made with different types of milk. *9.30am–5pm Mon-Fri*

Chihye Coffee: Relax with soft music and neutral colours. Chihye serves a range of drinks including great lattes, homemade cakes and toasts. *8am–7pm*

Reino: Tiny gem of a coffee shop open for decades, with a sweet, chain-smoking owner. Best visited solo or in groups of two. *11.30am–10pm Mon-Thu, hours vary Fri-Sun*

Yokohamaya: Enjoy dark roasts in this long-running basement *kissaten*. The owner's enthusiasm for coffee is infectious. *10am–7pm Mon-Fri, noon-6pm Sat & Sun*

BEST VIEWS OF ROPPONGI

There's no better way to comprehend Tokyo's vastness than from a sky-high vantage point.

Tokyo City View: Unparalleled photos from the 52nd floor of the Roppongi Hills Mori Tower. Catch Mount Fuji when it's clear.

Main Deck: The Main Deck of **Tokyo Tower** (p87) has expansive panoramic views at 150m, and a window in the floor. Courage required.

Top Deck: At Tokyo Tower's 250m-tall Top Deck, you'll see everything, bar the Tower itself.

Hills House Sky Room Cafe & Bar: Pay for a drink from the 34th-floor cafe and an entry fee to access the observation deck below.

Jade Room & Garden Terrace: Fine dining with a breathtaking front-row view of Tokyo Tower.

Graves of History

MAP P84

Calm place for reflection

Aoyama Cemetery (青山霊園; *tokyo-park.or.jp; free)* is a tree-lined space rich in history, and shines during cherry-blossom season. Dating back to 1874, it was named for the influential Aoyama family of the Gujō clan. Among the 126,000 souls who rest in the more than 14,000 tombs here are Meiji Restoration leader Ohkubo Toshimichi and local canine legend Hachikō. There's also a section for foreigners who made Japan home, including Italian engraver Edoardo Chiossone, designer of his adopted home's first banknotes.

A Magnificent Guest House

MAP P84

Palace for foreign dignitaries

Located within the Akasaka Estate, the **State Guest House** (迎賓館赤坂離宮; *geihinkan.go.jp/en/akasaka; adult/child ¥1500/free)* was built in 1909 in neo-Baroque style as the palace for Japan's then crown prince. It was renovated in 1974 into a state guest house with a Japanese-style annex,

EATING AROUND ROPPONGI: SWEET TREATS ⎯⎯ MAPS P81 & P84

Hocus Pocus: Nagatachō cafe with cake-like doughnuts with creative flavours like *sakura* lemon zest. *11am-6pm Mon-Fri, from noon Sat & Sun ¥*

Toraya Akasaka: This *wagashi* maker serves sweets and Japanese teas in its popular tea room, with gallery and shop. *9am-6pm Mon-Fri, from 9.30am Sat & Sun ¥¥*

Yelo: Try monster-sized *kakigōri* (shaved ice) in zany varieties like organic carrot mascarpone. *11.30am-2am Mon-Thu, hours vary Fri-Sun ¥*

Naniwaya Sōhonten: Savour crispy *tai-yaki* in classic red-bean-paste flavours at Naniwaya, running since 1909. Eat in or take away. *11am-7pm Thu-Mon ¥*

Zōjō-ji temple

The Japanese festival **Tanabata Matsuri** (七夕祭り) concerns the tale of two star-crossed lovers, Orihime and Hikoboshi, who can only meet once a year, on the seventh day of the seventh month, on the Milky Way. To commemorate, Japanese children (and adults, too) tie colourful paper strips *(tanzaku)* with their wishes onto branches of bamboo from mid-June.

Zōjō-ji's Tanabata celebrations are famed throughout Tokyo. By the time the main event rolls around, its Tanabata branches are full of paper wishes.

On 6 and 7 July, the temple creates its own 'Milky Way' of *washi* (Japanese handmade paper) lanterns that line the steps up to the entrance, attracting large crowds of *yukata* (light cotton kimono)-bedecked revellers.

and has since hosted foreign dignitaries, international conferences and summits. The palace features Italian marble, murals and *cloisonné* wall panelling, and was designated a National Treasure in 2009. Advance reservations are needed to visit the annex, but not for the main building and garden.

Soak up Zōjō-ji's History   MAP P84

A fascinating shrine and fantastic views

Around a half-hour's walk from central Roppongi is Shiba, where the impressive **Zōjō-ji temple** (増上寺; *zojoji.or.jp/en; free*) is located. This district flourished during the Edo period due to its proximity to the well-travelled Tōkaidō road, which connected Edo (present-day Tokyo) with Kyoto. Zōjō-ji is where the ruling Tokugawa shogunate worshipped following the temple's relocation to this district in 1598.

Sangedatsumon, Zōjō-ji's impressive front gate, is a designated Cultural Property dating back to 1622 – and Tokyo's oldest wooden structure, having managed to survive the Great Tokyo Air Raids of 1945. The site has a mausoleum housing

continues on p87

EATING AROUND ROPPONGI: OUR PICKS   MAPS P81 & P84

Bricolage Bread & Co: Be prepared to queue for delicious French bread and brunch-style dining. *7am-7pm Tue-Sun* ¥

Echigoya Genpaku Sohonzan: A lunchtime favourite: perfectly grilled fish, with rice, miso soup and pickles. *11am-4pm & 6-11pm Mon-Fri, 11am-2.30pm Sat* ¥

Gonpachi Nishi-Azabu: This restaurant, of Tarantino's *Kill Bill* fame, serves Japanese classics in a lively atmosphere. Book in advance for vegan sushi. *11.30am-3.30am* ¥¥

Common: Uber-cool Common offers brunch, dinner and cocktails daily, with lounge DJs Thursday to Saturday, and exhibitions by local artists. *8am-11pm* ¥

ROPPONGI & AROUND
KŌJIMACHI
13
Tunnel
Tunnel
Tunnel
Tunnel
Shinanomachi
KIOI-CHŌ
7
24
Tunnel
Shuto Expwy No 4
Benkei-
bori Moat
Nagatachō
Nagatachō
Akasaka-
mitsuke
Akasaka
Imperial
Property
NAGATACHŌ
Area not
open to
public
Aoyama-dōri
31
Meiji-
jingū
Gaien
5
Ichō-Namiki
30
Aoyama-dōri
Aoyama-
itchōme
17
Gaien-higashi-dōri
28
Hitotsugi-dōri
20
Akasaka
18
Aoyama-bochi-dōri (Cherry St)
19
41
Tamachi-dōri
39
AKASAKA
Loop Rd No 3
Aoyama-reien
(Aoyama
Cemetery)
Kotto-dōri
Nogizaka
Midtown
Garden
Hinokichō-
kōen
Gaien-nishi-dōri
1
Aoyama
Cemetery
Nogizaka
MINAMI-
AOYAMA
See
Central Roppongi
p81
Roppongi
Roppongi-
itchōme
Aoyama-
kōen
Roppongi
Crossing
Tunnel
Roppongi
Azabudai
Hills
Shuto Expwy No 2
teamLab
Borderless
Tunnel
2
Shuto Expwy No 3
40
Torii-zaka
AZABUDAI
NISHI-
AZABU
MOTO-
AZABU
ROPPONGI
6-CHŌME
TV Asahi-dōri
Azabu-Jūban-dōri
Azabu-
jūban
HIGASHI-
AZABU
36
38
Kurayami-zaka
32
27
Shuto Expwy
Loop Line
0   500 m
0   0.25 miles
N
Daikoku-zaka
Amishiro
Park
25
Azabu-
jūban

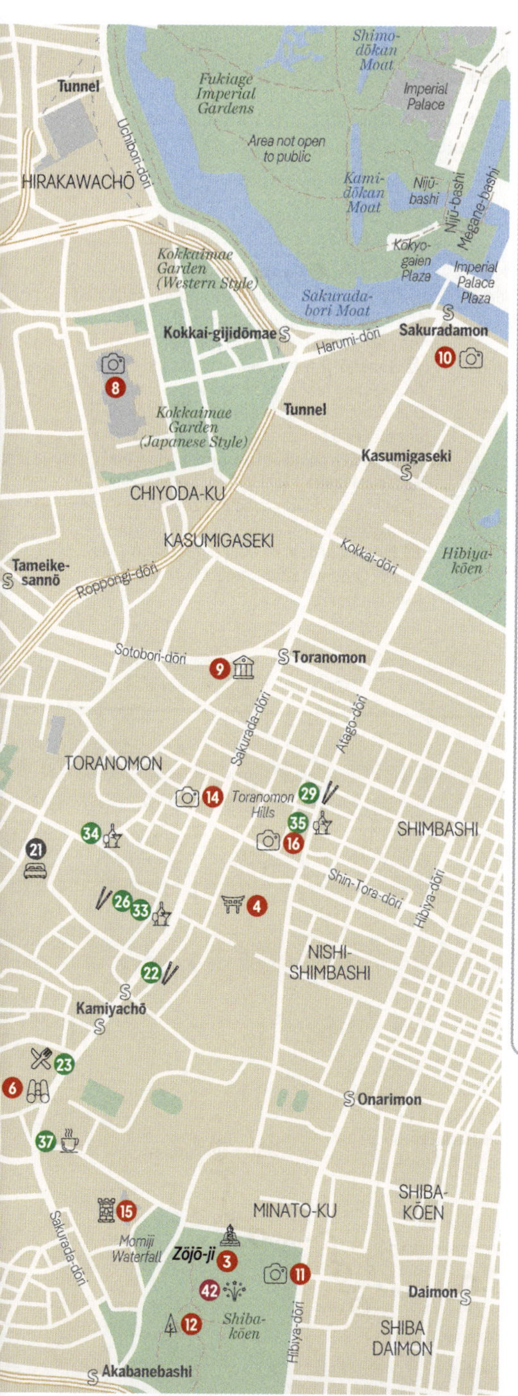

HIGHLIGHTS

1 Aoyama Cemetery
2 teamLab Borderless
3 Zōjō-ji

SIGHTS

4 Atago Jinja
see 2 Azabudai Hills
5 Hie-jinja
6 Hills House Sky Room Cafe & Bar
7 Hotel New Otani Japanese Garden
8 National Diet Building
9 National Museum of Territory and Sovereignty
10 Old Ministry of Justice Building
11 Sangedatsumon
12 Shiba Park
13 State Guest House
14 Tokyo Node
15 Tokyo Tower
16 Toranomon Hills

SLEEPING

17 9h Nine Hours Akasaka Sleep Lab
18 First Cabin Akasaka
19 Henn na Hotel Tokyo Akasaka
20 Hotel Hillarys Akasaka
21 Okura Tokyo

EATING

22 Echigoya Genpaku Sohonzan
23 Florilège
24 Hocus Pocus
25 Itohan
26 Jade Room & Garden Terrace
27 Naniwaya Sōhonten
28 Ramen Mozu
29 Toranomon Yokochō
30 Toraya Akasaka

DRINKING & NIGHTLIFE

31 Bar Luther
32 Chihye Coffee
33 Gold Bar at Edition
see 29 Memento Mori
34 Orchid
35 Rooftop Bar at Andaz Tokyo
36 Tokyo Confidential
see 29 Toranomon Brewery
see 35 Toranomon Distillery
37 Yokohamaya

ENTERTAINMENT

38 1Oak Tokyo
39 B-Flat
40 Cube
41 G's Bar
42 Tanabata Matsuri

AN INNER-CITY WALK THROUGH ROPPONGI'S ART & HISTORY

A typically-Tokyo mix of contemporary art, architecture, historically-relevant shrines and the pensive Aoyama Cemetery

START	END	LENGTH
Aoyama Cemetery	Mohri Garden	2km; 1hr

Begin wandering through the calm grounds of ❶ **Aoyama Cemetery** (p82) to the towers of Roppongi. Leave at its southernmost exit, and follow the path to ❷ **Calm & Punk**, a gallery showcasing contemporary art for free. Pop into ❸ **Miaki Gallery**, then ❹ **SNOW Contemporary**, two more free-entry galleries nearby.

Continue south, to gaze upon ❺ **The Wall** and **Art Silo**, two Nigel Coates buildings. The former imagines 'Romans in Tokyo', and is home to *Nishi Azabu Wall*, an 8m-high artwork by British artist Grayson Perry. Neighbouring Art Silo is a feat of engineering, being string-bean tall and thin.

Head up the ❻ **Ōyokochōzaka** – one of the area's many hills – with the Roppongi Hills Mori Tower in sight as you go. Follow the road to the top and when you reach it, you'll be facing ❼ **Senshō-ji**, a 400-year-old temple and the final resting place of the prodigal samurai Okita Sōji. From there, walk down to ❽ **Myōkyō-ji**, another Edo period shrine, and descend the steps to Roppongi Sakurazaka. Follow that down ❾ **Keyakizaka** – look out for Shigeru Uchida's *I Can't Give You Anything But Love* chair – and keep going. Finish at the Japanese-style ❿ **Mohri Garden**, looking out through Jean-Michel Othoniel's sculpture *Kin no Kokoro* (Golden Heart).

continued from p83

six of the Tokugawa shoguns, 1000 Jizō (Buddhist patron of travellers, children and the unborn) statues, and rotating exhibitions from the collection of 100 scrolls by artist Kano Kazunobu depicting the Five Hundred Arhats, as well as an impressive *daibonshō* (big bell) that is tolled twice a day: morning and night. Zōjō-ji also has unblemished views of Tokyo Tower (東京タワー; *en.tokyotower.co.jp; adult/child ¥1500/600)*, an impressive landmark.

Shiba Park (芝公園; *tokyo-park.or.jp/park/siba; free)*, on whose grounds Zōjō-ji stands, offers spectacular seasonal vistas courtesy of its zelkova, camphor, gingko, cherry and plum trees. The **Momiji Waterfall**, positioned between Zōjō-ji and Tokyo Tower, is particularly picturesque amid the autumnal foliage. The park also hosts occasional events near its Onarimon entrance, including a bi-annual Oktoberfest in spring and autumn.

Visiting Roppongi's Hills & Towers MAP P84

Embodying the future cityscape

Azabudai Hills (麻布台ヒルズ) is the newest development from the Mori empire, and includes the tallest building in Japan: the 327m-high Mori JP Tower. The four-building project aims to create a nexus of people-friendly green spaces by placing the Roppongi, Toranomon, Ark and Azabudai Hills complexes within walking distance of each other – increasing Tokyo's profile as a cutting-edge global city.

It's home to a range of fine-dining options, such as **Sushi Azabu** and **Florilège**; a gourmet food and drink market; and, notably, the **teamLab Borderless: MoriBuilding Digital Art Museum** *(teamlab.art/e/tokyo; from ¥3800)*. Run by digital art collective teamLab, the space includes a range of interactive installations. Set up by flower-filled waterfalls, dance with a team of *yōkai* (ghosts), be dazzled by a never-ending light show and look for hidden sunflowers.

A few blocks along is **Toranomon Hills** (虎ノ門ヒルズ), spread over four soaring skyscrapers comprising residential, retail and business, with countless attractions. One highlight is **Toranomon Yokochō**, with food stalls run by Japan's top restaurants. For lunch-goers, consider buying a *bentō* (boxed meal) and taking it to the outdoor Oval Plaza to picnic in the grass alongside the impressive 10m-high *Roots* statue, by Spanish artist Jaume Plensa. If you fancy staying late, join

JAPAN RADIO TOWER

The 333m-high transmission tower – you'll probably know it as **Tokyo Tower** – was built in 1958, the tallest tower in the world at the time. It was unabashedly modelled on France's Eiffel Tower, although it weighs half that of its Parisian counterpart.

Tokyo Tower came to life as the first major landmark in post-war Japan, an orange-and-white symbol of the nation's efforts to rebuild after WWII. Its design incorporates melted US tanks used in the 1950–53 Korean War, and today it puts on solar-powered light shows every evening.

These displays often literally symbolise peace, such as lighting in the colours of the South Korean flag to commemorate the anniversary of when ties between Japan and Korea were formalised.

EATING IN ROPPONGI & AROUND: DINNERTIME —————— MAPS P81 & P84

Ramen Mozu: Thin chewy noodles with a choice of salt and *shōyu* broths, *wagyū* ramen and vegetarian options. Topped with crispy fried shallots. *11am-11pm* ¥

Lilyan: Traditional soba noodles cooked in an open kitchen, alongside delectable natural wines and *nihonshū* (sake). *11.30am-2.30pm & 6-11pm* ¥¥

Florilège: Michelin-starred French cuisine centring on Japanese vegetables, helmed by chef Hiroyasu Kawate. *noon-3pm & 6-10pm Wed-Sun, booking required* ¥¥¥

Itohan: Beloved local spot serving *monja-yaki* – Tokyo's local take on Osaka's savoury pancake, *okonomiyaki* – for decades. *5-11pm Wed-Fri, 4.30-11pm Sat & Sun* ¥

SKY-HIGH URBAN SHRINES

Wanting to protect his capital from natural disasters, shogun Tokugawa Ieyasu ordered the construction of the **Atago Jinja shrine** (愛宕神社; *atago-jinja.com; free*), built in 1603 atop Atago Hill, Tokyo's highest mountain.

Enshrined deities include Homusubi no Mikoto (the God of Fire), and an 86-step staircase leads to the shrine. It earned the moniker the 'Stone Stairs of Success' after a samurai ascended it on horseback.

A 20-minute walk northward is **Hie-jinja shrine** (日枝神社; *hiejinja.net; free*), also fronted by a steep staircase. Guarded by monkeys rather than the usual lion-dogs or foxes, this shrine features a striking series of orange *torii* (entrance gates). In June of even-numbered years, the **Sanno Matsuri** festival is held here, complete with an ornate procession.

National Diet building

the Yokochō throngs for a nighttime drinking session at on-site spots such as the **Toranomon Brewery** for craft beer, **Toranomon Distillery** for craft gin, or **Memento Mori** for inventive cacao and chocolate-themed cocktails.

The space is also home to **Tokyo Node**, a creative complex covering five floors of Toranomon Hills Station Tower. It includes restaurants and cafes, such as Michelin-starred 49th-floor French **apothéose**, which has stunning views; and a gallery space that hosts impressive exhibitions using a 15m-high projection-mapped dome wall.

Exploring the Government District   MAP P84

Architecture and history of social protest

Straddling the neighbourhoods of Kasumigaseki and Naga-tachō, just south of the **Imperial Palace** (p60), this quiet district of government buildings offers several sites worth visiting for those interested in stepping off the well-trodden tourist path.

DRINKING AROUND ROPPONGI: COCKTAILS & MOCKTAILS   –MAPS P81 & P84

| **These:** Step into These's book-lined interior, choose a cocktail of fruits from the fruit basket, and whisper, read and sip the night away. *6pm-3am Mon-Sat, to 2am Sun* | **Rooftop Bar at Andaz Tokyo:** Admire sky-high views with sumptuous cocktails at Tokyo's highest rooftop bar. *5pm-midnight Sun-Thu, to 1am Fri & Sat* | **Gold Bar at Edition:** Sophisticated cocktails in a swish setting. Try the Plum and Basil Highball combining *umeshu* (plum wine) with Nikka whisky, basil and peach. *6pm-2am* | **Tokyo Confidential:** Innovative cocktails by award-winning bartenders in this hideaway; 'Only Fans' is a twist on the Pornstar Martini. *6pm-1am Mon-Sat, to midnight Sun* |

Many of the government buildings were previously Edo-period samurai dwellings, converted following the Meiji Restoration of 1868. An outstanding example of that era's architecture is the **Old Ministry of Justice Building** (法務省旧本館; *moj.go .jp/english/mojm-01.html; Message Gallery free*), designed in 1895 as the Edo-era residence of the Yonezawa Domain's Ue-sugi clan. Later used for several Ministry of Justice functions, it was designated as an Important Cultural Property in 1994.

Also of interest is the **National Diet Building** (国会議事堂; *tinyurl.com/36wvv7xc; free, advance reservation required*), finished in 1936 and renovated after a wartime firebombing. Large-scale demonstrations were held here in 1959 and 1960, and again in 1970, with hundreds of thousands protesting the US–Japan Security Treaty, which opened the door for US military bases on Japanese soil (particularly in Okinawa).

Many other citizen demonstrations have been held here in recent decades, advocating for issues including the protection of Japan's peace constitution and an end to nuclear power following the Fukushima nuclear disaster. While the protest fervour of days past has largely dissipated, small groups of demonstrators still occasionally gather while the Diet is in session in order to hand out flyers advocating their causes (occasionally with English translation).

Nearer to Toranomon is the **National Museum of Territory and Sovereignty** (領土・主権展示館; *cas.go.jp/jp/ryodo _eg/tenjikan; free*), a facility that offers a host of ways to learn about disputed territories – Senkaku Islands, Northern Territories and Takeshima – from Japan's perspective. A highlight is the modest immersive theatre, where visitors can get a feel for the nature of the islands.

BEST NIGHTLIFE SPOTS

Dance the night away at these clubs and bars, open till late.

1Oak: Three-storey hip-hop club showcasing DJs and artists from Japan and abroad. Dress to impress.

Cube: Dance to the excellent sound system in this tiny hidden club where local DJs spin underground electronic music.

Electrik Jinja: An understated jazz bar close to Billboard Live, where many performers stop by after their show for an informal after party.

G's Bar: Bob along to live jazz by pros from 8pm to 10.30pm at this friendly basement spot. Hang around after for great chats.

B-Flat: Enjoy live jazz, Latin and funk most evenings at this legendary dining bar that's been running since 2001.

Researched by Cherise Fong

EBISU, MEGURO & AROUND

WHERE HISTORY MEETS GASTRONOMY

Ebisu's charm draws on its heritage as the birthplace of Yebisu beer in 1889. Over a century later, the spirit of the brewery lives on.

Ebisu (恵比寿) is also one of the seven Japanese gods of fortune, who oversees fishing and commerce, and is habitually depicted with a jolly, laughing expression – an altogether befitting representation of the lively neighbourhood that is his namesake. Streets bubble with eateries and bars that cater to all manner of tastes, while a central plaza hosts community events. Just north, Daikanyama is clustered with stylish shops, restaurants and cafes that invite an afternoon of browsing. Meanwhile, Meguro (目黒) encompasses largely residential districts – some arty, some upmarket, some both – where Tokyo takes on a more local scale. And trendy, river-hugging Naka-Meguro flourishes in spring, and is pleasant all year round.

TIP

The tourist information centre near Naka-Meguro Station (Gate Town Building, underground level) is packed with information on local offerings; the Meguro City Guide Map recommends four separate walking tours covering culture, spiritualism, crafts/tea ceremonies, and art, while the Meguro Tourism Encyclopedia includes detailed explanations on sites of interest, including local temples and shrines.

FROM LEFT: MUSEIMAGE/GETTY IMAGES, BEIBAOKE/SHUTTERSTOCK

Tokyo Photographic Art Museum (p93)

See page 219 for places to stay in in Ebisu, Meguro and around

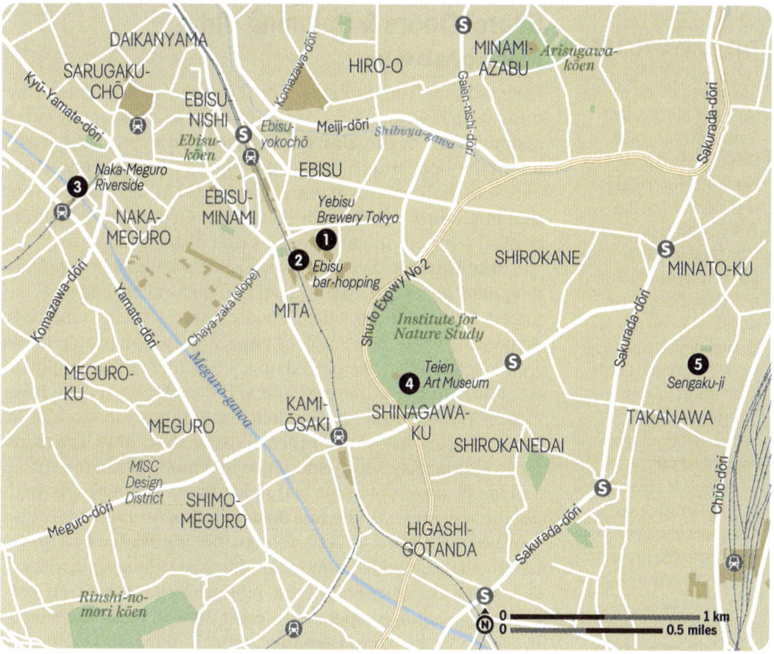

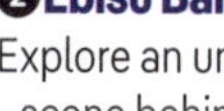

⭐ Highlights

❶ Yebisu Brewery Tokyo

Sample beer from the eponymous brewery that set the tone for the entire neighbourhood. **p93**

❷ Ebisu Bar-Hopping

Explore an underground scene behind hidden passageways or listen to soulful vinyl. **p92**

❸ Naka-Meguro Riverside

Stroll along the river frequented by well-dressed dogs, in or out of cherry blossom season. **p97**

❹ Teien Art Museum

Admire authentic art deco in a former imperial residence surrounded by lushly landscaped gardens. **p96**

▲❺ Sengaku-ji

Pay your respects to each one of the famous 47 Rōnin on their original gravesite with smoking incense. **p99**

🚶 Getting Around

Walking

The small streets of Ebisu and Daikanyama are easily walkable and quiet, as long as you don't mind the hills. Take a leisurely amble along the Meguro River.

Bicycle

Follow the waterways and railways for fluid rides across the neighbourhoods, especially the narrow pathways along the Tokyū Tōyoko train tracks.

Railway

One stop from Shibuya, Ebisu Station connects to three JR train lines and the Hibiya metro line, which extends from Naka-Meguro to Ueno and beyond.

THE TOKYO TOILET

Anyone who has seen the film *Perfect Days* will recognise Shibuya ward's eye-catching public restrooms from the **Tokyo Toilet** project, launched in 2020. Sixteen top architects and designers were commissioned to design public toilets from the ground up, in an effort to combine functionality, accessibility, cleanliness and safety.

The toilets come in different shapes, materials and textures, and the project has won many design awards, featuring structures conceived by architects such as Tadao Ando, Kengo Kuma and Sou Fujimoto. Among the most titillating toilets are two near Yoyogi Park designed by Shigeru Ban, whose transparent, pastel-hued stalls become opaque when locked. Four more designer Tokyo Toilets (p98) are near Ebisu Station.

Secret Doors & Spinning Vinyl
Bar-hopping in Ebisu

Downstream from Shibuya, Ebisu is full of side streets brimming with boutique bars, animated *izakaya* and many small restaurants. The tiny **Bar Trench** (*small-axe.net/bar-trench*), one of the pioneers of Tokyo's now vibrant cocktail scene, emits old-world bohemianism with a perfectly chilled playlist – but that might just be the absinthe talking. Original cocktails are crafted with botanical infusions and bitters.

At **Bar Martha** (*martha-records.com*), photography is prohibited, loud voices are discouraged and musical hegemony is enforced. It's hard to say which is more impressive: the nine-page whisky list or the collection of vinyl. Soulful songs on records from decades past are played on spot-lit turntables, amplified by giant vintage Tannoy speakers. For cocktails, try the fresh ginger Moscow Mule or the deliciously tangy Mango Mojito. On the other side of the railroad, little sister **Bar Track** offers a similar listening experience in a more intimate setting.

Ebisu is also known for its hidden bars, where simply finding the way in is half the fun. **Janai Coffee** (*janaicoffee.tokyo*) may be marked by a street-level sign, but it's fronted by a lower-basement decoy coffee stand that hides the passage into a classy speakeasy. Opposite Ebisu Park, pulling the handle of coin locker **A10** (*a10club.jp*) opens the secret door to dark stairs leading down to the bar of the same name. It may be noisy, but the drink menu includes many exquisite cocktails.

Noblesse Oblige
Indulge in Daikanyama

In the upmarket hills roughly triangulated by Shibuya, Ebisu and Meguro, **Daikanyama** (代官山) sometimes feels like a private playground that you have the privilege of patronising. The luxuriant Parisian apothecary **Officine Universelle Buly** (*buly1803.jp*) is right at home here, as is the sophisticated eyeglasses retailer **Globe Specs** (*globespecs.co.jp*) and the French restaurant **Chez Lui** (*chez-lui.com*). But the neighbourhood is built on many levels, both topographically and

continues on p97

EATING IN EBISU: FAVOURITES & CHEAP BITES

Tamjai Sangor: Hong Kong–style spicy, rich noodles with your choice of toppings. The *pīdan* (preserved egg) in garlic sauce steals the show. *11am-10pm* ¥

Chun Shui Tang: Taiwanese (bubble) teahouse in Daikanyama that also makes tasty *tantanmen*, hot-and-sour soup and other seasonal noodles. *11am-9pm* ¥

Ouca: Refined ice cream in Japanese flavours – sweet milk, black sesame, *kokutō* (cane sugar) or *kinako* (soy bean), served with roasted green tea and salty seaweed. *11am-11pm* ¥

Blue Seal: Okinawan ice-cream brand founded on a US military base in 1948, offering flavours such as salt cookie, sugar cane and *shiiquasa* sherbert. *11am-9pm* ¥

Afuri: The original location of this iconic ramen shop known for its *yuzu* salt broth. Also makes a tasty rainbow vegan ramen. *11am-5am* ¥

Blacows: A fitting tribute to Japan's premium 'black cow' *wagyū*. Mouth-watering toppings include gorgonzola with walnuts and fig sauce, and pesto. *11am-3pm & 5-9pm* ¥¥

Thanks Nature: Wholesome salads, thick smoothies and lovingly prepared fusion dishes with fine and fresh ingredients in a calm setting. *11.30am-11pm* ¥¥¥

Hemp Café Tokyo: Casual joint serving surprisingly gourmet, elegantly presented CBD delicacies and vegan fare by a specialised chef. *11am-3pm & 6-10pm* ¥¥¥

Yebisu Garden Place

The classically styled plaza of Yebisu Garden Place (恵比寿ガーデンプレイス) was inaugurated in 1994 on the site of the original Yebisu beer brewery. Most weekends, it hosts local events such as an organic farmers market, and there are outdoor movie screenings in summer and crystal illuminations in winter. Some nights, you can hear live jazz playing through the open terrace of the red brick BNP building.

Yebisu Garden Place

Taste Yebisu from the Tap

Yebisu, now a popular premium label under Suntory, is one of Japan's oldest beers. It was first brewed here in a red-brick factory in the 1890s, giving the neighbourhood its name. While the original factory closed in the 1980s, beer-making returned to Ebisu in 2024 with the opening of **Yebisu Brewery Tokyo** (*sapporobeer.jp*). The craft-sized facility produces Yebisu Infinity, a new 'prototype' beer for the label, which you can try alongside other limited-edition and seasonal brews at the in-house taproom. The free museum retraces the history of the brand through vintage bottles, photographs, posters and other original artefacts, such as Yebisu's striking wooden signboards from the 1920s.

Browse a TOP Museum Gallery

The **Tokyo Photographic Art Museum** (東京都写真美術館; TOP Museum; *topmuseum.jp; exhibition prices vary*) is undeniably a photographer's museum, with featured exhibitions often curated by photographers' associations. The three gallery spaces are each charged separately, making it easy to drop in for an exhibit – a retrospective of a major artist, a selection of documentary photos from the archives, or thematic shows from the collection. If you're feeling peckish, the ground-floor cafe serves homemade vegetable curry.

TOP TIPS

● For more Yebisu beer after taproom hours, head over to **Yebisu Bar Stand** (till 10pm).

● **Yebisu Garden Cinema** has an open cafe next to the lobby, for a quick coffee in a pleasant setting.

PRACTICALITIES

● *gardenplace.jp*

● 7am-midnight

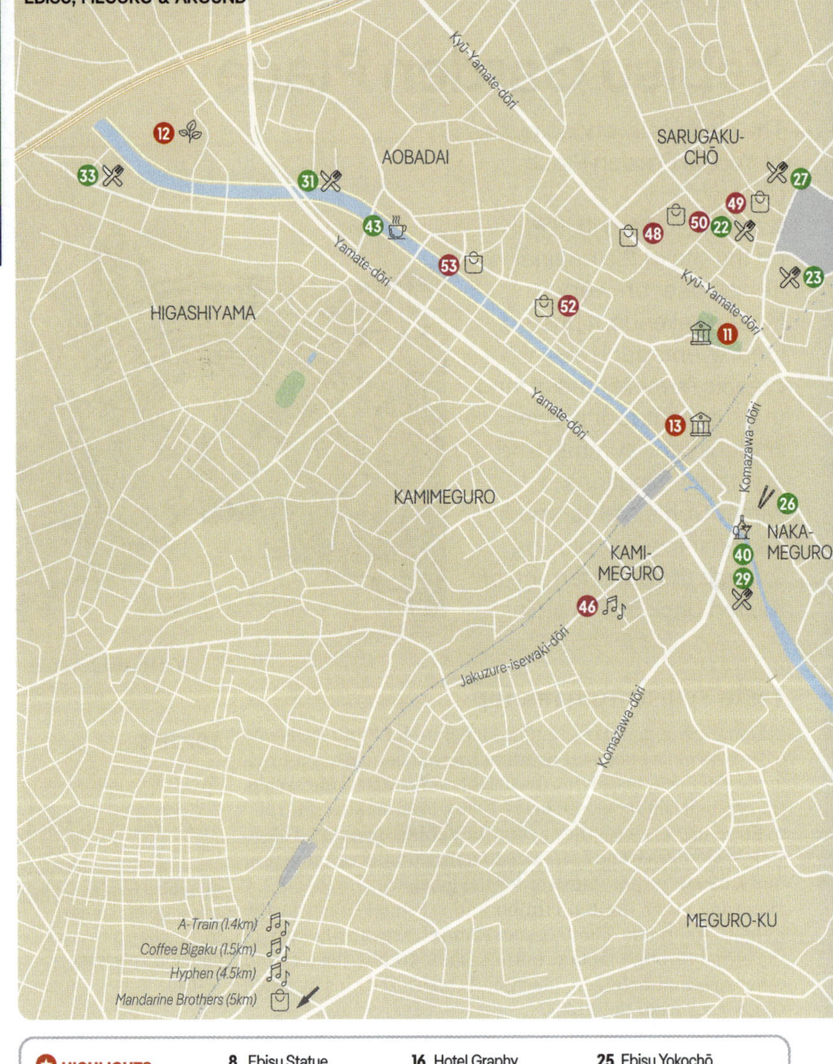

⭐ HIGHLIGHTS

1 Tokyo Metropolitan Teien Art Museum
2 TOP Museum
3 Yebisu Brewery Tokyo
4 Yebisu Garden Place

⭐ SIGHTS

5 Ebisu East Park toilet
6 Ebisu Park toilet
7 Ebisu Shrine
8 Ebisu Statue
9 Higashi Sanchōme toilet
10 Institute for Nature Study
11 Kyū Asakura House
12 Meguro Sky Garden
13 Sato Sakura Museum

⚫ SLEEPING

14 °C
15 Ebisuholic
16 Hotel Graphy
17 Prince Smart Inn

🟢 EATING

18 Afuri
19 Ăn Cơm
20 Blacows
21 Blue Seal
22 Chez Lui
23 Chun Shui Tang
24 Comodo
25 Ebisu Yokochō
26 Ensui
27 Hacienda del Cielo
28 Hemp Café Tokyo
29 Huit
30 Ouca
31 Riverside Club
32 Tamjai Sangor
33 Tempura Tango
34 Thanks Nature
35 Tooth Tooth Tokyo

<table>
<tr><td>

**DRINKING &
NIGHTLIFE**

36 AIO
37 Bar Martha
38 Bar Track
39 Bar Trench
40 Cabin
41 Janai Coffee

</td><td>

42 Log Road Daikanyama
43 Starbucks Reserve
    Roastery
44 Yebisu Bar Stand

ENTERTAINMENT

45 Blue Note Place
46 Rakuya
47 Yebisu Garden Cinema

</td><td>

SHOPPING

48 Daikanyama T-Site
49 Globe Specs
50 Green Dog
51 Officine Universelle
    Buly
52 Pegion
53 Snobbish Babies

</td><td>

see 48 Tsutaya Books
    Daikanyama

TRANSPORT

54 Ebisu Station Exit 4
55 Ebisu Station West Exit

</td></tr>
</table>

Teien Art Museum

Although the Teien Art Museum (東京都庭園美術館) often hosts compelling exhibitions – usually of decorative arts – its chief appeal lies in the building itself. It's an authentic art-deco structure and former princely estate built with Japanese craftsmanship in 1933, designed on the inside by leading French art-deco figures such as Henri Rapin and René Lalique, with much of the original interior intact.

CAITO/SHUTTERSTOCK

Tokyo Metropolitan Teien Art Museum

TOP TIPS

● Save extra time to lounge in the cafe or on the lawn.

● The very fancy **Comodo** restaurant, set inside the garden, serves lunch and dinner.

● For more of a nature walk in the forest, go next door to the Institute for Nature Study (p97).

PRACTICALITIES

● *teien-art-museum.ne.jp*

● 10am-6pm Tue-Sun

● exhibition/garden adult ¥1000/200

Visit the Manor

It was during the golden age of art deco that Prince Asaka Yasuhiko and Princess Nobuko stayed in France, and they wasted no time in commissioning the style's top designers to decorate their new residence in Tokyo. Even a century later, every room is a well-preserved wonder of art deco, showcasing fine wooden frameworks and furniture, glass relief doors and chandeliers, stained- and etched-glass panels, wood inlay floorings, and iron finishings on staircases and radiators. And with more than 20 types of stone in various colours and patterns, the entire building is like a sample book of domestically quarried stone materials. Witness the French Vert d'Estours green marble bathrooms.

Wander the Garden

It's no coincidence that the museum is named after its gardens, with a rich diversity of flora that is in bloom at almost any time of year. The lawn space and Japanese Garden have been preserved since Prince Asaka's family lived here, including the original Kouka (光華) Teahouse, completed by a master *suki-ya* carpenter in 1936. The More recently converted European Garden contains several large art sculptures.

continued from p92

commercially, from the hillside **Log Road Daikanyama** strip that includes a brewpub and a doughnut shop, to the rolling maze of independent boutiques around the area.

Daikanyama's main landmark is the large **T-site** (*store.tsite. jp*), centred around the triple-block **Tsutaya Books** – which, in addition to lifestyle and art books, manga, international magazines and an executive lounge bar, dedicates an entire wall to luxury fountain pens. The open-air T-site complex also includes a friendly e-bike shop, an organic health food store, a pop-up gallery space and. of course, a dog grooming salon. It's one of the few places in Tokyo where you'll see Tesla chargers, not to mention someone casually walking their pet pig on a leash.

For a more down-to-earth look inside a traditional wooden manor preserved from 1919, don't miss the hidden **Kyū Asakura House** (旧朝倉家住宅), a rare Taishō-era (1912–26) villa on the visible cusp of Western architecture, which was once the private residence of a local statesman.

Enjoy Wild Nature

Take in history and fab flora

Just outside the Teien Art Museum and Gardens, the rare natural forest of what is now the **Institute for Nature Study** (国立科学博物館; *ins.kahaku.go.jp*; *¥320*) has an even longer backstory. The property dates to the Edo period (1603–1868), when it served as the secondary home of the daimyō Matsudaira Yorishige. During the Meiji period (1868–1912) the manor was used to store military weapons and ammunition, before becoming the imperial estate Shirokane Goryōchi in the Taishō period. During all this time, the property was closed off to the general public, and the landlords pretty much let the local flora go wild. Since 1949, the area has opened to the public as a Natural Monument and Historic Site, home to some 500 native plant species.

Pretty in Pink

Stroll along the Meguro Riverside

The Meguro River runs through several quiet residential neighbourhoods before it flows into Tokyo Bay. The section west of Meguro Station is lined with cherry trees, and in spring, people gather on the paved promenades under the boughs for *hanami* (cherry blossom viewing parties). At **Naka-Meguro** (中目黒), the river narrows, and the flowering trees form a

BEST DOG APPAREL SHOPS

Snobbish Babies: Mix-and-match frilly tops and bottoms, rubber socks and booties, backpacks and branded sweatshirts, then buy yourself a blouse to match.

Pegion (ペギオン): Drawstring raincoats, chenille sweaters, ribbed hoodies for French bulldogs, three-quarter-length sleeve turtlenecks for Italian greyhounds and whippets.

Mandarine Brothers: Dress your dog in the Brothers' signature skin-tight cool body suit, then show it off in this Jiyūgaoka cafe as you snack on a bagel sandwich.

Green Dog: This comprehensive vet clinic and dog salon at T-site also carries a selection of casualwear, including UV-cut tech tees.

P2's First: Go to floor 6C inside **Hands Shibuya** for kimono-silk cat collars and cotton *yukatas*. Baseball fans, be sure to snag a dog-sized OHTANI 17 shirt.

EATING IN EBISU: BEST ATMOSPHERE

Hacienda del Cielo: Rooftop bar and terrace overlooking Daikanyama, serving modern Mexican fare with colourful cocktails. *11.30am-11pm* ¥¥¥

Tooth Tooth Tokyo: Dainty appetisers, game meat, sumptuous pastas and fancy drinks in a dramatic theatrical setting. *11.30am-3pm & 5pm-11.30pm* ¥¥¥

Ăn Cơm: Refined Vietnamese at a slick bar counter in Hiroo. Try the spring rolls: octopus with corn, chicken crab with plum. *11.30am-2.30pm & 5.30pm-11pm Sun & Tue-Thu* ¥¥¥

Tempura Tango: Friendly upstairs bar, where veggies are displayed like raw fish and delicate tempura dishes are paired with sake. Dogs welcome. *5pm-midnight* ¥¥¥

TOUR EBISU'S DESIGNER TOILETS

This walk takes you past four public restrooms from the Tokyo Toilet project, all permanently ensconced in Ebisu's glowing nightlife district.

START	END	LENGTH
Ebisu Station Exit 4	Bar Martha	1.4km; 25min

From **❶ Ebisu Station Exit 4**, turn right at the intersection and head up the street to the light stone-textured concrete **❷ Ebisu Park toilet** designed by Masamichi Katayama (Wonderwall), a nod to prehistoric Japan's river huts. Cross the street and continue past the tiny **❸ Ebisu Shrine**, then up a street lined with bars and restaurants.

Turn right and around the corner to grab a drink at **❹ Bar Trench** (p92), then head down to **❺ Ebisu Station's West Exit**, where you'll find the glowing white jewel box toilet designed by Kashiwa Sato. Beside it stands the bronze **❻ Ebisu Statue** by Shigeru Kinoshita depicting the smiling god of fortune holding a fat sea bream, symbol of prosperity.

Walk under the train tracks then left up the street and around the corner to see the triangular red Origata-inspired **❼ Higashi Sanchōme toilet** designed by Nao Tamura. Head down to the main street, turn left then right. The animated **❽ Ebisu Yokochō** will be on your right, opposite Afuri ramen (p92).

A few steps further inside **❾ Ebisu East Park** with its octopus slide is the white Squid Toilet, featuring a playfully sloped roof designed by Fumihiko Maki. Walk down the side street and turn left after **❿ Ouca** (p92) onto another main street lined with eateries. At the large intersection, turn off onto the quiet side street that leads to **⓫ Bar Martha** (p92).

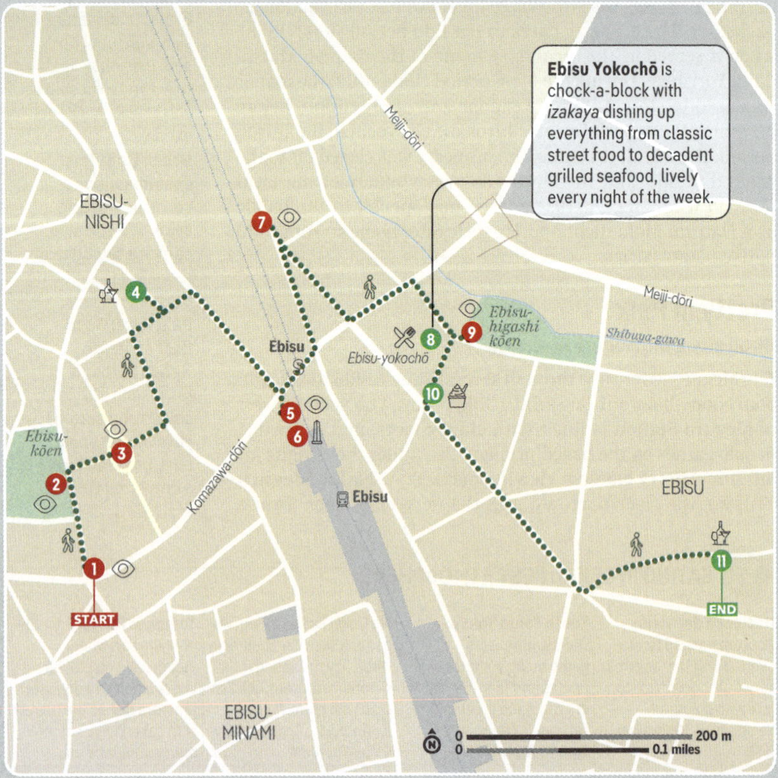

tunnel of pink, framed by festive red lanterns above *sakura* petals floating downstream. The river thrums with chaotic yet joyful energy, as street vendors hawk everything from strawberry champagne to hot kebabs. This stretch is particularly dense with fashionable cafes, bars and boutiques, making it a popular destination year-round. In case you come during the off-season, the compact **Sato Sakura Museum** (郷さくら美術館; *satosakura.jp; adult/child ¥800/free*) hosts a permanent collection of large-scale artworks that feature cherry blossoms in all their efflorescent glory, as well as related thematic exhibitions of *nihonga* (Japanese paintings).

At the western end of the Meguro River you'll find the landmark **Starbucks Roastery**, a behemoth steampunk coffee and tea haven designed by the ubiquitous architect Kengo Kuma. It's a lavish place to pause if your timing is right (outside festival season), as it has multiple open levels with wooden furniture in various arrangements, all the way out to the generous terraces on the 3rd and 4th floors overlooking the river. On the other side of the freeway, surrounded by a dizzying spiral of motorways, **Meguro Sky Garden** offers some respite from the traffic with meandering floral paths along the elevated landscape park.

Long Live the 47 Rōnin

Pay your respects at Sengaku-ji

The story of the **47 Rōnin** (赤穂義士; Akō Gishi) who conspired to avenge their master, Lord Asano – himself put to death after being tricked into pulling a sword on a rival – is legendary in Japan. As a result of their murderous raid, the masterless samurai were condemned to die, but allowed to commit seppuku (ritual disembowelment; an honourable death for a samurai). Their remains were buried alongside their master's at **Sengaku-ji** (泉岳寺; *sengakuji.or.jp*) in 1703. This solemn temple reserves a separate area to honour the 47 warriors on a hill behind the main building. If you want to visit the individual tombstones, each one inscribed with the *rōnin*'s name and age at death (the youngest was 16), donate a few hundred yen for a box of incense sticks. The smell of incense rising from the tombs is a sobering reminder of both the real human lives sacrificed in the name of loyalty and the legend that overshadows them.

For a more up-close and personal look at the 47 lads, pop into the on-site museum and annex, which exhibit the famous war drum, as well as detailed models of all the warriors, each with its own charismatic expression and posture – the better to commemorate each individual *rōnin* one by one.

BEST LIVE JAZZ CLUBS

Blue Note Place: Two-storey arcade seating in a red-brick building spotlighting both classic jazz and young musicians in Yebisu Garden Place.

Rakuya (楽屋): Restaurant setting for cabaret-style performances in Naka-Meguro, while enjoying fresh Thai or Vietnamese dishes.

Coffee Bigaku (珈琲美学): Owner-run live house with wooden decor, hosting dynamic jazz gigs around a grand piano in lively Gakugei Daigaku.

A-Train: Tiny New York–style bar serving sliders at the counters, where the musicians are so close you can almost reach out and touch them.

Hyphen: Old-fashioned jazz club for acoustic gigs with a full bar and an upright piano, small tables and a big sofa, in Jiyūgaoka.

EATING & DRINKING IN NAKA-MEGURO: ALONG THE RIVER

Riverside Club: Laidback industrial living room with an open kitchen, visible selection of liquors and soul music soundtrack. *11am-9pm* ¥¥

Huit: Classic French menu with wines. Time-honoured music complements the old-world decor. Save room for the Gâteau Nantais. *11.30am-8pm Tue-Sun* ¥¥¥

Cabin: Cosy bar with wood and fireplace, specialising in craft cocktails and whisky flights. Try the Lover's Club with Botanist Gin and raspberry. *6pm-midnight*

Ensui: (炎水) Eight counter seats, where Chef Ito shaves the aged fermented bonito for *katsuo-kombu dashi* in front of you, with exquisite seafood bites. *10.30am-9pm* ¥¥¥¥

Researched by Cherise Fong

SHIBUYA & SETAGAYA

YOUTH CULTURE AND CREATIVE ENERGY

Thanks to its iconic intersection, Shibuya could be a visual shorthand for Tokyo in the global imagination – pulsating with energy, in perpetual transformation.

A pilgrimage site for young people throughout Japan that also draws trendsetters from around the globe, Shibuya (渋谷) must be experienced to be believed. This once-suburban district has over just the past few decades developed into a dynamic centre for progressive youth culture and innovation, particularly in design, tech startups, fashion and performing arts. Throngs of humanity are in motion here – a phenomenon best observed at the famous Shibuya Scramble Crossing, which moves hundreds of thousands of pedestrians daily, as advertisements blare out from giant flashing 3D video screens and rolling loudspeakers tout the latest J-pop. Further afield in Setagaya (世田谷), the chaos gives way to a scattering of distinct neighbourhoods that are stylishly low-rise and low-key.

TIP

Visit one of the tourist information centres at Shibuya Station to pick up the Shibuya Map, plus an array of pamphlets detailing sites such as the local sentō (public baths) and nightlife spots. The one at Shibuya Fukuras also offers luggage storage, battery charging, airport-bus ticket sales and local tour information.

Shibuya streetscape

FROM LEFT: KINGMAYA STUDIO/SHUTTERSTOCK; VISUALSPACE/GETTY IMAGES

See page 219 for places to stay in Shibuya & Setagaya

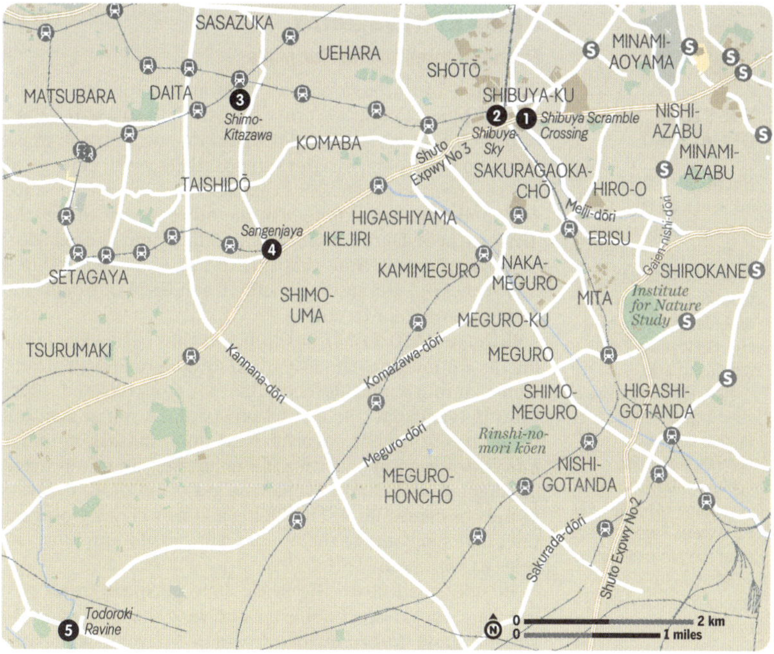

⭐ Highlights

❶ Shibuya Scramble Crossing

Immerse yourself in the sensory swarm of Shibuya's famous intersection. **p108**

❷ Shibuya Sky

View the neighbourhood and beyond from a sky-high perspective on a rooftop terrace. **p109**

▼ ❸ Shimo-Kitazawa

Find vintage clothes and other preloved treasures in Setagaya's bohemian zone. **p111**

❹ Sangenjaya

Explore a larger-than-life *yokochō* that developed organically out of Japan's postwar devastation. **p113**

❺ Todoroki Ravine

Bathe in a secluded forest along a meandering path in Tokyo's only natural ravine. **p112**

🚶 Getting Around

Walking

Given the density of people, shops and all-around stimulation in central Shibuya, Shimo-Kitazawa and Sangenjaya, these districts are best explored on foot, one step at a time.

Bicycle

West of central Shibuya, the streets narrow and stretch out toward the quieter suburbs. As long as you stay off the main roads, cycling is a breeze with a few rolling hills.

Railway

Shibuya Station is a major railway hub, with train lines segueing into subway lines and vice-versa. The Ginza metro line connects Shibuya to Asakusa, while Shimo-Kitazawa is just one rapid-express train stop away.

THE STORY OF HACHIKŌ

Hachikō (ハチ公) is the name of the Akita dog portrayed by the statue in front of Shibuya Station. It honours a beloved real-life dog whose story of loyalty is still famous today.

The original Hachikō would come to the station each day to meet his owner, Professor Ueno, after his commute home from work. Even after the professor's sudden death, Hachikō continued to visit the station every morning and evening, for the next nine years. A local newspaper ran the story, and the nation fell in love with the faithful dog.

The original statue, forever facing Shibuya Station, was inaugurated in 1934 – in the honorary presence of Hachikō himself, who passed away the following year.

Retail Extravaganza

Flagship stores and fashion malls

Shopping in Shibuya doesn't stop at the station, but it's a good place to start. Across the street, **Miyashita Park** (*miyashita-park.tokyo*) is a low-rise semi-open-air mall whose shops epitomise the district's trendsetting youth culture, all under a rooftop green space that stretches between a skatepark and a high-rise hotel. On the other side of the tracks, **Tower Records** (*towershibuya.jp*) offers eight packed floors of nonstop music. Note that this titanic Shibuya flagship, a rare successful vestige of the defunct cult US brand, dedicates its entire 6th floor to vinyl.

Shibuya PARCO (*shibuya.parco.jp*) has been a local fashion institution since the 1970s, and its 2019 renovation transformed it into a multi-level destination, from the landscaped rooftop terrace, to the exhibition space for young creators, to the hip basement *yokochō*. Next door, **Hands** (*shibuya.hands.net*) is a fun house for DIY hobbyists, home improvers, analogue gamers and anyone who geeks out on 12 different brands of dental floss. The Shibuya store's cleverly overlapping floors encourage the use of stairs, so you can burn calories as you shop.

Outside, head down the brick slope of **Spain-zaka** past sneakers, eyeglasses, bubble tea and vape shops, then up the street to **Loft** (*loft.co.jp*) for gift-worthy souvenirs and paper stationery in all its forms. The surrounding streets are occupied by countless big and small brand-name shops, all competing for your attention.

Shibuya By Night

Out and about from dusk to dawn

Just east of the elevated JR tracks, all-night *yokochō* drinking alleys come to life after sundown. **Nonbei Yokochō** (*nonbei.tokyo*) is Shibuya's original shabby-chic, retro drinking strip – a tiny lane packed with even tinier bars and *izakaya*, accessed from the ground up. Stretching alongside Miyashita Park at street level, **Shibuya Yokochō** (*shibuya-yokocho.com*) extends to outdoor terrace seating, with restaurants offering dishes from around Japan. The district's most famous nightclub is the warehouse-style **Womb** (*womb.co.jp*), specialising in techno and house. **Harlem** (*harlem.co.jp*) focuses on hiphop, while **O-East** (*shibuya-o.com/east*) spotlights Japanese

EATING IN SHIBUYA: GOURMET ESCAPES

Ukiyo: Seasonal Japanese ingredients are married with world spices. Booking essential. *Seatings at noon and 12.30pm Fri & Sat, 7 and 7.30pm Tue-Sat* ¥¥¥

Tofu Sorano: Sumptuous dishes featuring homemade tofu with various sauces and spices, from steamed and silky to crispy deep-fried. *5-10.45pm* ¥¥¥

d47 Shokudō: Celebrating Japan's 47 prefectures with regional ingredients and homestyle specialties, overlooking Shibuya Station. *11.30am-4pm & 6-9pm Thu-Tue* ¥¥¥

ätä: French-inspired Japanese seafood tapas using familiar ingredients in unfamiliar ways. Best seats are at the counter facing the open kitchen. *5pm-2am Mon-Sat* ¥¥¥

Shibuya Yokochō

bands – and includes the sleek, arty DJ Bar Azumaya (*azu maya.jp*), which serves sake and Japanese spice-accented cocktails. **White Space Lab** (*dj-bar-space.jimdofree.com*) is a smaller, chilled-out dance space that wraps up at midnight.

Karaoke, more than just a place to sing, is also an excuse to let loose, a bonding ritual, a reason to keep the party going past the last train and a way to kill time until the first one starts in the morning. Most parlours in Shibuya are open till around 6am. All have private rooms equipped with decent audio-visual systems and a wide selection of songs in Japanese and English. The **Karaoke-kan** (*karaokekan.jp*) on Center Gai and Bunkamura-dōri both have rooms with large windows directly overlooking the lively streets below.

Alternatively, sit back and relax with a cocktail at **Sound Bar Howl** (*wam-inc.jp/howl*), which projects golden-age Hollywood movies on the wall, along with (unrelated) pop music on the speakers. Vinyl records are also available for individual listening through headphones. The bar closes at 4.30am, just in time for you to catch the sunrise.

BEST PLACES TO LISTEN TO VINYL

LION (名曲喫茶ライオン): Classical music flowing from gargantuan speakers in a church-like cafe founded in 1926 for the ultimate sound scape.

Jazz & Coffee Masako: Old-fashioned jazz cafe in Shimo-Kitazawa with modern acoustics, a wall of LPs, period furniture and beaded curtains.

Route-1: Friendly, charming record bar near Meguro Sky Garden (p99) spinning mostly oldies but goodies from the 1970s and '80s.

Record Bar Analog: Cult sofa bar in Dōgenzaka where you can request one song from its retro collection, with a 90-minute seating limit.

Recoco: Two locations in Shibuya and Shimo-Kitazawa where you can play records at your own table. Just pick out an album and put on headphones.

EATING IN SHIBUYA: NOODLE SHOPS

MAP P104

Soba Maren: Hole-in-the-wall for a colourful bowl of soupless chewy soba topped with fresh ingredients and pork cubes. *11.30am-11pm Sun-Thu, to 3am Fri & Sat* ¥

Ramen Kamo To Negi: Wheat ramen in a broth made from select Japanese duck and spring onions, bringing out the umami of the fine meat slices. *10am-4am* ¥¥

Tokyo Tarako Spaghetti: Japanese dry noodles featuring raw and grilled cod roe. Pour hot *dashi* bonito broth into the bowl for even more flavour. *11am-10.30pm* ¥¥

Yamashita Honki Udon: Thick, chewy Sanuki udon served in various combos, some whipped and creamy, with crisp tempura and other side dishes. *11am-11pm* ¥

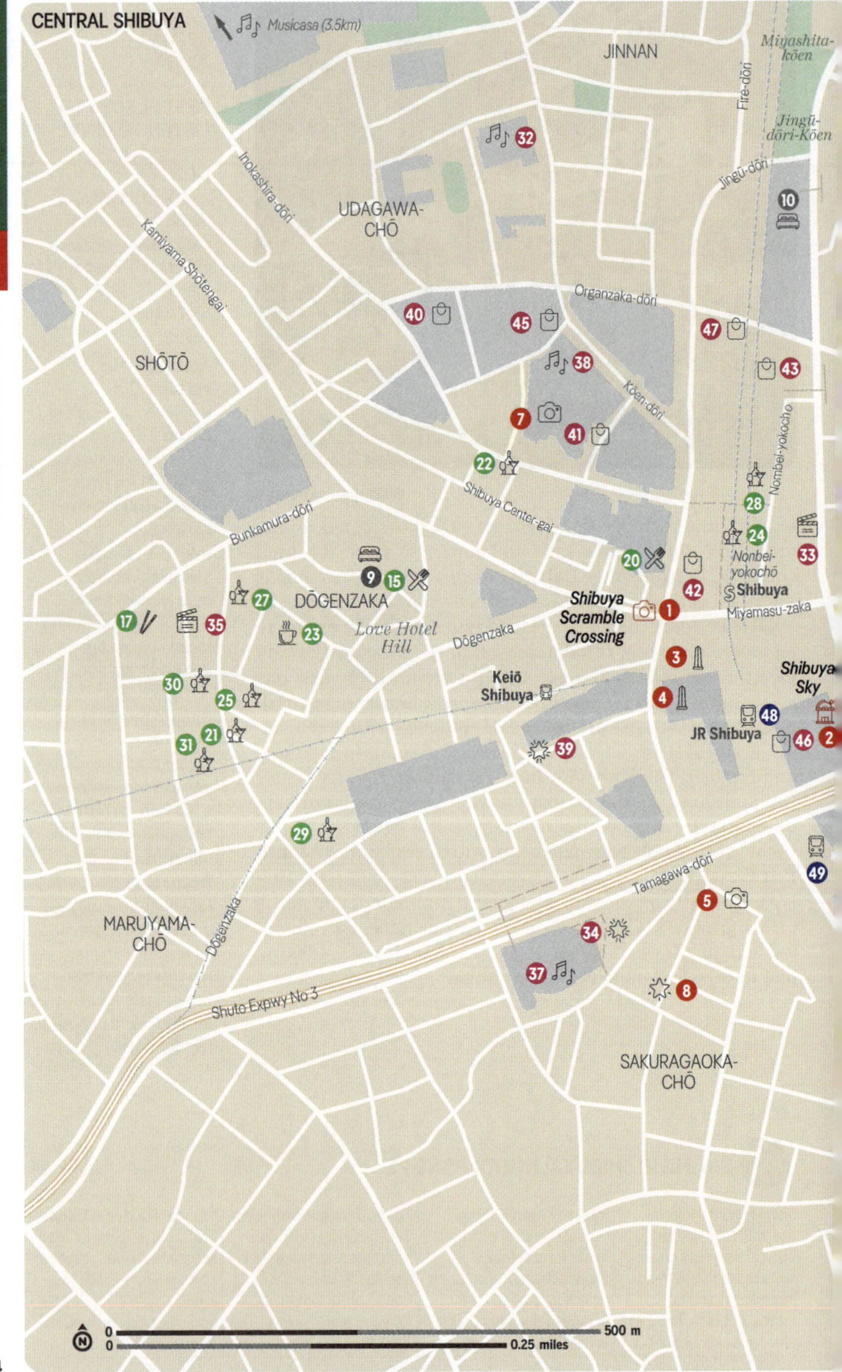
CENTRAL SHIBUYA
Musicasa (3.5km)
JINNAN
Miyashita-kōen
UDAGAWA-CHŌ
Jingū-dōri-Kōen
Fire-dōri
Jingū-dōri
Inokashira-dōri
10
Kamiyama Shōtengai
Organzaka-dōri
SHŌTŌ
40
45
47
Kōen-dōri
38
43
Nombei-yokocho
7
41
28
22
Shibuya Center-gai
24
Nonbei-yokochō
33
20
Bunkamura-dōri
9 15
Shibuya
27
DŌGENZAKA
42
Shibuya
17
35
Love Hotel Hill
Dōgenzaka
Scramble Crossing
1
Miyamasu-zaka
23
3
Shibuya Sky
30
Keiō Shibuya
4
25
48
21
39
JR Shibuya
46 2
31
29
Tamagawa-dōri
49
MARUYAMA-CHŌ
5
Dōgenzaka
34
37
SAKURAGAOKA-CHŌ
8
Shuto Expwy No 3
0   500 m
N
0   0.25 miles

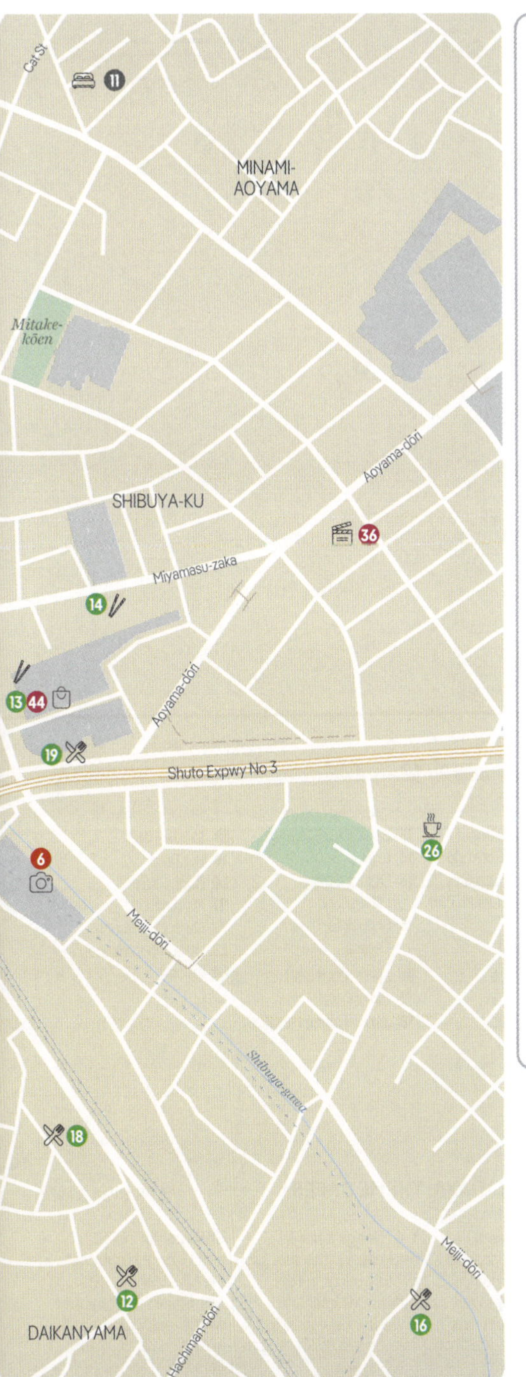

★ **HIGHLIGHTS**		23	LION
1	Shibuya Scramble Crossing	24	Nonbei Yokochō
2	Shibuya Sky	25	O-East
★ **SIGHTS**		26	Recoco
3	Hachikō Statue	27	Record Bar Analog
4	Myth of Tomorrow	28	Shibuya Yokochō
5	Sakurazaka-dōri	29	Sound Bar Howl
6	Shibuya Stream	30	White Space Lab
7	Spain-zaka	31	Womb

ACTIVITIES, COURSES & TOURS
8 Shibuya Saunas

SLEEPING
9 Hotel Indigo Tokyo Shibuya
10 Sequence Miyashita Park
11 Trunk Hotel Cat Street

EATING
12 ätä
13 d47 Shokudō
14 Ramen Kamo To Negi
15 Shibrewya
16 Shibuya Fureai Botanical Center
17 Soba Maren
18 Tofu Sorano
19 Tokyo Tarako Spaghetti
20 Yamashita Honki Udon

DRINKING & NIGHTLIFE
21 Harlem
22 Karaoke-kan

ENTERTAINMENT
32 Body & Soul
33 Bunkamura Le Cinéma
34 Cerulean Tower
35 Eurospace
36 Image Forum
37 JZ Brat
38 Koendori Classics
39 Tokyo Comedy Bar

SHOPPING
40 Hands
41 Loft
42 Magnet by 109
43 Miyashita Park
44 Shibuya Hikarie
45 Shibuya PARCO
46 Shibuya Scramble Square
47 Tower Records

TRANSPORT
48 Shibuya Station
49 Shibuya Station New South Exit

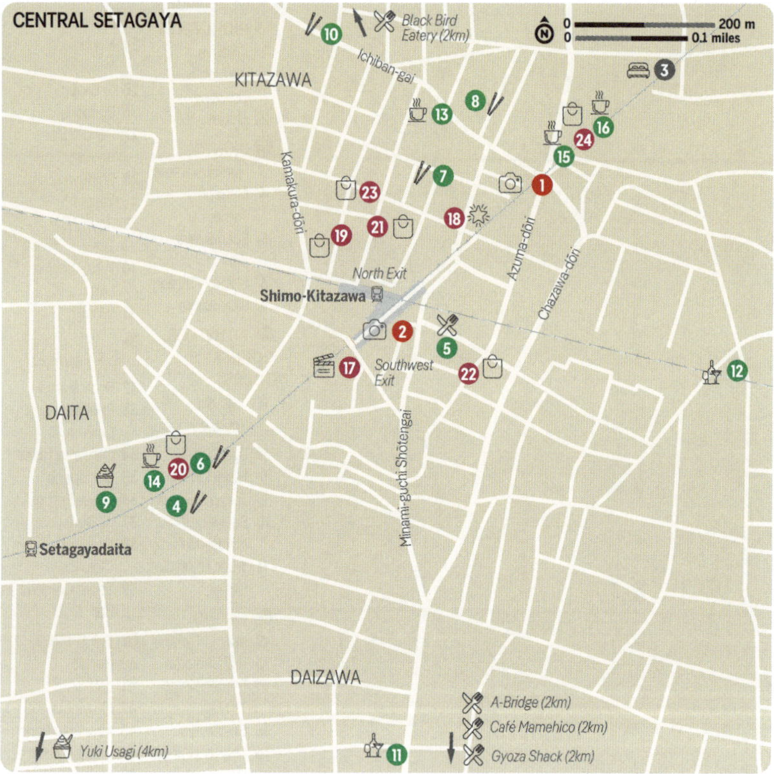

CENTRAL SETAGAYA

SIGHTS	6 Hakkō Department	13 Bear Pond Espresso	**SHOPPING**
1 Senrogai	7 Nijiro Curry Shokudo	14 fuzkue	19 Big Time
2 Shimo-Kitazawa	8 Rojira Curry Samurai	15 Ogawa Coffee Laboratory	20 Bonus Track
SLEEPING	9 Shiro-hige's Cream Puff Factory	16 Shimokita Chaen Ōyama	21 Flamingo
3 Mustard Hotel	10 Ten To Sen		22 Flash Disc Ranch
EATING	**DRINKING & NIGHTLIFE**	**ENTERTAINMENT**	23 Little Trip to Heaven
4 Andon	11 Bar Bodeguita	17 Cinema K2	24 Reload
5 Curry Spice Gelateria Kalpasi	12 Bar Gari Gari	18 Jazz & Coffee Masako	

EATING IN SHIBUYA & SETAGAYA: THEME CAFES — MAPS P104 & P106

Shibuya Fureai Botanical Center: Home-brewed beverages and organic pizza, set inside a multi-level community greenhouse. *11am-9pm* ¥¥

Shiro-hige's Cream Puff Factory: Totoro-shaped cream puffs and cookies fill this Ghibli-approved bakery in the forest near Shimo-Kitazawa. *10.30am-6pm Wed-Mon* ¥

Yuki Usagi: *Kakigōri* shaved ice in flavours such as strawberry cheese, with white chocolate 'snow bunny' ears, near Sangenjaya. *11.30am-8pm Tue-Sun* ¥

Shibrewya: Indigo hotel's bright lobby cafe serves alcohol, coffee, smoothies, and gourmet waffle lollipops shaped like Hachikō. *10.30am-9pm* ¥¥

Stand & Deliver

Open mic nights

If you happen to be a travelling artist who's itching to perform, a few live houses welcome visiting performers on open mic nights. Or just come and watch. **Black Bird Eatery** (*blackbirdtokyo. com*) in Sasazuka hosts an open mic for acoustic musicians every 4th Friday of the month in a friendly community atmosphere (with homemade curry). In Ikenoue near Shimo-Kitazawa, at the smoky underground **Bar Gari Gari** (*cinemabokan.com*), Joy and Sam host the monthly 'Drunk Poets' night for poetry in English, spoken or slammed, with occasional musical accompaniment. For the more comically inclined, **Tokyo Comedy Bar** (*tokyocomedybar.com*) in the Renga building near Shibuya Station hosts regular 90-minute open mic line-ups of short (five-minute) stand-up acts in English and Japanese.

Jazz with a Japanese Twist

Live music with traditional instruments

Check out the schedules of independent live music venues around Shibuya, and you might be surprised to find acts featuring traditional Japanese instruments playing in collaboration with more conventional jazz and classical instruments. At **Body & Soul** (*bodyandsoul.co.jp*), a few times a year the young flautist Fuefuki Kana leads a lively 'Shinobue Jazz' concert spotlighting her signature bamboo flutes, often with guest musicians playing koto (zither) or *kotsuzumi* (hand drum).

The hidden **Koendori Classics** (*koendoriclassics.com*) is a favourite venue of Yukihiro Issō, the legendary virtuoso player of the *nō* flute, who delights with his nimble-fingered improvisations and shocks with his experimental noise band. On a quiet hillside in Yoyogi Uehara, the concrete **Musicasa** (*musicasa.co.jp*) classical concert hall has hosted performances by Earth Voice (*wadaiko* drumming plus singing and strumming on the rare Amami *sanshin*), and B-Come (びかむ), an extraordinary ensemble of *biwa*, *shakuhachi*, koto and percussion. Even the luxury jazz club **JZ Brat** (*jzbrat.com*) has welcomed the jazz *shakuhachi* player Reikan Kobayashi.

Reviving Sauna Culture

See the designer chic Shibuya Saunas

In Japan, where onsen have been a part of life since ancient times, standalone saunas have only more recently gained traction with the younger generation. Once associated with older men and capsule hotels, then as added value to *sentō* and beauty spas, the latest sauna boom can be attributed to a successful manga by Katsuki Tanaka that was adapted into a popular TV drama in 2019. Sadō (サ道, 'The Way of Sauna') focuses on three men whose social interactions all revolve around sauna culture, with episodes including scenes shot in various saunas around Japan, especially in Tokyo. The trendy-chic **Shibuya Saunas** on Sakurazaka-dōri was designed under the supervision of Katsuki Tanaka himself.

MYTH OF TOMORROW

Many of Tokyo's major train stations have interesting public artworks, but Shibuya Station has a mural worth seeking out. **Myth of Tomorrow**, created in 1967 by Japanese artist Tarō Okamoto, depicts (in abstraction) the atomic bomb exploding over Hiroshima.

It has a fascinating backstory: the haunting, 30m-long work was originally commissioned for a Mexican luxury hotel, but went missing when the hotel was left unfinished two years later. After the mural eventually turned up on the outskirts of Mexico City in 2003, it was transported to Japan for much-needed restoration, then finally in 2008, permanently installed inside Shibuya Station.

Look for it spanning the wall of the elevated passage facing the Shibuya Scramble Crossing.

Shibuya Scramble Crossing

One of Tokyo's most iconic sights is a sprawling intersection where pedestrians scramble across from multiple directions. It's a mesmerising sight, especially when seen from above. If the crossing looks familiar, maybe that's because it has appeared in countless films. Several hundred people on average cross at once, from selfie-shooting tourists to weekend shoppers to anyone who wants to join in the fray.

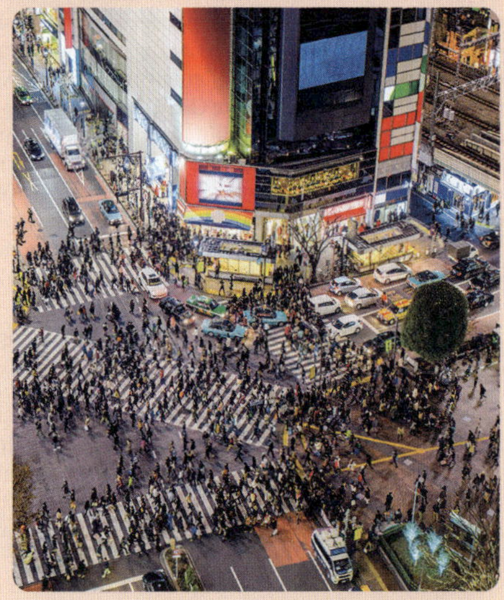

Shibuya Scramble Crossing

Dive into the Intersection

Situated at the Hachikō exit of labyrinthine Shibuya Station, the Shibuya Scramble Crossing is a starburst nexus of people flowing in all directions with both apparent chaos and balletic precision. Enter at ground level, get caught up in the swarm, and feel the rush of pure adrenaline that is getting to the other side.

Scramble for Views

The crossing can be viewed from various heights above street level. Inside **Shibuya Station**, look for (free) views of the intersection from the elevated passage across from the Tarō Okamoto mural. For a more immersive view closer to the action, **Magnet** mall's 2nd-floor Hoshino Coffee offers front-row mezzanine seats from its long wooden counter. Across the street, take the escalators past Starbucks up to the Share Lounge on the 3rd and 4th floors (the ¥1870 hourly rate includes unlimited snacks and soft drinks) for a much more intimate window seat, especially at night. Back at Magnet, head straight up to the 7th floor for late-night views with drinks and DJs, or to the dedicated 8th-floor open-air roof deck (¥1800 admission includes one drink).

TOP TIPS

● Don't linger long in the intersection, as the green light gives pedestrians only just enough time to cross.

● To experience the crossing without the crowds, go after midnight, once the last trains have stopped running.

TOP EXPERIENCE

Shibuya Sky

At 229m above the ground, the 46th-floor rooftop that crowns the district's tallest building, Shibuya Scramble Square, overlooks Shibuya Scramble Crossing, the entire neighbourhood and beyond to the horizon. Both inside and out, it's a delightful experience by day or night.

Shibuya Sky

Step Out on Shibuya's Highest Rooftop

Shibuya Sky has both indoor and outdoor observation decks. The indoor lounge is pleasantly bright and temperature-controlled, but the open-air roof deck is the clear highlight. The transparent barriers all but disappear in photos, and the roof features other clever design elements, such as hammocks built into the deck. Easily identifiable landmarks include Tokyo Tower and Tokyo Skytree. Use the giant compass to guide you (Mt Fuji is due west) and follow the white stripes to the corners for the best photo ops. Sunset tickets sell out especially fast, so book early. Time-slotted tickets guarantee no overcrowding, but there is no time limit for enjoying the views.

View the Sky after Dark

Between April and December, a dedicated part of the terrace becomes The Roof, a seasonal bar open from late afternoon, with limited seats by reservation only. As well as morning yoga or pilates, periodic evening events include live music, DJ evenings and star-gazing parties. Catch the nightly light show on the hour and half-hour from 7pm. Last admission is at 9.20pm.

TOP TIPS

● The outdoor roof deck may close without notice due to extreme heat, wind or other sudden changes in weather conditions.

● Next to the 14/F exit, Kagurazaka Saryo cafe offers more panoramic views.

● Seek out views in a more intimate setting from the 11/F Share Lounge.

PRACTICALITIES

● *shibuya-scramble-square.com/sky*

● 10am–10.30pm

● adult ¥2700, advance purchase after 3pm ¥3400, child ¥1200

SHIBUYA ON FOOT, ABOVE THE CROWDS

For every tourist who makes a beeline for the Shibuya Scramble Crossing, at least a dozen locals are set on avoiding it. Get to know life beyond the crossing.

START	END	LENGTH
Shibuya Station New South Exit	Shibuya Stream	2.5km; 40min

From Shibuya Station's **1 New South Exit,** turn right and go down the escalators to the street. Walk up **2 Sakurazaka-dōri**, whose resident cherry blossoms are illuminated each spring, passing Shibuya Saunas on your left. At the top, turn right and walk across the street toward the **3 Cerulean Tower**, which houses JZ Brat and a *nō* theatre in the basement. Take the escalator up and cross the foot bridge over the highway. Make your way to the intersection with **4 Sound Bar Howl** (p103) on the corner.

Cross the street and walk downhill, dodging fans outside **5 O-East** (p102) on your right, before scanning the large movie poster of **6 Eurospace** (p113) on your left. Turn right on Bunkamura-dōri, cross the big shopping avenue, then turn right into the narrow street that leads to **7 Hands** (p102). Climb around the corner up the hill onto Organzaka-dōri and continue past **8 PARCO** (p102) on your right. Cross Kōen-dōri and walk down the hill, where you can't miss **9 Tower Records** (p102) on the corner.

Walk under the train tracks and along the open-air rooftop of **10 Miyashita Park** (p102), not far above the street-level *yokochō*. At the other end, cross the intersection to **11 Hikarie**, take the escalator up to the 2nd floor, then turn around and walk across the elevated passage into **12 Scramble Square**. From here you can either head straight up or down the escalators back into Shibuya Station, or turn left past the elevators and flow right into **13 Shibuya Stream**.

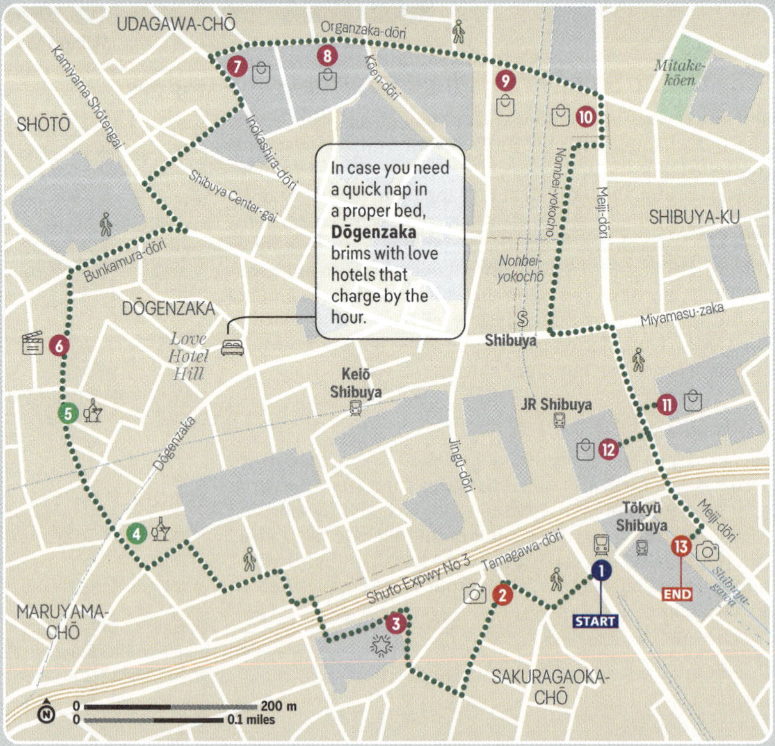

Subcultural Shimo-Kitazawa MAP P106

Bargain haven where artists thrive

The bohemian enclave of **Shimo-Kitazawa** (下北沢) is just a short train ride away from Shibuya Station on the Keiō Inokashira line, but has a very distinct vibe. Once farmland, the area has a fascinating historical trajectory.

After the Great Kantō Earthquake of 1923, an influx of new residents arrived, including intellectuals and writers. An active black market sprang up during the post-WWII devastation, then when several independent theatre companies were founded here in the 1980s, artists, actors and musicians were added into the mix.

The neighbourhood gradually developed into the pedestrian-centred maze of fringe cafes and food shacks, vintage clothing, vinyl records and other thrift shops, independent live venues and arts spaces that remains the core of Shimo-Kitazawa today.

One of these shops, **Flash Disc Ranch** (+81-3-34140421), with its extensive collection of vintage vinyl, was briefly featured in the 2024 film *Perfect Days* (look for the colourful cartoon sign at the foot of the staircase). **Bear Pond Espresso** (*bearpondespresso.com*), opened in 2009 by New York–trained and acclaimed barista Katsuyuki Tanaka, was featured in the mouth-watering 2014 documentary *A Film About Coffee*. Notwithstanding, Shimo-Kitazawa is perhaps best known in the mainstream for its well-stocked, smartly curated secondhand clothing shops, such as **Big Time** (*bigtime.jp*), **Flamingo** (*flamingo-online.jp*) and **Little Trip to Heaven** (*littletriptoheaven.jp*).

Since the Odakyu line train tracks were moved underground in 2013, Shimo-Kitazawa's more recently revamped (if not gentrified) **Senrogai** ('Railroad St') comprises a long expanse of greenery, including an open space near the east exit where weekend festivals and flea markets are held. Nearby is the chic new **Reload** (*reload-shimokita.com*) shopping complex, which includes the elegant **Shimokita Chaen Ōyama** (*shimokita-chaen.com*), managed by 10th-grade tea masters, the Kyoto-imported **Ogawa Coffee Laboratory** (*oc-ogawa.co.jp*), where you can reserve quality beans to roast and brew your own coffee, and the **Mustard Hotel** (*mustardhotel.com*), where every room has a record player.

WATERWAYS & RAILWAYS

Tokyo's waterways suffered from extensive post-war industrial pollution and were further blighted by the urban planning of the 1964 Olympics, when they were covered with highways and concrete. In an effort to reverse this history, Shibuya aimed to rediscover its hidden rivers by making them more accessible. Opened in 2018, the **Shibuya Stream** complex stretching along the narrow Shibuya River at the foot of Google Japan is the gateway to a riverside path leading toward Ebisu that's lined with both community garden plots and new small businesses. Like **Miyashita Park** (p102), **Senrogai** (p113) and **Log Road Daikanyama** (p97), it's also part of a growing trend to convert former railway tracks into long strips of chic eateries that do particularly well at lunch time.

THE GUIDE

SHIBUYA & SETAGAYA

EATING IN SHIMO-KITAZAWA: CURRY SHOPS MAP P106

| **Rojira Curry Samurai:** Hearty coconut soup curry topped with a roster of fresh vegetables and roots, along with chicken on the bone. *11am-3.30pm & 5.30-9pm* ¥ | **Curry Spice Gelateria Kalpasi:** Colourful plates of curries, pickles and spices to mix into wild rice. Finish off with homemade gelato. *11.30am-9pm Fri-Wed* ¥ | **Nijiro Curry Shokudo:** Rainbow window eatery serving large plates loaded with curry and veggies over rice. Wash down with a sweet lassi. *noon-9pm* ¥ | **Ten To Sen:** Big bowls of thick spicy curry soup ramen overflowing with fresh vegetables, meats and burdock. *11.30am-3pm & 5-8.30pm* ¥ |

Todoroki Ravine

The Todoroki Ravine (等々力渓谷) is a cool and tranquil urban oasis, carved out by the Yazawa River at the southern end of the Musashino Plateau. Named after the reverberating sound of its waterfall, this geological marvel in southern Setagaya is Tokyo's only ravine. Its meandering path stretches approximately 1km along the floor of the valley.

Todoroki Ravine

TOP TIPS

● If parts of Todoroki are closed due to maintenance, view the ravine from bridges at street level.

● Take a break at the peaceful **Setsugetsuka** (雪月花) teahouse by the stream.

● Also try **Otto**, a casual Italian restaurant perched directly on the gorge.

PRACTICALITIES

● *city.setagaya. lg.jp/02075/9082.html*

● Japanese Garden 9am-5pm Mar-Oct, 9am-4.30pm Nov-Feb

● free

Follow a Secluded Path

As you descend the steps into the gorge, listen for wild bird-song, and look for the exquisite *komorebi* effect, created by sunlight filtering through the foliage, under a tangled canopy of zelkova, oak and maple trees. Points of interest along the path include picturesque bridges and a well-preserved 'tunnel tomb' from the 7th-century Kofun period. The **Chigo Daishi-dō** pavilion enshrines a striking stone sculpture depicting the founder of the Shingon school of Buddhism, Kobo Daishi – as a praying, gold-plated child – who, according to local lore, discovered the ravine following a prophetic dream.

Take a Spiritual Promenade

The **Fudō-no-taki** waterfall pours forth from the mouths of twin dragons, where Shintō and Buddhist worshippers once engaged in ascetic bathing practices. Up the stairs, **Todoroki Fudōson** is a Shingon Buddhist temple whose spacious grounds are particularly impressive amid springtime cherry blossoms or blazing autumn leaves. Across the stream, climb the stone path to the Shōin drawing room built in 1961 surrounded by a small **Japanese Garden**, for a moment of pure tranquillity.

Across the station, the award-winning **Bonus Track** (*bonus-track.net*) plaza features vegan food, **Andon** (*shimokita.andon.shop*) sake, rice balls and porridge sourced from Akita Prefecture, **fuzkue** (*fuzkue.com*) dedicated reading cafe where silence is golden, and the **Hakkō Department** (*hakko-department.com*) restaurant-grocer devoted exclusively to fermented food and drink. Bonus Track also hosts regular events, such as DIY workshops, craft markets and firecrackers in summer.

Sangenjaya's Glowing Alleyways MAP P114

Larger-than-life *yokochō*

South of Shimo-Kitazawa, and just a couple stops away from Shibuya Station on the Den-en-toshi line, is the centuries-old watering hole of **Sangenjaya** (三軒茶屋). Its name refers to the original 'three teahouses' where Edo-period travellers once came to seek rest and refreshment with tea and sake. Sangenjaya was a mid-journey stopping point for walking pilgrimages to the Ōyama Afuri shrine in Isehara, Kanagawa Prefecture. Two of the former teahouses still exist today, albeit in different forms: the pottery shop **Tanakaya To-en** (田中屋陶苑) on Chazawa-dōri near Sangenjaya Station, and the *izakaya* **Shigaraki** (志が良喜), housed in an elegant black wooden building on Setagaya-dōri.

Sleepy in the daytime, Sangenjaya comes alive around dusk. Wander along its lantern-lit backstreets to discover a mix of cozy *izakaya*, modern bars and creative fusion restaurants, from smoky *yakitori* joints to stylish wine bars to regional curry parlours. This is a great place to experience Japan's original culture of *yokochō* – the ramshackle alleyways lined with food stalls and shops that sprang up as people rebuilt their livelihoods following the devastation of the war. **Sankaku Chitai** (三角地帯, Triangle Zone) is packed with tiny eateries and drinking holes, while the surrounding streets are also home to numerous night spots with a bit more space.

For a free view of the area and the western Tokyo skyline, head up to the Sky Carrot observation deck on the 26th floor of **Carrot Tower**.

TOP INDEPENDENT FILM HOUSES

Image Forum: Old-school art-house cinema showing Japanese and international independent films and thoughtful documentaries. No food or drinks allowed.

Eurospace: Housed inside a film school, with a tendency for edgy, progressive and festival circuit programming. Occasional Q&A with filmmakers.

Bunkamura Le Cinéma: Arty cafe parlour perched above Bic Camera at Shibuya Station, favouring European indie productions and auteur retrospectives.

Cinema K2: Inside the Tefu Lounge on the south side of Shimo-Kitazawa Station, featuring 4K projections of films d'auteur.

Shimotakaido Cinema: Community theatre projecting a wide range of films – old and new, cult and classic, animated, musical, experimental.

EATING & DRINKING IN SANGENJAYA: FAVOURITES — MAPS P106 & P114

Café Mamehico: Delectable home cooking and dainty desserts made with quality ingredients, set in an artfully decorated chic wooden interior. *9am-9pm* ¥¥

A-Bridge: Lively rooftop cafe-bar hidden above a shady alleyway serving cocktails and a wide array of food, from creative appetisers to ratatouille. *noon-11pm Thu-Tue* ¥¥

Gyoza Shack: Specialising in *gyōza* stuffed with natural ingredients, boiled, fried, even sweet: Umeboshi Shiso, Pumpkin Gorgon Honey. *5pm-midnight* ¥

Bar Bodeguita: Run by Japanese twin siblings who grew up in Cuba, serving authentic Cuban food and cocktails, plus live salsa music. *hours vary Wed-Sun* ¥

SHIBUYA & SETAGAYA

SIGHTS

1. Gōtokuji Temple
2. Sangenjaya
3. Sankaku Chitai
4. Setagaya Hachiman Shrine
5. Shōin Jinja

ACTIVITIES, COURSES & TOURS

6. Carrot Tower

EATING

7. Café Mamehico
8. Gyoza Shack
9. Ogura-An
10. Ukiyo
11. Yuki Usagi

DRINKING & NIGHTLIFE

12. A-Bridge
13. Log Road Daikanyama
14. Route-1
15. Shigaraki

ENTERTAINMENT

16. Black Bird Eatery
17. Musicasa
18. Shimotakaido Cinema

SHOPPING

19. Boroichi Market
20. Tanakaya To-en

TRANSPORT

21. Setagaya Line

Retro Tram Ride

Visit Setagaya in 10 stations

One of Tokyo's only two remaining tram lines, the **Setagaya line** *(sg50th.tokyo)* has been successfully operating since 1969. In 2019 it became Japan's first urban railway line to be fully powered by renewable energy. Departing from Sangenjaya Station, the hyperlocal 5km route winds through 10 residential neighbourhoods and connects with three different train lines, offering a leisurely way to explore Setagaya's more understated attractions.

No doubt the most popular station is Miyanosaka, home to the famous **Gōtokuji Temple** (豪徳寺; *gotokuji.jp*), considered to be the origin of Japan's famous *maneki-neko* (beckoning cat) used to attract customers and good fortune. (The Setagaya line even celebrated its 50th anniversary by adding a cat-themed tram to its fleet.) Once you enter the forested temple grounds, head over to Honojo to see thousands of white *maneki-neko* figurines in all different sizes placed by visitors as offerings. Down the hill on the other side of the station, past the preserved 1925 tram car, **Setagaya Hachiman Shrine** (世田谷八幡宮; *80000.or.jp)* hosts a ceremonial sumo match every September.

Shōin-jinja-mae Station is named after the resident shrine dedicated to Yoshida Shōin, a spiritual leader of the Meiji Restoration who was executed for treason at age 29. In summer, **Shōin Jinja** *(shoinjinja.org)* installs a wooden trellis to hang dozens of colourful *furin* (wind chimes) offerings, gently swaying and tinkling in front of the main hall. The road leading to the temple is lined with pâtisseries and small shops selling gourmet rice crackers and other souvenirs.

Accessible from both Setagaya and Kamimachi Stations, the 440-year-old **Boroichi Market** *(city.setagaya.lg.jp/02072/10108.html)* attracts hundreds of thousands of people to browse its 700 stalls peddling antiques, secondhand clothing and other vintage items, over two days every December and January.

At the north terminal station and ancient post town of Shimo-Takaido, grab a freshly baked *taiyaki* (fish-shaped pastry) at **Ogura-An** *(oguraan.com)* and catch an indie flick at **Shimotakaido Cinema** *(shimotakaidocinema.com)*. From here, a short ride on the Keiō train line will take you straight to Shinjuku.

LOCAL FESTIVALS

The weeklong **Shimo-Kitazawa International Puppet Festival** *(sipf.jp)* animates neighbourhood theatres and streets with edgy, countercultural performances in February, while the **Shimo-Kitazawa Music Festival** *(shimokita-fes.com)* showcases local indie rock in July.

In September, the **Reitaisai Festival** *(kitazawamatsuri.wixsite.com/kitazawahachiman)* takes place at Kitazawa Hachimangū shrine, featuring *taiko* and *kagura* dances.

Local independent films are screened during the **Shimo-Kitazawa Film Festival** *(shimokitafilm.com)* in October. English subtitles are minimal, but side events include music and food.

The **Shimo-Kitazawa Curry Festival** *(curryfes.com)*, also in October, celebrates this famed local dish. Fancy a squid ink or kiwi curry? You got it.

Researched by Rob Goss

HARAJUKU & AOYAMA

FASHION, ART AND ARCHITECTURE

Fashion and style come in all guises in this trendsetting part of Tokyo – from streetwear and youth trends to haute couture and cutting-edge art and architecture.

Artistic and refined – with a healthy dose of creative edginess thrown into the mix – Harajuku (原宿) and Aoyama (青山) defy easy description and hold appeal for a range of ages and tastes. Slicing through the area is Omotesandō-dōri, home to some of the city's most luxurious shopping, while nearby is Takeshita-dōri, the epicentre of Japan's ever-shifting youth trends, and its iconic culture of *kawaii* (cuteness). Adding a striking contrast is Yoyogi Park, one of Tokyo's most beloved spots for communing with nature and lively urban festivals. Next to that comes another change of pace at the magnificent Meiji-jingū, a shrine in vast natural surroundings that was built for the Emperor Meiji and his spouse, Empress Shōken.

TIP

The Harajuku Tourist Information Centre, located in the HIS building near the Takeshita-dōri exit of Harajuku Station, is an excellent place to procure local maps and pamphlets, store luggage, buy drinks and souvenirs, and peruse information on everything including upcoming tours and events.

FROM LEFT: ANTHONY PLUMMER/LONELY PLANET, AGUSTIN.PHOTO/SHUTTERSTOCK

Prada Aoyama (p124)

See page 219 for places to stay in Harajuku & Aoyama

⭐ Highlights

❶ Meiji-jingū
Visit the century-old spiritual home to the souls of Emperor Meiji and Empress Shōken. **p126**

❷ Yoyogi Park
One of Tokyo's favourite spots for kicking back in the grass and attending urban festivals. **p125**

❸ Nezu Museum
Browse a wonderful collection of Asian antique artworks, then stroll the lush garden. **p119**

◀ ❹ Takeshita-dōri
Weave through the crowds to discover the city's latest youth trends. **p118**

❺ Omotesandō
Take in the high-end boutiques and architectural gems along one of Tokyo's swankiest streets. **p118**

🚶 Getting Around

Train
Harajuku is one stop from Shibuya on the JR Yamanote line (and two stops from Shinjuku). The station, while small and easy to navigate, can get very crowded.

Metro
Meiji-jingūmae (Chiyoda and Fukutoshin lines) is adjacent to JR Harajuku Station and Omotesandō (Chiyoda, Ginza and Hanzōmon lines) is at the Aoyama end of the street. Aoyama can also be accessed by Gaienmae Station on the Ginza line.

Walk
It's a 15- to 20-minute walk from Harajuku and Aoyama to Shibuya.

On the land that now encompasses Omotesandō Hills, once stood Dojunkai Aoyama Apartments, a Bauhaus-inspired building from 1926 that housed shops and galleries.

While Omotesandō Hills retains a small-scale replica of the beloved structure, campaigners decried the new complex as soulless – a form of gentrification that was the antithesis to everything the bohemian Dojunkai represented.

Dojunkai was also one of the few local buildings to survive the US military fire-bombing of 1945 that destroyed Tokyo's eastern neighbour-hoods and large swathes of Omote-sandō – and killed hundreds. A peace statue comm-emorating this turbulent time stands at the intersection of Omotesandō and Aoyama-dōri. If you want to see an area that escaped the carnage of WW2 and has dodged urban redevelopment, there's Yanaka (p180) on the east side.

Shop Till You Drop

Stroll along Omotesandō-dōri

Extending southeast from Harajuku Station to the Nezu Museum, and passing through the Omotesandō, Harajuku and Aoyama districts, shopping along this road reigns supreme – and the fashionistas and luxury buyers who flock here from around the globe ensure prime people-watching.

Start at Meiji-jingūmae subway station, then head along **Omotesandō** (表参道) towards the Meiji-dōri intersection, where two neighbouring retail outlets offer ample opportunities to part with your cash. Spread over half a dozen floors (plus 'half' floors), **Laforet Harajuku** (*laforet.ne.jp*) houses an extensive lineup of cool fashion brands, while **Tokyu Plaza** (*tokyu-plaza.com/omokado*) offers a chilled-out rooftop terrace called Omohara Forest.

Continuing southward, Omotesandō-dōri and the surrounding streets are lined with shops and restaurants to suit all budgets and tastes. Down one of these, you'll find all manner of reasonably priced Japanese textiles, ceramics and crafts to take home as souvenirs at the iconic **Oriental Bazaar** (*orientalbazaar.co.jp*), an antiques and souvenir store that has been in Omotesandō since 1951, when many of its customers were US Occupation affiliates.

Back on the main street, nearby is the upmarket shoppers' pilgrimage point, **Omotesandō Hills** (表参道ヒルズ; *omotesando hills.com*). Designed by architect Ando Tadao, and featuring sharp, sleek designs, the complex houses high-end fashion giants including Yves Saint Laurent, Valentino, Bvlgari and Dior, along with numerous smaller jewellery, fashion and cosmetics brands, and both Japanese and overseas eateries. Just don't plan on visiting too early – most stores and cafes don't open until 11am.

A Deep-dive into Harajuku Style

Explore Takeshita-dōri

Takeshita-dōri (竹下通り; *takeshita-street.com*) is best known as the locus of the goth and lolita scenes that flourished in the early 2000s. But it's no one-hit-wonder: for half a century, this meandering lane – lined with small boutiques and free of car traffic – has been a beacon of creative style. Other looks incubated here include the rainbow-bright, super-*kawaii* (cute) *'decora'* style that ruled Harajuku in the 1990s.

EATING IN HARAJUKU: INSTAGRAMMABLE SNACKS

Marion Crêpes: Get classic Harajuku crêpes stuffed with whipped cream and sliced fruit at Marion Crêpes on Takeshita-dōri. *10am-9pm* ¥

Totti Candy Factory: Magnificent, photogenic rainbow cotton-candy swirls are one of Takeshita-dōri's new wave of sweets. *10am-7pm Mon-Fri, 9am-8pm Sat & Sun* ¥

Strawberry Fetish: The latest sweet to take Harajuku by storm is the Chinese *tanghulu* – skewers of sugar-glazed fruit. *10am-8pm Mon-Fri, from 9am Sat & Sun* ¥

Micasadeco & Cafe: Super-fluffy soufflé pancakes, one of the most popular things to eat in Harajuku. Expect to queue. *11am-5pm Mon-Fri, 10am-6pm Sat & Sun* ¥

Nezu Museum

GOLDEN GINGKO

Tokyo's official tree is the ginkgo, called *ichō* in Japanese – once you realise this you'll see the motif of the fan-shaped leaves everywhere. For a couple of weeks around late November and early December, the trees turn a dazzling shade of yellow and carpet the pavements in gold when the leaves fall.

The most famous display is along the aptly named **Gingko Avenue** (いちょう 並木; *Ichō-namiki*) in Aoyama, near the Gaienmae subway stop. Another good local spot is along the western edge of Yoyogi Park, near Yoyogi-kōen Station.

Just brace yourself for the smell of the gingko nuts when they fall to the ground and begin to decompose – many liken it to rancid butter or vomit.

While nowadays most fashion scenes are online, Takeshita-dōri remains a pilgrimage site for teens from all over Japan, and it can get absolutely jammed in the afternoons. Remnants of fashion trends past can be found here and there, alongside more contemporary shops. Still committed to being extra, it's an especially good place to shop for fun accessories (like animal-shaped backpacks) and colourful basics like socks and tights.

Nezu & Beyond

Exploring local art museums

While walking around Aoyama, make sure to give yourself an hour for one of the finest museums in the area. First opened in 1941, the **Nezu Museum** (根津美術館; *nezu-muse.or.jp; adult/child from ¥1300/1000*) houses the private collection of entrepreneur and art connoisseur Nezu Kaichirō. It includes over 7400 antique Asian works reflecting his eclectic tastes, which span mediums including ceramics, calligraphy and Buddhist sculpture. The 2009 renovation by renowned architect Kengo Kuma added a striking bamboo-grove border and a

EATING IN HARAJUKU & AOYAMA: COMFORT FOOD

Harajuku Gyōza-rō: Long-running favourite for all-day plates of *gyōza*, served fried or boiled. There's often a queue but service moves quickly. *11.30am-9pm* ¥

Kyūshū Jangara: Sample thin noodles, tender *chāshū* (roast pork) and rich broth for which Kyūshū-style ramen is famous. Try the vegan version, too. *10am-10pm* ¥

Maisen: Famed for *tonkatsu* (breaded, deep-fried pork cutlets) and its old public bathhouse setting. Eat in, or takeaway delicious *tonkatsu* sandwiches. *11am-9pm* ¥¥

Sakura-tei: Cook your own savoury *okonomiyaki* pancakes at this colourful place in the funky Design Festa gallery (p123). Has all-you-can-eat lunch deals. *11am-11pm* ¥¥

⭐ HIGHLIGHTS

1 Meiji-jingū
2 Nezu Museum
3 Omotesandō
4 Ōta Memorial Museum of Art
5 Yoyogi-kōen

⭐ SIGHTS

6 Design Festa
7 Dior Omote-sandō
8 Gingko Avenue
9 Meiji-jingū Gyoen
10 Omotesandō Hills
11 Prada Aoyama
12 Space Banksia
13 Spiral Building
14 Takeshita-dōri
15 Taro Okamoto Memorial Museum
16 Tokyu Plaza

⭐ ACTIVITIES, COURSES & TOURS

17 Shimizu-yu

⬤ SLEEPING

18 Dormy Inn Premium Shibuya Jingūmae
19 Tokyu Stay Aoyama Premier
20 Trunk Hotel Cat Street

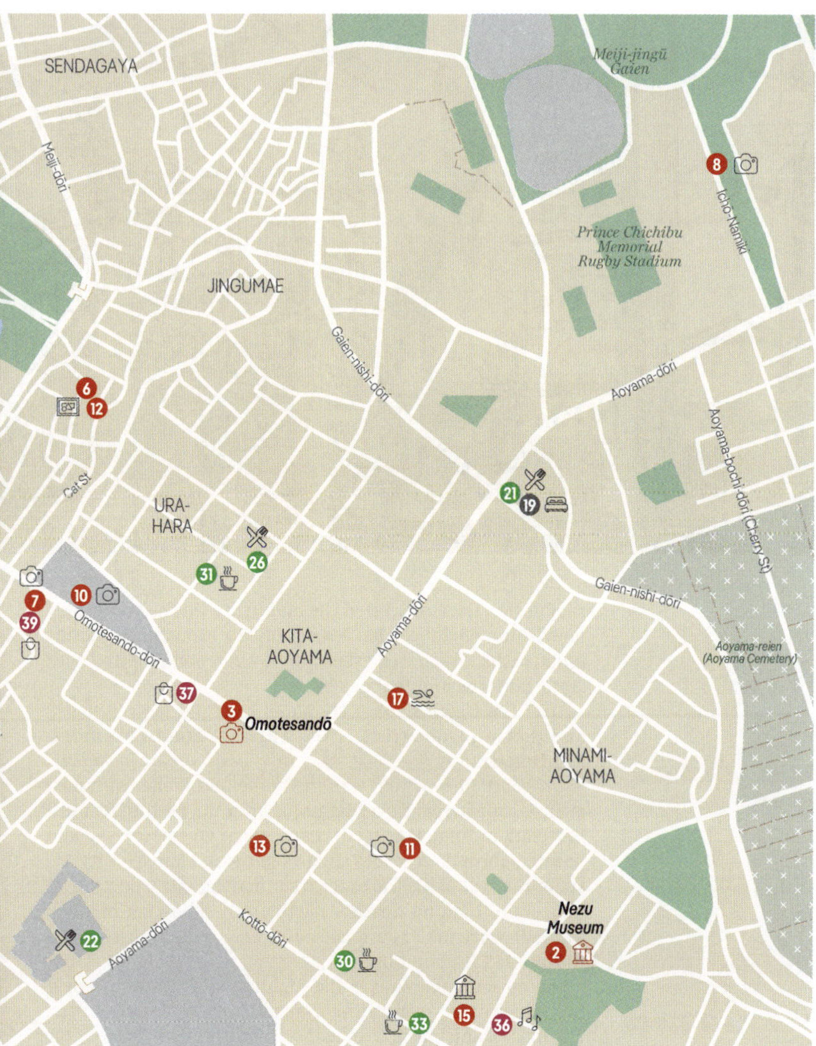

	EATING		
21	Citron	**28** Micasadeco & Cafe	**31** Higuma Doughnuts x Coffee Wrights
22	Farmers Market @UNU	**see 6** Sakura-tei	**32** Little Nap Coffee Stand
23	Harajuku Gyōza-rō	**29** Strawberry Fetish	**33** Matsubaya Saryō
24	Initial	**see 29** Totti Candy Factory	**see 13** Sakurai Japanese Tea Experience
25	Kyūshū Jangara	**DRINKING & NIGHTLIFE**	**34** Sarutahiko Coffee The Bridge
26	Maisen	**30** Aoyama Flower Market Green House	**35** The Roastery by Nozy
27	Marion Crêpes		

EATING

21 Citron
22 Farmers Market @UNU
23 Harajuku Gyōza-rō
24 Initial
25 Kyūshū Jangara
26 Maisen
27 Marion Crêpes
28 Micasadeco & Cafe
see 6 Sakura-tei
29 Strawberry Fetish
see 29 Totti Candy Factory

DRINKING & NIGHTLIFE

30 Aoyama Flower Market Green House
31 Higuma Doughnuts x Coffee Wrights
32 Little Nap Coffee Stand
33 Matsubaya Saryō
see 13 Sakurai Japanese Tea Experience
34 Sarutahiko Coffee The Bridge
35 The Roastery by Nozy

ENTERTAINMENT

36 Blue Note Tokyo

SHOPPING

37 Bottega Veneta
38 Laforet Harajuku
39 Oriental Bazaar

roof design that integrated the building with the stunningly flourishing onsite garden – save time to meander its picturesque paths, which wend their way around ponds dotted with stone lanterns and teahouses.

After the Nezu, stroll a couple of hundred metres south, and down a side street is the **Taro Okamoto Memorial Museum** (岡本太郎記念館; *taro-okamoto.or.jp; adult/child ¥650/300*), which was the home and atelier of famed avant-garde artist Taro Okamoto, from the mid-1950s until his death in 1996. During his early years, Okamoto lived and painted abroad, in places such as Paris and Mexico City. He spent the rest of his life and career in deep introspection on matters of life and death – particularly following his own difficult wartime experiences and his studio's destruction in the 1945 firebombing.

The museum showcases the highlights of Okamoto's oeuvre, which spans everything from abstract art to surrealism. His most iconic piece, a splashy structure titled *Tower of the Sun*, was unveiled at the 1970 Osaka World Expo. His *Myth of Tomorrow* (p109), a work depicting the scene of an atomic bomb explosion, was lost for decades in Mexico City – and later

EATING & DRINKING IN AOYAMA & HARAJUKU: TEA & SWEETS

Aoyama Flower Market Green House: Florist serving floral-themed herbal beverages and edible flower-flecked dishes in a flowery setting. *10am-9pm* ¥

Initial: Decadent sculptural parfaits, with seasonal fruit and rich soft-serve; gelato and fruit sandwiches, too. *noon-10pm Mon-Fri, from 11am Sat & Sun* ¥

Matsubaya Saryō: Kotto-dōri tea shop blending traditional and modern aesthetics, with bonsai on the tables and high-grade Japanese teas and sweets. *10am-6pm* ¥¥

Sakurai Japanese Tea Experience: Chic salon offering tea with sweets, and tea cocktails week-days after 7pm. Best to reserve. *11am-11pm Mon-Fri, to 8pm Sat & Sun* ¥¥

Design Festa

FARMERS MARKETS

Farmers markets can be a great way to get to know a place – through its food producers, mainly – and **Farmers Market @ UNU** (*farmersmarkets. jp*), held in front of the United Nations University (UNU) campus along Aoyama-dōri, is no exception.

Taking place most Saturdays and Sundays from 10am to 4pm all year long, it features farm-fresh goods from growers throughout the country, along with baked delights, crafts, food trucks and occasional live music.

The markets are an opportunity to chat with vendors and learn more about Japan's local food culture.

rediscovered in a warehouse in 2003. The enormous, restored painting is now displayed inside Shibuya Station, just outside the gates to the Inokashira line.

At the other end of Omotesandō-dōri, just behind the landmark LaForet building, lies the **Ōta Memorial Museum of Art** (太田記念美術館; *ukiyoe-ota-muse.jp; adult/child from ¥1000/free*). Comprised largely of the collection amassed by businessman Seizo Ota V, the museum features around 14,000 *ukiyo-e* (woodblock prints) from legendary artists of the genre, including Katsushika Hokusai and Utagawa Hiroshige. The works on display are rotated regularly, according to specific themes – recent exhibitions have featured cats, kimono and cultural connections to China.

For art with a younger, edgy feel, also stop by **Design Festa** (*designfestagallery.com; free*) in Harajuku. This self-titled 'Harajuku Art Village', established in 1998, consists of east and west galleries, plus a cafe-bar and on-site *okonomiyaki* restaurant. The complex also offers opportunities for artists to display their original works, and for visitors to try their hand at mural painting.

DRINKING IN HARAJUKU & AOYAMA: BEST COFFEE

Little Nap Coffee Stand: Alongside Yoyogi Park, this delightful pocket cafe serves strong coffee brews (try the macchiato) and baked goods. *9am-7pm*

Higuma Doughnuts X Coffee Wrights: An airy cafe in the backstreets of Omotesandō with moreish doughnuts and speciality coffee. *11am-6pm Thu-Tue, from 10am Sat & Sun*

The Roastery by Nozy: Espresso drinks made from beans carefully sourced and roasted in-house, right on Cat St. Try the espresso-flavoured soft-serve. *10am-8pm*

Sarutahiko Coffee The Bridge: Located upstairs, inside the renovated Harajuku Train Station, this cafe is the digital nomad's dream. *8am-10pm*

TAKE A STROLL THROUGH AOYAMA

This tour uncovers unique museums and eateries, along with buildings designed by some of Japan's most respected architects.

START	END	LENGTH
Gaienmae Station	Meiji-jingūmae Station	4km; 2hr

Begin at **1 Gaienmae subway station**, then walk along Aoyama-dōri toward Aoyama. If you need coffee or a quick bite, stop at **2 Citron**, a French cafe that does a great quiche. Next, you could break for a bath at **3 Shimizu-yu**, one of a dwindling number of *sentō* (public baths) in Tokyo, before exploring fashionable Aoyama. For that, take a left at the next major intersection, and prepare to be wowed by the nearby shimmering glass crystal tower housing luxury fashion giant at **4 Prada Aoyama**. Around here you can browse boutiques and galleries, before reaching the magnificent **5 Nezu Museum** (p119) and its collection of antique Asian artworks. Heading south, you'll pass famous jazz club **6 Blue**

Note Tokyo, after which you can take a right and head up Kotto-dōri towards Aoyama-dōri. Next, browse art exhibits and eclectic shops at the nearby **7 Spiral**. Its 5th-floor Sakurai Japanese Tea Experience (p122) offers an intriguing window into tea culture, featuring onsite-roasted *hōjicha* (roasted green tea) and sophisticated tea-based cocktails (reservations recommended). Lastly, head up Omotesandō-dōri to see the area's architectural standouts, including **8** Ito Toyo's **Bottega Veneta** and **9** Sejima Kazuyo's **Dior**. After the boutiques and complexes along Omotesandō, grab a train at **10 Meiji-jingūmae subway station** – or add on more of the sights in this chapter.

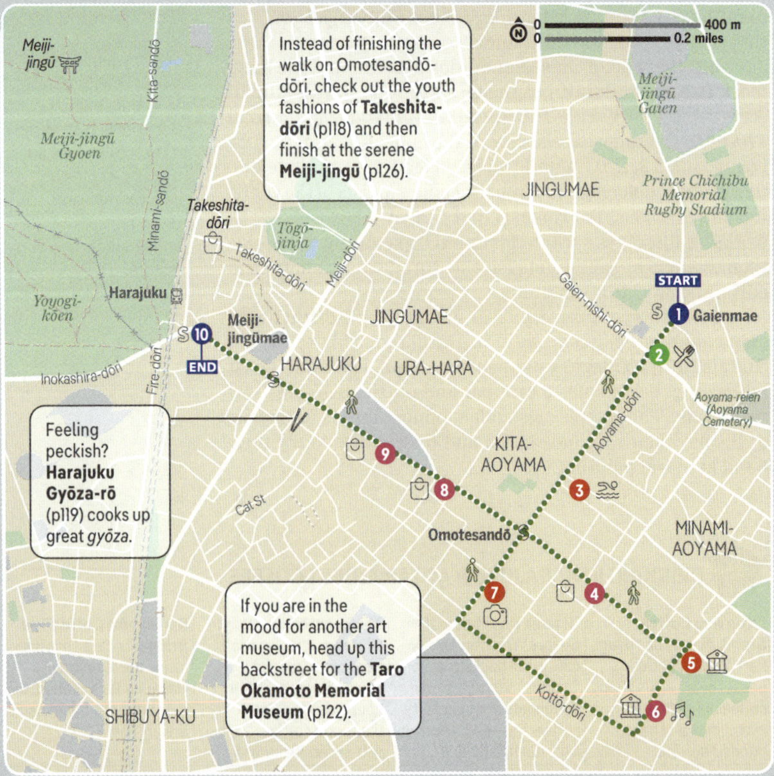

Located just adjacent is **Space Banksia** *(space-banksia. com)*, a cafe–art gallery hosting rotating exhibitions, film screenings and pop-ups featuring local artists and creators – check the website for upcoming schedules.

Explore Yoyogi Park

Prime people-watching

Once the site of a post-WWII US military barracks, and later the 1964 Tokyo Olympics Village, **Yoyogi-kōen** (代々木公園; *tokyo-park.or.jp/park/yoyogi; free*) is where Tokyoites head for picnicking, sports, music sessions or just plain lounging. On Sunday afternoons, a legendary troupe of rockabilly dancers performs near the Harajuku entrance, complete with slicked-back, Elvis-style hairdos. Also held here on many weekends are farmers markets, featuring everything from organic produce to clothing to lifestyle goods, while the lively international festivals held in the park showcase the cultures and cuisines of Tokyo's foreign residents, from Peru to Jamaica to Thailand.

Clean Up at a Neighbourhood Bathhouse

A *sentō* soak

Keen to take a break from the hustle and bustle and dip your toe into Japanese bathing culture? Then while out and about in Aoyama, you could drop by **Shimizu-yu** (清水湯; *shimizuyu.jp; adult/child from ¥550/200)*, a *sentō* with a crisp, modern look and a variety of amenities, including rain showers, jet baths and two saunas. Given that *sentō* are traditionally no-frills bathhouses where locals come with their own soap and towels, you'll need to pack wash gear or pay extra for the 'sauna course with rental towels' *(¥1330)*, which will give you access to everything plus essentials like soap and shampoo.

As for bathing etiquette, *sentō* follow the same rules as *onsen* (p35), and the most important thing to know is that you need to clean up at the showers and rinse well before getting into the soaking tubs. Shimizu-yu is open from noon until midnight (until 11pm on weekends) and closed on Fridays. Unfortunately, visitors with tattoos are not allowed entry.

THE FOOD OF THE JAPANESE DIASPORA

Japan has one of the world's largest communities of Brazilians outside of Brazil – and vice-versa.

This is down to the history of revolving-door immigration between the two countries, wherein numerous Japanese set sail for Brazil in the early 1900s to seek better economic opportunities – and their children and grandchildren did the same, in reverse, when Japan's government issued working visas in 1990 to those with at least one Japanese grandparent. These *nikkei* (Japanese-descended) Brazilians have brought the cuisine of their homeland to Japan – just as their parents and grandparents took the cuisine of Japan to Brazil.

A top favourite is *churrasco* (Brazilian-style slow-roasted barbecued meat) at restaurants like Barbacoa, which has locations in Aoyama and elsewhere in Tokyo.

MICHAEL GORDON/SHUTTERSTOCK

Meiji-jingū

Meiji-jingū

The lush grounds of the 100-year-old Meiji-jingū (明治神宮) is considered a must-see – and it rarely disappoints. This monumental Shintō shrine made of unvarnished timber is ensconced in a 69-hectare forest (bigger than Yoyogi Park) and is a wonderful example of how Shintō sites are designed to function in harmony with nature, even in the heart of one of the world's great metropolises.

DON'T MISS

The Towering *Torii* Gates

Hand-washing Font

The Main Sanctuary

Votive Tablets

Meiji-jingū Gyoen

Under the Torii

The entrance to Meiji-jingū is marked by the first of three towering **torii**, the elegant, somewhat pi-shaped gates that indicate the entrance to sacred Shintō ground. From here, you follow a wide gravel path that winds through a dense thicket of trees, and in about 15 minutes you'll reach the main sanctuary – a lantern-lit hall with a dramatic, copper roof that occupies a clearing beyond the final, monumental gate.

PRACTICALITIES

- *meijijingu.or.jp*
- free
- sunrise–sunset

A Modern Classic

While the whole scene appears timeless, Meiji-jingū is actually a relatively modern creation. Founded in 1920, it's dedicated to Emperor Meiji and Empress Shōken, whose reign (1868–1912) coincided with Japan's transformation from isolationist, feudal state to imperialist nation. The forest is of similar vintage, created from hundreds of trees donated from all over Japan and planted by volunteers. Considered sacred and designed to flourish over generations, the forest has been left untouched ever since. For this reason, you can't stray from the path.

Manners & Customs

Shrines are part of the Shintō tradition, but are non-exclusive. There are no prohibitions on visiting, just an imperative to be respectful; this means refraining from behaviours that might be considered disruptive (like eating, drinking, smoking or talking loudly). Photos are allowed, but not around the main hall or the kiosks, or of people praying.

There are a number of customs associated with visiting shrines; nothing is obligatory, but they can add to the experience and serve as a sign of respect. For example, on your left just before the final *torii*, there's a **font** where it's customary to rinse your hands before entering the inner sanctuary. At the **main sanctuary**, you can join visitors in greeting the *kami* (Shintō gods) with bows, hand claps and a small offering.

Leave a Wish

To the right of the main sanctuary, you'll see racks of **votive tablets** – surrounding a magnificent camphor tree – on which messages are written. These are called *ema* and you can purchase them from the kiosks on the perimeter of the courtyard. Use one of the pens provided, then add yours to the chorus of prayers, wishes and notes of gratitude in multiple languages. The kiosks also sell *omamori* (amulets), silken pouches holding prayers for luck or protection. These might be for success in school entrance exams, safe childbirth, a happy union or safe travel. As Meiji-jingū is popular with international tourists, the amulets are labelled in English. Note that the kiosks only accept cash – most cost ¥1000 or ¥1500.

The Iris Garden

Midway along the gravel path, the grounds also have an oft-overlooked garden, **Meiji-jingū Gyoen** (明治神宮御苑), which predates the founding of the shrine. Once part of a feudal estate, and later an imperial property, it has strolling paths, benches for contemplative breaks and a pond with colourful koi and sunning turtles. A highlight is the iris garden; it's one of the personal touches added by Emperor Meiji, who designed it to please the empress. The couple often frequented the garden, which is cited as a reason this location was chosen for the shrine. Admission is ¥500, and it is usually uncrowded – except in June when the irises bloom.

SIGNS OF OVERTOURISM

With overtourism an increasingly pressing issue for Tokyo and other popular parts of Japan, tourist behaviour is becoming a major talking point. Meiji-jingū is no exception. You'll notice the lower parts of the *torii* here now have protective covers. That's because in 2024 an American tourist made headlines for all the wrong reasons by carving letters into one of the sacred pillars.

TOP TIPS

● Want to time your visit for a ceremony? At 8am and 2pm daily, you can see the *nikku-sai* ritual, a ceremonial offering of food and prayers to the *kami*.

● You can avoid the crowds by coming early on a weekday, but be aware that most shops, cafes and attractions in nearby Harajuku and Omotesandō won't be open until 10am or 11am.

● Remember this is a sacred area. That means following the well-signposted rules about photography in the main sanctuary, not eating or smoking on the grounds, and being quiet and respectful.

Researched by Louise George Kittaka

WEST TOKYO & AROUND

LAIDBACK NEIGHBOURHOODS AND WILD NATURE

Head west to discover some of the city's most intriguing districts, then onward to the Tama region's colourful temples, unique museums and natural wonders.

Your westward journey begins with Nakano (中野区), home to the *otaku* (geek) haven of Nakano Broadway. Next is Suginami (杉並区), which encompasses Kōenji (高円寺), known for its activist history and vintage stores; Ogikubo (荻窪), packed with ramen shops; and Nishi-Ogikubo (西荻窪), with a thriving antiques scene. The Tama Region (多摩地域) begins with stylish Kichijōji (吉祥寺), with Inokashira Park and the beloved Ghibli Museum. Explore Tokyo's living history at the Edo-Tokyo Open Air Architectural Museum and Chōfu's temple town of Jindai-ji (深大寺). Further out is the nature-rich Okutama (奥多摩), where activities include hiking, rafting and camping.

TIP

Take your time exploring the neighbourhoods along the Chūō line for a particularly laid-back slice of Tokyo life. Featuring abundant peaceful temples and shrines, unique shops and cafes, and lively *yokochō* lined with bars and eateries, many tucked underneath and alongside the train tracks, these neighbourhoods brim with atmosphere.

FROM LEFT: MICHAEL YEO/SHUTTERSTOCK, TANYA JONES/SHUTTERSTOCK

Nakano Broadway (p130)

See page 219 for places to stay in West Tokyo

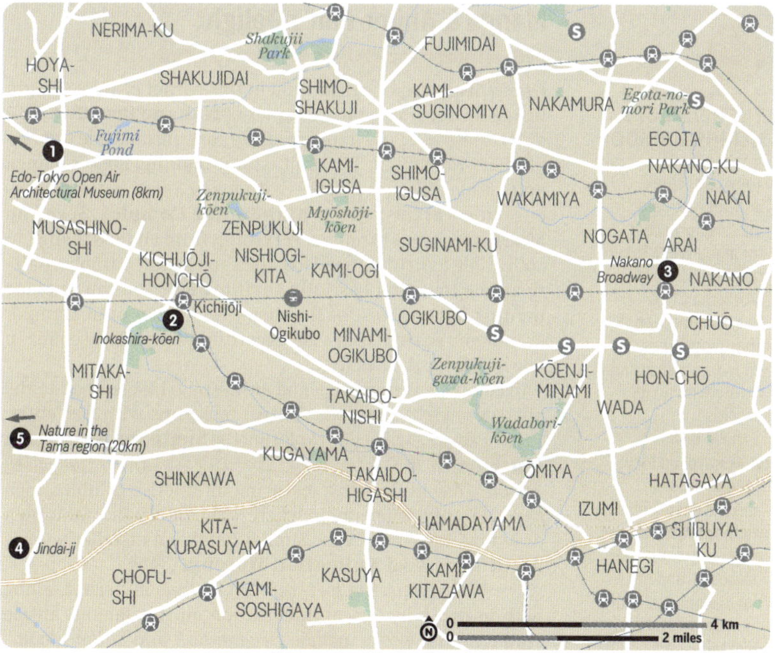

⭐ Highlights

❶ Edo-Tokyo Open Air Architectural Museum
Step into centuries past with a tour of faithfully reconstructed buildings and hands-on demonstrations. **p133**

❷ Inokashira-kōen
Explore a pondside shrine and the enchanted world of legendary animator Miyazaki Hayao at the Ghibli Museum, Mitaka. **p134**

❸ Nakano Broadway
Dig for all sorts of anime and manga treasure inside this subcultural hub. **p130**

❹ Jindai-ji
Savor the charm of Tokyo's second-oldest temple and wander the historic streets. **p135**

▲❺ Tama region
Follow trails through Tokyo's glorious nature, from mountain peaks to river valleys. **p140**

🚶 Getting Around

Train
Most major points of interest are easily accessed on the Chūō and Keiō lines (from Shinjuku) and the Keiō Inokashira line (from Shibuya).

Car
To explore the natural wonders of Okutama, where public transport may be infrequent or inconvenient, a car can be an easy and cost-effective option.

Bicycle
Rental cycles can be a great choice once you reach your destination, with bicycle-sharing or city-run rental services available at many major stations.

THE HEART OF A NEIGHBOURHOOD

Tokyo has sleek and sophisticated malls aplenty, but for many West Tokyo neighbourhoods along the Chūō line, the traditional shopping street known as a **shōtengai** is where local life unfolds.

These covered walkways run for several blocks and are lined with mom-and-pop stores, speciality shops and eateries – and not a car in sight. Typically found near stations in established residential areas, *shōtengai* are more than just places to shop – they're community hubs and often the focus of local festivals and events.

Schoolchildren call out greetings to shopkeepers on their way home and elderly residents can count on a listening ear. Stretching for 650m from Asagaya Station, the **Asagaya Pearl Centre** is one fine example.

Manga & Anime Fan's Delight

Feed all comic and cartoon desires in Nakano

Otaku of all stripes can go wild in this corner of Tokyo. Begin inside the retro shopping complex of **Nakano Broadway** (中野ブロードウェイ; *nakano-broadway.com*) just outside Nakano Station's North Exit. The multi-storey building houses manga and anime offerings galore – with many found in the numerous outlets of the popular **Mandarake Complex**. Spend an afternoon sifting through everything from endless manga to collectible figurines to video games to cosplay paraphernalia to anime toys, and basically anything else you can imagine nerding out on. Most of the shops don't open until 11am, or even noon, so time your visit accordingly, or enjoy a coffee in one of the local cafes first.

To complete your manga and anime pilgrimage, head to the adjacent neighbourhoods for two museums with free entry. Fans of all ages will enjoy exploring the **Suginami Animation Museum** (杉並アニメーションミュージアム; *sam.or.jp/english_home; free*) in Ogikubo, featuring interactive exhibits, such as a DIY animation studio where you can produce your own drawings and voice-overs. Similar hands-on installations are found at the **Toei Animation Museum** (東映アニメーションミュージアム; *museum.toei-anim.co.jp; free*) in Nerima, along with in-depth historical information on this famous anime studio, whose works include *Dragon Ball* and *Sailor Moon*.

Cultural Exploration in Ogikubo

A rhapsody in green

The lovely and secluded **Ōtaguro Park** (大田黒公園; *ogikubo3gardens.jp/ootaguro; free*) in Ogikubo features paths flanked by ginkgo trees, a koi-filled pond, and an adjacent pavilion and teahouse. Once the residence of musician and music critic Ōtaguro Motoo (1893–1979) – credited with helping to establish Ogikubo's classical music culture – the green space was created after he bequeathed the grounds to Suginami City. While the park normally closes at 5pm, it stays open until 9pm from late November to early December for autumn foliage viewing, when the enormous illuminated trees reflect on the surface of the pond to stunning effect (*entry for the light up adult/child ¥300/100*).

EATING IN & AROUND NAKANO: OUR PICKS

Kawanaka-ya: A tiny, lantern-adorned and packed Higashi-Kōenji eatery serving *yakitori*, with sake to wash it down. *5-11pm Mon & Wed-Fri, from 4pm Sat & Sun* ¥

Pao Caravan Sarai: This Higashi-Nakano Afghan restaurant serves skewered meat and vegetables amid traditional decor. *5-11pm Wed-Mon* ¥¥

Lou: Portland-inspired Nakano cafe with a leafy terrace featuring coffee drinks, scrumptious desserts, craft beers and natural wines. *8am-4pm Thu-Tue* ¥

Gion: The decor in this photogenic cafe near Asagaya Station echoes Japan's Shōwa era, with classic Japanese cafe fare to match. *8.30am-2am Mon-Sat, from 9am Sun* ¥

WEST TOKYO

HIGHLIGHTS

1 Ghibli Museum, Mitaka
2 Inokashira-kōen

SIGHTS

3 Asagaya Pearl Centre
see 2 Benzaiten Shrine
4 Nakano Broadway
5 Ōtaguro Park
6 Suginami Animation Museum

EATING

7 Cocktail Shobo
8 Gion
9 Handsome Shokudō
10 Henri Fabre Café
see 2 Iseya Kōen-ten
11 Kawanaka-ya
12 Lou
13 Nakadaya
14 Nikuyorozu

15 Pao Caravan Sarai
16 Pepa Cafe Forest
17 Shinozaki
18 Where is a Dog?
see 22 Yonchōme Café
19 Yummy

DRINKING & NIGHTLIFE

20 B²
21 Coffee Amp the Roaster
22 Poem Mano a Mano Coffee
23 Woodberry Coffee

SHOPPING

24 Antique Street
25 Kōenji Pal Shopping Street
26 Look Street
see 12 Mandarake Complex
see 7 Shiroto no Ran

NISHI-OGIKUBO'S RETRO CHARM

Nishi-Ogikubo sits between Ogikubo and Kichijōji on the Chūō line. Managing (so far) to avoid the commercialisation of neighbouring Kichijōji, the district has everything from vinyl records to eyeglass stores to French-style bistros where you're likely to see elegant older couples out dining.

It has long been known as an affluent neighbourhood where numerous elite businesspeople and military officers lived or owned second homes, many of which were sold off after WWII and forming, as a result, the roots of the district's numerous antique shops.

A good place for browsing is north of the train station at **Antique Street** (骨董通り), where shops sell curios of all sorts, including *ukiyo-e* (woodblock prints) and porcelain wares.

Ramen shop, Ogikubo

Home of Tokyo's Ramen

Eat your fill around Ogikubo Station

Cheap and filling, ramen shops began proliferating in Ogikubo after WWII, dishing up inexpensive sustenance with a side of comfort to a recovering population. Known for its signature soy sauce broth and fish-based stock, Ogikubo set the standard for what many now think of as 'Tokyo ramen'. Its cultural impact even reached the silver screen: the 1985 cult classic *Tanpopo*, directed by Itami Jūzō, follows a truck driver who helps revive a struggling ramen shop, drawing inspiration from the neighbourhood's ramen ethos. Today, ramen in Ogikubo is more than a meal – it's a way of life. The main area for ramen tasting is around **Kyokai-dōri** (Church Street) on the north side of Ogikubo Station.

Kōenji's Unique Shops & History

A neighbourhood of subculture and activism

Kōenji's streetscape is a fascinating mix, encompassing record stores, barber shops, tattoo parlours, fruit stands, ramen stalls, artisan studios, pocket parks, micro-bars and live music joints.

DRINKING IN WEST TOKYO: WHERE TO GET GREAT COFFEE

Coffee Amp the Roaster: Stylish Kōenji shop along Look St serving a lineup of coffee and espresso drinks, plus beans to go. *11am-6pm Tue-Sun*

Woodberry Coffee: Flagship Ogikubo shop of this small-batch, sustainable roastery, with hearty dishes and coffee with beans sourced from El Salvador. *8.30am-7pm*

B²: Coffee roastery and bakery adjacent to Kichijōji's Excel Hotel Tokyu, offering tasty cafe fare. The lattes are fabulous. *8.30am-6pm*

Poem Mano a Mano Coffee: A local fixture for almost 50 years, this cafe pairs excellent coffee with luscious desserts. The fruit sandwiches are a speciality. *10am-8pm* ¥

You never quite know what lies around the next corner. It is also arguably Tokyo's top spot for vintage clothing, and for a particularly populated stretch of shops offering great finds, head down the covered **Kōenji Pal Shopping Street** near the station's south exit, and **Look Street** (the open-air section lying beyond it).

Whether it's the numerous establishments housed here, inside renovated *kominka* (traditional wooden structures), or the elderly residents out doing their afternoon shopping, wandering Kōenji's streets is to breathe in decades of history. Resembling an earthier version of Shimo-Kitazawa, both neighbourhoods have followed similar trajectories in drawing vocal anti-establishment types into their folds. Many of the recycled goods shops have been home to activist collectives, including **Shiroto no Ran** (素人の乱, 'Amateur Riot'), who organised anti-nuclear demonstrations in the area following the Fukushima Nuclear Disaster in 2011.

Also held in Kōenji in 2016 and 2023 was September's No Limits festival, with 10 days of events and art exhibitions on the interconnected problems of war, refugees, racism, overdevelopment and poverty.

Preserving the Past

A walk through architectural history in Koganei

Time travel back to the Edo era (1603–1868) and right through to the Shōwa (1926–1989) period at the **Edo-Tokyo Open Air Architectural Museum** (江戸東京たてもの園; *tatemonoen.jp; adult/child ¥400/free*), which (as its name suggests) features historic restored, preserved and reconstructed buildings – some of which were lost in their day to earthquakes, fires, wartime fire-bombing or urban development. Structures include thatched-roof farmhouses, private homes, villas of feudal lords and aristocrats, a teahouse and assorted businesses. Traditional craft demonstrations also take place, along with rotating exhibitions. Closed Mondays.

Seeking the Stars

Probe the unseen universe in Mitaka

Dedicated to 'solving cosmic mysteries', the **National Astronomical Observatory of Japan** (国立天文台; *nao.ac.jp*) – headquartered in Mitaka and maintaining campuses throughout the Japanese archipelago and overseas – holds regular stargazing parties that are open to the public. Led by its

KŌENJI AWA ODORI FESTIVAL

There is always something new to see in Kōenji. From local art projects and street-art initiatives to installations, dance performances and theatre productions, this neighbourhood is teeming with creativity.

It's perhaps at its most artistic during the **Kōenji Awa Odori** festival, held annually on the last weekend of August. Kōenji's version of the festival – which originated in Tokushima Prefecture – is one of Japan's liveliest and wildest. The first Kōenji Awa Odori took place in 1957 as a way to revitalise the town, which it has done with great success.

Today the event draws massive crowds – some 1.3 million spectators – as well as amazing performances from 12,000 dancers, alongside plentiful street food.

EATING IN KŌENJI: BEST ARTISTIC CAFES

Cocktail Shobo: Atmospheric literary cafe, offering food and cocktails based on recipes from famous novels. *6-11pm, plus noon-3pm Sat & Sun ¥*

Henri Fabre Café: Join the Kōenji literati at this spacious 2nd-floor place at Za Koenji Theatre, where colourful cafe classics are served. *11.30am-7pm ¥*

Yonchōme Café: This Kōenji institution has delivered pasta, burgers, seasonal drinks and lush desserts, amid retro lamps and tile art, since 1987. *11.30am-midnight ¥*

Yummy: Delightful dining bar dishing up hearty sets and great desserts, against a backdrop of smooth jazz. *11am-3.30pm & 5-9pm Mon & Wed-Fri; 11am-9pm Sat & Sun ¥*

INOKASHIRA'S MYTHIC MUSE

Inokashira Park was established in 1917 on land gifted to the people of Tokyo by Emperor Taishō (1879–1926).

Another regal presence in the park is **Benzaiten**, the namesake of the photogenic shrine tucked away on the northwest side of the pond. Known as a river goddess, sites dedicated to her worship are typically found near bodies of water.

Benzaiten is the sole female member of the Seven Lucky Gods of Japanese mythology, a sort of divine supergroup which spread good fortune throughout the country. However, according to a local legend, she also has a jealous streak and may try to break up couples who venture out on the lake in rental boats.

astronomers-in-training, each gathering has a different viewing target, utilising the observatory's 50cm telescope to observe the moon's craters, Jupiter's Galilean moons and the rings of Saturn, as well as harder-to-detect phenomena such as star clusters and cosmic dust. Availability is via an online lottery application. As explanations include only limited English, it's best to have a translation app on hand. The campus is also open daily to visitors *(10am to 5pm; free)*, and its lush grounds include the formerly operational 20cm Telescope Dome, Observatory History Museum and Solar Tower Telescope.

Discovering the Treasures of Inokashira-kōen

Ghibli Museum and art markets

Sandwiched between Nishi-Ogikubo and Mitaka City is the district of Kichijōji, whose main attraction is the spacious **Inokashira-kōen** (井の頭恩賜公園; *gotokyo.org/en/spot/624/index.html; free*), one of Tokyo's best and most popular parks. The park encircles a large pond, and perched at the edge is the small, vermillion-red **Benzaiten Shrine**, which dates back to the Heian period (794–1185). The pond is fringed with cherry trees and is one of the city's best spots for *hanami* (cherry-blossom viewing). Inokashira-kōen is also popular with birdwatchers, although one of the most frequently spotted varieties isn't feathered at all: the swan-shaped pedal boat. These quirky rides are a favourite among couples and families, and there are always lines during cherry-blossom season. Traditional rowboats are also available to rent if you prefer a slightly less ostentatious vessel *(from ¥600)*. The park hosts art markets on weekends, where local crafters sell their wares and lively performers keep the crowds entertained.It's also a fantastic picnic spot, so grab skewers from an iconic Kichijōji establishment: the adjacent **Iseya Kōen-ten** *yakitori* (chicken skewers) shop. Alternatively, **Pepa Cafe Forest** offers tasty Thai food (and cool art) right inside the park.

Needing no introduction is the iconic **Ghibli Museum, Mitaka** (ジブリ美術館 *ghibli-museum.jp; adult/child ¥1000/700*), located inside the sprawling Inokashira-kōen. Founded by legendary animators Miyazaki Hayao and Takahata Isao, Studio Ghibli has produced delightful films, such as *Spirited Away* and *My Neighbor Totoro*, that have become icons of the genre. Beginning with the museum's playful architecture and special in-house animation welcome-screening, along

EATING IN WEST TOKYO: OUR PICKS FOR A HEARTY MEAL

Handsome Shokudō: A local fixture since 2001, this colourful place dishes up Thai fare along Nishi-Ogikubo's Willow Alley. *lunch 11.30am-3pm Tue-Sun, dinner hours vary* ¥

Nakadaya: Chow down on fresh *maguro* (tuna) at the counter of this joint inside Kichijōji's station-front Harmonica Yokochō. *11am-9pm Mon-Fri, to 8pm Sat & Sun* ¥

Shinozaki: A friendly family-run restaurant in Kichijōji featuring *unagi* (eel) steamed and grilled over hot coals, and served in lacquered boxes. *noon-2pm & 5-8pm Fri-Tue* ¥¥

Nikuyorozu: Feast on fragrant chargrilled meat and vegetables at this atmospheric restaurant tucked behind Mitaka Station. *noon-2pm & 5-11pm* ¥¥

Inokashira-kōen

with numerous interactive exhibition spaces and the chance to thumb through the notebooks where the studio's masters plied their craft, even anime newbies will be drawn into the enchanted world of Ghibli. It's important to note that visits to the Ghibli Museum require advance reservations – tickets are not sold onsite, so plan ahead. Tickets for the following month are released at 10am (Japan time) on the 10th of each month and may sell out quickly.

History, Nature & Onsen in Chōfu

A serene temple, hot springs and handicrafts

In the city of Chōfu (調布市), and just a short bus ride away from the Ghibli Museum, is **Jindai-ji** (深大寺), the second-oldest Buddhist temple in Tokyo after Sensō-ji (p192), dating back to 733. At the temple, observe the powerful fire ritual at Ganzan-Daishi Hall, held twice daily on weekdays and three times daily on weekends. The ceremony is conducted to offer protection and answer prayers. The adjacent streets invoke the era of Edo – make sure to enjoy a lunch of soba noodles

TOP OUTDOOR SPOTS FOR FAMILIES

Check out these nature-rich locations for family fun.

Shōwa Memorial Park (p137): Go wild on the vast and imaginative playscapes in Tachikawa.

Hossawa Falls: Ranked among Japan's top 100 water-falls, with four cascading tiers accessible via a pleasant 15-minute walk. In Hinohara Village.

Akigawa Valley: Especially beautiful in autumn, it's also ideal for camping, fishing and barbecues. Rent everything you need from multiple operators.

Nippara Limestone Caves: Enjoy the colourful illuminations inside, where the temperature stays a cool 11°C year-round.

Mitake Valley: A popular destination for kayaking, with several companies offering guided tours.

EATING IN WEST TOKYO: HEALTHY BITES

Café Slow: Longstanding purveyor of 'slow living' in Kokubunji, with a menu featuring scrumptious organic lunches. *11.30am-6pm Tue-Sun* ¥

Kurumed Coffee: A whimsical spot near Nishi-Kokubunji Station serving sandwiches and creative desserts, many of them starring walnuts. *11am-7pm Sun-Wed, to 8pm Fri & Sat* ¥

Where is a Dog?: Kichijōji cafe with a gluten-free menu, plus vegetarian/vegan options. Check out the story behind the name. *noon-3pm & 5-8pm Wed-Fri, noon-8pm Sat & Sun* ¥

Ocio Healing Space & Café: A store near Higashi-Koganei Station serving coffee and baked goods. It offers Thai massage in the connected space. *11am-7pm Tue-Sat & 2nd & 4th Sun* ¥

AN EYE FOR GOOD FORTUNE

Daruma dolls are symbols of good luck, said to be modelled after Bodhidharma, the monk credited with founding Zen Buddhism.

Typically made of papier-mâché, the round figures have blank eyes. After purchase, the left eye is filled in when a wish is made, the right when it comes true.

During the Edo period (1603–1868), memorial events started to be held at Jindai-ji temple to honour Ganzan-Daishi, a 10th-century monk who protected people from misfortune. The temple became a popular site for buying and blessing *daruma*, a tradition that continues today.

The lively annual **Jindai-ji Daruma Market** is held on 3 and 4 March, attracting visitors from across the region.

(for which this area is famous) and stroll the adjacent **Jindai Botanical Gardens** (神代植物公園; *adult/child ¥500/free*).

A short stroll from Jindai-ji is the onsen of **Yumori no Sato** (湯守の里; *yumorinosato.com; adult/child ¥1080/650*). Indulge in this experience of natural hot-spring bathing, which has a calm, waterfall-laced garden setting and the mineral-rich waters drawn from 1500m underground. The nine onsite baths are crafted from a range of natural materials, including bamboo and cypress wood, and are open from 10am to 10pm, seven days a week. Also nearby is **Daru-chan no Ouchi** (だるチャンのおうち), a tiny, colourful shop and atelier devoted to *daruma* dolls, symbols of good luck that have come to be associated with Jindai-ji. The temple hosts the Daruma Market every March but groups of up to four can try making a *daruma* year-round with the staff at Daru-chan (*reservations required; instagram.com/daruchan_noouchi; ¥5500*).

Those interested in Japanese crafts will also enjoy taking a hands-on paper-making workshop. *Washi* (traditional Japanese paper), crafted from materials including the fibres of the mulberry plant, is both durable and stylish. Just east of Okutama on the western edge of Tokyo, **Hinode Washi** (ひので和紙; *hinodewashi.tokyo/activity_english.html; from ¥8000*) offers you the chance to create your own *washi*. The friendly proprietor begins by giving a tour of the mulberry trees on his grounds, and then leads the workshop in his atelier. Make reservations via the website.

Hidden Walks

Urban strolling in Kunitachi

The city of Kunitachi (国立市) offers one of the metropolis' most pleasant (and least-known) urban walks. Exiting Kunitachi Station, head south along Daigaku-dōri, a broad avenue flanked by cherry and gingko trees. On the left are numerous unique shops, including **Antique John** (*antiquejohn.thebase. in*), which sells vintage kimono, used clothing, antique furniture and miscellaneous goods, and **Watermark Arts & Crafts** (*watermark-arts.com*), a small graphic art gallery that opens during exhibitions (check website for scheduling). The road ends at Yaho Station, and the entire walk takes about 30 minutes (without stops). If you're lucky, you'll do the walk during peak *sakura* (cherry blossom) season among a heavenly swirl of raining petals.

A Storybook World

The feline queen of Tama

Sanrio Puroland (サンリオピューロランド; *puroland.jp; adult/ child from ¥3900/2800*) is an indoor theme park at Tama Center (多摩センター) which celebrates the whimsical world of Hello Kitty and her friends. Created in 1974 by designer Shimizu Yuko, Hello Kitty has since become a global icon of cuteness and friendship. This colourful, storybook-like park offers photo ops, character greetings, themed performances and a couple of (very gentle) rides. For families with young

Shōwa Memorial Park

WHY I LOVE WEST TOKYO & BEYOND

Louise George Kittaka, Lonely Planet writer

Having lived in this area for over 20 years and raised my family here, I've developed a strong affection for West Tokyo and what lies beyond. Life in my suburban bed town truly offers the best of both worlds – easy access to the energy of the city alongside the calm of nature.

I can jump on a train and be in bustling Shinjuku in less than 30 minutes, or drive in the opposite direction to find mountain trails, quiet forests and cobalt-blue rivers in an hour.

The Tama region also afford plenty of opportunities to indulge in two of my favourite pastimes: flower-viewing and hiking to Okutama's waterfalls.

kids and lovers of *kawaii* (cute) culture, it could well be the cat's whiskers. Tickets can be bought online or at the entrance, but may sell out in advance. The park is often closed on Wednesdays and Thursdays; check the online calendar for latest information.

Urban Meets Rural in Shōwa Memorial Park

Tokyo's largest park

Before diving deep into the Okutama area on Tokyo's western perimeter, take a minute for Tachikawa (立川市), a destination sitting along the urban-rural divide and offering sites that are well worth a stop-off. Just a short 15-minute stroll from Tachikawa Station is the picturesque **Shōwa Memorial Park** (昭和記念公園; *showakinen-koen.jp; adult/child ¥450/free*), Tokyo's largest park, built to commemorate Emperor Shōwa's (Hirohito) 50th year on the throne – the park's Memorial Museum is also worth a visit. With expansive sports fields and picnicking areas, Japanese gardens, dramatic autumn foliage and periodically held illumination events, this is a fantastic spot to escape the thrum of the capital's sprawl. It's also a superb location to indulge in the Japanese pastime of flower viewing – and not just for cherry blossoms. From spring through autumn, a never-ending parade of flowers bloom, including tulips, nemophila, poppies, irises, hydrangeas, sunflowers and cosmos.

At the edge of the park (back towards the station) is **Green Springs** (グリーンスプリングス; *greensprings.jp*), a spacious shopping complex framed by a manicured lawn and dotted with upmarket shops and cafes. A 120m water cascade and a musical fountain add to the multisensory experience. Also held here is a summertime open-air cinema, with some films geared towards children.

Stroll Through a Temple Town

Soak up the history of Chōfu's atmospheric Jindai-ji neighbourhood. Founded in 733, **Jindai-ji temple** was named after Jinja Daio, a water god said to have helped two young lovers unite. Their grateful son, the monk Manko Shonin, built the temple to honour the benevolent deity. Jindai-ji is easily reached by bus from Chōfu or Kichijōji Stations. You'll start your walk at Jindai-ji's Main Gate, walk three to four hours, and finish at Yumori no Sato onsen.

As you enter the temple complex through the ❶ **Main Gate** (山門) , note the photogenic thatched roof. Built in 1695, the gate survived a great fire in 1865 and is the oldest building on the grounds. Proceed to the ❷ **Bell Tower** (鐘楼), once used for timekeeping. The current bell is a modern replica from 2001, replacing the original cast in 1376, which is preserved elsewhere on the site. Turn left to reach the ❸ **Main Hall** (本堂), where a statue of Amida Nyorai, a central figure in Pure Land Buddhism, is enshrined. The present hall was reconstructed in 1919 after earlier versions were lost to major fires in 1646 and 1865.

Behind and left of the Main Hall stands the ❹ **Ganzan-Daishi Hall** (元三大師堂), enshrining a large figure of the revered

Jindai-ji Temple

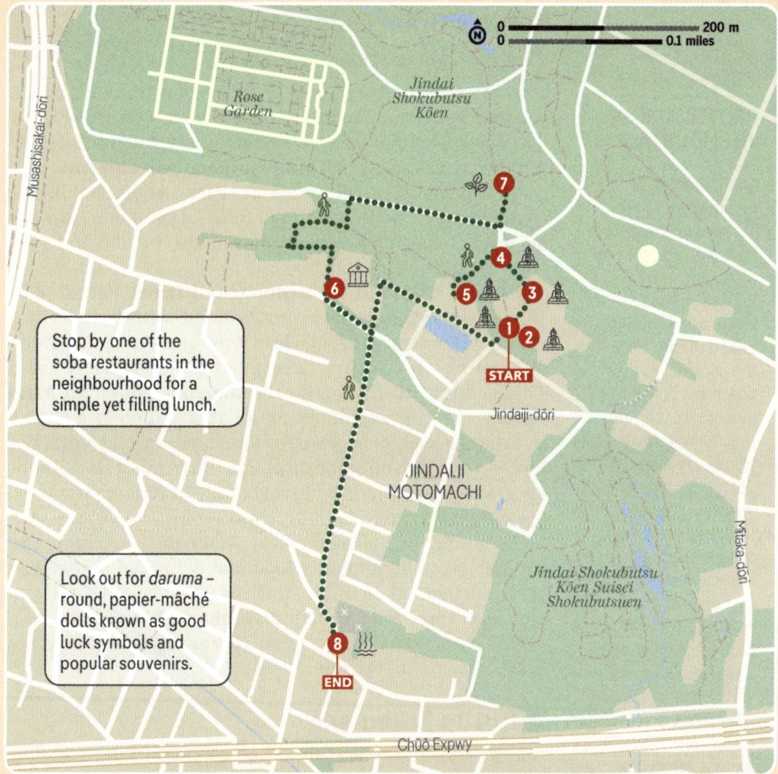

10th-century monk Ganzan Daishi, believed to have divine powers and to bring good fortune. The statue is generally shown only once every 25 years – the next unveiling is in 2034. Enter the **⑤ Shakadō** (釈迦堂) to view the precious Hokuhō Buddha statue, discovered here in 1909 but believed to date back to the 7th century – making it older than Jindai-ji itself. Just how this designated National Treasure ended up at the temple remains a mystery.

Exit via the Main Gate and take some time to explore the surrounding streets, lined with shops selling crafts, trinkets and sweets. Stop by the picturesque **⑥ Jindai-ji Waterwheel Museum** (深大寺水車館) for insight into prewar rural life. Soba noodle production requires both quality buckwheat and pure water. Thanks to the area's abundant springs, buckwheat thrived around the temple and proved easier to grow than rice, giving rise to the many soba restaurants found here today.

Head along the left side of the temple complex, then walk through the North Gate to reach the nearby entrance of **⑦ Jindai Botanical Gardens** (神代植物園). Highlights at this extensive park include a plethora of seasonal flower displays, tropical greenhouses and the elegant fountain courtyard. The gardens are particularly lovely in autumn, when Tokyo's largest rose garden bursts into bloom.

Complete your day with a relaxing soak in the hot springs at **⑧ Yumori no Sato** (湯守の里), a short walk south of the Main Gate. Both indoor and outdoor baths are available, and towels and loungewear can be rented for a small fee.

PROTECTORS OF THE MOUNTAIN

Long a centre for mountain worship, Takao-san is said to be home to some of Japan's more unusual creatures – long-nosed goblins called **tengu**. They are considered the guardians of the mountain's faith and the attendants of Izuna Daigongen, the principal deity at Yakuō-in temple.

Visitors to the temple will see representations of two kinds of *tengu*: smaller ones with crow-like beaks, and larger versions with very prominent noses.

Tengu are also connected to another famous Takao landmark, the huge and unusually shaped Takosugi ('octopus cedar'). According to legend, when the tree heard it was in danger of being cut down to clear a path to Yakuō-in, it pulled in its roots. This amazing feat was attributed to the *tengu*.

Tokyo's Great Outdoors

Wilderness within the capital's borders

Tokyo's western region, Tama, is the gateway to scenic nature, which only becomes more lush the further west you go. The outdoor opportunities here are boundless, and include hiking the sacred peaks of **Takao-san** and **Mitake-san** (御岳山, in Chichibu-Tama-Kai National Park). Additional hiking routes can be enjoyed along the trails of Okutama (奥多摩), meaning 'Deep Tama', where you can also indulge in lots of river rafting and camping.

Located on Mt Mito, the **Hinohara Citizens' Forest** (檜原都民の森; *gotokyo.org/en/spot/270/index.html*) features a variety of hiking trails through lush forest, including the Waterfall Course – Tokyo's first designated 'Forest Therapy Road'. This gentle path leading to the gorgeous 30m-high **Mito Falls** (三頭大滝), is suitable for all ages and offers a chance to experience *shinrin-yoku*, or forest bathing. The practice involves walking mindfully through the woods, taking in the natural sights, sounds and scents to help reduce stress and promote relaxation.

The abundance of fresh, clear water in this region also lends itself to high-quality food and drink. So if your legs get tired, then take a wasabi tour in Okutama, or visit the region's sake breweries, including **Ishikawa Shuzō** (石川酒造; *tamajiman.co.jp*) in Fussa and **Nozaki Shuzō** (野崎酒造; *kisho-sake.jp*) in Akiruno.

A Trip up Takao-san

Tokyo's favourite mountain and hiking spot

Takao-san (高尾山) makes a perfect nature break from the city, and is easily reached in under an hour from Shinjuku via Takaosanguchi Station. There are options to suit all ages and levels of fitness – don't be surprised if sprightly octogenarians power-walk past you on their way to the summit.

Hikers can choose from multiple routes, with well-paved **Trail No 1** being the easiest and most popular, while those with hiking experience might prefer one of the more rugged paths for a more adventurous expedition. While you can climb from the bottom, most people take advantage of the cable car or chairlift to get halfway up the mountain before starting their hike. The departure point for both is a short walk from Takaosanguchi Station. During autumn, the

EATING IN THE TAMA REGION: GREAT JAPANESE FOOD

Head Temple Takao-san Yakuo-in: Trek part way up Mt Takao to be rewarded with *shōjin-ryōri* (Buddhist vegetarian cuisine). Reservation essential. *11am-2pm* ¥¥

Ikada: This restaurant in Ōme serves generous portions of grilled chicken, plus jumbo-sized *onigiri* (rice balls). *11am-5pm Sat-Wed* ¥

Hinadoriyama: Japanese-style restaurant in Hachiōji offers charcoal-grilled dishes in private rooms, with food arriving on small boats along a canal. *11am-8.30pm Thu-Tue* ¥¥

Yusui: Serving handmade soba and tempura near Jindai-ji temple, this spot is pricier than average, but the queues speak for its quality. *10.30am-6pm Mon-Wed, to 7pm Fri-Sun* ¥¥

Tengu statue, Takao-san

forest blazes with colour, and the trails become crowded with leaf-peepers, particularly on weekends. Visiting on a weekday is recommended during peak autumn foliage.

One of the main points of interest is atmospheric **Yakuō-in** (薬王院; *takaosan.or.jp/english*), a Buddhist temple founded in 744. For centuries, it has been a spiritual centre where pilgrims prayed for protection and success. You'll pass a variety of stalls selling trinkets and snacks as you approach Yakuō-in, and from there it's about 15 minutes to the summit. With a bit of luck, you might catch panoramic views stretching as far as Mt Fuji on a clear day.

There are plenty of restaurants to choose from at Takao-san, most of them clustered at the base or along Trail 1. The mountain's signature dish, *tororo* soba – noodles topped with sticky grated yam – was once eaten by pilgrims for stamina.

Next to Takaosanguchi Station is the **Takao 599 Museum** (*takao599museum.jp*), a free-entry facility with educational exhibits on local nature and history, while the nearby **Trick Art Museum** (*trickart.jp/english*) offers optical illusion photo ops. Finish off your day with a soak in the hot springs at **Keio Takaosan Onsen Gokurakuyu** (*takaosan-onsen.jp*).

SPECIAL NATURE OF OKUTAMA

With more than 15 years in Okutama, New Zealander **Mike Harris** operates Canyons, an outdoor adventure company. *canyons.jp/en/areas/okutama/canyons-okutama*

At the western edge of the Tama region, Okutama presents a surprising expanse of pristine nature. This area is an outdoor enthusiast's paradise, offering activities like pack-rafting on clear rivers, navigating gorges while canyoning or exploring scenic trails hiking and climbing.

A key attraction is Mitake-san, featuring a notable shrine with stunning views overlooking Tokyo, alongside opportunities for traditional *shukubō* (temple lodging) for an immersive stay. The region boasts exceptional food and drink, including wild venison, craft beers and fine sake from the historic breweries, providing an authentic taste of the area.

EATING IN & AROUND OKUTAMA: OUR CAFE PICKS

Hinohara Terrace: Colourful plate lunches, pizzas and desserts in nature-rich surroundings. Try to get a terrace seat. *9am-6pm Mon-Fri, from 11.30am Sat & Sun* ¥¥

Dorapu Blue: A cosy hillside cafe in Hikawa where the owner prepares every dish, from flavourful curries to homemade desserts. *10am-5pm Thu-Mon* ¥

Okutama Riverside Café Awa: Relax on the terrace with lovely views of the Tama River. A small but varied menu, including vegetarian options. *11am-3pm Wed-Sun* ¥

Vancouver Coffee: A stylish, cyclist-friendly cafe in Akiruno with modern minimalist decor, serving coffee and fresh pastries. Cash only. *11.30am-5pm Sat-Thu* ¥

Researched by Louise George Kittaka

SHINJUKU & NORTHWEST TOKYO

THE BEATING HEART OF TOKYO

With its eclectic mix of skyscrapers, shopping malls, nightlife and spacious parks, there's always something new to discover – day or night – in bustling Shinjuku.

Shinjuku (新宿) is a place with two faces – to the west are windowed office buildings and high-rises; to the east, glitzy department stores, and a world of neon lights. A passageway of sorts, Shinjuku is where people from all walks of life gather. From here, follow the tracks on one of Tokyo's busiest trains – the Yamanote line – and you'll arrive at Northwest Tokyo. Ikebukuro (池袋), a youthful area boasting big stores and arcades, is Northwest Tokyo's hub. Running between Shinjuku and Ikebukuro is Meiji-dōri avenue, and along it, two less-populated though equally vibrant neighbourhoods: Shin-Ōkubo (新大久保) and Takadanobaba (高田馬場), where good food can be had at just about any corner.

TIP

Navigating through Shinjuku and Ikebukuro stations can be overwhelming, even for locals. Google Maps will often tell you which station exit is closest to your destination. Follow station signage carefully and keep to the left side of walkways. Rush hour is 7.30–10.00am and 5.30–8.00pm.

Shinjuku streetscape

FROM LEFT: HANNEKE WETZER/SHUTTERSTOCK, DEREKTEO/SHUTTERSTOCK

See page 220 for places to stay in Shinjuku & Northwest Tokyo

⭐ Highlights

❶ Shinjuku Gyoen

This imperial garden is a must-see during cherry-blossom season, between March and April. **p144**

▶❷ Godzilla Head

A symbol of Kabukichō, Godzilla is coolest at night, when its eyes glow red. **p167**

❸ Golden Gai

Choose from dozens of small shanty bars to slip into and strike up a conversation. **p148**

❹ Kabukichō

Experience the glitz and the grit of Shinjuku's eclectic after-dark playground. **p151**

❺ Hanazono Shrine

Join visitors offering prayers at a serene shrine that has served the area for centuries. **p145**

🚶 Getting Around

Train

The JR Yamanote, Chūō-Sōbu and Saikyō lines stop at Shinjuku Station, as do the Odakyu and Keiō lines. Take the Yamanote line to Shin-Ōkubo, Takadanobaba and Ikebukuro.

Metro

Shinjuku Station is served by the Marunouchi, Toei Shinjuku and Toei Ōedo lines; the first two also stop at Shinjuku-sanchōme Station, which is connected to Shinjuku via underpass.

Walk

Your own two feet are often the quickest and easiest way to get to the major points of interest around Shinjuku.

WHY I LOVE SHINJUKU

Winnie Tan, Lonely Planet writer

I called Shinjuku home for eight years. Though it was initially the department stores and the neighbourhood's vibrant nightscape that drew me in, walking through the station's underpasses became an unexpected hobby of mine. What started out as attempts to avoid the elements on hot or rainy days resulted in many happy discoveries.

With Shinjuku's rapidly changing landscape, the same underground exits can lead to completely new shops and buildings, and not being able to navigate them with a smartphone can make the experience all the more exciting.

Even after eight years, I'm still not convinced that I uncovered it all – it really is that big.

The World's Busiest Train Station

MAP P146

A sprawling beast

Shinjuku (along with Ikebukuro and Shibuya) was designated a sub-centre of Tokyo in 1958. The following years saw the area undergo rapid development, eventually becoming the busy giant it is today; and there's no sign of it slowing down. But look just slightly beyond the tantalising pull of Kabukichō (p151), the high-tech billboards near the stations and the beautiful shop windows, and you'll also see a neighbourhood that's a slice of everyday Tokyo – where people live, eat, work and go to school.

Almost everyone who's ever been to the capital will have been to Shinjuku Station (新宿駅). Serving around 3.5 million people per day across 11 train lines, the amount of foot traffic that passes through its halls is nothing short of mind-boggling. And as if the station itself and the never-ending sea of commuters aren't imposing enough, the buildings that make up the station complex sit atop a maze of underground passages and exits that can take you from one end of Shinjuku to another, without ever needing to surface above ground. These passages feed directly into prominent shopping hotspots: department stores **Lumine EST** (*lumine.ne.jp/est*), **Odakyu** (*odakyu-dept.co.jp*), **Isetan** (*mistore.jp/store/shinjuku.html*) and electronics giant **Bic Camera** are all connected via an underpass. A shopping arcade that exists entirely underground, **Subnade** (*subnade.co.jp*) sits under the outer threshold of Kabukichō and is accessible via the same underpass from Shinjuku. The **NEWoMAN** (pronounced 'New Woman'; *newoman.jp*) commercial centre is connected directly to the gates of the New South Exit, the station's newest wing.

While the station's hallways can get rather cramped, the New South Exit is where commuters surface for fresh air and a snack. Exit from the station turnstiles here and you'll come to an open plaza overlooking the station's train tracks, and a bust of Japan Rail's adorable mascot at **Suica Penguin Square**. On a nice day, you'll see locals seated here basking in the sunshine, coffee from one of the nearby cafes in hand.

The City's Green Haven

MAP P146

Feudal lord's residence turned urban oasis

Smack bang in the centre of an otherwise concrete jungle, **Shinjuku Gyoen** (新宿御苑; *adult/child ¥500/free*) is a welcome respite for Tokyo's residents. A former feudal lord's

DRINKING IN SHINJUKU: WHERE TO GET COFFEE

MAP P146

Blue Bottle Coffee Shinjuku Cafe: Shinjuku's premier coffee stand. Always busy; get coffee to go and drink it at the terrace. *8am–9pm Tue–Sat, to 8.30pm Sun*

Tsubakiya Coffee Shop Shinjuku: Retro and cosy Japanese Western–style cafe with classic coffee and cakes. A perfect place to relax with a good book. *8am–4.30pm*

Verve Coffee Roasters: Located in the NEWoMan shopping mall by the New South Exit, this cafe serves up an impressive range of coffee drinks and light meals. *7am–10pm*

Coffee Swamp: Hidden away on the Nishi-Shinjuku side of the station, this unpretentious little roastery is well worth the walk. *8–11am & noon–3.30pm*

Shinjuku Gyoen

residence from the Edo period, this green space was converted into an imperial garden in 1906, before opening its doors to the public in 1951. You could easily spend a few hours strolling along the winding paths that take you through the park's three distinct garden styles (French formal, English landscape, Japanese traditional). And for when you need something to fuel up with, there are several restaurants and cafes dotted within the grounds that provide a welcome break. You can also simply do like the locals do, and find a spot to stretch out in as you enjoy a coffee and a good book – or an afternoon siesta.

In spring, the park is one of Tokyo's best spots to witness the beauty of the cherry blossoms – there are over a thousand *sakura* trees here, from 65 different species. This, however, also means that things can get quite crowded, and advance online ticket reservations (through the park's website; *env.go .jp/garden/shinjukugyoen*) with a designated time slot may be required during peak cherry-blossom season, though visitors are free to buy a ticket at the gate any other time of the year.

Another photogenic spot for cherry blossom viewing is **Hanazono Shrine** (花園神社; *hanazono-jinja.or.jp*). Just

continues on p148

RITE OF SPRING

Hanami, or 'flower viewing', is the much-loved Japanese tradition of enjoying cherry blossoms in full bloom. Every spring, people flock to parks and temple grounds with friends, family or co-workers to sit under the trees, eat, drink and soak up the beauty of the season.

The flowering of the cherry blossoms is a big event, and many follow the forecast closely to time their *hanami* just right. All you really need is a picnic sheet and something to eat – anything from a fancy *bentō* box to a quick snack from the convenience store will do.

Some major cherry-blossom sites hold evening light-up events, where the illuminated blossoms take on an ethereal quality that feels particularly magical.

🍸 DRINKING IN SHINJUKU: COCKTAILS WITH A VIEW — MAP P146

Roof Top Bar & Terrace G: Come at happy hour (until 7pm) and watch the sun set over Shinjuku. Near Higashi-Shinjuku Station. *5pm-4am Mon-Sat, 2-10.30pm Sun*

Jam 17 Dining & Bar: Sleek and urban bar on the 17th floor of Kabukichō Tower with unique Japan-themed cocktails. *5pm-1am (11.30am-10pm for dining)*

Unoya Nishi-Shinjuku Nomura Building: Enjoy drinks and dinner at this elegant *izakaya* with stunning views from the 49th floor. *5-11pm Mon-Sat, to 10pm Sun*

86: A contemporary take on a New York speakeasy, this stylish cocktail bar sits atop the 17th floor of the Kimpton Shinjuku. *8-11pm Sun-Thu, to 1am Fri & Sat*

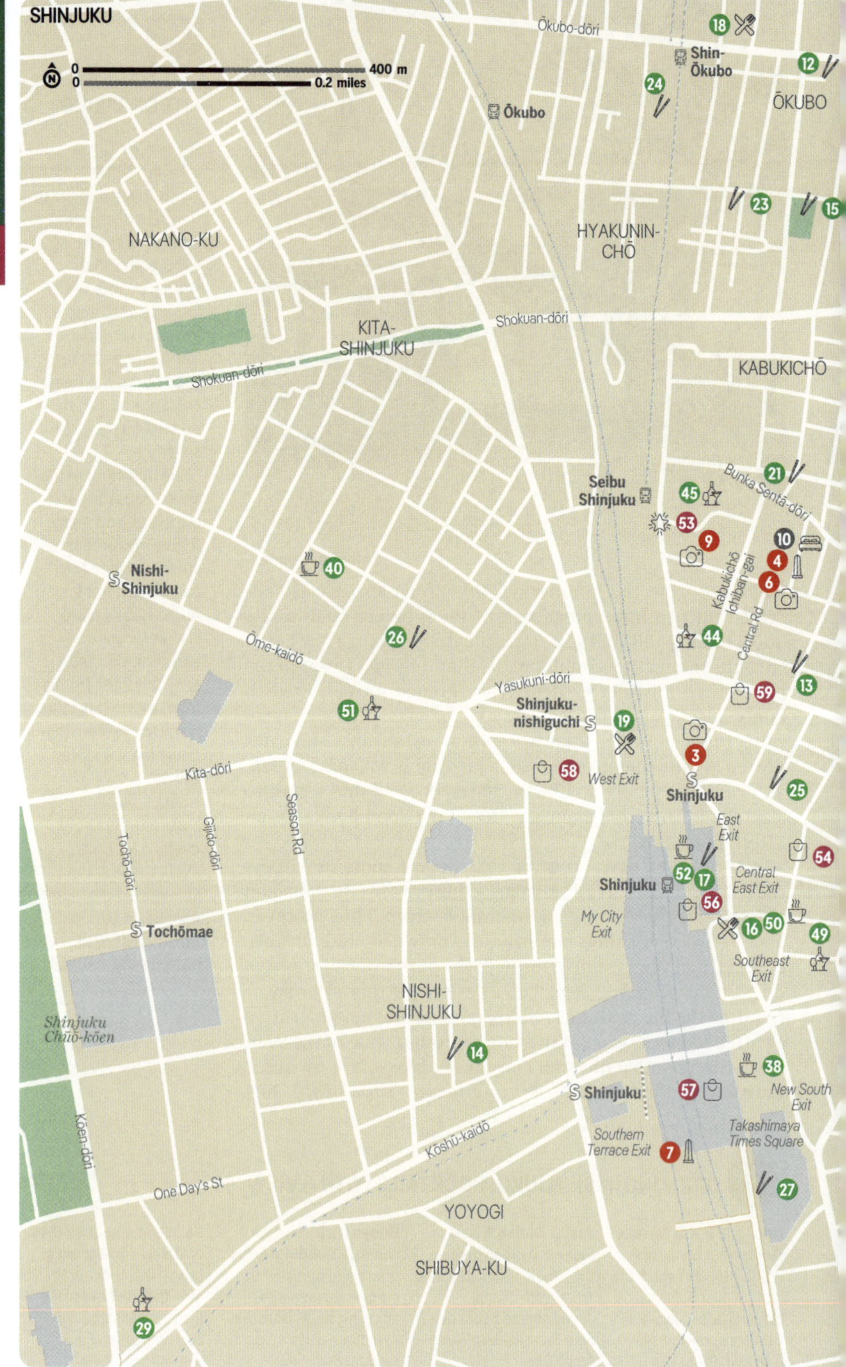
SHINJUKU
0   400 m
0   0.2 miles
N
NAKANO-KU
Ōkubo-dōri
Shin-Ōkubo
ŌKUBO
Ōkubo
HYAKUNIN-CHŌ
KITA-SHINJUKU
Shokuan-dōri
Shokuan-dōri
KABUKICHŌ
Bunka Sentā-dōri
Seibu Shinjuku
Nishi-Shinjuku
Ōme-kaidō
Kabukichō Ichiban-gai
Central Rd
Yasukuni-dōri
Shinjuku-nishiguchi
West Exit
Kita-dōri
Season Rd
Gijidō-dōri
Tochō-dōri
Shinjuku
East Exit
Central East Exit
Shinjuku
My City Exit
Tochōmae
Southeast Exit
NISHI-SHINJUKU
Shinjuku Chūō-kōen
New South Exit
Shinjuku
Takashimaya Times Square
Southern Terrace Exit
Kōshū-kaidō
Kōen-dōri
One Day's St
YOYOGI
SHIBUYA-KU
18
12
24
23
15
21
45
53
9
10
4
6
44
59
13
51
26
19
58
3
25
54
52
17
56
16
50
49
14
57
38
7
27
29

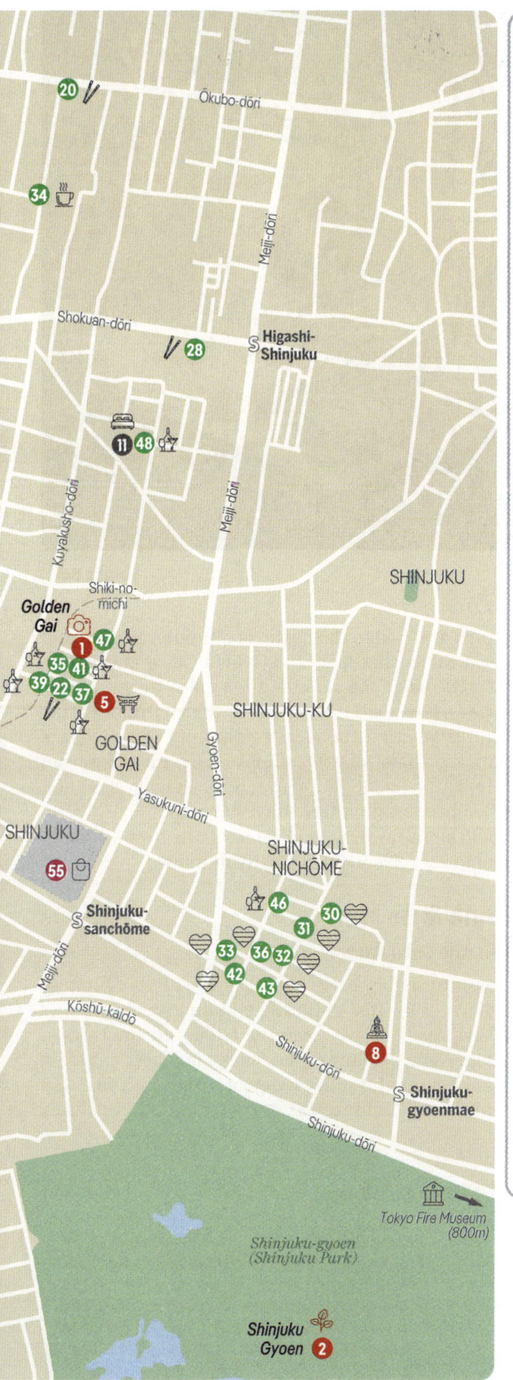

Ōkubo-dōri
Meiji-dōri
Shokuan-dōri
Higashi-Shinjuku
Kuyakusho-dōri
Meiji-dōri
Shiki-no-michi
SHINJUKU
Golden Gai
GOLDEN GAI
Gyoen-dōri
SHINJUKU-KU
Yasukuni-dōri
SHINJUKU
Shinjuku-sanchōme
SHINJUKU-NICHŌME
Meiji-dōri
Kōshū-kaidō
Shinjuku-dōri
Shinjuku-gyoenmae
Shinjuku-dōri
Tokyo Fire Museum (800m)
Shinjuku-gyoen (Shinjuku Park)
Shinjuku Gyoen

★ HIGHLIGHTS
1 Golden Gai
2 Shinjuku Gyoen
★ SIGHTS
3 Cross Space Shinjuku
4 Godzilla Head
5 Hanazono Shrine
6 Kabukichō
7 Suica Penguin Square
8 Taisō-ji
9 Tokyo Mystery Circus
● SLEEPING
10 Hotel Gracery Shinjuku
11 Shinjuku Granbell Hotel
● EATING
12 Delica Ondoru
13 Gyūkatsu Aona
14 Himawari Sushi
15 Jongno Hotok
16 Kichiri
17 Komeraku
18 Macapresso Tokyo
19 Omoide Yokochō
20 Pungumu
21 Ramen Jirō
22 Ramen Nagi
23 Shin-chan
see 14 Shinjidai
24 Somuo Shin-Ōkubo
25 Sushi Zanmai
26 Taiwan Saki Mensen
27 Tsukiji Tamasushi
28 Yakiniku Shinjuku Kōei Honten

● DRINKING & NIGHTLIFE
29 86
30 Adezakura
31 Aiiro Cafe
32 AiSOTOPE Lounge
33 Arty Farty
34 Bam Bi Coffee
35 Bar Cinema Club
36 Bar Goldfinger
37 Bar Plastic Model
38 Blue Bottle Coffee Shinjuku Cafe
39 Champion Bar
40 Coffee Swamp
41 Death Match in Hell
42 Dragon Men
43 Eagle Tokyo Blue
44 Hanbey
45 Jam 17 Dining & Bar
46 New Sazae
47 Open Book
48 Roof Top Bar & Terrace G
49 Torikizoku
50 Tsubakiya Coffee Shop Shinjuku
51 Unoya Nishi-Shinjuku Nomura Building
52 Verve Coffee Roasters

● ENTERTAINMENT
53 Kabukichō Tower
● SHOPPING
54 Bic Camera
55 Isetan
56 Lumine EST
57 NEWoMan
58 Odakyu
59 Subnade

THAT GOLDEN GLOW

Just beyond the neon lights of Kabukichō, Golden Gai offers an authentic slice of nostalgic drinking culture. What began as a black-market zone after WWII, gradually became a gathering place for writers and artists, especially after a 1950s crackdown on prostitution.

Thanks in part to local preservation efforts, Golden Gai has retained its postwar character. Several buildings destroyed in a major fire in 2016 were carefully restored to their original condition. Each of the area's tiny bars has its own distinctive personality and loyal customers, and a new generation of owners is putting its stamp on the scene.

Today, many bars welcome visitors from around the world, and where locals and tourists rub shoulders in a congenial atmosphere that transcends language.

KHAIKHOLUN VAIPHEI/SHUTTERSTOCK

Golden Gai

continued from p145

a few minutes' walk from the bustle of Shinjuku Station and right around the corner from the Golden Gai nightlife district, this serene place can come as a (very pleasant) surprise. For centuries, Hanazono has served as the guardian shrine of Shinjuku, protecting the local community of merchants and artisans who have long worshipped here. Entering from the main approach on Meiji-dōri avenue, the vivid vermillion *torii* gate leads you into a tree-filled space that feels far removed from the usual frenetic pace of life nearby, although it can become very lively during festival times.

Sing, Drink & Be Merry — MAP P146

Friday night, the Shinjuku way

Drinking culture is big here. As a transport hub, Shinjuku is where many Tokyoites naturally end up after work – its multiple bars ready to welcome the tired and the thirsty. The bars here come in many styles: smoky Japanese *izakaya*, small karaoke bars and quiet hangouts where it's just you and the bartender. **Golden Gai** (ゴールデン街) is a densely

EATING IN SHINJUKU: LATE-NIGHT GRUB — MAP P146

Gyūkatsu Aona: Fill up on *tonkatsu* (tender slices of beef breaded and deep fried) at this store near Kabukichō. *11am-11.30pm* ¥¥

Ramen Nagi: A busy store in Golden Gai serving fragrant *niboshi* (dried fish) ramen – a popular way to round off a night of drinking. *24hr* ¥

Ramen Jirō: Decadent *tonkotsu* (ramen noodles in pork bone broth) piled with meat and vegetables to fuel you for the rest of the night. *11.30am-2.30am Thu-Tue* ¥

Yakiniku Shinjuku Kōei Honten: Get your fill of *yakiniku* (grilled meat) and *hormone yaki* at any time of the night at this friendly spot, located on Shinjuku's east side. *11am-7am* ¥¥

packed complex of six lanes crammed with over 200 tiny bars, and visiting the ones on the 2nd floor involves a precarious climb up a creaky wooden staircase. **Champion Bar** (*onecoinbarchampion.com*) sits right at the entrance of the area and draws tourists in with its ¥500 drinks and loud karaoke; while it's a good place to start, we suggest squeezing through the alleyways or venturing upstairs to find the real gems. These might not come as cheap – some places ask for a cover charge (*¥500 to ¥1500*), and drinks usually cost ¥700 and up, but it's worth it.

Some things to keep in mind here: it's safer to assume that the bars here are cash-only, so make sure to have enough on hand, and everyone in the group must order a drink, even if it's a non-alcoholic one.

Night-time at Nichōme

MAP P146

LGBTIQ+ Hangouts

Shinjuku Nichōme (新宿二丁目), colloquially known as 'Nichōme' or 'Nichō', is Tokyo's largest nightlife area specifically catering to the LGBTIQ+ community. About a 10-minute walk from Shinjuku's Golden Gai, the area was a red-light district during Japan's post-war years, and when sex work was outlawed in 1958, gay bars began taking over the premises that were once occupied by brothels. The exact number is up for debate, but it's believed that up to 500 bars now occupy this 300-sq-metre area.

There are a number of well-known destinations that are hotspots for locals, expats and tourists: **Aiiro Cafe** (*aliving .net/aiirocafe*) is one of the most popular, staffed by friendly, international members of the community and offering all-you-can-drink beer at happy hour for the unbeatable price of ¥1000. This corner venue spills out onto the street – look for the rainbow *torii* (entrance gate) outside and the people drinking underneath. For the ladies, **Bar Goldfinger** (*linktr.ee/goldfingertokyo*) and **Adezakura** (*adezakura. tokyo*) are open exclusively to women on weekends – Goldfinger also has free popcorn and karaoke. For go-go boys, drag queens, bear nights, K-pop nights and themed events, check out what's happening on the weekends at **AiSOTOPE Lounge** (*aisotope-lounge.net*) or **Eagle Tokyo Blue** (*eagletokyo.com*). And for a night of dancing, head to **Dragon Men** (*instagram .com/dragon.men*) or **Arty Farty** (*artyfarty.jp*).

A NIGHT OUT IN NICHŌME

Koh, a Japanese local, shares his top tips.

Start your night at **Aiiro Cafe**, one of the best places to meet locals and foreigners alike.

New Sazae is where I go to groove with the most eclectic group of humans to the best retro tunes.

While many bars here cater to different genres and fetishes, most are traditional Japanese counter bars run by a 'mama'. Being able to speak even a little Japanese can go a long way.

Nichōme is one of the friendliest LGBTIQ+ communities out there. My advice is to first meet and chat with us locals, and we can direct you to whatever tickles your fancy.

DRINKING IN SHINJUKU: THEMED BARS OF GOLDEN GAI

MAP P146

Death Match in Hell: Take a trip to the underworld at this classic horror- and death-metal-themed bar; all drinks aptly priced at ¥666. *8pm-3am Mon-Sat*

Bar Cinema Club: This cinema-themed bar has plenty of vintage film posters and autographs to admire while you drink. *5pm-5am*

Open Book: The grandson of award-winning author Komimasa Tanaka runs this sleek bar that's lined with books. Try the signature lemon sour. *8-11.55pm Mon-Sat, to 11.30pm Sun*

Bar Plastic Model: This cosy bar is filled with nostalgic music and books. You can pick a record to play from the wide range lining the counter. *8pm-5am Mon-Sat, to 2am Sun*

THE GUIDE

SHINJUKU & NORTHWEST TOKYO

SIGHTS
1 Otome Road

SLEEPING
2 Hotel Metropolitan Ikebukuro
3 Vessel Inn Takadanobaba

EATING
4 Animate Cafe
5 Dōgen
6 Menya Musashi Takatora
7 Menya Sou
8 Ramen Yamaguchi
9 Tori Paitanmen Kageyama
10 Watanabe

SHOPPING
11 Animate Ikebukuro Flagship Store
12 Gashapon Department Store
13 K-Books
14 Lashinbang
15 Pokémon Center Mega Tokyo
16 Sunshine 60
17 Sunshine City

Kanpai at the Izakaya MAP P146

Cold beer, hot skewers

A place to stay and drink alcohol – that's what *izakaya* roughly translates to. Often referred to as a Japanese bar or tavern, the *izakaya* is a mainstay of society. It's where friends and colleagues come together and chat over drinks, food and the sound of clinking glasses, accompanied with shouts of '*Kanpai!*' (cheers). Unlike typical bars, there is hardly ever any socialising between different groups of customers. In fact, some larger *izakaya* opt to offer even more privacy, with cubicles and screens that separate different groups.

Whether it's to unwind with colleagues, gather for a post-game celebration or have a simple catch-up, the *izakaya* is the locals' hangout. The establishments themselves make these spots a satisfying experience, and they offer all-you-can-drink alcohol, fried food and savoury *yakitori* (chicken skewers) that wash down nicely with a cold mug of beer. Franchises like **Torikizoku** (*welcome.torikizoku.co.jp*) are popular and great for first-timers and tourists for their friendly atmosphere and easy tablet ordering system (not to mention delicious *yakitori*). But to get the authentic *izakaya* experience, head to a *yokochō* – tucked-away side alleys lined with these down-to-earth drinking spots. In Shinjuku, that place is **Omoide Yokochō** (思い出横丁; *shinjuku-omoide.com*), near the station's West Exit.

Kabukichō, Nocturnal Neighbourhood MAP P146

Neon lights and karaoke mics

By day, **Kabukichō** (歌舞伎町) is just your average part of town that sometimes seems a bit quiet and empty; but nightfall is when it truly shines – quite literally. With its seedy veneer, it might come across as a little daunting, though most bars here are fine. The name comes from a 1940s idea to build a venue here for kabuki – a classical form of Japanese theatre; the plan wasn't realised but the moniker stuck. A typical night here begins with all-you-can-drink beer and cocktails to get the buzz going, followed by a wander down its streets. For some Tokyoites, a good evening is one that ends here in the wee hours, stumbling out of a bar with your voice hoarse from belting out the very best karaoke anthems. Many are equipped with karaoke machines that are cheap (¥100 per song) or free to use, and everyone's always welcome to sing along – it doesn't matter how well you can carry a tune. However, it's always a good idea to check a reviews on Google prior

IZAKAYA 101

Your host will show you to either a table or a tatami mat area – remove your shoes in the latter. A damp towel is offered for your hands and you'll have time to check the menu before the server takes your order.

Many *izakaya* also serve an appetiser known as *otōshi*. These are automatically brought to the table shortly after customers are seated. They cost a small fee per person, which locals consider a sort of tip or cover charge.

Rather than individual meals, dishes are shared among the group, making it easy to sample a range of flavours.

Finally, when looking for an *izakaya*, beware of touts – they are illegal, but crop up in areas like Kabukichō.

EATING & DRINKING IN SHINJUKU: IZAKAYA CHAINS MAP P146

Torikizoku: Relaxing atmosphere and tasty *yakitori* (skewers). Many outlets in neighbourhoods like Shibuya and Shinjuku. *3pm-4am Mon-Fri, from 1pm Sat & Sun* ¥¥

Kichiri: The decor is a modern twist on traditional Japanese style, and the extensive menu has options to please most dietary needs. *5-11pm Sun-Thu, to 2am Fri & Sat* ¥¥

Hanbey: Retro 1950s to 1970s-themed *izakaya* with an extensive menu that even includes crickets. *5pm-midnight* ¥¥

Shinjidai: A no-frills *izakaya* that's among the city's cheapest, hence its popularity with students. *5pm-5am Mon-Thu, from 2pm Fri, from noon Sat & Sun* ¥¥

THE NOSTALGIA OF OMOIDE YOKOCHŌ

Omoide Yokochō (思い出横丁) presents a passage into the past. With its dim lantern-lit alleys crammed with shops and *izakaya* that haven't changed for at least half a century, it's a rare piece of Shinjuku that has somehow evaded the city's rapid, modern developments.

Its name even sounds romantic – *omoide* translates to 'memory', harkening back to a simpler era. But before it was Omoide Yokochō, it was Lucky St, a post-war-era black market of shops that stood back-to-back, separated only by wooden shutters.

Even the ubiquity of *yakitori* and *motsuyaki* (grilled offal) shops here can be traced back to this era, where offal wasn't rationed and could therefore be consumed in greater quantities.

Restaurant, Kabukichō (p151)

to going, just as an extra precaution. As mentioned for other establishments, many accept only cash, and each person is expected to order a drink.

Taste the World in Shin-Ōkubo

MAP P146

Eat at Tokyo's kitchen

Just one stop away from Shinjuku on the Yamanote line, **Shin-Ōkubo** is a lively neighbourhood that locals refer to as Koreatown. Riding on K-pop's wave of popularity, it attracts plenty of young adults and teenagers who come to shop for their favourite idol merchandise, buy Korean beauty products and try the latest fried-cheese snack. Shin-Ōkubo's roots, however, began in the 1980s when a large community of people who worked at Kabukichō, the majority of them Korean, took residence in the area. And while Korean barbecue and fried-chicken restaurants still occupy the main avenue of Shin-Ōkubo, this is also one of Tokyo's most multicultural neighbourhoods – secreted in the side streets are Taiwanese restaurants, Indian supermarkets and Vietnamese *banh mi* stalls, all catering to a community looking for a taste

EATING IN SHIN-ŌKUBO: OUR PICKS FOR KOREAN FOOD ——— MAP P146

Pungumu: Stylish Korean barbecue restaurant with lots of variety. Can get very busy, especially on weekends. *11am-11pm Sun-Thu, to 11.15pm Fri & Sat* ¥¥

Jongno Hotok: Stop by this street stall for some piping hot *hotteok* (Korean stuffed pancakes) and cheese-stuffed corn dogs. *10.30am-7.30pm* ¥

Shin-chan: Generous servings of crispy, juicy fried chicken. It's open till late – perfect for those late-night cravings. *11.30am-midnight* ¥¥

Delica Ondoru: With options ranging from fried chicken and Korean barbecue to spicy stews, this restaurant is great for when you're looking to try a bit of everything. *24hr* ¥¥

of home. Start with a light brunch: **Somuo Shin-Ōkubo**'s dishes taste just like they would in Thailand, and **Taiwan Saki Mensen** (*instagram.com/saki_mensen_888*) serves up bowls of delicious oyster *mee sua* (flour vermicelli). Then, spend the afternoon trying some decadent sweets – we love **Macapresso Tokyo** (*macapresso.com*) for the chunky macarons and the fluffy pancakes at **Bam Bi Coffee** (*instagram.com/bam_bi_coffee*) – before popping into one of the many Korean restaurants for dinner.

Tuck into the City's Best Ramen

MAP P150

Noodles get experimental in Takadanobaba

Hot, greasy, satisfying and cheap, ramen was originally introduced by Chinese immigrants to Japan. Over time, local chefs adapted it to Japanese tastes, experimenting with regional broths and toppings, and today ramen is both a culinary art form and one of Japan's most familiar and economical dishes. You won't have trouble finding good ramen in Tokyo, but for one of the city's best noodle stops, head to the neighbourhood of **Takadanobaba**, just two stops away from Shinjuku Station. As a favourite hangout for university attendees, ramen fits right into the landscape of this lively student area. Young people here aren't just looking for cheap and inexpensive meals – they're also at the forefront of new culinary trends, often knowing the best spots for the most flavourful bowls or innovative takes. If there's a line out the door, chances are students found it first.

Ramen connoisseurs might find that one visit to Takadanobaba won't suffice. The number of ramen shops and fierce competition in the area mean that everyone has their own personal favourite, but for good old fashioned ramen, you can't go wrong with the soy-sauce-based noodles at **Ramen Yamaguchi** (*ramen-yamaguchi.com*). To try broth that really packs a punch, go for *tsukemen* – a sub-type of ramen where the noodles are served alongside a bowl of thick, flavourful broth for dipping. Our best picks are **Menya Musashi Takatora** (*menya634.co.jp*) for its porky broth and ample servings of meat, and **Watanabe** (*watanabestyle.com*) for broth with a rich, fishy taste.

For a different flavour profile from the usual *tonkotsu* (pork bone) based broths, **Tori Paitanmen Kageyama** (*kageyamarou.com*) specialises in ramen in a rich chicken soup, while **Menya Sou** (*menya-sou.com*) is recommended for its salt ramen and tasty balance of chicken and seafood flavours. And

K-POP LOVE AFFAIR

Japan's young people love international pop music as much as their parents did at their age, but while the older generation leaned into Western artists, today's youth are looking closer to home: South Korea's irresistible **K-pop**.

With catchy tunes, high-energy performances and just enough English to be cool, K-pop hits have steadily outperformed Western songs on Japan's music charts in recent years. And like the country's own idol scene, many K-pop stars emerge from a rigorous training system. They're expected to maintain impeccable behaviour and a friendly, approachable persona – something many young Japanese find easy to relate to.

This popularity shows no sign of slowing down, as seen in the growing influence of K-pop-inspired culture in the streets of Shin-Ōkubo.

EATING IN SHINJUKU: WHERE TO GET FISH & SUSHI

MAP P146

Tsukiji Tamasushi: A comfortable sushi restaurant inside Takashimaya, offering set meals with assorted sushi as well as à la carte orders. *11am-10pm* ¥¥¥

Himawari Sushi: A cheerful conveyor-belt sushi shop in Nishi-Shinjuku with a wide variety of dishes to suit all tastes. *11am-3pm & 5-10pm Wed-Mon* ¥¥

Komeraku: Stop by for a light lunch of *ochazuke* (rice eaten with broth) at this casual restaurant inside the Lumine EST shopping mall. *11am-10pm* ¥

Sushi Zanmai: A popular national chain that's a step up from conveyor-belt sushi restaurants, offering good quality at an affordable price. *11am-11pm Tue-Sun, to 10pm Mon* ¥¥

OWL CITY

Owls are a common sight in Ikebukuro, in the form of statues, mascots and shopfront decorations. The most likely reason for this is a bit of word play – the *bukuro* in 'Ikebukuro' sounds like *fukurō* – the Japanese word for 'owl'.

You won't have much luck spotting real owls here, due to the urban build-up, but some say that Ikebukuro was once a spot where owls liked to congregate. Other sources cite the round, pouch-like area where ponds formed as the origin for the neighbourhood's name, as *ike* and *bukuro* translates to 'pond' and 'pouch', respectively. No traces of these bodies of water are left, though, as the last remaining pond dried out after WWII.

RUDIMENCIAL/GETTY IMAGES

Shin-Ōkubo (p152)

although it's pricier than average, head to **Dōgen** (*facebook .com/dohgen*) to try its rich beef ramen made with slices of *wagyū*.

Colourful Museums in Shinjuku   MAPS P146 & P150

The world of Yayoi Kusama and Tokyo's blazing history

From psychedelic polka-dotted pumpkins to mirrored infinity rooms, few works are as instantly recognisable and captivating as those of artist Yayoi Kusama. Having had an impressive career spanning over 70 years, with numerous exhibitions across the globe, saying that Kusama is a powerhouse is an understatement. With her exhibitions frequently drawing large crowds, it might be surprising to find that the **Yayoi Kusama Museum** (草間彌生美術館; *yayoikusamamuseum. jp; adult/child ¥1100/600*) is nestled in a quiet residential area of Waseda (早稲田) – just one station away from Takadanoba-ba. The small, five-floor space, dedicated entirely to her works, holds two new exhibitions a year. To visit, you must purchase a ticket in advance, with a designated entry slot.

Step inside the Yotsuya Fire Station near Yotsuya-Sanchōme Station and explore the history of firefighting in Japan at the **Tokyo Fire Museum** (消防博物館; *free*). You'll trace the evolution from Edo-period fire brigades to today's emergency response, with antique uniforms, historic fire trucks and even a real rescue helicopter suspended from the ceiling. Try your hand at fire engine simulators, explore hands-on displays and snap a photo in firefighter gear. This museum will captivate younger members of the family, as well as anyone with an interest in transportation and urban culture.

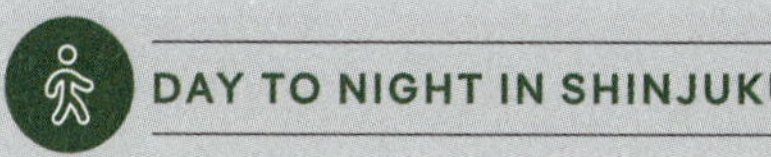

DAY TO NIGHT IN SHINJUKU

Get acquainted with the many layers of this vibrant neighbourhood on a walk through Shinjuku's most iconic spots.

START	END	LENGTH
Suica Penguin Square	Golden Gai	3.5km; 3-4hr

Start with a view of the train tracks and skyscrapers at **1 Suica Penguin Square** (p144), located just outside Shinjuku Station's New South Exit. Then, make your way down to ground level towards **2 Shinjuku Gyoen Shinjuku Gate** (p145) for a walk through the park. Next, head northwest in the direction of Shinjuku-dōri Avenue to **3 Isetan** (p144) for some shopping. Continue down the avenue until you come to an intersection in front of **4 Cross Space Shinjuku**, atop of which sits a 3D billboard often featuring cats and other adorable characters. Push north and continue past Yasukuni-dōri avenue.

As you come to another intersection, you'll see the **5 Godzilla Statue** peeking out from behind the Hotel Gracery. Head towards it, and you'll find yourself in **6 Kabukichō** (p151). Turn left in front of Hotel Gracery and continue west to find **7 Tokyo Mystery Circus** (東京ミステリーサーカス), where some escape rooms and puzzles are available in English. Adjacent is Shinjuku's newest landmark, **8 Kabukichō Tower**, which houses a hotel and entertainment facilities. As evening falls, head east from here along the backstreets of Kabukichō towards **9 Hanazono Shrine** (p145) for a bit of quiet. Finally, round off your explorations with a drink at one of **10 Golden Gai's** (p148) many bars.

Pedestrians rule on Sundays at **Shinjuku-dōri**, which is closed to vehicular traffic from noon until evening.

Don't miss the lovely selection of premium pastries and food on the basement floor (B1) of Isetan.

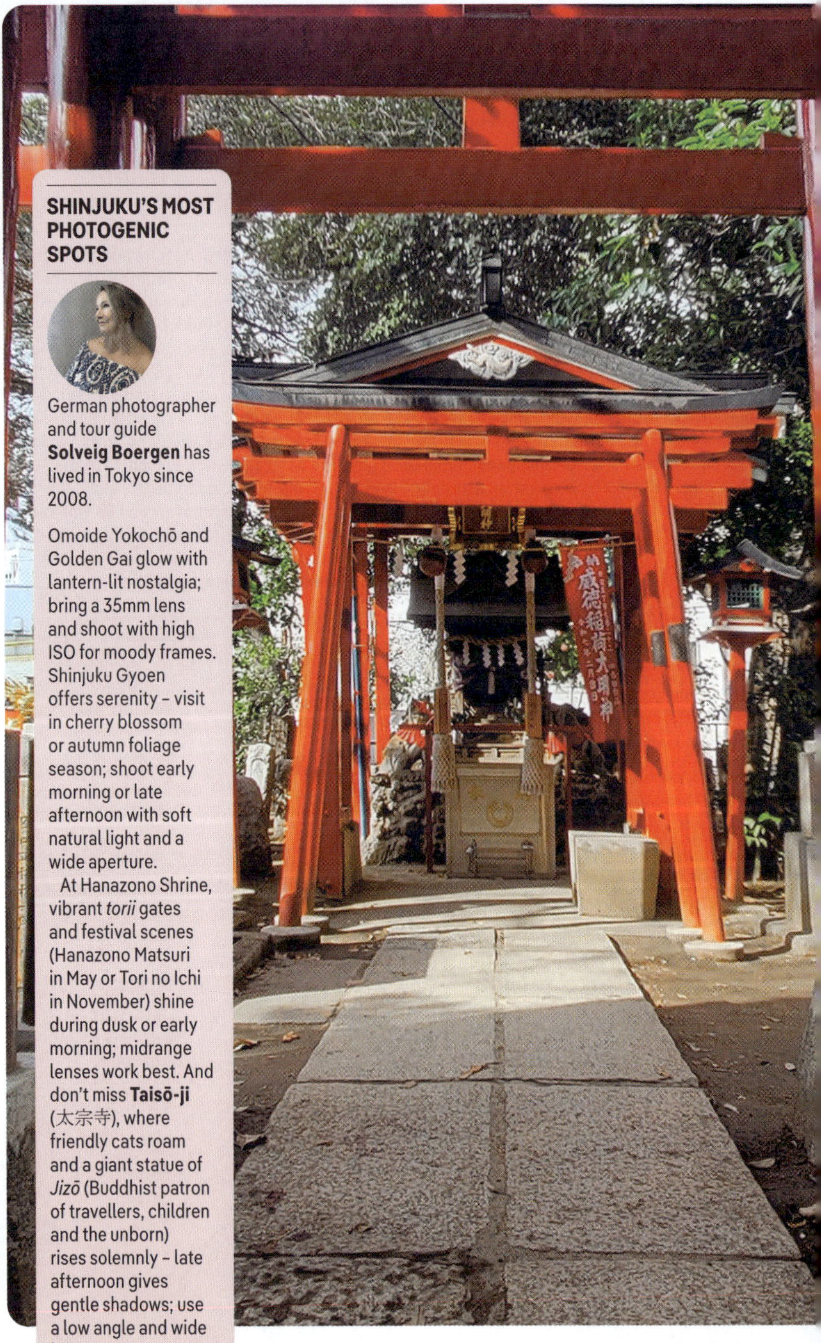

SHINJUKU'S MOST PHOTOGENIC SPOTS

German photographer and tour guide **Solveig Boergen** has lived in Tokyo since 2008.

Omoide Yokochō and Golden Gai glow with lantern-lit nostalgia; bring a 35mm lens and shoot with high ISO for moody frames. Shinjuku Gyoen offers serenity – visit in cherry blossom or autumn foliage season; shoot early morning or late afternoon with soft natural light and a wide aperture.

At Hanazono Shrine, vibrant *torii* gates and festival scenes (Hanazono Matsuri in May or Tori no Ichi in November) shine during dusk or early morning; midrange lenses work best. And don't miss **Taisō-ji** (太宗寺), where friendly cats roam and a giant statue of *Jizō* (Buddhist patron of travellers, children and the unborn) rises solemnly – late afternoon gives gentle shadows; use a low angle and wide lens.

Hanazono Shrine (p145)

Pop-Culture Shopping at Ikebukuro   MAP P150

Anime and Pokémon lovers, unite

Ikebukuro, part of Toshima ward, ranks as the city's second-busiest transit hub after Shinjuku. The station is flanked by two major department stores – Tobu on the west and Seibu on the east – which double as convenient orientation points in this vibrant district. If the neighbourhood of Akihabara is for *otaku* (geeks), then Ikebukuro is also for *otaku*; but more specifically, those who enjoy manga, anime and games geared towards a female audience. In Akihabara, you have mecha robots and the season's hottest mainstream characters; in Ikebukuro, you have bookshelves and arcades stocked with the merchandise of well-dressed male anime idols and cute characters. **Otome Road**, literally 'Maiden Road', is a street occupied by some of Japan's foremost comics and merchandise stores, like **K-Books** (*k-books.co.jp*). The **Animate Cafe** (*animatecafe.jp*) is also here, with special collaborations held every month. While not on Otome Road itself, an *otaku*'s trip to the area isn't complete without a stop at the **Animate Ikebukuro Flagship Store** (*animate.co.jp/shop/ ikebukuro*). Spanning 10 floors, there are event halls, a gallery and a theatre. **Lashinbang** (*lashinbang.com/special/ 1223*), a major chain specialising in secondhand anime and manga goods, has several shops clustered a few minutes walk from Otome Road.

For lovers of cute characters, and for those travelling with children, **Sunshine City** (*sunshinecity.jp*) is the place to go. **Pokémon Center Mega Tokyo** (*pokemon.co.jp*) is located here, and as well as being stocked full of the latest merchandise, it has a dedicated space for card tournaments, and the Pokémon Go Lab, where players of the mobile game can hang out. There's also the adorable Pikachu Sweets, a takeout cafe with Pokemón-themed offerings. For other merchandise, Kiddy Land, the Disney Store, the Ghibli Store and the One Piece Mugiwara Store all have outlets here.

For other fun things to do, check out the world's largest collection of capsule toys and pick up a quirky souvenir or two at the **Gashapon Department Store**, or head up to the observation deck on the 60th floor of **Sunshine 60** (*adult/child ¥1100/900*). There's also a rooftop aquarium.

TO SLURP OR NOT?

Slurping ramen is a perfectly acceptable part of the dining experience – and a practical one, too. The noodles are served in piping hot broth, and slurping draws in air to help cool them, reducing the risk of burns. It also lets you eat quickly, which is important for time-starved office workers or late-night diners trying to catch the last train home.

Some people swear that slurping enhances the flavour, too. While you might hear that it shows appreciation to the chef, that's a misconception – most are too focused on preparing the next bowl to notice or care.

Whether you slurp or not is up to you; the ramen will taste delicious either way.

Researched by Manami Okazaki

KŌRAKUEN & AKIHABARA

ANIME, BOOKS AND ENDLESS ENTERTAINMENT

Akihabara, sometimes called 'Akiba', is the destination for electronics and anime, while Kōrakuen is the home of Tokyo's most popular baseball team.

Akihabara (秋葉原) is where fans of manga and anime come to bask in the glory of their favourite media and buy exclusive merchandise. Giant arcades, bookstores and merch shops draw the most attention. Kōrakuen (後楽園) is most notably home to Tokyo Dome, an indoor stadium where Tokyoites flock to see concerts and baseball games. In the vicinity of Tokyo Dome City is the serene Koishi-kawa Kōrakuen, one of Tokyo's oldest and most beautiful gardens. Near Kōrakuen, the cobbled streets, shrines and old-fashioned shops of Kagurazaka offer a glimpse into the past. South of Tokyo Dome City is Jimbōchō, the world's largest book district with over 150 bookstores.

FROM LEFT: NATCHAMAS/SHUTTERSTOCK, INFANTRYDAVID/SHUTTERSTOCK

Tokyo Dome (p160)

See page 220 for places to stay in Kōrakuen & Akihabara

⭐

Highlights

❶ Tokyo Dome

Even if you aren't into baseball, it's worth going to a game to experience the jubilant energy. **p160**

❷ Akihabara Radio Kaikan

Shop here for anime merchandise, trading cards, model kits and viral idol goods. **p163**

❸ Akagi-jinja

A sleek, modern structure in Kagurazaka, redefining what a shrine should look like. **p166**

❹ Komiyama Shoten

Incredible selection of fine art and rare photography books. Also sells prints and posters. **p169**

❺ Akihabara Radio Center

Old alley lined with shops selling vintage tech and electronic parts. **p163**

🚶

Getting Around

Train

To get to the centre of Akihabara, follow the signs at the station for the Electric Town Exit. The JR and Tsukuba Express stop at Akihabara. The Tokyo Dome area is accessible via Kōrakuen, Suidobashi and Iidabashi.

Subway

Jimbochō is easily reached via the Hanzomon, Toei Shinjuku and Toei Mita subway and the JR to Kanda. Kagurazaka is also directly next to Iidabashi Station (East Exit for Japan Rail; Exit B3 for Tokyo Metro).

Walking

At the weekends, much of Akihabara is blocked off to traffic, so walking around is the way to go. We suggest walking from Jimbochō to Akihabara.

JAPANESE BASEBALL 101

While sumo is considered to be the national sport, it's baseball that has captured the popular imagination, and no doubt stars such as Shohei Ohtani's spectacular performance abroad has created a new generation of fans.

The game was introduced into Japan in 1872 by an American teacher and is still a beloved school sport. The two top pro level leagues are the Central and Pacific, each with six teams, and they play 144 games from March to October. While similar to the US major league, they use a smaller bat on a smaller strike zone and field.

The fervour for the regional teams is intense; the most heated rivalry takes place between the Osaka Hanshin Tigers and the Tokyo Giants, but the atmosphere is jolly rather than aggressive.

Striking out at Tokyo Dome

MAP P161

The capital's baseball stadium

Completed in 1988, **Tokyo Dome** (東京ドーム; *tokyo-dome.co.jp/dome/*) is an indoor baseball stadium that doubles as a concert and event venue holding up to 55,000 spectators. Home to the Tokyo Giants, this is the best place in the city to catch a baseball game. It has also served as a historic space for big international artists and ginormous conventions. The **Baseball Hall of Fame & Museum** (*baseball-museum.or.jp; adult/child ¥800/500*) has excellent displays of photos, uniforms and baseball bats.

Thrills, Spills & Relaxation

MAP P161

Fun at Tokyo Dome City

It's an impossible-sounding feat for somewhere as densely packed as Tokyo, but **Tokyo Dome City** (東京ドームシティ; *tokyo-dome.co.jp*) somehow manages to cram in the baseball stadium a roller rink, an onsen (hot springs) spa, a theme park, a shopping mall and more – all in one place. Because Tokyo Dome is a major sports and event venue, the whole complex can get rather packed on weekends and game days, but weekdays here are relatively quiet. Lots of indoor and outdoor kid-friendly rides and attractions at the theme park make it a great place for families with younger children to hang out, but there's something for thrill seekers, too. **Thunder Dolphin** (*¥1800, 1-day passports also available*) is the only major roller coaster in central Tokyo, and it takes riders down a vertiginous plunge before zipping through a hole in **LaQua** (ラクーア) shopping centre. **Korakuen Hall**, next to Tokyo Dome, is a well-known venue for Japanese martial arts, MMA and wrestling matches – recently, the popularity of women's professional wrestling is taking over – action-packed melodrama and dazzling outfits.

Koishikawa Kōrakuen Gardens

MAP P161

Serene gardens in the city

First established as a garden for Lord Tokugawa Yorifusa's spare Edo residence in 1629, **Koishikawa Kōrakuen** (小石川後楽園; *tokyo-park.or.jp/park/koishikawakorakuen; adult/child under 12 ¥300/free*) is the oldest *daimyō* (feudal lord) garden. Tall office buildings now rise above its treetops, but

EATING IN KŌRAKUEN & AKIHABARA: TSUKEMEN SPOTS — MAPS P161 &162

Tsujita Akihabara: Slippery, slurp-worthy *tsukemen* (dipping noodles) served alongside a thick, delicious broth. *11am-9.30pm* ¥

Mensho Tokyo: Chewy, freshly made noodles served in lamb knuckle and pork bone broth. Near Tokyo Dome. *11am-11pm Wed-Sun* ¥

Tokyo Style Noodle Hotate Biyori: Clear and light *tsukemen* broth made from Hokkaido scallops. *hours vary* ¥

Menya Musashi Bujin: Incredibly hearty *tsukemen* joint loved by locals. Its most popular item has a chunk of pork in it. *11am-10.30pm Mon-Sun* ¥

HIGHLIGHTS

1 Koishikawa Kōrakuen

SIGHTS

2 Akagi-jinja
3 Baseball Hall of Fame & Museum
4 Engetsu-kyo Bridge
5 Korakuen Hall
6 Tokyo Dome
7 Zenkoku-ji

SLEEPING

8 Book Hotel Jimbocho
9 Toggle Hotel
10 Tokyo Dome Hotel

EATING

11 Agezuki
12 Curry Bondy
13 Gavial
14 Majicurry
15 Mensho Tokyo
16 Sabouru
17 Tonkatsu Kenshin

DRINKING & NIGHTLIFE

18 Bumpōdō Gallery Cafe
19 Glitch Coffee & Roasters
20 Jimbōchō Book Center

ENTERTAINMENT

21 Tokyo Dome City
22 Yarai Noh Theatre

SHOPPING

23 Gallery Soumei-do
24 Genkido
25 Hara Shobo
26 Kitazawa Bookstore
27 Komiyama Shoten
28 Magnif
29 Nanyodo
30 Ogawa Tosho
31 Ohya Shobo

SIGHTS
1 Kanda Myōjin

ACTIVITIES, COURSES & TOURS
2 Super Potato Retro-kan

SLEEPING
3 BnA STUDIO Akihabara
4 Under Railway Hotel

EATING
5 Ippe Koppe by Tonkatsu Aoki
6 Maidreamin Akihabara Electric Town-exit Store
7 Marugo
8 Menya Musashi Bujin
9 Tokyo Style Noodle Hotate Biyori
10 Topca
11 Tsujita Akihabara

DRINKING & NIGHTLIFE
12 Final Fantasy Eorzea Cafe
13 Game Bar A-Button
14 Mogra

ENTERTAINMENT
15 GiGO
16 Taito Station

SHOPPING
17 Akihabara Gachapon Hall
18 Akihabara Radio Center
19 Akihabara Radio Kaikan
20 BicCamera
21 Hareruya 2
22 K-Books
23 Mandarake Complex
24 Seekbase
25 Sofmap
26 Tamashii Nations
27 Yellow Submarine
28 Yodobashi Camera

EATING & DRINKING IN AKIHABARA: THEMED CAFES & BARS —MAP P162

Maidreamin Akihabara Electric Town-exit Store: Franchise with several branches. Maids often stand outside and give a taste of their cutsie antics. *hours vary* ¥¥

Final Fantasy Eorzea Cafe: A cafe that replicates the *Final Fantasy* role-playing game with cheap food. *10.45am-11pm*

Game Bar A-Button: Retro game-themed bar in Akihabara; chock-full of consoles, controllers and all things video game. *6-11pm*

Mogra: Even if you aren't into clubbing, this anime soundtrack and J-pop venue has a great vibe (dancing, rather than sitting around drinking). *hours vary*

in certain secluded spots, it's easy to imagine what the garden might have looked like centuries ago, when the *daimyō* walked its grounds. Much of the scenery within it is based on other beautiful locations throughout Japan, while traditional Chinese influence can be seen, too – an example of which is the curved **Engetsu-kyo Bridge**. Designed by Chinese Confucian scholar Zhu Zhiyu and shaped like a full moon, the bridge exists in its original form from the Edo period.

Akihabara Electric Town

MAP P162

Otaku central

It's a sight every *otaku* (geek) recognises – neon arcades, colourful buildings topped with anime character billboards and maid cafes – this area just outside the 'Electric Town' JR train exit encapsulates the essence of Akihabara. But before Akiba was a town for anime geeks, it was (and still is) a tech-geek heaven. With many of the area's most prominent shops and entertainment complexes, like **Akihabara Radio Kaikan** (p166), located here, it's also the best place to begin your neighbourhood exploration. For the best experience, visit on a Sunday, when the adjacent **Chūo-dori avenue** (中央通り) is open exclusively to pedestrians from 1pm.

Shop Gadgets & Gizmos

MAP P162

The 'electric' in Electric Town

From Akihabara Station, your gateway to the neighbourhood is through the Electric Town Exit – a very apt name for what Akihabara actually was when it got its start: in the postwar years, the neighbourhood emerged as *the* place to go for radio parts and other electronics, when radios were an essential part of daily life. The popularity of Akihabara as an electronics destination later paved the way for larger shops dealing in consumer appliances, when TVs and washing machines came along in the 1960s. To catch a glimpse of Akihabara's humble beginnings, head to **Akihabara Radio Center** (*radiocenter.jp*) near the station – it's a remnant of those postwar era shops that now sell electronic parts, walkie-talkies and other gizmos.

Japan's big-box electronics retailers all have outlets in Akihabara: **Yodobashi Camera** (*yodobashi.com/ec/store/0018/*), **Bic Camera** (*biccamera.co.jp*) and **Sofmap** (*sofmap.com*) have big presences in the neighbourhood and are popular with both tourists and locals. Well-stocked and accessible,

STEP INTO A WORLD OF FANTASY

Owing to Akihabara's reputation for being a fantasyland for asocial people with a penchant for escapism, there are many entertainment services for solitary people, in what is often described as the 'intimacy economy'.

An ubiquitous sight around Akihabara are the staff working at maid cafes – spaces that are meant to serve as a temporary respite from everyday life. Everything from the interior decor down to the staff costumes and mannerisms are such that customers can place themselves in a world different to their own.

The earlier maid cafes were established here in the 2000s, and the number has only expanded since. The emphasis here is on women in French maid outfits serving customers in the most cheerfully subservient way possible.

EATING IN AKIHABARA & KAGURAZAKA: TOP TONKATSU — MAPS P161 & P162

Marugō: Expect lines at this famed Akihabara *tonkatsu* institution, but it's worth the wait: every bite is a crispy, fatty delight. *11.30am-3pm Wed-Sun* ¥¥

Ippe Koppe by Tonkatsu Aoki: Local Akihabara *tonkatsu* spot, the speciality is fried to perfection. Also try the *katsu* curry. *11am-8pm Mon-Sun* ¥

Tonkatsu Kenshin: Perfectly juicy, crispy, light coloured *tonkatsu* with marbled fat at this popular Kagurazaka store. *11.30am-2pm & 5-7pm Mon-Fri* ¥¥

Agezuki: Savour the balance of pork, cabbage and rice in this Kagurazaka favourite. Solo travellers welcome. *11.30am-2.30pm & 5.30-9pm Wed-Mon* ¥

VERTICAL CITIES & ZAKKYŌ BUILDINGS

Discover the multi-tenant buildings urbanist and sub-culture scholar **Joe McReynolds** (*@joeschmoefro*) likens to 'walking into a narrow back alleyway in Akihabara, but vertically.'

Zakkyō are vertical commercial buildings where each floor hosts one or more completely different business. A single *zakkyō* like Radio Kaikan can pack dozens of different microbusinesses into one compact building, making the cityscape three-dimensional.

Zakkyō extend the commercial street vertically, allowing intimate spaces and subculture niches to hide behind their glowing facades and cheap upper-floor rents. They are perfect incubators for the *otaku* and electronics subcultures that have long defined the neighbourhood.

The building type matches these micro-spaces for specialised communities.

they're excellent for duty-free shopping, and for checking out all the latest gadgets. For those who like to tinker with their tech, an interesting experience is to go trawling through the 'junk' stores. As their name might suggest, these places carry an array of outdated hardware, like CD drives, cables and other PC periphery. They can often be found along Akihabara's back streets, behind the taller buildings along Chūo-dōri.

Figures & Games Galore   MAP P161

Fun at the arcade

Arcades, or 'game centres' as they're called in Japan, are convenient places to stop by for a quick bout of fun. Brightly coloured, with plenty of crane-game cabinets stocked with famous characters that are immediately visible from the street, they stand ever ready to entice pedestrians into spending some spare ¥100 coins. These entertainment complexes are in most neighbourhoods around Tokyo, but Akihabara has a high concentration of them. The big arcade chains are here, including **GiGO** and **Taito Station**. Don't miss the latest rhythm games, where the entire family can enjoy playing the piano, *taiko* drum and dancing machines like Dance Dance Revolution, or simply watch the pros streaming their astonishing skills.

Also scattered around Akihabara and wider Tokyo are *gacha* machines (sometimes called *gachapon*), which dispense random capsule toys and trinkets for around ¥200 to ¥500 apiece. The best *gacha* arcade is the **Akihabara Gachapon Hall**, although electronic shops like Bic Camera and Yodobashi Camera (p163) also have them.

Akihabara Gachapon Hall

The Geek's Haven

MAP P162

From electronics to anime

From dingy post-war alleys featuring shops lined with radio parts and wires to a booming centre drawing visitors from across the globe who all share a love for Japanese subcultures, Akihabara has certainly come a long way. The neighbourhood today is teeming with shops, most of them occupying multiple storeys, catering to one kind of *otaku* or another. A term that is often translated as 'geek', *otaku* also refers to enthusiasts of a certain (often niche) interest, but the most common usage of the term refers to those who love exactly what Akihabara offers: anime and manga. For *otaku* shoppers looking to snag merchandise of their favourite anime characters – whether it's a new launch or a rare exclusive – Akihabara is the best place to go.

A few steps away from Akihabara Station is **Akihabara Radio Kaikan** (秋葉原ラジオ会館; *akihabara-radiokaikan.co.jp*), a landmark of the neighbourhood. Here, you'll find a dizzying array of trading cards, books, dolls and figurines, tech and audio equipment, and more. The nine floors of retail are packed full with merchandise, brought to you by big retailers like **K-Books** and hobby shop **Yellow Submarine**. If manga and *dōjinshi* (unofficial comics) are what you're looking for, you'll find it at **Animate** or **Melonbooks**; both are along Chūo-dori (p163). **Mandarake Complex** (*mandarake.co.jp/dir/cmp*) is a must see for collectibles such as toys, games, vintage items and rare manga.

GACHA CAPSULE TOYS

Gachapon (also called *gashapon*) are the omnipresent capsule toys dispensed by vending machines that are available in a mind-boggling arrays of designs.

First imported from the US in 1965, they originally sold toys and sweets for just ¥10. In the late 1970s, toymaker Bandai started to make ¥100 items. Now the quality is quite high, especially those made by **Kaiyōdō**, which has a store on the 5th floor of Radio Kaikan. **Qualia**, founded by Yuya Ogawa, features designs that are wonderfully absurd. Ogawa says he has to 'constantly think about how we can surprise and excite our customers when they open the capsules, and it is with this spirit we focus on craftsmanship.'

The most iconic *gacha* arcade is the chaotic **Akihabara Gachapon Hall** (*akibagacha.com*).

VIRTUAL & HOLOGRAM IDOLS

If there's one idol whose influence is omnipresent in Akihabara, it's the ubiquitous **Hatsune Miku**. Miku is the virtual mascot for singing software Vocaloid and the global community of users have collectively made her a cultural phenomenon.

She's able to sell out concerts where a hologram of her likeness appears on stage – even opening for Lady Gaga. Easily recognisable for her long aqua pigtails, the virtual singer's face is on everything from dolls to badges.

In her first five years she made more than ¥10 billion in revenue. Her YouTube features user-created songs as well as official collaborations and has over 400 million views. Nowadays the culture of V-tubers and hologram idols is burgeoning, with many cyber celebrities taking over humans.

K-Books on the 3rd floor of Radio Kaikan is one of the best places to see this trend.

Explore Tokyo's Former Geisha Quarter

MAP P161

Shrines, cafes and kimono

The neighbourhood of **Kagurazaka** (神楽坂) is located on a hill, and on either side of the sloped street that runs through the centre is a collection of quaint shops, cafes, restaurants and cobbled lanes that promise more to discover for its visitors. Once a *hanamachi* – a pleasure quarter where geisha entertained – much of Kagurazaka retains a traditional Japanese 'look' that is suggestive of what the area might've been like in the decades and centuries prior. Yet, scattered among the kimono and tableware shops and classy *ryōtei* (traditional, high-class Japanese restaurants) are French bistros and bakeries – all signs of the sizeable French expatriate community that settled here.

The best way to begin your journey through the neighbourhood is to start from Kagurazaka Station (Exit 1a) and make your way to **Akagi-jinja** (*akagi-jinja.jpI*), a modern shrine designed by famed architect Kengo Kuma in natural wood and glass. Then, continue eastward in the direction of Iidabashi Station on a charming walk that will take you past supermarkets, cafes and other small local businesses. The neighbourhood is also a great place to pick up some authentic souvenirs – thrift for some recycled kimono, browse locally made tableware or pick up freshly roasted tea at Rakuzan, a teashop that's just across the street from the 400-year-old **Zenkoku-ji** temple (*kagurazaka-bishamonten.com*). If visiting in summer, the **Awa-Odori Festival**, which features a long line of dancers performing a lively traditional dance through the main street of the neighbourhood, is a must-see. In mid-October, the wonderfully quirky **Kagurazaka Bakeneko Matsuri** takes place, a huge parade where everyone is dressed as supernatural cats. The **Yarai Nōh Theatre** (*yarai-nohgakudo.com*) offers both traditional and progressive *nō* performances.

Books & Coffee at Jimbōchō

MAP P161

Tokyo's treasure trove of old books

There's one thing **Jimbōchō** (神保町) is known for, and that's secondhand books. Sandwiched in an area between Tokyo Dome City and the Imperial Palace, it's a neighbourhood with a casual, down-to-earth vibe, as well as over 150 bookstores with a collective inventory of over 10 million books,

EATING & DRINKING IN JIMBŌCHŌ: BEST CAFES

MAP P161

Bumpodō Cafe Gallery Cafe: Cosy cafe and art gallery inside a stationery shop. Snag a sunny window seat for the best reading spot. *11am-6.30pm*

Sabouru: This cafe's interior is reminiscent of a comfy log cabin and is full of rustic charm. Try the Neapolitan spaghetti and colourful cream sodas. *11am-7pm Mon-Sat* ¥

Jimbōchō Book Center: Stylish cafe-bookstore popular for work and study. A digital-nomad hangout with great puddings. *9am-7pm Mon-Fri, from 10am Sat & Sun* ¥

Glitch Coffee & Roasters: A modern option serving serious coffee aficionados top-quality offerings. *9am-7pm* ¥

A COLLECTOR'S MINDSET AKIHABARA TOUR

Akihabara is the place where the market caters to aficionados collecting according to their obsessions, rather than simply consuming trends.

START	END	LENGTH
SEEKBASE building	Super Potato	1.5km; 2½hr

This tour will give you a peek into the collector's mind. Start at the ❶ **SEEKBASE** building. Browse the Godzilla and old-school anime toys at Mandarake CoCoo. Also visit the excellent vintage camera shop 2ndBase and vinyl store RECOfan on the same floor.

Still under the train tracks, towards Akihabara Station, ❷ **Tamashii Nations** make high-quality anime and robot figures with meticulous builds.

Inside the ❸ **Radio Kaikan** (p163) building, the 2nd-floor ASTOP is unusual in that it leases out boxes to people who sell off their collections.

Each box is a peak into the collector's brain. On the 4th floor, you'll see model car kits; some of the most popular are Japanese drift cars. On the 5th floor at Uchūsen Toys, there's a glass case filled with bears called Bearbrick; all have the same shape, but each one is a collaboration with a famous artist or brand.

Across Chūo-dōri is the trading cards shop ❹ **Hareruya 2**, with six floors of Pokemon cards – with the world's largest inventory. Continue on to ❺ **Super Potato**, with its great range of retro gaming consoles and games.

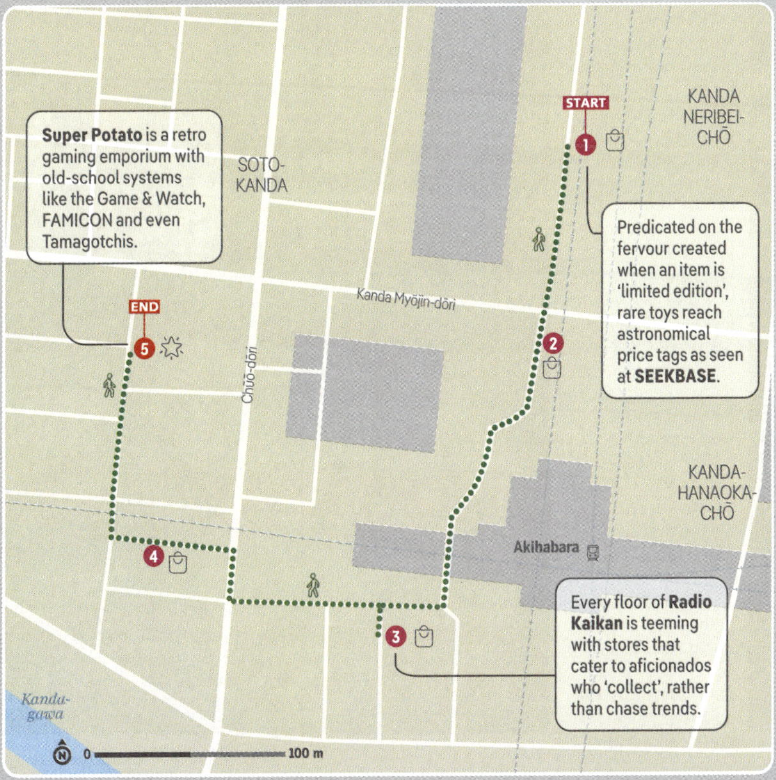

Super Potato is a retro gaming emporium with old-school systems like the Game & Watch, FAMICON and even Tamagotchis.

Predicated on the fervour created when an item is 'limited edition', rare toys reach astronomical price tags as seen at **SEEKBASE**.

Every floor of **Radio Kaikan** is teeming with stores that cater to aficionados who 'collect', rather than chase trends.

AKIHABARA'S SHRINE

The **Kanda Myōjin shrine** (神田明神; *kandamyoujin.or.jp*), a seven-minute walk from Akihabara Station's Electric Town Exit, was founded in 730 CE near present-day Ōtemachi.

With a nearly 1300-year history, it is said that Tokugawa Ieyasu, founder of the Tokugawa shogunate, paid respects to the Shinto gods there.

The shrine moved to its current location in 1616, and it's now a popular spot among visitors to Akihabara, who pray for love, luck and prosperity. Some of the *ema* – small votive plaques that are petitions for assistance from the shrine's resident deities – feature anime- and manga-style drawings made by visitors.

The biannual **Kanda festival**, which takes place on odd-numbered years in mid-May, is one of Tokyo's three most famous festivals, with costumes processions and rowdy parades.

Kanda festival

many featuring art and photography. The shelves are stuffed entirely with old tomes in every genre and category available, housed mostly in historic buildings. There's no telling what you might find here – every shop has its own eclectic selection, from novels, foreign languages and history to technical manuals. Bookstores like the excellent **Komiyama Shoten** offer incredible selections of fine art and rare photography books. It also sells prints and posters, plus fashion titles, so even without knowing Japanese, there is a day's worth of treasures to trawl through. English books can be found in select shops like **Kitazawa Bookstore** (*kitazawa.co.jp*) and **Ogawa Tosho**. Most of these are along Yasukuni-dōri. The district is also known for woodblock print stores such as **Hara Shobo** and **Gallery Soumei-do**, which sell contemporary prints as well.

Spend some time sifting through the neighbourhood's many bookshelves; then, with a book or journal in hand, a *kissaten* (coffee shop) is the next place to go. These can be found quite easily around the area, and range from modern and minimalist to cosy and retro. Some of the cafes here also double as bookstores. Drop in for a slow cuppa, some melon cream soda or an old-style *purin* custard pudding topped with bitter caramel sauce – then crack open a book and whittle the afternoon away in quiet, caffeinated bliss.

Jimbōchō Curry Town

MAP P161

Sample some of its 50 curry shops

Sweet and creamy, served on moist Japanese white rice – depending on who you talk to, Japanese curry is either a filling comfort food or a bland concoction lacking in heat.

What can be said is that it is dissimilar to its origins as an Indian dish brought to Japan by the British Empire during the Meiji era. Japanese curry uses a roux of flour and thickener, giving it a stew-like texture.

While it was initially served in elite eateries, by the early 20th century it became an affordable meal in households. Jimbōchō has over 50 curry shops, both Japanese as well as spicier versions.

The **Kanda Curry Grand Prix** in November is a festival that showcases the best in the region.

MAGNIF, A HAVEN FOR MAGAZINES

Magnif is a shop in Jimbōcho, but rather than books, it specialises in vintage fashion and lifestyle magazines. Its collection of over 10,000 ranges from subculture to couture from the 1940s to 2000s.

Owner **Yasunori Nakadake's** (@magnif_zinebocho) favourite era is the '90s, and there are plenty of old-schoolstyle magazines from the golden era of fashion print media. Nakadake says 'the appeal of magazines is their beauty owing to the printing techniques. Also, once it is printed, the content, including the advertising, can't change, so it becomes a time capsule.'

Bookstores he recommends are **Genkido**, as the prices aren't swayed by online trends; **Nanyodo**, with its beautiful storefront; and **Ohya Shobo**, which specialises in rare books.

 **EATING IN JIMBŌCHŌ: JAPANESE CURRY** ———— MAPS P161 & 162

Curry Bondy: Meaty, fruity, spicy curries and delicious puddings. A favourite literati haunt. *11am-9.30pm Mon-Fri, 10.30am-10pm Sat & Sun* ¥

Topca: Spicy curries with melt-in-the-mouth chunky meat and vegetables. *11am-3.30pm & 5.30-10.30pm Mon-Fri, 11.30am-6pm Sat & Sun* ¥

Gavial: More like stew than a curry, with large cubes of beef or pork and a mellow roux. *11am-9pm Wed-Sun, to 4pm Mon* ¥

Majicurry: The ultimate comfort food. Filling Japanese-style curry with breaded *tonkatsu* or hamburger patties on top. *11am-10pm* ¥

Researched by Rob Goss

UENO & YANESEN

ART AND CULTURE IN OLD TOKYO

With a mix of top museums, retro vibe and traditional ways, these east-side neighbourhoods are a whole different experience to central Tokyo.

If you love art and culture, make a beeline for Ueno (上野). The focal point, Ueno Park, is home to several temples and shrines, the country's largest museum and a handful of other major institutions. A short walk away is Ameya-yokochō, one of Tokyo's liveliest marketplaces, with an eclectic collection of eateries and bargain shops that draws the crowds. Northwest of Ueno is a distinctly quieter bunch of small neighbourhoods collectively known as Yanesen (谷根千). Here, you'll find cafes and art galleries in humble buildings that have miraculously survived earthquakes, wars and modernisation efforts, thus preserving an 'old Tokyo' feel that's rarely seen in the city nowadays.

TIP

All museums close at 5pm, with las entry at 4.30pm; note that Ueno Park and its museums can get quite crowded on weekends. It's possible to walk from Ueno to Yanaka, and vice versa — in which case, begin your journey from Nippori Station.

Benten-dō (p178), Ueno Park

FROM LEFT: RINTARO KANEMOTO/FOR LONELY PLANET, PAOLO GIANTI/SHUTTERSTOCK

See page 220 for places to stay in Ueno & Yanese

⭐ Highlights

❶ Tokyo National Museum

Get a crash course on Japanese art and history at the country's largest museum. **p176**

❷ Ameya-yokochō

Go bargain hunting in the city's liveliest street market. **p179**

❸ Yanaka Ginza

Take a break from modern-day Tokyo with a stroll along this retro shopping street in Yanesen. **p180**

▲❹ Rikugi-en

Unwind in an elegant Edo-era garden known for its beautiful autumn leaves. **p183**

❺ Ueno Park

Hop between museums, explore shrines and temples, or just chill out at this sprawling park. **p173**

🚶 Getting Around

Subway

Ueno is on Tokyo Metro's Hibiya and Ginza lines, the latter of which is handy if you are planning to combine Ueno with some time in nearby Asakusa (p184).

Train

Several JR lines serve Ueno, including the Yamanote loop line, which connects with Tokyo, Shibuya, Shinjuku and other stations. The Yamanote goes to Nippori for Yanaka, Komagome for Rikugi-en, and Sugamo.

Walking

With so much in and around Ueno Park, you can cover all the sights on foot, and even add on a walk around Yanesen for a full day out.

SAVE ON ADMISSIONS

If you are planning on visiting a lot of museums and galleries during your time in Tokyo, pick up a **Grutto Pass**. For ¥2500 you get access to 102 facilities around the capital, either for free or at a discounted price. Many of the city's art and history museums are covered, including all in Ueno Park. You can buy the pass at any of the participating facilities, or online at *rekibun. or.jp/en/grutto*.

You can opt to have a physical card or download the pass in an app, and it's valid for two months after you first use it – usually. There's a 31 March cut-off each year, so there's not much point buying one in late March.

An Afternoon of Culture

Museum-hopping in Ueno Park

Nowhere else in Tokyo has a collection of museums quite as varied and impressive as Ueno – all of them located in the vast grounds of **Ueno Park**. The best starting point is **Tokyo National Museum** (東京国立博物館; *tnm.jp; adult/child ¥1000/ free; p176*) in the park's north, home to six buildings that house collections ranging from prehistoric Japanese art to temple treasures, and even artefacts from across Asia and the Middle East. Make the Japanese Gallery (Honkan) your first stop, checking out the Japanese art dating from prehistory to the 19th century on the 2nd floor before making your way to the galleries downstairs. After that, look inside the Heiseikan building to see the *haniwa* (earthenware figures), and then visit the **Museum Garden** and its historic teahouses. Also worth seeing is the **Gallery of Hōryū-ji Treasures**, which features objects from the ancient Buddhist temple Hōryū-ji, many of which are officially classed as National Treasures and Important Cultural Properties.

Near the TNM, a popular destination for those with children is the **National Museum of Nature & Science** (国立科学博物館; *kahaku.go.jp; adult/child ¥630/free*) – its permanent exhibit showcases dinosaur fossils and taxidermied animals and plants native to the island. It can get crowded on weekends, however, and while there is English signage on exhibits, it can be a bit sparse. As you get closer to Ueno Station, you'll see the **National Museum of Western Art** (国立西洋美術館; *nmwa.go.jp/en; adult/child ¥500/250*), which has an impressive collection of Western paintings from the 17th to the early 20th centuries, including pieces by Monet and Renoir. For modern art, you could make your way to **Tokyo Metropolitan Art Museum** (東京都美術館; *tobikan.jp/en; prices vary*); the permanent exhibition is free to visit.

Last, but not least, is the **Shitamachi Museum** (したまちミュージアム; *taitogeibun.net/english/shitamachi; adult/ child ¥300/100*), which reopened in 2025 after a multi-year refurbishment. Located by the southern end of Shinobazu Pond, the three small floors here give a vivid insight into Ueno's past, including reconstructions of homes and animated streetscapes on the 1st floor. On the 3rd floor are a few traditional toys to try, including *kendama* and spinning tops.

DRINKING IN UENO: BEST PLACES FOR COFFEE

Up to You Coffee: On the eastern side of Ueno, on route to Kappabashi-dōri, stop for a coffee made by latte-art world champion barista Takehiro Okudaira. *10am-6pm*

Café Lapin: Charming old-school cafe that roasts its own beans and serves *kissaten* fare such as sandwiches and cakes. *7am-5pm Mon-Sat*

Social Good Roasters: This stand in Ueno Station serves hand-drip brews and more. It offers careers to people with disabilities. *8am-9pm Mon-Fri, from 9am Sat & Sun*

Everyone's Cafe: A handy stop in Ueno Park for coffee, herb teas, light meals and desserts. Has outdoor seating when the weather is nice. *10am-9pm Mon-Fri, from 9am Sat & Sun*

Kiyomizu Kannon-dō

Temples & Shrines in the City

Ancient sacred spaces

Despite Tokyo's hyper-modern and urban nature, centuries-old shrines and temples somehow fit right into its landscape, all still beautifully preserved and maintained. Ueno Park has some of the capital's most prominent within walking distance of each other, while Yanesen is home to the city's oldest places of worship.

The grandest of them all is the gilded **Ueno Tōshō-gū** (上野 東照宮; *uenotoshogu.com/en; adult/child ¥500/200*). Built in 1627 in memory of Tokugawa Ieyasu, founder of the Tokugawa shogunate, the structure has survived earthquakes and wars, and represents Edo-era architecture at its finest. A short walk through the park grounds will take you to **Kiyomizu Kannon-dō** (清水観音堂; *kiyomizu.kaneiji.jp; free*), one of Tokyo's oldest temples, built in the image of Kiyomizu-dera in Kyoto. At the back of the temple, facing Shinobazu-ike pond, is a pine tree with branches shaped in a perfect circle to resemble a full moon. Called *tsuki-no-matsu* (moon pine), it's a symbol that has made its way onto several Edo-era woodblock prints,
continues on p178

GOSHUIN-ATSUME

Most shrines and temples have a *goshuin*: a unique seal stamped in vermillion. **Goshuin-atsume** (literally 'collecting seals') used to be a practice of more devout travellers that has surged in popularity, particularly among younger people, as a way of keeping a physical memento of a trip.

Special booklets (*goshuincho*) are used to collect these seals, on which a shrine or temple will stamp their name and inscribe the date. Donations are requested in return, usually ranging from ¥300 to ¥500.

If you fancy collecting some of your own, *goshuincho* are now sold in stationery stores and at temples and shrines – the pages are made of card and fold out like an accordion.

EATING IN UENO: WHERE TO GET A FILLING MEAL

Isen Honten: This venue invented *katsu-sando* – sauce-covered pork-cutlet sandwiches. Also serves *tonkatsu* set meals. *11.30am-3pm & 4.30-8.10pm Thu-Tue* ¥¥

Kamachiku: Udon shop specialising in *kama-age* udon (noodles served in the cook pot). Housed in a restored warehouse in Nezu dating from 1910. *11.30am-2pm & 5.30-8pm Tue-Sat* ¥

Nagaoka-ya: *Izakaya* serving Spanish fare like paella and delicious, juicy lamb chops fresh off the grill, plus craft beers on tap. *5-11pm Mon-Fri, from 4pm Sat & Sun* ¥¥

Ueno Menya Musashi Bukotsu Sōden: Thick *tsukemen* (dipping noodles) topped with generous servings of pork. You could also order ramen. *11.15am-10.15pm* ¥

HIGHLIGHTS
1 Asakura Museum of Sculpture
2 Tokyo National Museum

SIGHTS
3 Benten-dō
4 Gallery of Hōryū-ji Treasures
5 Hagiso
6 Kiyomizu Kannon-dō
7 National Museum of Nature & Science
8 National Museum of Western Art
9 Nezu-jinja
10 SCAI the Bathhouse
11 Shitamachi Museum
12 Tennō-ji
13 Tokyo Metropolitan Art Museum
14 Ueno Park
15 Ueno Tōshō-gū
16 Yanaka Ginza
17 Yanaka-reien
18 Yūyake Dandan

SLEEPING
19 Hotel Resol Ueno
20 Nohga Hotel
21 Sawanoya Ryokan

EATING
22 Amane Saryō
see 5 Hagi Cafe
23 Isen Honten
24 Kamachiku
25 Karutaya
26 Nagaoka-ya
27 Nezu-no-Taiyaki
28 Onigiri Cafe Risaku
29 Shin Uguisu-tei
30 Ueno Menya Musashi
31 Usagi-ya
32 Yanaka Komichi

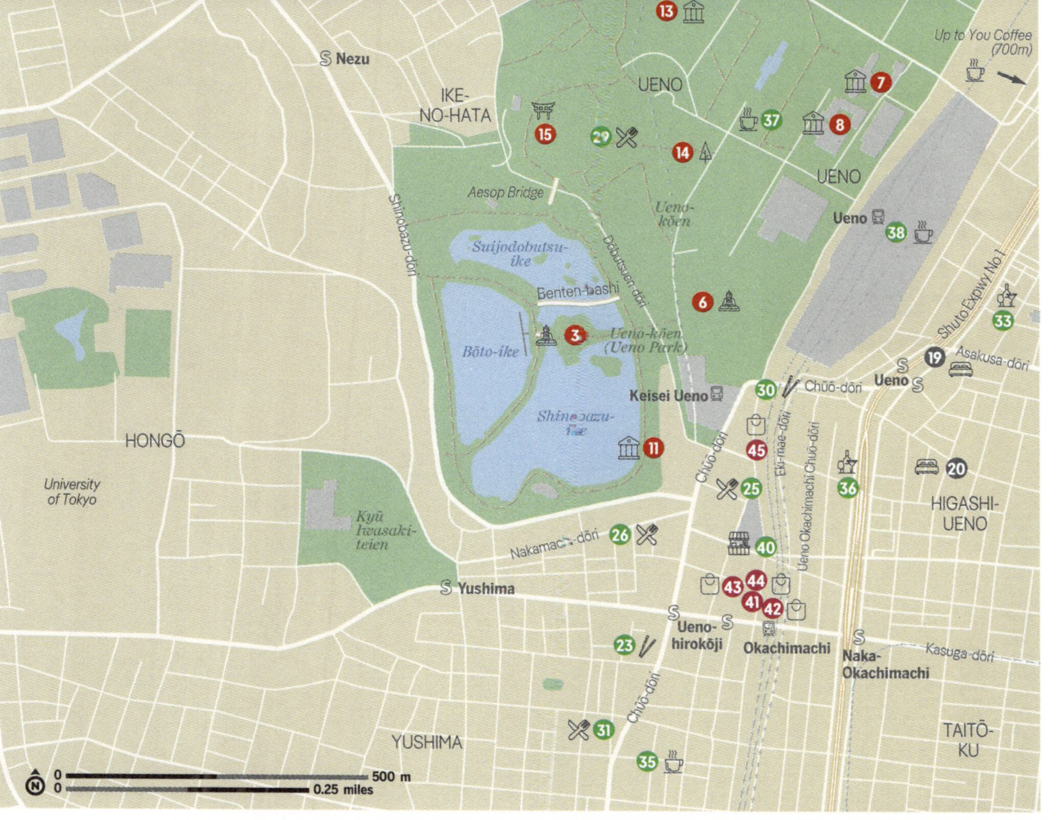
DRINKING & NIGHTLIFE
33 Bar Bookshelff
34 Bousingot
35 Café Lapin
36 Cocktail Works Ueno
37 Everyone's Cafe
38 Social Good Roasters
39 Yanaka Beer Hall

SHOPPING
40 Ameya-yokochō
41 Don Quijote Okachimachi
42 London Sports
43 Niki no Kashi
44 Sasugaya
45 Shimura Shōten
46 Yubiningyō Shōkichi
S Nezu
IKE-NO-HATA
UENO
Up to You Coffee (700m)
15
29
37
7
14
8
UENO
Aesop Bridge
Ueno-kōen
Ueno
38
Shinobazu-dōri
Suijodobutsu-ike
Benten-bashi
Dōbutsuen-dōri
6
Bōto-ike
3
Ueno-kōen (Ueno Park)
Shuto Expwy No.1
33
19
Asakusa-dōri
Ueno
S
Keisei Ueno
Shinobazu-ike
30
Chūo-dōri
45
Chūo-dōri
25
Eki-mae-dōri
Ueno Okachimachi Chūo-dōri
36
20
HIGASHI-UENO
HONGŌ
11
University of Tokyo
Kyū Iwasaki-teien
Nakamachi-dōri
26
40
S Yushima
43 44
41 42
S Ueno-hirokōji
S Okachimachi
23
Okachimachi
Naka-Okachimachi
Kasuga-dōri
YUSHIMA
Chūo-dōri
31
35
TAITŌ-KU
N
0   500 m
0   0.25 miles

Tokyo National Museum

Historic Highlights

The Honkan (Japanese Gallery) is designed to give visitors a crash course in Japanese art history from the Jōmon era (13,000–300 BCE) to the Edo era (1603–1868 CE). The works on display here are rotated regularly, to protect the more fragile ones and to create seasonal exhibitions, so you're always guaranteed to see something new.

Buy your ticket from outside the main gate then head straight to the Honkan with its sloping tile roof. Stow your coat in a locker and take the central staircase up to the 2nd floor, where the exhibitions are arranged chronologically. Allow two hours for this tour of the highlights.

The first room on your right starts from the beginning with ancient Japanese art. Pick up a free copy of the brochure *Highlights of Japanese Art* at the entrance. The exhibition starts here with the **1 Dawn of Japanese Art**.

Continue to the **2 National Treasure Gallery**. 'National Treasure' is the highest distinction awarded to a work of art in Japan. Keep an eye out for more National Treasures, labelled in red, on display in other rooms throughout the museum.

Moving on into the Heian era (794–1185 CE), considered the first flourishing of what we think of as Japanese culture, stop to admire the **3 courtly art**. Next is the medieval art: ink brush scrolls, tea ceremony pottery and **4 samurai armour and swords**; and then the **5 ukiyo-e and kimono** of the 17th and 18th centuries.

Head to the ground floor, where rooms are arranged by theme (such as lacquerware). Particularly noteworthy is the collection of **6 Japanese sculpture** and the **7 Ainu and Ryūkyū cultural artefacts**.

Finish your visit with a look inside the enchanting **8 Gallery of Hōryū-ji Treasures**.

6 Japanese Sculpture (Room 11)
Many of Japan's most famous sculptures, religious in nature, are locked away in temple reliquaries. This is a rare chance to see them up close.

7 Ainu and Ryūkyū Collection (Room 7)
Japanese culture is often considered a monolith, but before Japan colonized Hokkaidō (home of the indigenous Ainu people) and the Ryūkyū Empire, both had their own rich cultures.

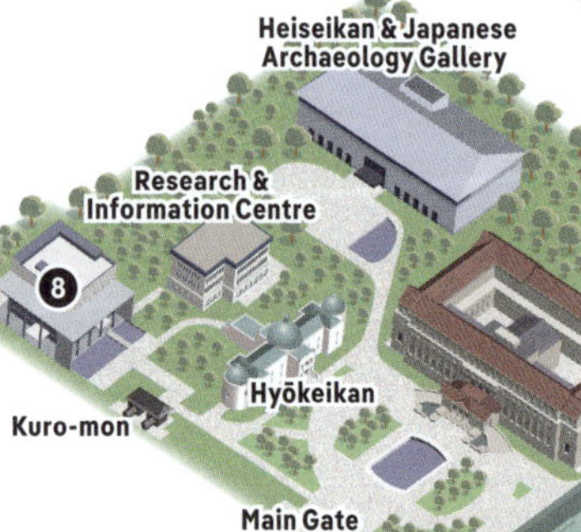

8 Gallery of Hōryū-ji Treasures
Surround yourself with miniature gilt Buddhas from Hōryū-ji, one of Japan's oldest Buddhist temples, founded in 607. Don't miss the graceful Pitcher with Dragon Head, a National Treasure.

❹ Samurai Armour & Swords (Rooms 5 & 6)

Glistening swords, finely stitched armour and imposing helmets bring to life the samurai, those iconic warriors of Japan's medieval age.

❸ Courtly Art (Room 3)

Literature works, calligraphy and narrative picture scrolls are displayed alongside decorative art objects, which allude to the life of elegance led by courtesans a thousand years ago.

❺ Ukiyo-e & Kimono (Room 10)

Chic silken kimono and lushly coloured *ukiyo-e* (woodblock prints) are two icons of the Edo-era. *Ukiyo-e* – means the 'floating world' or world of fleeting beauty and pleasure.

Honkan (Japanese Gallery) 2nd Floor

❷ National Treasure Gallery (Room 2)

A single, superlative work from the museum's collection of 88 National Treasures (perhaps a painted screen, or a gilded, hand-drawn sutra) is displayed in a serene, contemplative setting.

Museum Garden & Teahouses

Honkan (Japanese Gallery)

Tōyōkan (Gallery of Asian Art)

Honkan (Japanese Gallery) 1st Floor

❶ Dawn of Japanese Art (Room 1)

The rise of the imperial court and the introduction of Buddhism changed the Japanese aesthetic forever. These clay works from previous eras show what came before.

GIFT SHOP

The museum gift shop, on the 1st floor of the Honkan, has an excellent collection of Japanese art books in English.

MUSEUM GARDEN

The museum garden is open all year-round and features some historic teahouses. Note that the garden may close earlier than the museum does.

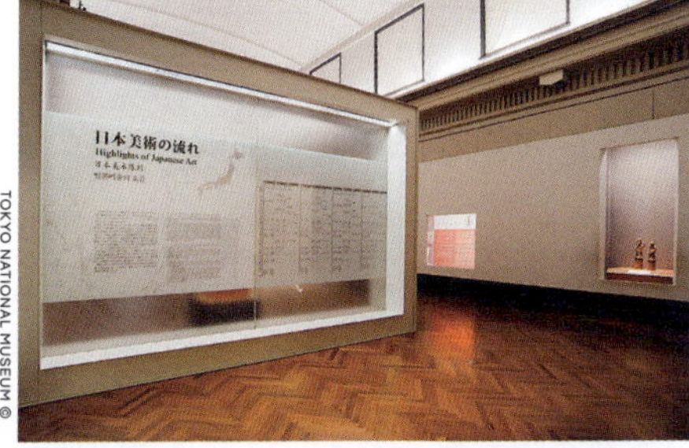

A MAN & HIS DOG

Maybe it's because I'm owned by a Shiba, but every time I visit **Ueno Park** (p172), I'm struck by the bronze statue of a man and a dog, standing together high on a pedestal. The man in question is **Saigō Takamori**, dubbed 'the last true samurai' for his role in the Meiji Restoration and then Satsuma Rebellion – the failure of which in 1877 led him to commit seppuku (ritual suicide). Unusually, he's depicted here in kimono rather than military attire, taking a stroll with his canine companion Tsun.

Records don't say what kind of dog Tsun was, just that he was a foreign breed with floppy ears and a black and white coat.

SANNE DOST/SHUTTERSTOCK

Nezu-jinja

continued from p173

though the tree we see is a recreation – the original was destroyed in a typhoon during the Meiji period. Nestled in the centre of the lotus-covered Shinobazu-ike pond is **Benten-dō** (辯天堂; *free*), built to resemble Hōgon-ji, a temple on an island of the massive Lake Biwa in Shiga Prefecture.

Northwest of Ueno in Yanesen is the vermillion **Nezu-jinja** (根津神社; *nedujinja.or.jp; usually free but ¥200 for the azalea garden in spring*), with a line of *torii* (entrance gates) and bushes of blooming azaleas. Built in 1706, it's one of Tokyo's oldest shrines, and an Important Cultural Property. The best time to visit is around April to May, when the grounds are pink and white with azalea blooms and food vendors set up on the grounds for the annual azalea festival.

Celebrating the Seasons in Ueno Park

Festivals of all kinds

The ample space at Ueno Park and its many green spaces make it the perfect gathering place for festivals throughout the year. While the major ones often happen during spring and summer, cultural events are held throughout the year at

EATING IN UENO & YANESEN: SWEET SNACKS

Karutaya: There's only one item on offer at this famous Ameya-yokochō stall: the *miyako-manjū*, a pastry filled with white bean paste. *12.30-8pm Wed-Mon ¥*

Nezu-no-Taiyaki: Small neighbourhood store selling *taiyaki* – bean-filled pastry shaped like *tai* (sea bream), which explains the red fish on the shop sign. *10am-2pm Mon-Fri ¥*

Shin Uguisu-tei: Tea-house inside Ueno Park dating to 1915. Try the matcha with *uguisu dango* – soft, traditional sweets with a bean-paste filling. *10am-5pm Tue-Sun ¥*

Usagi-ya: Century-old bakery sells fluffy *dorayaki* (pancake-like pastries filled with bean paste) and cute bunny-shaped *usagi-manjū* (sweet dumpling pastries). *9am-6pm Thu-Tue ¥*

the **Takenodai Square**, just across the road from the Tokyo National Museum (p176) – on one visit for this book, there was a Taiwanese food festival with dozens of colourful food stalls. The festival that draws the most crowds is the **Ueno Sakura Matsuri** around late March to early April, when the garden paths are lined with lanterns that light up below the cherry blossom trees along Sakura-dōri. If you're visiting Japan between early April and May, check out the **Botan Matsuri** (peony festival) at Ueno Tōshō-gū to see the beautiful flowers in bloom. Despite the heat and humidity, summer is Tokyo's peak season of festivals, and Ueno gets in on the act with the **Ueno Natsu Matsuri**, a month-long celebration that brings plenty of events and shows from mid-July, including traditional dance and idol performances, and even pro wrestling. There's also an antique market and other street stalls near Shinobazu Pond during the event.

Wending Through the Yokochō

The foodie and bargain-hunter's paradise

A *yokochō*, in its typical definition, means a narrow side street off the main road, but nowadays, they're associated with *izakaya* (Japanese pub-eateries) and street stalls, and as places where people can sit, drink and unwind. Of all the well-known *yokochō* in Tokyo, **Ameya-yokochō** (アメヤ横丁; *ameyoko.net*) is one of the largest, with over 400 stores crammed onto the street stretching between Ueno Station and Okachimachi Station.

Like other *yokochō* in the capital, Ameya-yokochō can trace its advent to the period after WWII, when it was a black market that sold food at a time when supplies were scarce. As for its name, there are two different hypotheses: some say it was from the sweet stores that opened here when sugar was considered a luxury (*ameya* means 'sweet shops'); others think 'Ameyoko' may have been short for 'America Yokochō', as many of the black market goods were supposedly obtained from American GIs stationed in Tokyo during the occupation years.

Ameyoko is a lively open-air marketplace. Shops here sell everything from candy to shoes, jackets and perfume. Many non-Japanese eateries have also set up here, doling out kebabs and *xiao long bao* (soup-filled Chinese dumplings) from their stall windows. Once things get up and running after 10am, the alley possesses an atmosphere not often seen in other major parts of Tokyo, in that it's uncurated, a little overwhelming and somewhat chaotic – it seems to operate to a different

GOTTA CATCH 'EM ALL

There are plenty of sculptures, buildings and green spaces to admire in Ueno Park, but you might want to keep an eye on the ground, too. That's because there are two **Pokéfuta** – manhole covers that feature Pokémon – outside two museums: the Tokyo National Museum and the National Museum of Nature & Science.

These colourful manhole covers appear in select locations across the country, with the two in Ueno being the only ones near downtown Tokyo. Besides being very cute and on theme (the covers feature Baltoy and Bronzor, which resemble the ancient artefacts at the Tokyo Museum, and dinosaur-like Tyrunt), these manholes serve as Pokéstops on the (still popular in Japan) smartphone game, *Pokémon Go*.

EATING IN YANESEN: COOL CAFES

Amane Saryo: Cosy cafe housed in a beautifully renovated old residence close to Nezu Shrine. Light meals and cakes available. *11am-6pm Thu-Mon* ¥

Hagi Cafe: Part of a complex in Yanaka that includes a gallery and hotel; good spot for a healthy Japanese breakfast. *hours vary* ¥

Yanaka Komichi: Can't decide between coffee or ice cream? Have both at this kiosk tucked down an alley off Yanaka Ginza. *11am-6pm Mon-Fri, from 10am Sat & Sun* ¥

Onigiri Cafe Risaku: Several dozen varieties of *onigiri* (rice-ball snacks) served with miso soup to put a pep in your step. *9am-8pm Thu-Tue* ¥

BEST AMEYOKO BARGAINS

Niki no Kashi: This large sweets and confectionery store sells a dizzying array of products that make perfect souvenirs.
Don Quijote Okachimachi: Vibrant shop packed with all sorts of goods, from snacks and quirky souvenirs to adult toys.
Sasugaya: A thrift store where you can get bargains on brand-name bags and even secondhand whisky.
Shimura Shōten: A little bargain shop that sells assorted chocolate by the bagful at ¥1000. Shopkeepers will make a big show of dropping the candy in the bag.
London Sports: Discount sportswear store with brand-name products. You might have to sift through the jumble, but it can be well worth it.

set of rules, and in keeping with that theme, bargaining is allowed at some stores. Though the alley feels like a fairly long stretch, it takes a little less than 10 minutes to get from one end to the other, so it's easy to take a little time to walk down the length of the *yokochō* before deciding where to eat and what to buy.

Old Tokyo Charms in Yanaka

Slip back in time

If the hustle and bustle of the city gets a bit too hectic, take a breather in sleepy **Yanaka** (谷中), a neighbourhood that retains an unassuming, old-timey charm that is rarely seen now in modern-day Tokyo. Largely undamaged by natural disasters and WWII bombings, Yanaka almost appears to exist in its own bubble – despite its close proximity to the highly developed Ueno, you'll mostly find wooden buildings, humble temples and understated neighbourhood shophouses here; a combination that gives the impression of a town left untouched by modernity.

The liveliest part of town is **Yanaka Ginza** (谷中銀座; *yanaka ginza.com*), a narrow shopping street lined with butchers and produce shops, souvenir stores and small cafes sitting at the foot of **Yūyake Dandan** (夕やけだんだん) – the photogenic 'Sunset Steps' you'll walk down on your way here from Nippori Station. The street has a friendly neighbourhood vibe that's helped along by the many cats that can be found along the stretch in the form of sculptures atop shop roofs, as merchandise in stores, and actual furry felines that may occasionally be found roaming about.

Another spot here that's worthy of a slow weekday afternoon's exploration is **Yanaka-reien** (谷中霊園; *tokyo-park .or.jp/reien/yanaka; free*) – one of the city's largest cemeteries and the resting place of many notable Tokyoites, including the last shogun, Tokugawa Yoshinobu. Near where the cemetery begins – just south of Nippori station – is **Tennō-ji** (天王寺; *free*), a temple founded sometime between 1394 and 1427, which is best known for a seated statue of Buddha cast in bronze. Unless you come when the cherry blossoms are in flower around late March to early April, the cemetery is an incredibly peaceful place to explore. As are Yanaka's backstreets, which feature in the walk on p182.

DRINKING IN UENO & YANESEN: OUR PICKS

Cocktail Works Ueno: Beautiful bar built to look like an urban kitchen, with inventive craft cocktails. *6pm-3am Mon-Sat, 5-11pm Sun*

Bousingot: A funky cafe-bar in Sendagi that doubles as a used bookstore. *6-10pm Wed-Mon*

Bar Bookshelff: A place for book lovers, by book lovers, so order a cocktail and sip it over a read. *6pm-1am Tue-Fri, from 3pm Sat & Sun*

Yanaka Beer Hall: Charming old building not far from SCAI the Bathhouse. It has its own brews on tap, including wheat beer and heavier IPA. *11am-8pm Tue-Sun*

Yanaka Ginza

Art in the Suburbs

Everyday galleries

Ueno Park (p172) may have all the big museums, but Yanesen has a charming collection of small art museums and galleries that provide a more casual and intimate setting in which to appreciate the works. Among the standouts, **SCAI the Bathhouse** (*scaithebathhouse.com/en; free*) is a contemporary venue that occupies – as its name suggests – an old bathhouse in Yanaka. While the exhibition space inside is modern, the gallery has kept its traditional Japanese facade, and since its establishment in 1993, it has hosted both Japanese and foreign artists. Down a sidestreet off of Yanaka Ginza, another space for contemporary pieces is **Hagiso** (*hagiso.com/hagiso; free*), an old apartment building that's been converted into a cafe/art gallery/salon/hotel. Stop by for a cup of coffee, then check out the displays – a new exhibition by a local artist goes up here every month and a half or so.

A few minutes away is the **Asakura Museum of Sculpture** (朝倉彫塑館; *taitogeibun.net/asakura; adult/child ¥500/250*), which was the former studio and residence of famed sculptor Fumio Asakura. Among his works, you'll find bronze sculptures of famous Japanese figures, and cats, which Asakura was particularly fond of. **Yubiningyō Shōkichi** (指人形笑吉; *shokichi. main.jp; ¥700 for puppet shows*) is another workshop in Yanaka where artist Mitsuaki Tsuyuki creates his incredibly lifelike hand puppets. While here, don't miss the puppet show – six are staged on days the store opens, if three or more people turn up. The exact schedule is on their website. They even take commissions, if you have ¥40,000 handy to get a puppet made in your likeness. All these are closed on Mondays, and some also close on additional days, so check websites before going.

THE RESIDENTS OF YANAKA-REIEN

As well as being the resting place for Japan's last shogun, the sprawling **Yanaka-reien** is home to many other historic figures – famous and infamous. There's author and poet Higuchi Natsuko (1872–96), whose image appears on older versions of the ¥5000 banknote in recognition of her influence on modern Japanese literature – new ¥5000 notes feature Umeko Tsuda, a pioneer in women's education.

You might also stumble upon the headstone of Nicholas of Japan (1836–1912), the Russian cleric who introduced the Eastern Orthodox Church to Japan.

More gruesome is the story of Reien resident Takahashi Oden (1848–79), who after poisoning her husband was the last Japanese woman to be executed by beheading.

CHRISTIAN MUELLER/SHUTTERSTOCK

A STROLL AROUND YANESEN

This walk takes in several Yanesen highlights but also meanders through the area's narrow backstreets.

START	END	LENGTH
Nezu Station	Nippori Station	4km; 3hr

Go left from Exit 1 of **1 Nezu Station** and in a few minutes you'll be at the side street that leads to **2 Nezu-jinja** (p178), one of the oldest and most photogenic shrines in the city. Continuing on the main road, you'll pass Sendagi Station and then see a post office across the road. Heading up the side street next to the post office will take you to the bottom of **3 Yanaka Ginza** (p180), the area's old shopping street, lined with family-run stores.

Just before you get to the flight of steps at the top end of the street, take a right down to **4 Hagiso** (p181), a cafe-gallery-hotel where you can check out the latest art exhibition and grab a coffee or light lunch. Now in the maze-like backstreets of Yanaka, take the first left after Hagiso and follow it as it winds by several minor temples. In a few minutes, you'll be at Suwadai-dōri, which you can follow right – passing a mix of old homes, small stores and cafes – and then take the left fork down to **5 SCAI the Bathhouse** (p181), a contemporary art gallery housed in an old public bathhouse. From here, backtrack a couple hundred metres, then take a right onto Sakura-dōri. This will lead you through the peaceful grounds of **6 Yanaka-reien** (p180) cemetery and then to **7 Tenno-ji** (p180) – a temple with an impressive bronze-cast Buddha statue – before reaching **8 Nippori Station**.

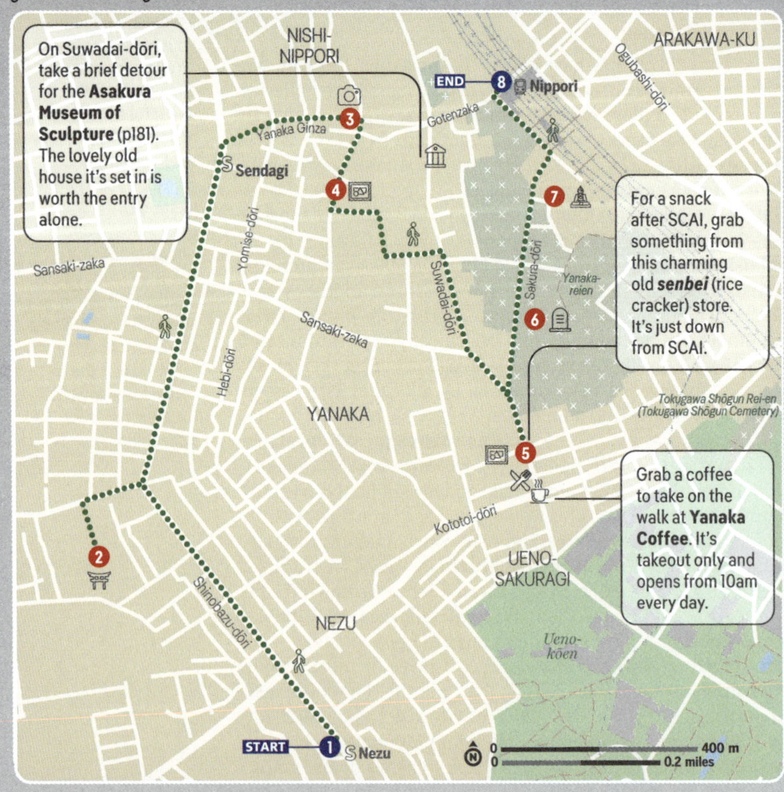

Stroll an Edo-era Garden

Unwind at Rikugi-en

Five stations away from Ueno on the Yamanote line, nestled in the quiet residential area of Komagome, is **Rikugi-en** (六義園; *tokyo-park.or.jp/teien/en/rikugien; adult/child ¥300/free*), one of Tokyo's most elegant strolling gardens. It was built in 1702 by Yoshiyasu Yanagisawa, a close confidant of Japan's fifth Tokugawa shogun, and was given the name 'Rikugi-en' as a nod to the six categories of Chinese poetry. Building on the poetic theme, the garden was then designed to depict 88 scenes from classical poetry, and though only 32 remain, the result is nevertheless still stunning.

Walking from scene to scene, you'll find ponds, stone bridges, wooded walkways and trickling streams that provide a full sensory experience. With the sound of the city relegated to a distant hum, it's like being transported away from Tokyo's urban bustle, even if some scenes now have modern buildings acting as unintentional borrowed scenery beyond Rikugi-en's grounds. For a break from strolling, you could also stop at the Fukiagajaya teahouse for matcha and a seasonally designed *wagashi* (Japanese sweet).

While Rikugi-en is well worth an hour at any time of year, it's at its most beautiful in the autumn months, when the maple leaves turn auburn and start to fall. To celebrate the season, the garden is lit up in the evenings between late November and early December, and the place takes on a mysterious beauty not seen during the day – though you will be sharing the otherwise peaceful garden with hundreds of others.

Shopping with Seniors

Visit Granny's Harajuku

If you can't get enough of casual, friendly neighbourhood vibes, head over to **Jizō-dōri** shopping street (地蔵通り商店街) in Sugamo, one stop on from Komagome. Lovingly nicknamed 'Granny's Harajuku', the 800m-long street is lined with chiropractors and shops selling wares mostly aimed at seniors, including hats, mobility aids and fashions that range from floral to leopard-skin in style.

Things to look out for as you amble up and down the street include the bright red storefronts of the several branches of Maruji, selling supposedly auspicious *aka-pantsu* (red underwear), and numerous outlets specialising in *shio-daifuku* (rice cakes filled with sweet and salty bean paste) – the Sugamo equivalent to Harajuku's crêpes. You might also spot Sugamon, the neighbourhood's beloved duck mascot, who often appears on promotional banners.

Rob Goss, Lonely Planet Writer

In the two decades I've lived in Tokyo, it's always been the Shitamachi (p172) where I've most felt at home. Yanaka (p180) is a wonderful example. The narrow side streets here take you on a journey to small temples and offer up glimpses of daily life. You'll stumble upon galleries and cafes housed in old buildings and find family-run shops that have been in business for generations.

Things move more slowly; more quietly, too. It's so different to Tokyo's image as a modern, crowded metropolis that it's always at the top of my list when people ask where they should visit. It's the perfect place for a grabbing a takeout coffee and heading off for an aimless stroll.

ASAKUSA & SUMIDA RIVER

LASTING TRADITIONS AND HISTORIC SIGHTS

Asakusa (浅草) is all about keeping the old ways of Tokyo alive. Though a lot about the area is catered towards tourists, locals love it too.

Let the scent of incense waft over you as you step up to Tokyo's most ancient temple, Sensō-ji, while strolling through the neighbourhood streets in a kimono. Within walking distance of the temple is Kappabashi, where chefs and home cooks alike go to find cooking equipment and tableware. Move south along Sumida River (隅田川) and you'll arrive at Kuramae, a neighbourhood of both traditional and modern artisans who work from small studios and run shops stocked with handmade items. Further south is Ryōgoku, where tournaments for Japan's national sport – sumo – take place, as well as the Edo Tokyo Museum, which takes you through the history of the city.

TIP

You can explore Asakusa, Kappabashi and Kuramae on foot – there are also walkways along Sumida River where you can get a splendid view of the city. And for Tokyo Skytree, buy tickets online in advance, as they're cheaper.

Sumo tournament (p186)

See page 220 for places to stay in Asakusa & Sumida River

⭐ Highlights

❶ Sensō-ji
Tokyo's oldest temple and the traditional symbol of the city, dating back to the 7th century. **p192**

❷ Tokyo Skytree
A modern icon – the view from the observation deck is unbeatable. **p186**

❸ Kuramae
Quiet neighbourhood near Asakusa occupied by artisans and their ateliers. **p195**

❹ Ryōgoku Kokugikan
Experience the thrill of Japan's national sport at either a match or morning practice. **p186**

▲ ❺ Kappabashi
An incredible concentration of artisanal wares related to cooking and tableware. **p190**

🚶 Getting Around

Train
For Asakusa use the metro Ginza line, the Asakusa line as well as the Tsukuba line. The JR Chūō line serves the Sumida region, and the Toei Oedo line stops at Kuramae Station.

Walk
The most convenient way to get around is by walking. Meander around the backstreets and small alleyways with local eateries and shops, and peek into residential life.

Rickshaw
While being pulled along on a carriage on wheels might not be immediately appealing, the experience of riding a rickshaw offers an filmic way to experience the district.

SUMO & SHINTŌ

An ancient sport dating back some 1500 years, the origins of sumo are rooted in religion: bouts were originally performed as a Shintō ritual for the gods in return for a bountiful harvest and were seen as a way to please the deities. In the oldest historic record, the Kojiki published in 712, there is mention of gods wrestling.

Before sumo was practised as a sport, matches took place at shrines and temple grounds, during *matsuri* (festivals). Even today, the *yokozuna* wrestlers wear folded pieces of paper, a Shintō symbol to suggest that something is sacred.

The spectacle is shrouded in ritual and a ring entering purification ceremony takes place each day, giving the impression that more than a show of strength, sumo is a display of discipline, reverence and philosophy.

Enter the Arena

MAP P187

Watch a sumo battle

Standing by the banks of Sumida River, **Ryōgoku Kokugikan** (両国国技館; *kokugikan.sumo.or.jp*) is Japan's national sumo wrestling stadium. For 15 days in January, May and September each year, the giant fighters step onto the sacred *dohyō* (wrestling ring) here to fight, all in a bid to move up the ranks. You'll know it's tournament season when you see colourful flags called *nobori* hoisted on bamboo sticks along the stadium's exterior – these have the fighters' names written on them, with the name of their sponsor underneath.

It's a clash of the titans – the fighters have trained tirelessly for years in preparation for the tournament, and each bout lasts mere minutes, if not seconds. Today's sumo matches are still very ritualistic and tied to the Shintō faith: above the *dohyō* is a roof resembling a Shintō shrine suspended in mid-air; and before facing their opponent, the *rikishi* (fighters) scatter a handful of purifying salt into the ring and rinse their mouths in another rite of purification.

Tickets for each tournament go on sale roughly one month before the day of the event (*sumo.or.jp/EnTicket; adult/child from ¥2500/500*). If you don't manage to snag one before they sell out, 400 general admission tickets go on sale at 8am at the stadium's box office on the day of the tournament. Junior wrestler matches begin earlier, with the main event featuring the country's wrestling superstars and the *yokozuna* (the highest-ranking sumo) starting in the afternoon. There are several sumo *dojo* (training centres) across Sumida and Taito wards such as **Arashio Beya** *(arashio.net)* that offer the opportunity to see morning practices (check its homepage for details).

Tokyo Skytree

MAP P187

The top of the capital

At 634m, **Tokyo Skytree** (東京スカイツリー; *tokyo-skytree.jp; adult/child from ¥2600/950*), designed by famed architect Tadao Ando, is the tallest tower in the world. It resembles something out of a sci-fi anime as the exterior latticed metal lights up at night in disco colours. It was completed in 2012 and altered the skyline of the downtown Tokyo area with its brilliant presence. The needle-like structure serves as a telecommunications and broadcasting tower to Tokyo's millions of inhabitants, and at the top are two observation decks: one

EATING AROUND ASAKUSA: BEST EDO-STYLE FOOD ⸻ MAPS P187 & P191

Dote no Iseya: Housed in a classic wooden building, the place serves saucy, hearty, Edo mae tempura. *11am-2.30pm Thu-Mon* ¥¥

Namiki Yabusoba: Delicious soba shop founded in 1913 with a strong soy dipping sauce; it's popular so expect to line up. *11am-7pm Fri-Tues* ¥¥

Irokawa Unagi: Watch the chef cooking over the charcoal and savour the fluffy, smoky *unagi* (eel) at this eatery established in 1861. *11.30am-2pm Mon-Sat* ¥¥

Asakusa Midori Sushi: A sushi joint that locals love. Unpretentious with large toppings. *5pm-11pm Mon-Sun* ¥¥

ASAKUSA & SUMIDA RIVER

HIGHLIGHTS
1 Edo-Tokyo Museum
2 Ryōgoku Kokugikan
3 Tokyo Skytree

SIGHTS
4 Great Kantō Earthquake Memorial Museum
5 Japanese Sword Museum
6 Kyū-Yasuda-teien
see 23 Sumida Aquarium
7 Sumida Hokusai Museum
8 Tokyo Metropolitan Memorial Hall

SLEEPING
9 Cyashitsu Ryokan Asakusa
10 Sumida Nagaya

EATING
11 Asakusa Ichimon
12 Bon
13 Dote no Iseya
14 Enshūya Takao
15 Sasaya Cafe
16 Vegan Cafe PQ's
17 Yakiniku Beast

ENTERTAINMENT
18 Kazunoya Oiwake

SHOPPING
19 Ink Stand
20 Inkimono
see 19 Kakimori
21 Sumida Edo Kiriko Museum
22 SyuRo
23 Tokyo Solamachi
24 Tsubame Kobo

EATING IN ASAKUSA: BEST LOCAL EATERIES — MAP P187

Asakusa Ichimon: Wonderfully atmospheric traditional hotpot restaurant. *6-10pm Mon-Fri, 5-10pm Sat & Sun* ¥¥

Enshūya Takao: Casual, downtown-style *izakaya* open since 1926 and loved by locals. *6pm-midnight Thu-Mon* ¥¥

Yakiniku Beast: Specialising in sweet Ota beef and raw beef sushi. Also has excellent *yuzu* cold noodles. *5-11pm Mon-Fri, 1-3.30pm & 5-11pm Sat & Sun* ¥¥

Kazunoya Oiwake: A *shamisen* (traditional lute) bar where you can enjoy lively performances and a laidback vibe. *5.30-11pm Tue-Sun* ¥¥

Tokyo Rickshaw (*tokyorickshaw.com*) is one of the most popular rickshaw operators, and around 30% of the drivers are women in their 20s who build up a following on socials. **Miyu Iijima** (*@miyu chimu_rickshaw*) is one such driver. She says her impetus to start was actually trying it herself as a tourist: 'The driver was so kind and welcoming and I thought, I want to be someone who gives that kind of warm impression.'

She says her job involves rickshaw operations, learning about the history, hospitality and physical training, but most of the skill is in maintaining balance. She says the best thing about the Asakusa area are the people.

'Locals are very warm and encouraging. You often hear nearby shopkeepers yelling "keep it up!"'.

at 350m, the other at 450m. The 360-degree views you get across the city and out to Tokyo Bay are truly spectacular. The best time to go is just before sunset – head up while it's light to see Tokyo in all its glory, then watch the city lights go on as the sun creeps below the horizon.

A Day at Skytree

MAP P187

Sky-high entertainment

Tokyo Skytree (p186) (*tokyo-skytree.jp*) draws most people in with its awesome architecture and commanding views of the city – on the observatory deck, you're at the highest point of this densely populated metropolis, and from up here, buildings look like matchboxes, and cars are but mere specks.

After a trip up the tower, venture beneath the structure to **Tokyo Solamachi** (東京ソラマチ; *tokyo-solamachi.jp*), a shopping and entertainment complex that's a popular destination for locals and tourists, particularly those with children. Aside from the shops (over 300 mostly midrange Japanese and international brands) and restaurants, the **Sumida Aquarium** (*sumida-aquarium.com; adult ¥2500, child from ¥800*)

EATING IN ASAKUSA & SUMIDA: BEST NAKAMISE SNACKS —— MAP P191

Funawa Nakamise Shop: A selection of sweet potato *wagashi*. Try the soft serve with its divine texture. *10am-6pm* ¥

Tokiwadō Kaminari-okoshi: Puffed rice crackers going back to the Edo era in flavours like green tea and almond. *10am-6.30pm* ¥

Kimuraya Ningyō-yaki: Sweet sponge cakes made in a metal mould in front of your eyes, filled with red bean. *10am-6.30pm* ¥

Nakamise Kineya: Delicious salted rice crackers with an unique texture – it's difficult to stop eating them. *9.30am-6.30pm* ¥

Tokyo Skytree

and a **planetarium** *(planetarium.konicaminolta.jp, adult/ child ¥1800/1200)* are also located here, plus there's a sizeable play area on the 5th floor.

For souvenirs, head down to the 4th floor, where you'll find franchise stores for some of Japan's most popular gifts. Shopping here can feel somewhat less authentic than buying similar items elsewhere, but it's good when you're short on time or need to get some last-minute purchases. Pop-culture aficionados will want to stop by the **Pokémon Centre** *(pokemon.co. jp/shop/pokecen/skytreetown)* and the adorable **Kirby Café** *(kirbycafe.jp)*. There's even more character merchandise elsewhere in the building – near the food court are stores dedicated to beloved characters like Snoopy, Miffy and Rilakkuma. And if all that browsing and shopping is leaving you peckish, there's a wonderful selection of sweets and confectioneries on the 2nd floor. Other dining options are also plentiful here; light bites are on the 1st floor, and restaurants are on the 6th. But for those special occasions, there's no better place to celebrate than the restaurants with a view, halfway up Tokyo Skytree, on the 30th to 32nd floors.

THE FOOD OF EDO

Four foods are said to be representative of **Edo food culture**: sushi, tempura, *unagi* (eel) and soba. That's not to say that these foods didn't exist prior to the Edo period – *unagi*, for example, is believed to have been consumed since ancient times – but the Edo period was when these dishes were perfected.

A common theme among Edo dishes is the use of fresh seafood as the main ingredient, usually taken straight from the bay and prepared quickly and simply in order to negate the need for refrigeration.

People also used great amounts of rice at this time, with the average person consuming up to 5 *gō* (about 750g uncooked) of rice per day.

EATING IN ASAKUSA & SUMIDA: BEST VEGAN

MAPS P187 & P191

Sasaya Cafe: Spacious cafe in a converted warehouse with a terrace area; delicious vegan plates. *8.30am-6pm Mon-Sun* ¥

Vegan Cafe PQ's: Big but cosy option that specialises in photogenic, colourful curries. Also a queer-friendly space. *11am-5pm Thu-Mon* ¥

Bon: Well presented, sophisticated vegan meals inspired by Buddhist cuisine. *noon-3pm & 6-9pm Mon,Tue & Fri, noon-3pm & 5-8 pm Sat & Sun* ¥¥

Marugoto Vegan Dining Asakusa: Simple comfort vegan meals such as plates and curries. *11.30am-3pm & 6-9pm* ¥

Shopping at Kappabashi

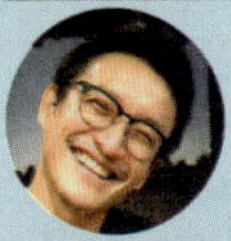

MAP P191

Stock up your kitchens

Whether you're a professional in search of state-of-the-art tools or a home cook looking to purchase that special utensil that'll last a lifetime, **Kappabashi-dōri** (かっぱ橋道具街) is the place to go. Straddling the neighbourhoods of Asakusa and Ueno, this 800m street specialises in all things culinary – you'll know you're here when you see the huge statue of a chef looking down from his perch atop a building.

Along the street and in the side alleys are approximately 160 stores stocking everything from knives, kitchen gadgets and lacquerware to pots, souvenirs and – most interesting of all – plastic food samples. Inside these plastic-food-sample shops, you'll find the ultra-realistic bowls of noodles so often seen outside restaurants in the city; some are available as souvenirs for you to take home. Outlets like **Ganzo Shokuhin Sample-ya** (*ganso-sample.com/en*) also hold workshops (*¥3000*) for visitors to try their hand at making one of these food samples in-store, though sessions are held only in Japanese.

Start at the excellent **Dengama** (*dengama.jp*) ceramics store and make your way up the road. Along the way, there is the excellent **Hashito** (*hashitou.co.jp*), which is like a museum of chopsticks with various wood types. **Tsuchi-ya** (*tsuchi-ya.jp*) has a beautiful selection of glassware, including Edo-*kiriko* cut glass, made in Sumida. **Majimaya** (*majimaya.com*) has a ginormous selection of baking goods, with hundreds of cookie moulds, and **Kanaya Brush** (*kanaya-brush.com*) sells traditional brushes for calligraphy, beauty and cleaning. There's an English map and directory of Kappabashi's shops available to download (*kappabashi.or.jp/en/*).

Marvel at Traditional Japanese Arts

MAP P187

Swords, glass and woodblock prints

In the Edo era (1603–1868), the neighbourhoods of present-day Asakusa and Sumida River were part of an area known as *shitamachi*: this was where the common people lived, and where many merchants and artisans set up their stores and studios. The legacy of Edo-era crafts is still visible today in the Sumida area, from textiles to dolls to hair ornaments.

Ukiyo-e, or 'pictures of the floating world', are prints made using meticulously carved blocks of wood that were popular during the Edo period. None are more recognisable than

continues on p194

DRINKING IN KURAMAE: BEST CAFES

MAP P191

Dandelion Chocolate: Enjoy a coffee or hot chocolate with a delectable selection of chocolate made in its factory. *10am-7pm*

Coffee Wrights Kuramae: Roastery and quaint upstairs cafe with a constantly changing selection of single origin roasts. *11am-4pm Wed-Fri, 10am-5.30pm Sat & Sun*

marble Kuramae: Stylish designer cafe with delicious cheesecakes. Has a quiet ambience and is perfect for relaxing with a book. *9am-7pm*

Hatcoffee: Supremely cute latte 3D art specialists; they can also do dog portraits if you show them a pet photo. *10am-9pm Tue-Sun*

HIGHLIGHTS
1 Sensō-ji

SIGHTS
2 Kaminari-mon

SLEEPING
3 Asakusa Saunaland
4 Asakusa View Hotel

EATING
5 Asakusa Midori Sushi
6 Funawa Nakamise Shop
7 Irokawa Unagi
8 Kimuraya Ningyō-yaki
9 Marugoto Vegan Dining Asakusa
10 Nakamise Kineya
11 Namiki Yabusoba
12 Tokiwadō Kaminari-okoshi

DRINKING & NIGHTLIFE
13 Coffee Wrights Kuramae
14 Dandelion Chocolate
15 Hatcoffee
16 Leaves Coffee Roasters
17 marble Kuramae

SHOPPING
see 8 Bunkoya Ōzeki
18 Dengama
19 Ganzo Shokuhin Sample-ya
20 Hashito
21 hibi 10 Minutes Aroma
22 Jiyūcho
23 Kanaya Brush
see 20 Kappabashi-dōri
24 Kurodaya
25 Maito Kuramae Store
26 Majimaya
27 mt lab.
28 Nakamura Tea Life Store
29 Proto Utsuwa to Takaramono
30 Sakai Kokodō Ukiyo-e Gallery
see 8 ukeroku
31 Tsuchi-ya

191

Sensō-ji

TOP EXPERIENCE

Sensō-ji

Tokyo's oldest temple, Sensō-ji, is to the city what the Colosseum is to Rome: you simply have to see it. Built in the 7th century, the temple enshrines Kannon, the Goddess of Mercy (hence why it's also known as Asakusa Kannon-dō). Legend says that the original Kannon statue for which the temple was built was fished out of the Sumida River.

DON'T MISS

Kaminari-mon

Kannon-dō

Five-Storey Pagoda

Nakamise-dōri

Omikuji

Kimono rental

Nakamise-dōri

While the 250m avenue **Nakamise-dōri** (仲見世通り) leading up to the temple is mostly rife with souvenir kitsch (think nylon kimonos), there are still many gems that reflects the districts' artisanal legacy such as **Kurodaya,** a paper shop with handcrafted paper, **Bunkoya Ōzeki** leather shop (just adjacent to the main strip), the **Sakai Kokodō Ukiyo-e Gallery**, and **Sukeroku**, a folk toy store that specialises in auspicious miniature figurines. The street also has numerous traditional snacks.

PRACTICALITIES

- *senso-ji.jp/english*
- free
- grounds 24hr

Kaminari-mon

Kaminari-mon (雷門) is your gateway to the temple. You'll see a gigantic red lantern hanging above the entrance, almost close enough to touch. The lantern weights an impressive 700kg; step right up to it to see an intricately carved dragon on its underside. Flanking the doorway are statues of two deities: Fujin, the God of Wind, and Raijin, the God of Thunder. Both are enshrined as protectors of the gate (against natural disasters). The original gate was built in 942 CE and has been rebuilt several times – the current incarnation dates back to 1960.

Five-Storied Pagoda

As you continue towards the main temple hall, a pagoda emerges into view from the left. Known simply as the **Five-Storied Pagoda** (五重塔), the structure was first built in 942 CE along with the original Kaminari-mon, but fires and disasters over the centuries have seen it rebuilt multiple times. The pagoda was considered to be one of the city's finest during the Edo period and was an important landmark of Asakusa that appeared often in art of the time. The top storey of the tower houses a **Śarīra** – a relic of the Buddha's remains.

Kannon-do

Breathe in the incense as you approach **Kannon-do**, the Main Hall, then climb the steps and enter the worship area. If you'd like to make an offering, drop a coin into the wooden box at the top of the steps. Originally built by the third shogun, Tokugawa Iemitsu, Kannon-do was a designated National Treasure before it was destroyed in WWII air raids – the structure that stands today was rebuilt in 1958. There is an altar in the temple's outer sanctum, while the temple's namesake, the goddess Kannon, is enshrined within its inner sanctum.

Omikuji

Part of the quintessential Japanese temple experience is getting an *omikuji* – a written form of fortune telling. There are silver canisters and numbered cabinets within the halls of Kannon-do and in its outer courtyard. Getting your fortune told is a matter of dropping ¥100 into a wooden box, shaking the canister until a numbered stick falls out, then checking its corresponding cabinet drawer. The slip of paper found inside will have your fortune written on it in English and Japanese. Don't be dismayed if you get a bad fortune, locals in the know will warn you that Sensō-ji is notorious for it. Just fold the paper up and tie it to a rack nearby to ward the misfortune away.

KIMONO RENTALS

While there are concerns about cultural appropriation, Japanese locals are more than overjoyed to see tourists wearing and appreciating kimonos. Many services offer photoshoots with authentic kimono and *yukata* (lighter versions) in the Asakusa area (it's highly recommended that you don't try to do it yourself). The selection and styling is all part of the fun and they suit all body types. **Inkimono** in Asakusa take excellent photos of the kimonos they style.

TOP TIPS

● Sensō-ji is almost always crowded. You'll have a bit more breathing space earlier in the day or at night as the lights stay on until 11pm. Without the crowds, the temple is wonderfully atmospheric.

● Go during festival time when you can see the true gusto of downtown Tokyo come alive. Aside from the major festivals, there are many fairs, like the resplendent **Hagoita** (shuttlecock) fair in December and the **Chinese Lantern Plant** fair in July.

● A lot of the souvenirs sold at Nakamise-dōri are similar; get a good look on your way to the Main Hall, then shop on your way out.

COMMUNITY IN KYOJIMA

Ayumu Haitani, muumuu cafe owner, Kyojima, Sumida.

I moved here because I was able to rent an old property at a low cost with the freedom to renovate, which made it easier to try out ideas. Through that, I've also met many people who share similar values. There are many in the community who value communication and mutual respect and I think the connections are maintained in a loose, comfortable way.

I think Kyojima is a really unique area with all kinds of people, and a sense of connection that's largely influenced by the buildings and layout that have remained since the area was spared from wartime destruction. Compared to newer houses, which prioritise privacy, the older houses naturally bring people closer together.

continued from p190

The Great Wave off Kanagawa, which depicts an enormous sweeping wave alongside Mt Fuji. Its artist, Katsushika Hokusai, was born in Sumida, and the neighbourhood is where he spent a large portion of his long life. The **Sumida Hokusai Museum** (すみだ北斎美術館; *hokusai-museum.jp; adult/child ¥1500/free*) in Ryōgoku takes you through the artist's life and works through his prints (replicas) and interactive displays. It also features a model of Hokusai's former studio in Sumida. In the same neighbourhood is the **Japanese Sword Museum** (刀剣博物館; *touken.or.jp/museum; adult/child ¥1000/free*), which houses swords ranging from the centuries-old to more modern creations. Some of those on display are National Treasures, with blades that are sharp and pristine, despite their age.

Next door is the **Kyū-Yasuda-teien**, a compact and resplendent Japanese-style garden which dates back to 1691 (an excellent view is available from the 2nd floor verandah of the Sword Museum).

For a peek at more accessible art pieces, it's worth making a trip to the **Sumida Edo Kiriko Museum** (すみだ江戸切子館; *edokiriko.net; free*) – it's small and really more of a shop, but it's one of the few speciality stores in the city keeping the late-Edo-period artform of *kiriko* (cut glass) alive. It's also where you'll see real craftspeople at work, cutting intricate designs and traditional motifs into glassware. They do workshops here, too, where you can try your hand at creating Edo-*kiriko* glass – it makes for a nice personalised souvenir.

Step Back into Old Edo
MAP P187

Edo life and history

The **Edo-Tokyo Museum** (江戸東京博物館; *edo-tokyo-museum.or.jp*) isn't just great for history buffs – detailing the story of the capital from the Edo period to the modern day, it's an essential visit for anyone interested in getting a more in-depth understanding of the city and how it's been shaped by its past. The museum is right next to Ryōgoku Kokugikan (p186).

A five-minute walk away is the sombre **Yokoamicho Park** (*tokyoireikyoukai.or.jp*), home to the **Tokyo Metropolitan Memorial Hall**, designed by architect Chuta Ito, which commemorates the 58,000 victims of the Great Kantō Earthquake of 1923 and the WWII bombings. It's an impressive building, and the video that plays on loop inside shows footage of these events.

The park also has the **Great Kantō Earthquake Memorial Museum** (*free*), an excellent history exhibition with artefacts from these tragedies, as well as photojournalism and artworks by citizens. As harrowing as these events were, these monuments give a deeper understanding of the city and the mentality of the people.

Kyū-Yasuda-teien

Crafts & Coffee at Kuramae

MAPS P187 & P191

The modern artisan district

Despite its proximity to ever-bustling Asakusa, **Kuramae** is quiet, even on weekends. This neighbourhood is where many artisans and craftspeople have their studios, and many small factories and manufacturers are headquartered here, giving Kuramae a reputation of being a 'maker's town'. Numerous shops and studios are in close proximity to each other, in particular a plethora of leather-ware stores (see p246 for more). If you appreciate great design and love elegant, handmade items, it's here you'll find that special piece for your wardrobe, that perfect pen for your writing desk, or that small-batch roasted coffee for your morning joe.

Begin your journey at stationery store **Kakimori** (カキモリ; *kakimori.com*) – there's a beautifully illustrated map of the neighbourhood available for free here, featuring notable shops and studios in the area. Kakimori makes beautiful pens and custom notebooks that are very popular among locals – you'll need a reservation to get your own custom-designed notebook made on weekends. Right upstairs is **Ink Stand**, where you can blend your own one-of-a-kind ink. On the way there, you'll also pass by **Jiyūcho** (*jiyucho.tokyo*), a little letter shop where you can write a letter to your future self (reservation required). Also nearby is **Tsubame Kobo**, where you'll find hand-dyed and woven scarves.

For an afternoon pick-me-up, grab a coffee at **Leaves Coffee Roasters** – the beans are fresh from their own little roastery nearby. Tea drinkers can check out **Nakamura Tea Life Store** for organic green tea – direct from the owner's farm in Shizuoka – that comes in cool tin canisters.

BEST ARTISAN SHOPS IN KURAMAE

Proto Utsuwa to Takaramono: A ceramics and decorative craft store with mini exhibitions featuring up-and-coming makers.

Maito Kuramae Store: Every piece of clothing in this boutique is made from organic materials, and it's all hand-dyed in Japan using natural dyes derived from plants.

SyuRo: Homeware shop stocked with pieces by local artisans that are built to last. Products range from interior accents to personal care items.

hibi 10MINUTES AROMA: hibi is an incense store that sells matches that give off exquisite scents, combining matchmaking from Harima with traditional incense from Awaji.

mt lab.: A *washi* (Japanese paper) masking tape emporium, featuring tape of every iteration that can be used for letter writing, home decoration, journals and art.

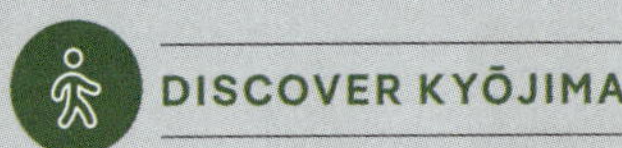

DISCOVER KYŌJIMA

Discover Kyōjima, a small community in Sumida ward that was largely spared from fire bombings.

START	END	LENGTH
Art & Nepal	Denki-yu	1.5km; 1½hr

Kyōjima is dense with tiny alleyways and cul-de-sacs, packed with streetlife both human and feline. Recently it has seen many creators and artists go to great lengths to retrofit old buildings to save the area from development and fortify a sense of local community.

Start at ❶ **Art & Nepal**, a Nepali restaurant inside a traditional *kōminka* house that doubles as an art space called Kyojima Eki. On either side of the street are examples of post-war **nagaya**, a type of vernacular wooden row house that once accommodated artisans and labourers. Go down *kendama yokochō* street to visit ❷ **muumuu cafe**. Other spaces on the same road with DIY

upgrades include tea shop ❸ **Satellite Kitchen**, and ❹ **wn penguin**, an upcycling shop.

Further along is a traditional linear shopping street called **Kira Kira Shotengai**, where there are numerous art studios and shops, such as ❺ **Kamos**, an indie bookstore, ❻ **NANZO**, a ceramics and art space inside a former futon bedding store, and ❼ **Maskshop OMOTE**, a shop selling both traditional and contemporary masks. Don't miss the traditional eateries still going strong that line these streets. The walk can end at ❽ **Denki-yu**, a spacious *sentō* public bathhouse that is known for appearing in the Wim Wenders film *Perfect Days*.

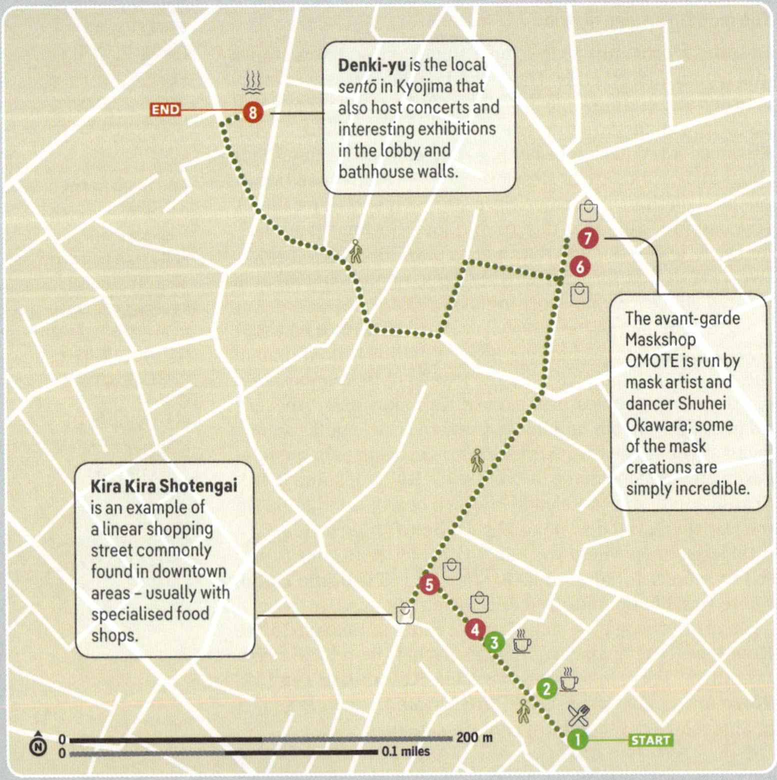

Sanja Matsuri

Causes for Celebration

MAP P191

Festivals in Asakusa

If you find yourself in town when it's *matsuri* (festival) season, then you're in for a treat. Many of these celebrations are grand affairs that draw massive crowds, and in Tokyo, few are bigger and more extravagant than those in Asakusa.

At Sensō-ji (p192), it starts with **hatsumōde**. At midnight on 31 December, the bell at Bentenyama within the temple grounds is struck 108 times to usher in the new year, a ritual that takes about 40 minutes to complete and draws massive crowds. **Setsubun** is a day in February that marks the beginning of spring. It's Japanese custom to throw beans on this day – a ritual believed to ward off demons and bad luck. Here, notable figures and even celebrities get involved, flinging beans off a raised platform to the crowds below.

One of Tokyo's largest festivals, **Sanja Matsuri**, a Shintō festival dedicated to the founders of Sensō-ji, sees over two million spectators. Occurring in May, rowdy festival enthusiasts carry *mikoshi* (portable shrines) through the streets. Over the three days of bedlam, expect to see *taiko* (drum) performances, dancers, local geisha and *matsuri* participants with full body tattoos in celebration mode.

Tokyo's festivals often occur in summer – the **Shitamachi Tanabata Matsuri**, around July 7th; the **Tōrō Nagashi**, mid-August when candle-lit lanterns are placed into Sumida River; and the **Sumida River Fireworks Festival**, on the last Saturday of July. Huge crowds donned in gorgeous summer *yukata* (cotton kimonos) gather to watch the pyrotechnics, but even from afar, it's possible to see these impressive explosions. During the month of August, many of the local temples and shrines also host **Bon Odori** dance festivals.

ASAKUSA INK

At Sanja Matsuri, no doubt one of the most impactful sights is that of spirited locals showing **full-body tattoo suits** while wearing *fundoshi* loincloths. Japanese tattooing has a long history in the district since the Edo era, alongside the culture of *ukiyo-e* woodblock prints.

Many of the dramatic tattoos seen at Sanja Matsuri are by Asakusa Horikazu — both the late father and son.

'The dramatic motifs found in Japanese tattooing are predominantly based on *ukiyo-e*,' Horikazu explains. 'Before *matsuri* season is the busiest time for me and people are eager to complete their suits to show them off.'

Horikazu uses the *tebori* (hand poked) technique. He describes the *sumi* ink used for the work as something that is 'alive' and gradually improves with time.

'The black settles to produce a blueish patina – that is the indelible quality of Japanese traditional tattoos.'

Researched by Rob Goss

ODAIBA & TOKYO BAY

CUTTING-EDGE ART, ONSEN AND FAMILY FUN

The capital's bayside features numerous attractions, from theme parks and shopping centres to a thriving fish market, hot-spring baths, visionary art works and canal-side galleries.

In the last few decades, Tokyo Bay (東京湾) has undergone a renaissance of sorts. Once industrial, Tennōzu Isle (often called Tennoz) has become an arty hangout with multiple major galleries. Similarly, Toyosu is now home to fancy apartment blocks, a sprawling mega mall, and popular attractions like Toyosu Market and the teamLab Planets digital art museum. And what to say about Odaiba (お台場)? An artificial island built in the 1800s as part of the Tokyo's defences, it's now (after periods of disuse) one of the city's most attraction-packed family days out – the place to find amusement centres, kid-friendly museums, and plenty more.

TIP

If possible, time your visit to Odaiba and Tokyo Bay with one of the many festivals held here, including Tennoz Canal Fes (spring); Odaiba Lantern Festival (July); ArtBay Tokyo Art Festival (September); Fiesta Mexicana (September); Hawaiian-style Aloha Nui Festival (dates vary); and Rainbow Fireworks Festival (December).

FROM LEFT: KAVRAM/SHUTTERSTOCK, HIROSHI-MORI-STOCK/SHUTTERSTOCK

Odaiba

See page 221 for places to stay in in Odaiba & Tokyo Bay

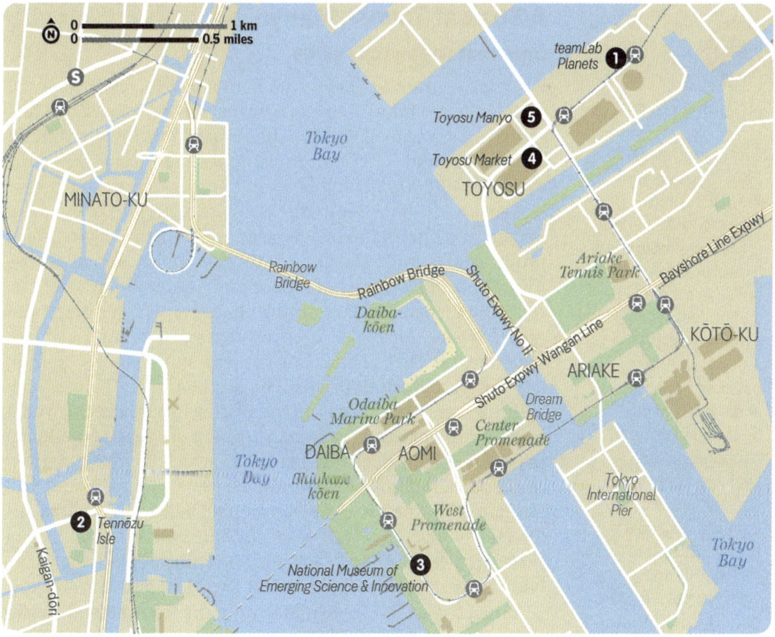

⭐ Highlights

❶ teamLab Planets

Immerse yourself in digital art installations and sensorial explosions of a mind-boggling nature. **p203**

❷ Tennōzu Isle

Explore a bayfront island host to numerous festivals and dotted with contemporary galleries. **p205**

❸ National Museum of Emerging Science & Innovation

Endless futuristic exhibits pushing the boundaries of cosmic possibilities. **p203**

◀ ❹ Toyosu Market

Get up super early for the tuna auction and piles of feast-worthy fresh sushi. **p200**

❺ Toyosu Manyo

Take a soothing soak in this high-rise bathhouse with sweeping city views. **p200**

🚶 Getting Around

Subway

Use the Rinkai line for Tennōzu Isle. It also has a couple of stops in Odaiba – Tokyo Teleport Station and Kokusai Tenjijō Station. The Yurakuchō line serves Toyosu and Tsukishima.

Train

The Yurikamome line, running between Shimbashi and Toyosu, has multiple stops in Odaiba. It comes with great bay views as it crosses Rainbow Bridge

Walking

Once you are in Tennōzu Isle, Odaiba or Toyosu, it's easy to get around each area on foot. You'll only need public transport to go between these main districts.

MONJA STREET

One station away from Toyosu on the Yurakuchō subway line, the Tsukishima (月島) neighbourhood is known for one of Tokyo's most distinctive dishes – **monjayaki** (もんじゃ焼き). A runny batter of flour, water and *dashi* that can be mixed with diced cabbage, meat, seafood, cheese, and numerous other combos, it's cooked on a griddle plate until gooey and sticky, then you eat it off the griddle using little metal spatulas that never quite seem to give you quite enough of the moreish *monja* in one mouthful.

If you want to know how popular it is, Tsukishima's aptly named Monja Street is home to 50 or so *monjayaki* specialists (many also serving *okonomiyaki* pancakes). Despite so much competition, they seemingly do a roaring trade.

A Soak at Toyosu Manyo

MAP P201

Onsen bathing and city views

Previous visitors to Tokyo who bemoaned the closure of the popular Tokyo Edo Monogatari onsen will be delighted at this spanking-new, albeit smaller spa across from Toyosu Market: **Toyosu Manyo** (豊洲万葉; *tokyo-toyosu.manyo.co.jp; adult/child ¥3850/2000*). You'll be even happier that one part of it is free – a 7th-floor footbath with views across to Rainbow Bridge and the high-rise cityscape of central Tokyo. For a proper soak, pay for the main bathing complex. Spread across nine floors, it has a mix of indoor and outdoor baths, saunas, relaxation rooms with reclining chairs, a manga library and places where (for extra fees) you can get Thai and Chinese massages. It isn't cheap, but you can cut costs by coming early: it's almost half price if you are in and out before 9am.

The process of visiting is an interesting experience too: you'll be asked to change into a *yukata* gown or *samue* (similar to pyjamas) and be given a locker key to which anything you buy in the souvenir store, cafe or elsewhere in the bathhouse will be charged for payment upon leaving. Unlike many baths, it's also tattoo-friendly. Well, sort of. Staff will sell you stickers (*¥110 each*) to cover body art, and you can enter as long as any body art can all be covered by just two 11cm by 20cm stickers.

Connected to the Toyosu Manyo is the Edo-themed **Senkyaku Banrai** (千客万来; *toyosu-senkyakubanrai.jp*), which has three floors of restaurants and a few shops. There's lots to choose from, including sushi, but except for a few noodle joints and sweet sellers, you will be paying a substantial tourist premium to eat here. If you visit Toyosu Manyo as part of the Toyosu walk on p204, you'll find a good selection of restaurants with better prices at LaLaport, about 20 minutes away.

Get up Early for Toyosu Market

MAP P201

The iconic tuna auction

Following its relocation from Tsukiji Market in 2018, the morning tuna auction at **Toyosu Market** (ザ・豊洲市場; *toyosu-market.or.jp/en; free*) is now more of an organised (some might stay sterile) affair compared to the chaos of days past. Still, if you don't mind getting up early, it's worth observing the live event – which gets started around 5.30am – even if it's now happening behind glass windows.

No reservation is required to watch from two floors above the auction floor, where you'll be away from the smells and

EATING IN ODAIBA & THE BAYSIDE: OUR PICKS

MAPS P201 & 202

Monja Kondō: Opened in 1950, the oldest *monja* restaurant in Tsukishima is still one of the most popular. *5-10pm Mon-Fri, from 11.30am Sat & Sun* ¥¥

Ramen Kokugikan: This area in Odaiba's Aqua City complex brings together six popular ramen restaurants, each serving a different style. *11am-8pm Mon-Fri, to 9pm Sat & Sun* ¥

Soholm: French-inspired menu of meat and seasonal vegetables, with natural wines and craft beer in verdant surroundings. *11am-4pm & 5-9pm Thu-Tue* ¥¥

TY Harbor Brewery: Stylish canal-side complex with fusion restaurant and onsite craft-beer brewery. *11.30am-3pm & 5.30-10pm Mon-Fri, 11.30am-4pm & 5.30-10pm Sat & Sun* ¥¥

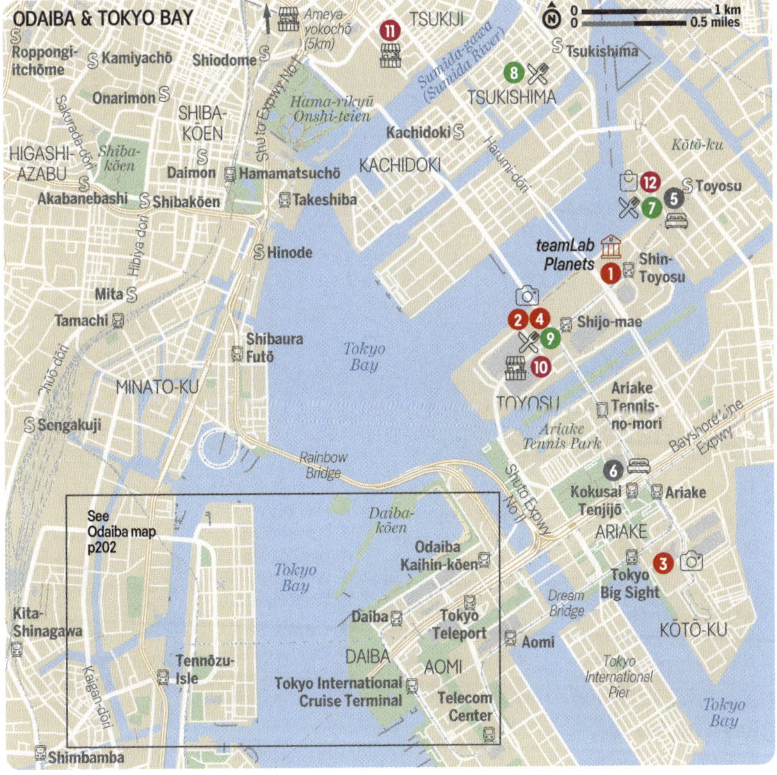

THE GUIDE

ODAIBA & TOKYO BAY

EATING IN ODAIBA & TOKYO BAY: COFFEE OR A SNACK — MAPS P201 & 202

Blue Bottle Coffee Toyosu: Grab espresso, matcha latte or a grilled sandwich at this waterside cafe by Urban Dock LaLaport. *8am-7pm* ¥

Breadworks Tennoz: A bakery-cafe in the TY Harbor building, serving coffee, tea and herbal infusions, along with patisseries and light meals. *8am-8pm* ¥

Toyosu Naraya: On the ground floor of the Senkyaku Banrai complex, Naraya has *teishoku* (set meals) and desserts like parfait with matcha ice cream. *10am-10pm* ¥

Decora Creamery: Multicoloured candy floss that you can even order as a topping for soft-serve ice cream. *11am-8.30pm Mon-Fri, 10am-9.30pm Sat & Sun* ¥

sounds of the proceedings. You'll need to apply in advance via an online lottery system, however, to visit the observation deck, located just above the auction floor. While this is also partially separated by a pane of glass, it nonetheless provides an authentic sensory experience.

One thing to keep in mind is that the auctions kick off before the trains starts running, so unless you are staying nearby, you'll need to budget for a taxi to get there. If you are more interested in strolling around lively market stalls, head to Tsukiji Outer Market (p75) or Ameya-yokochō (p179) instead.

Creative Events at Tokyo Big Sight   MAP P201

Amazing events all year

Located near Ariake Station, **Tokyo Big Sight** (東京ビッグサイト) is a sprawling convention centre that's won numerous awards for its construction and design, which most notably features a main building that looks like it's made with four inverted pyramids. Japan's largest venue of its kind, it packs a busy year-round calendar. Annual events include the Design Festa extravaganza – Asia's largest art-themed gathering – which is held in both spring and autumn and attracts creative types in numerous genres; AnimeJapan, which brings together anime and manga professionals, cosplayers and fans from across the globe in March, and Comiket, which does the same in both summer and winter; and the Tokyo Marathon Expo, featuring running gear and apparel, held in late February.

Futuristic Art at teamLab Planets   MAP P201

Mind-bending digital exhibits

Created by the teamLab collective, and a sister exhibit to teamLab Borderless in Azubadai Hills, the Toyosu digital art installation of **teamLab Planets** (チームラボプラネッツ; *teamlab.art; adult/child from ¥3600/1500*) similarly provides a sensorial explosion via truly fantastical imagery and experiences. The rooms are all differently themed, with one consisting of knee-deep water through which you walk barefoot amid darting koi and blooming flowers, and another where you are surrounded by multicoloured bouncing spheres. The ambient music also adds to the otherworldly effect. Just be sure to book in well advance.

Science Made Fun at the Miraikan   MAP P202

Universe-probing exhibits

Kids and adults alike will find something to love at this cutting-edge Odaiba museum. Known in Japanese as **Miraikan** (未来館; *miraikan.jst.go.jp; adult/child ¥630/210*) and known elsewhere as the **National Museum of Emerging Science & Innovation**, the mind-expanding installations cover everything from 3D simulations of Earth spinning out into space to a dome theatre (extra fee) exploring the concept of inter-dimensionality. Additional exhibits include a replica of the International Space Station, and a model that does a deep-dive into the workings of the internet. It's all very hands-on and comes with ample English explanations and guidance. But, if you've got used to the idea that museums and galleries in Japan tend to close on Mondays, the Miraikan has a trick up its sleeve: it closes Tuesdays.

Family Fun in Odaiba   MAP P202

Child-friendly attractions and nature

If you fancy a fun, family day out, take the Yurikamome line over **Rainbow Bridge** (レインボーブリッジ) to the Odaiba waterfront, where entertainment comes in all shapes and sizes. In particular, you'll find three huge malls here that are ideal for keeping kids busy on a rainy (or hot) day – DiverCity, Decks Tokyo Beach and Aqua City Odaiba. Each is full of not just stores and restaurants, but also amusement centres and museums.

At **DiverCity** (ダイバーシティ東京プラザ; *mitsui-shopping -park.com/divercity-tokyo*), toddlers will appreciate the small **Unko Museum** (*unkomuseum.com; adult/child from ¥2000/1100*), which manages to connect the bodily function of poop with Japan's *kawaii* (cute) culture through displays that include dung-shaped animals and a poop factory.

CENTURIES OF RECLAMATION

Tokyo Bay has been a work in progress for centuries. Reclamation began in the 1590s, when landfill from Edo Castle was used to house the Tokugawa shogunate's large entourage of warriors, artisans and merchants.

Jump forward to 1853, when US Commodore Matthew Perry's warships steamed into Edo Bay, demanding Japan open its borders to trade, and the Japanese responded by creating six cannon-laden islands – known as Odaiba.

During subsequent decades, mountains of waste were then piled into Tokyo Bay to make additional islands and piers. These included Toyosu, from where energy companies powered the ever-growing metropolis. Others were used to distribute supplies following the Great Kantō Earthquake in 1923 and wartime air raids in 1945.

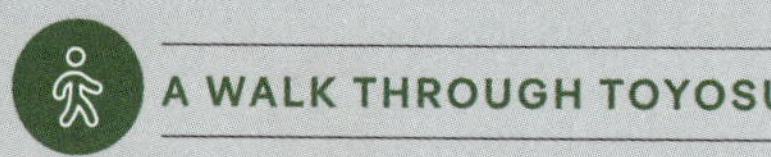

A WALK THROUGH TOYOSU

This walk mixes a couple of Toyosu's big attractions with some local vibes and one of Tokyo's signature budget feeds.

START	END	LENGTH
Shijo-mae Station	Tsukishima Station	4km; 3hr

Once you come out of ❶ **Shijo-mae Station**, you'll be just a few minutes from ❷ **Toyosu Manyo** (p200), where you could enjoy a free, rooftop footbath or pay for a dip in a soothing hot-spring. After that, head east along the main road to Shin-Toyosu Station, next to which is the superb ❸ **teamLab Planets** (p203) and its immersive digital art installations.

Just Toyosu Manyo and teamLab can make for a full morning or afternoon out, but if you want to stretch your legs a bit, follow the waterside path east to Toyosu for ❹ **Urban Dock LaLaport**, a mega-mall packed with stores selling high-street

fashions, sporting goods, cosmetics and interior goods. It also has restaurants, a cinema and other attractions, and it'll give you an insight into how some Tokyoites spend their downtime.

After that, go north, initially following the riverbank and then heading over ❺ **Harumi Bridge**, and you'll soon be in Tsukishima, a residential area built (like most of the bay area) on reclaimed land. Tsukishima's claim to fame is a dish called *monjayaki* (p200), which you can get from one of 50 specialist restaurants on or near ❻ **Monja Street** (p200). Once fed, you're only a few minutes from ❼ **Tsukishima Station**.

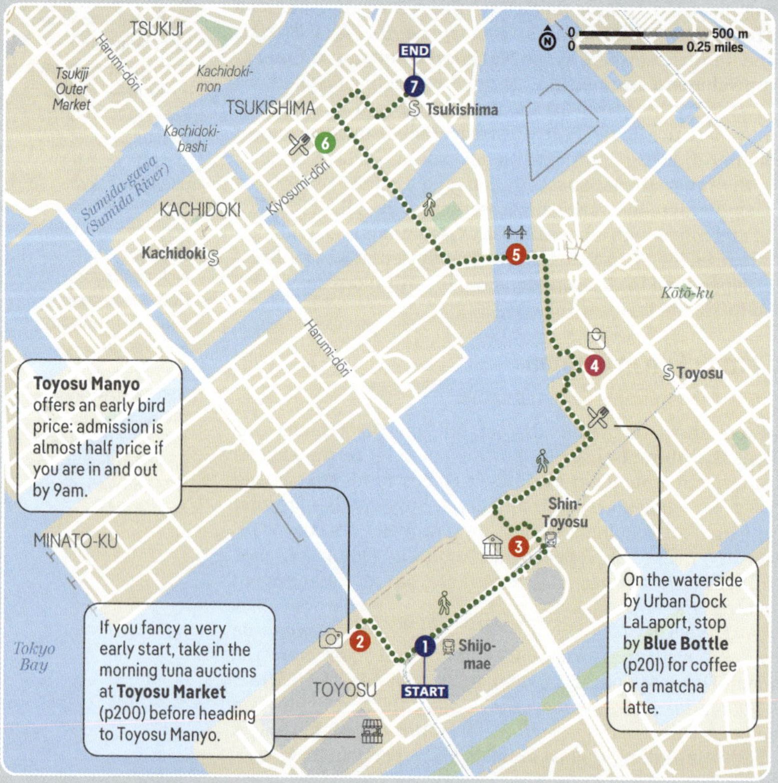

Toyosu Manyo offers an early bird price: admission is almost half price if you are in and out by 9am.

If you fancy a very early start, take in the morning tuna auctions at **Toyosu Market** (p200) before heading to Toyosu Manyo.

On the waterside by Urban Dock LaLaport, stop by **Blue Bottle** (p201) for coffee or a matcha latte.

Fronting the DiverCity complex, you'll also see the the 20m-high **Unicorn Gundam** statue, which switches into destroyer mode 10 times a day – the night-time shows are best, as they include video projections.

A little to the north, **Decks Tokyo Beach** (デックス東京ビーチ; *odaiba-decks.com*) is home to **Tokyo Joypolis** (*tokyo-joypolis.com; 1-day passport adult/child ¥5800/4800*), an indoor amusement centre offering VR experiences alongside plentiful rides and games. On the same floor is a compact **Legoland Discovery Centre** (*legolanddiscoverycenter.com/tokyo; from ¥3000)* that's geared to smaller children. Next to Decks, **Aqua City Odaiba** (アクアシティお台場; *aquacity.jp*) is less action-packed, but is where you'll find Ramen Kokugikan (p200), if you want to try multiple types of ramen under the same roof. Afterwards, you aren't far from the National Museum of Emerging Science & Innovation (p203), where you can add some educational fun to the day.

Art Offerings along Tennōzu Isle MAP P202

Thriving art scene and scenic waterways

A tiny island encircled by canals, and one of the few remnants of the 1850s' fortresses built to protect the city, **Tennōzu Isle** (天王洲アイル) has seen several large-scale conversions. Most recently, it transformed from an industrial district to a burgeoning art hub that makes full use of its attractive waterways. Central to this story are the behemoth Terrada Warehouses, built by the Terrada family after they purchased the remains of a local factory destroyed by WWII bombings. When Tokyo Bay underwent redevelopment in the 1990s, the languishing warehouses were infused with new life, as they were used to store luxury items such as art and wine. The former, in particular, is central to Terrada's forward-thinking vision, which makes Tennōzu Isle great for an afternoon of gallery-hopping.

A good place to start is the **Terrada Art Complex** (*terrada-art-complex.com; usually free, some exhibitions charge admission)*, a pair of warehouses that feature rotating content at more than a dozen onsite showrooms. These include the **Maki Gallery** (*makigallery.com)*, whose past shows have included Anomaly, which involved 'building burgers', created by edgy art-collective Chim-Pom in an open interrogation of Tokyo's never-ending cycle of demolition and construction. After that, you can stroll to more Terrada-run venues and spaces nearby, including the **WHAT Museum** (*what.warehouseofart.org; adult/child ¥1500/free)* for exhibitions from the warehouse collections; **WHAT café** (*cafe.warehouseofart.org; free)*, which sells work from up-and-coming artists; and **Pigment Tokyo** (*pigment.tokyo)*, a multifaceted art shop showcasing 4500 pigments and 600 paintbrush types. Art also infuses the island more generally, with unique sculptures fronting the canal-side boardwalks, where you'll also find several nice cafes and bistros, and poetry nestled within shrubbery.

BANKSY, THE OLYMPICS & SOCIAL PROTEST

In 2021, the Who is Banksy? exhibition ran concurrently with the Tokyo Olympics at one of Terrada's warehouses. That wasn't Banksy's first Tokyo foray. In November 2019, an image of a rat holding an umbrella was found on a flood barrier near the Olympic Village.

Thought to be a Banksy original, interpretations flourished. Was it critiquing capitalist excess? Depicting modern loneliness?

Although Japanese authorities have zero tolerance for unapproved street art, Tokyo's governor Koike Yuriko tweeted excitedly about the piece. This, along with Terrada's later Banksy exhibition, suggested that social protest was acceptable only when contained within galleries – or if it involved a celebrity.

If borders had not been sealed due to COVID-19, would Banksy have delivered one of his artworks with an anti-Olympics twist?

Side Trips from Tokyo

Fine examples of Japan's iconic shrines, statues, cities and natural sights can all be found within two hours of central Tokyo.

Places

Mt Fuji p206

Hakone p208

Kamakura & Enoshima p209

Kawagoe p210

Yokohama p210

Narita Town p213

Nikkō p214

Looking for a change in scenery, or escape into nature and tradition? You won't have to go far – some of Japan's best sights are easily accessible from the capital. Comfortable trains take you directly to most of them and back in time for dinner. Journey north to beautiful forested Nikkō and see the country's most ornate shrine. Swap skyscrapers for the charming Edo townscape of Kawagoe. Stand in the shadow of Kamakura's giant Buddha and feel the salty breeze off the coast of Enoshima. Feel like a kid again as you climb aboard ships and visit fun museums in Yokohama. And for the truly unmissable sight – bask in the glory of Mt Fuji from the shores of Kawaguchi-ko, and marvel at the otherworldly landscape of Hakone as you float over plumes of volcanic steam.

TOP TIP

Many train companies sell discounted 'free pass' ticket packages that include a return trip from Tokyo and unlimited transport at the destination.

Mt Fuji

TIME FROM TOKYO: **90 MINS** 

Climbing Japan's Mountain

Hiking to the summit of the legendary **Mt Fuji** requires an overnight stay, unless you're an expert climber. (If you do want to ascend Fuji, most visitors depart from the Subaru Fifth Station and stay overnight in a mountain hut.) But for those looking for a more laid-back trip to see Japan's most celebrated mountain up close, there are still plenty of viewing spots and activities around Fuji Five Lakes (the surrounding lake towns).

The most popular of the Five Lakes is **Kawaguchi-ko** (河口湖), which can be reached on the direct Fuji Excursion train (included in the JR Tokyo Wide Pass) from Shinjuku (p142) in just under two hours. Renting a car is also a good option and allows for more flexibility. At Kawaguchi-ko, the best vantage point is up at the critter-themed observation deck via the **Mt Fuji Panoramic Ropeway** *(mtfujiropeway.jp; adult/child ¥1000/500)*. Here, you'll see Mt Fuji and the nearby mountain ranges reflected in the lake below. **Ōishi-kōen** (大石公園) also offers great views of the mountain framed by various flowers and shrubbery, depending on the season. For a bit of extra adventure, explore the **Narusawa Ice Cave** (鳴沢氷穴; *mtfuji-cave.com; adult/child ¥350/200*) and **Fugaku Wind Cave**

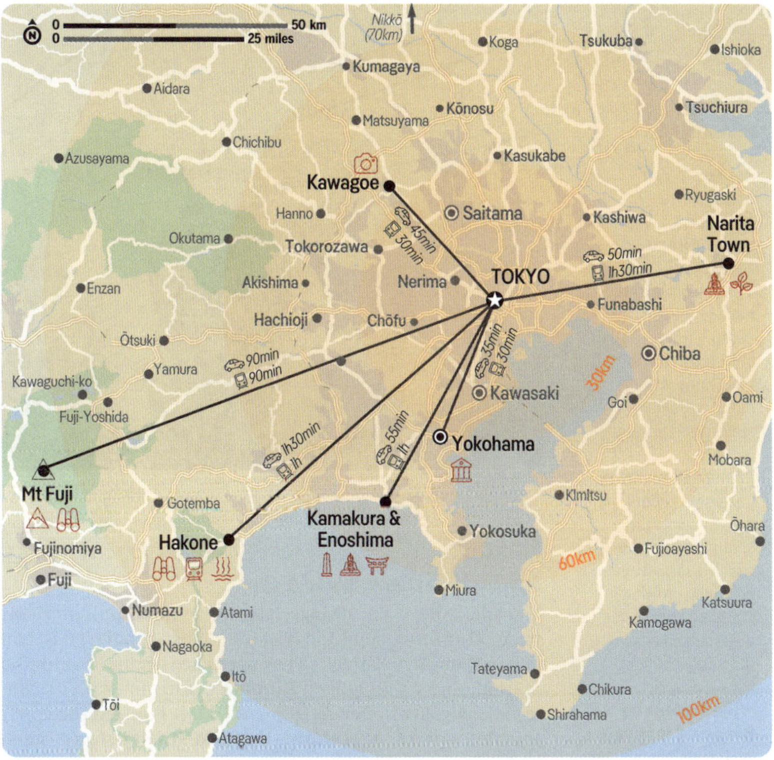

(富岳風穴; *mtfuji-cave.com*; *adult/child ¥350/200*), along with a foray into the surrounding **Aokigahara Forest** (青木ヶ原樹海).

The town of **Fuji-Yoshida** (富士吉田) also offers captivating panoramas of Mt Fuji – most popular of which is atop the hill at **Arakurayama Sengen-kōen** (新倉山浅間公園), where keen photographers willingly climb the 400-or-so steps in order to snap pictures of the mountain framed by seasonal foliage and the red **Chūrei-tō Pagoda** (忠霊塔; *chureito-pagoda.com*). The peak also looks photogenic at **Honchō-dōri** (本町通り), a road running through Fuji-Yoshida that is flanked by retro shops – a view some may recognise from the Japanese drama *The Hot Spot*. Before you leave, visit **Kitaguchi Hongū Fuji Sengen-jinja** (北口本宮冨士浅間神社; *sengenjinja.jp*), right at the end of Honchō-dōri, where for centuries people have come to pray before ascending Mt Fuji.

EATING AROUND MT FUJI: LOCAL DISHES

Hōtō Fudō: Shareable cauldrons of *hōtō* – thick knife-cut noodles in miso stew – enjoyed in a cavernous hall. *11am-7pm* ¥

Mimasu Shokudō: Humble restaurant serving delightfully chewy Yoshida udon in a hearty, savoury broth. A speciality of Fuji-Yoshida. *11.30am-3pm & 5-9pm* ¥

Matsuya Sabō: Feel at home with coffee, matcha and homemade cakes and pastries in a rustic *kominka* (Japanese-style home). *noon-6pm* ¥

Fuji Tempura Idaten: Try crispy, fried, locally grown vegetables or the signature Fuji-shaped tempura, Fujisan Tendon. *7pm-midnight* ¥

THE FUJI PILGRIMAGE

Before any Fuji ascent, it was essential for pilgrims to visit **Kitaguchi Hongū Fuji Sengen-jinja**. Dating back to the 8th century (reconstructed in the 1800s), this shrine is dedicated to Sakuya-hime, goddess of the mountain.

A majestic pathway lined with cedars guides you to the shrine's main gate, which is rebuilt every 60 years, growing in size. Two impressive one-tonne *mikoshi* (portable shrines) here are carried in the **Yoshida no Himatsuri festival** on 26 August to mark the end of the climbing season and offer thanks for protecting climbers for another year.

Head to the rear of the shrine through the wooden *torii*, and you'll see the original starting point of the Yoshidaguchi Trail up Mt Fuji.

ZEN S PRAROM/SHUTTERSTOCK

Hakone Ropeway

Hakone

TIME FROM TOKYO: **90 MINS** 

Scenic railways and splendid views

Volcanic valleys, hot springs, lush forests and stunning vistas make **Hakone** one of the best (and most popular) day-trip destinations out of Tokyo. The experience begins at Shinjuku Station, where the Odakyu **Romancecar** train, with its panoramic windows offering glimpses of Mt Fuji and the countryside, departs for **Hakone-Yumoto Station**. Once there, lunch options and tasty snacks abound in this onsen town.

From here, hop on the switchback **Hakone-Tōzan Railway** – which zigzags its way up steep mountain inclines to Gōra – taking in the forest views along the way. Next up is a tram-like cable car, ascending up another hill to Sōunzan Station, where you'll transfer onto the **Hakone Ropeway** *(hakonenavi.jp; adult/child ¥2000/700)* to **Ōwakudani** volcanic valley (大涌谷; *owakudani.com*). Have your camera ready here, as the transition from lush green forests to the sulphuric, steaming volcanic landscape hits when you least expect it – though you'll certainly smell it coming. No trip here is complete without sampling the *kuro onsen tamago*. These eggs are boiled in the volcanic water below, where the sulphur reacts with the eggshells, turning them black. Each egg, upon consumption, is said to extend one's lifespan by eight years.

EATING IN HAKONE: OUR PICKS

808 Monsmare: Delicious wood-fired pizzas with a satisfyingly chewy crust – near Hakone-Yumoto Station. *11am-2.30pm & 5-9pm Thu-Mon* ¥

Kamameshi Soba: Fuel up for your day trip with homemade soba and udon with a side of tempura at an affordable price. *11am-5pm Thu-Tue* ¥

Togendai View Restaurant: Enjoy mild *katsu* (pork cutlet) curry or *omurice* (rice-stuffed omelette) with views of the lake and ferries. *10am-4pm* ¥

Nukafuku: Vegan and gluten-free rice-bran doughnuts in assorted seasonal flavours. Inside Nakamura-ya souvenir shop, near Gōra Station. *11am-4pm Fri-Tue* ¥

Ōwakudani was created 3000 years ago when Kami-yama, a mountain in Hakone, erupted and collapsed. The eruption also formed the lake, **Ashi-no-ko** (芦ノ湖). The journey to the lake is another ride on the Hakone Ropeway, bound for Togendai Ropeway Station. The cobalt-blue crater-lake is famous for the exquisite view of Mt Fuji reflected on the still waters and visible on clear days (winter mornings are the most likely).

Sightseeing cruises depart directly from the station and you'll get some of the best viewing points from the upper decks, including the red *torii* of **Hakone-jinja** (*hakonejinja. or.jp*), which sits on the lake. Finish up the day by looping back to Hakone-Yumoto Station by bus.

Kamakura & Enoshima

TIME FROM TOKYO: **60 MINS** 

Famed statue, shrines, and seaside views

You could stand in the shadow of a giant Buddha statue, visit shrines, enjoy calming seaside views and hop across tide pools all on the same day trip through **Kamakura** (鎌倉) and **Enoshima** (江ノ島). A capital dating back to medieval Japan, Kamakura is roughly 60 minutes south of Tokyo. Here, the 93-tonne, 11.4m-high bronze Great Buddha **Daibutsu** (鎌倉大仏; *kotoku-in.jp/en; adult/child ¥300/150*) watches over the domain. It's a sight to behold, and for a small fee, you can walk inside the sculpture to see the statue's structural seams (but not much else). After visiting Daibutsu, turn back towards Hase Station and visit **Hase-dera** (長谷寺; *hasedera. jp; adult/child ¥400/200*), a temple complex dating back to 736 CE. Set on a hill, it's a gentle hike up to the main hall, Kannon-do, and there's plenty of lush greenery and beautiful garden views along the way.

When you're ready for sun and sea on the island of Enoshima, hop on the Enoden train to Enoshima Station. It's another 20-minute scenic walk across a bridge to the island itself, where visitors are greeted by the bronze *torii* to the island's eponymous shrine, **Enoshima-jinja** (江島神社; *enoshima jinja.or.jp*) dedicated to the goddess Benzaiten. There's only one way through the island – up the hill (you could also take the escalators, for a fee). And unless you catch a boat on the other side, you'll have to double back down later.

For the full adventure, keep following the path down to the **Iwaya Caves** (岩屋洞窟; *adult/child ¥500/200*). On the way, you'll come across the craggy rocks of the island's shoreline and touch the waves as they collect in the tide pools. For a

EATING & DRINKING IN KAMAKURA: COFFEE & SNACKS

Cheeers Coffee: Sleek cafe tucked away near the Great Buddha, pouring seriously good oat lattes and jasmine tea. *10am-6pm Tue-Thu, Sat & Sun* ¥

Iwata Coffee Shop: Kamakura's oldest retro cafe creates fluffy pancakes, reputedly adored by John Lennon and Yoko Ono. *9.30am-6pm Thu-Mon* ¥

Toshimaya: Baking delightfully light dove-shaped Hato Sabure butter cookies near Kamakura Station since 1894. *9am-7pm Thu-Tue* ¥

Ekiyoko Bake: Pretty tarts, scones and seasonal treats right outside of Hase Station – equally yummy as they are photogenic. *10am-6pm* ¥

A BRIEF HISTORY OF KAMAKURA

Kamakura was once Japan's ancient capital. It was the headquarters of Minamoto no Yoritomo, a power-hungry warlord. He chose Kamakura for its strategic location, close to his allies and protected by the sea and mountains.

He became the first shogun in 1192 after defeating his rivals, the Taira clan. Without an heir, power passed to the family of Yoritomo's wife, the Hōjō. The Hōjō clan ruled Japan from Kamakura until 1333 when they were overthrown by Emperor Go-Daigo, restoring Kyoto as the capital.

Kamakura then shrank, becoming a small town again by the Edo period.

It regained popularity in modern times when a railway line connected it to Tokyo, becoming a summer resort for wealthy Tokyoites.

more relaxing option, there's the **Sea Candle** (江の島シーキャンドル; *enoshima-seacandle.com; adult/child ¥800/400*) observation deck, nestled on the grounds of the well-manicured **Samuel Cocking Garden** (江の島サムエル・コッキング苑; *adult/child ¥500/¥250 on event days, otherwise free*).

Kawagoe

TIME FROM TOKYO: **30 MINS** 

Stroll through Little Edo

With charming streets lined with old warehouses and buildings that harken to yesteryear, **Kawagoe**, dubbed 'Little Edo', is a welcome reprieve from the bustle of Tokyo. Hop on the Tōbu Tōjō rail line from Ikebukuro Station, and you'll be there in just 30 minutes. For the quintessential Kawagoe sight, walk to **Kurazukuri-no-machinami**, a street lined with clay-walled black storehouses built after a great fire that destroyed a third of the town in 1893. Many of the buildings house restaurants, cafes and shops peddling delectable treats to snack on throughout the day. Also look out for **Toki-no-kane**, a wooden tower with a bronze bell that is a landmark of Kawagoe. Though it has been rebuilt several times over the last 400 years, the current bell tower was constructed in the 1890s and still chimes four times a day.

To the east is **Hikawa-jinja** (*kawagoehikawa.jp*) – a popular spot to pray for blessings associated with love and matchmaking – said to have been built in the 6th century. Marking its entrance is a towering *torii*, one of Japan's largest. From here, it's a 10-minute walk to **Honmaru Goten** (*adult/child ¥100/free*), once part of the vast Kawagoe Castle complex. Built in 1848, the structure served as the official residence and administrative office of the *daimyō* (feudal lord). Across the street is the **Kawagoe City Museum** (*adult/child ¥200/ free*) which, while modest in size, has some interesting exhibits giving guests an overview of the city's history.

Yokohama

TIME FROM TOKYO: **30 MINS** 

Noodles museum, ships and model trains

Yokohama (横浜) is so close to central Tokyo (an easy 30-minute train ride on multiple lines), yet it has its own style, with a playful side that appeals to young hearts. Even if you have never pondered noodle history before, there is enough to keep everybody smiling at **Cup Noodles Museum** (*cupnoodles-museum.jp; adult/child ¥500/free*), a nine-minute walk from Minatomirai

EATING & DRINKING IN KAWAGOE: OUR PICKS

Kanetsuki Udon Kinchō: Try the signature handmade udon, with sweet potato incorporated into the noodles, giving it a chewy texture. *11am–3pm Tue–Fri, to 4pm Sat & Sun ¥*

Koedo Osatsuan: Crispy, wafer-thin sweet potato chips served in a cup so you can snack while you walk. *10.30am–4.30pm Mon–Fri, to 5pm Sat & Sun ¥*

Nagamine-en Wahōan: Have an afternoon break with matcha and *wagashi* (Japanese-style sweets) in this old storehouse-turned-tea shop. *10am–5pm ¥*

Matcha Arata: Streetside kiosk preparing delicious matcha lattes, crêpes, and other refreshing drinks. Along Kashiya Yokochō. *10am–4pm Mon–Fri, to 5pm Sat & Sun ¥*

YOKOHAMA'S MARITIME HERITAGE ON FOOT

Get the most out of your day in Yokohama by exploring it on foot. This tour is packed with great views and historical sights.

START	END	LENGTH
Nippon Maru	NYK Hikawa Maru	3.5km; 2–3hr

Take in the harbour views and embark on a tour of Yokohama's maritime history on this walking tour, beginning at the **①** **Nippon Maru Sailing Ship** (p212), a retired training vessel for navy cadets that survived WWII. The nearby **②** **Yokohama Port Museum** gives you a crash course on the city's history as a port town. Go east via **③** **Kishamichi Promenade** to reach **④** **Akarenga Sōkō**, two converted redbrick warehouses that served as Customs Inspection Houses for Yokohama's 1920s shipping activities. Inside are stylish restaurants and shops.

Cross the bridge south and admire the harbour's boats at **⑤** **Zō-no-hana Park**, where the port of Yokohama was first opened. Continue on and you'll arrive at **⑥** **Yokohama Customs Museum**. Along with the nearby **⑦** **Kanagawa Prefectural Government Office** and **⑧** **Yokohama Port Opening Memorial Hall**, these three buildings were dubbed 'Queen', 'King', and 'Jack' respectively by sailors of the time, after poker cards. Head towards **⑨** **Yokohama Port Opening Square** and see the all-white **⑩** **Yokohama Kaigan Kyōkai**, Japan's first Protestant Church. Continue eastwards through **⑪** **Yamashita-kōen** and enjoy a stroll with harbour views until you reach **⑫** **NYK Hikawa Maru**, a luxury liner that ferried Japanese passengers to Seattle in the 1930s and later served as a hospital ship during WWII.

THE GUIDE

SIDE TRIPS FROM TOKYO

KAWAGOE FESTIVAL

Kawagoe Festival, also called **Kawagoe Hikawa Matsuri**, is the town's biggest celebration with a near 400-year history. On the third Saturday and Sunday of October each year, a parade of ornate, multi-tiered floats carrying life-sized dolls of gods and important figures, musicians and performers make their way through the town, accompanied by spectators and much merriment.

It is said to be an example of how major festivals would have looked like during the Edo period, and some floats used in the festival in fact date back to then.

The best time to see the event is on the Sunday evening, when the Hikkawase – the climax – occurs. Here, the floats face each other and performers battle it out in energetic displays. Visit the **Kawagoe Festival Museum** to see some of the floats up close.

Station. It's an ode to the 1956 invention of instant ramen by Momofuku Ando. Design lovers can ogle the packaging of virtually every Cup Noodle created across the decades in a gleaming display. Other rooms, with lots of childlike kookiness, will easily keep kids amused, and creating your own Cup Noodle packaging and ingredients is worth it, even just for the chic transparent gift bag.

Yokohama Cosmo World (*cosmoworld.jp*), also at Minatomirai, is a theme park that will delight the young ones and keep them occupied for an hour or so. You'll also get beautiful views of Yokohama at night from atop the ferris wheel. Adventurous visitors can buy a ticket and climb aboard the **Nippon Maru** (*nippon-maru.or.jp; adult/child ¥600/300*), a former training ship. You'll have access to most of the vessel – including views into the engine room and captain's quarters.

Train fans can head south of Yokohama Station to one of Japan's best collections of model trains and memorabilia: **Hara Model Railway Museum** (*hara-mrm.com; adult/child ¥1500/750*) brings together a collection by train maker and fanatic Hara Nobutaro; the lit-up night-time cityscapes, replete with tiny people, are captivating. Finish with dinner or snacks at the largest **Chinatown** in Japan, and pay a visit to **Kantei-byō** (*yokohama-kanteibyo.com*), an ostentatious shrine dedicated to a deity of business.

WHERE TO EAT IN YOKOHAMA: EAST & WEST

ToKi: Pull up at the bar for authentic spicy Sichuan-style 'sword-cut' noodles and dumplings without the tourist tax. *10.30am-9.30pm ¥*

Banwarō: Meat and vegetarian Taiwanese dishes done properly, especially *mapo* tofu, turnip cakes and dumplings. *11.30am-8pm Tue-Sun ¥*

Penny's Diner: American-style diner dishing out delicious burgers in a fluffy brioche bun. Near Nihon-Ōdōri Station. *11.30am-6pm Mon & Wed-Fri, to 8pm Sat & Sun ¥*

800° Degrees Artisan Pizzeria: Try the five-course artisan lunch. The menu has creative pizzas with local ingredients, but you can also customise your own. *11am-10pm ¥¥*

Narita Town

TIME FROM TOKYO: **90 MINS**

A historical temple and Edo streets

Most travellers today associate **Narita** (成田) with the airport. But for centuries, travellers and pilgrims from across the country have found themselves here too – en route to the grand Narita-san Shinshō-ji. Located in Chiba Prefecture, about an hour and half away from Tokyo (and a 10-minute train ride from Narita Airport), the town of Narita offers a glimpse of Edo culture, grand temple structures and extensive gardens that make it worth the half-day trip.

Ride to JR Narita or Keisei Narita Stations, and start your exploration along **Omotesandō** (表参道), a boutique street that winds like an eel (so locals say). *Unagi* (eel), of course, is the speciality here – and the 20-minute journey on foot down the sloped street is often punctuated by the smoky fragrance of charcoal-fired eel wafting from storefronts. Many of the 150 or more buildings along Omotesandō have been kept, or been restored to, the Edo style of architecture.

At the end of Omotesandō is **Narita-san Shinshō-ji** (成田山新勝寺; *naritasan.or.jp*) – a grand Buddhist temple complex you can't miss. Established in 940 CE, it is one of the largest temple grounds in Japan and houses several important cultural properties, including a beautiful three-storied pagoda, and Gaku-dō, a structure displaying old votive tablets. Behind the temple structures is a vast and tranquil Japanese garden that makes for a gentle afternoon trek. The **Narita Museum of Calligraphy** (*naritashodo.jp; adult/child ¥500/free*) is also located within the grounds and houses a collection of Japanese calligraphic works, though English signage can be sparse.

A major reason why Narita-san Shinshō-ji became a popular pilgrimage spot during the Edo period was **Ichikawa Danjūrō**, a popular kabuki actor of the time, and one of the most influential figures of the craft. It's said that the actor had prayed to the deity of Shinshō-ji, Fudō Myōō, for a child. After having been blessed with one, Ichikawa performed in a play in tribute to the temple that became a big hit among the masses. He later adopted the yagō (guild name) Narita-ya, after the temple. Ichikawa's long line of descendants – all kabuki actors – remain closely tied to the temple and Narita town.

A life-sized stone statue of Ichikawa Danjūrō VII sits under the Gaku-dō on the temple grounds.

Winnie Tan, Lonely Planet writer.

When I need a break from busy Tokyo, I hop on the slow train to Yokohama and spend the day walking the city and enjoying the views. There's always something to do here that suits whatever mood I'm in. I get a childish thrill making my own cup noodles at the Cup Noodles Museum.

When I need an escape from city life, I imagine what life might have been like in a different time while looking at the old houses in the Yamate Italian Garden.

After a full day on my feet, it's easy to find something delicious to reward myself with – whether it's delicious Chinese food, or pastries and pancakes at the area's many cute cafes.

EATING IN NARITA TOWN: UNAGI & MATCHA DESSERT

Kawatoyo Honten: Sit at low tables in a 1917 building for *unajyu* – chargrilled eel on rice. Expect a queue. *10am-5pm* ¥¥

Manpuku-tei: Can't decide between rice or noodles? Get *unajyu* with a side of homemade soba here. *10am-3pm Tue-Sun* ¥

Yamanoakari: Get cute, tea-based dessert and *kakigōri* (shaved ice) in gourmet flavours here, near Narita-san Shinshō-ji. *10am-4pm Fri-Wed* ¥

Narita Cha-ya Tabane-no-shi: Try the assortment of green matcha crêpes, filled with matcha cream, and topped with matcha powder. *10am-6pm Mon-Fri, from 9.30am Sat & Sun* ¥

Tōshō-gū

TOP EXPERIENCE

Tōshō-gū

Tōshō-gū (東照宮) is an extravagant shrine honouring the founder of the Tokugawa shogunate, Tokugawa Ieyasu (1543–1616). Ieyasu's grandson, Tokugawa Iemitsu, had the original structure (completed in 1617) renovated by celebrated artists of the day to dramatic effect, seen across its carved and decorated buildings. Tōshō-gū is the star attraction of Nikkō, a forested town reachable in under two hours from Tokyo's Asakusa on the Tobu Railway.

DON'T MISS

Okusha

Kara-mon

Yōmei-mon

Gohonsha

Sanzaru

Nemuri-neko

Kami-jinko

Omote-mon

Gojūnotō

Gates & Pagoda

The shrine's first gate is **Ishi-dorii**, which dates to Tōshō-gū's original construction. To the left is the 34.3m-tall **Gojūnotō**, an 1819 reconstruction of the five-storey pagoda first built here in the 17th century. After the ticket booths, the next gate is **Omote-mon**, guarded on either side by Deva kings.

Outer Courtyard

Continue to the outer courtyard for **Sanjinko**, the 'Three Sacred Storehouses', built in the *azekura-zukuri* style of architecture,

PRACTICALITIES

● *visit-tochigi.com/plan-your-trip/things-to-do/714*

● adult/child ¥1600/550

● 9am-5pm Apr-Oct, to 4pm Nov-Mar

which comprises horizontally stacked logs. On the upper storey of Kami-jinko, the 'Upper Storehouse', are relief carvings of elephants by the highly-esteemed Kanō Tan'yū, done as he imagined them to look, having never seen elephants in real life.

Monkeys

Look to your left to see **Shinkyūsha**, the 'Sacred Stable'. It's crowned with relief carvings of **Sanzaru**, the allegorical 'hear no evil, see no evil, speak no evil' monkeys who demonstrated the principles of Buddhist morality. These monkeys are also the unofficial symbol of Nikkō.

Crying Dragon

In the far left corner of the courtyard is **Honji-dō**. Look upwards for the ceiling painting of **Nakiryū**, the 'Crying Dragon'. Monks demonstrate the hall's acoustic properties by clapping two sticks together, and the dragon ®roars' (a bit of a stretch) when the sticks are clapped beneath its mouth.

Yōmei-mon

Ascend to Tōshō-gū's – and Japan's – most elaborately decorated gate, **Yōmei-mon** (陽明門). The National Treasure boasts over 500 carved images depicting folk tales, mythical beasts and Chinese sages, restored to its original and brilliant white and gold. On the inside of the gate, you'll notice that one of the pillars is upside-down, deliberately installed that way so as to ensure the gate remains 'imperfect' and thus warding off evil.

Inner Courtyard

A gold-accented, white second gate, **Kara-mon** (唐門), also a National Treasure, leads to the shrine's inner courtyard. The walls on the sides of both gates have fantastic carvings, including peony arabesques. There are also many stone lanterns around the complex that were gifted by loyal *daimyō* (feudal lords).

Gohonsha

The main shrine, **Gohonsha**, is built in the H-shaped *gongenzukuri* style, with its **Honden**, 'Main Hall', and **Haiden**, 'Hall of Worship', connected by a stone corridor. This is where the spirits of Tokugawa Ieyasu, Toyotomi Hideyoshi and Minamoto-no-Yoritomo are enshrined. Take off your shoes and step inside these halls, with paintings done by famous artists of the time, and a ceiling-painting pattern from the Momoyama period; note the 100 dragons. *Fusuma* (sliding door) paintings depict a *kirin* (a mythical beast that's part giraffe, part dragon).

Cat Carving & Inner Shrine

On the right is another gate, **Sakashita-mon** (坂下門). It's decorated not with dragons or phoenixes but with the sleeping cat **Nemuri-neko**: look up or you might miss the carving, one of the most famous in Japan, and attributed to the legendary artist Hidari Jingorō. Beyond it, 207 stone steps lead to **Okusha**, the inner shrine, where the tomb of Ieyasu lies under a 5m-tall five-storey pagoda cast of weathered gold, silver and bronze. A **tree** here is said to grant wishes (for a coin offering).

COLOURFUL RESTORATION

The first stage of the shrine's restoration work was undertaken in 2007 and unveiled in 2019. The work continues in sections, and most structures are now brilliant in colour, as they would have looked in the 17th century, when bold designs and vivid hues were popular.

Some of the painstaking traditional techniques include using white paint made from powdered shells.

TOP TIPS

● As Tōshō-gū is one of Japan's most famous attractions, it gets crowded. Ideally, arrive just before it opens. Alternatively, crowds thin out and the light is more photogenic half an hour before closing.

● Be prepared with sturdy shoes and clean socks. There are long, steep flights of stairs outdoors (with zero wheelchair access), and you have to remove your shoes to enter the main shrine.

● There are ticket machines and manned ticket kiosks; both have separate queues.

● The nearby **Nikkō Tōshō-gū Museum** holds valuable personal items that belonged to Tokugawa Ieyasu, though is quite small.

Where to Stay

From hipster neighbourhoods to laidback suburbs and bustling transport hubs to nightlife centres, there's an ideal area to stay for everyone in Tokyo.

Where to Stay If You Love...

Iconic sights, historic stores & modern luxury

Marunouchi & Nihombashi (p54) Some of the city's plushest hotels, easy access to the Imperial Palace and Tokyo Station, and long-established retailers and restaurants.

Fine dining & shopping

Ginza & Tsukiji (p66) Michelin-starred restaurants, high-end stores and accommodation prices to match.

Nightlife, design & contemporary art

Roppongi & Around (p78) It's not cheap staying here, but you'll be surrounded by contemporary art venues, great clubs and bars, and sleek urban complexes.

Creative cuisine, trendy cafes & hip boutiques

Ebisu, Meguro & Around (p90) The place to stay for stylish shops, creative vibes and design hotels.

Youth culture, clubbing & creative hangouts

Shibuya & Setagaya (p100) Youthful bars and clubs, cool neighbourhoods and a good range of accommodation options, even if they lean on the pricey side.

Fashion, art & architecture

Harajuku & Aoyama (p116) Style in multiple forms, from youth trends to haute couture and cutting-edge architecture.

Laidback neighbourhoods & nature

West Tokyo & Around (p128) Not the most convenient of areas to stay, but ideal for anyone interested in alternative neighbourhoods and being closer to nature.

Bar hopping, crowds & LGBTIQ+ venues

Shinjuku & Northwest Tokyo (p142) An eclectic mix of accommodation options and attractions, from bustling bars and the city's main Gaybourhood to the calm of Shinjuku Gyoen.

Pop culture, anime & amusement parks

Kōrakuen & Akihabara (p158) The centre of all things *otaku* (geeky), plus one of the city's finest gardens and the Tokyo Dome City entertainment complex.

Museum hopping, parks & retro vibes

Ueno & Yanesen (p170) Budget and midrange accommodation, top museums, a lively street market and great transport links to the rest of the city.

Tradition & historic sights

Asakusa & Sumida River (p184) Major attractions like Senso-ji and Tokyo Skytree, down-to-earth neighbourhoods and Tokyo's sumo heartland. Affordable accomodation too.

Family fun & futuristic art

Odaiba & Tokyo Bay (p198) Family-friendly attractions and a growing art scene, though an inconvenient base for exploring the rest of the capital.

Hotel Indigo, Shibuya (p219)

Marunouchi & Nihombashi

RYOKAN

Hoshinoya Tokyo ¥¥¥

MAP P58

Beautiful ryokan in Marunouchi combining urban and traditional Japanese aesthetics. Natural hot-spring baths.

MIDRANGE COMFORT

Hotel Ryumeikan Tokyo ¥¥

MAP P58

Former ryokan turned business hotel conveniently close to Tokyo Station. Rooms are not large but service and amenities are above average for the price.

Hotel Monte Hermana Tokyo ¥¥

MAP P58

Small but well-designed rooms just five minutes from Tokyo Station. Great value for money.

TOP-END STYLES

Palace Hotel Tokyo ¥¥¥

MAP P58

Spacious rooms and impeccable service at this stylish five-star hotel overlooking the Imperial Palace moat.

Ginza & Tsukiji

BOUTIQUE

Muji Hotel Ginza ¥¥¥

MAP P71

Boutique hotel by Japan's favourite lifestyle store, Muji. Entirely furnished and stocked with Muji products.

MIDRANGE COMFORT

Hotel Monterey La Soeur ¥¥

MAP P71

Midrange hotel decorated in a charming French apartment design. Good-sized rooms for the neighbourhood.

Agora Tokyo Ginza ¥¥

MAP P71

Simple, modern and minimalist rooms near Kabuki-za. Perfect for some relaxation.

Dormy Inn Premium Ginza ¥¥

MAP P71

Recently renovated hotel featuring a real onsen hot springs bath, plus complementary post-onsen ice cream and evening ramen.

Roppongi & Around

BUDGET

Hotel Hillarys Akasaka ¥¥

MAP P85

A charming, low-budget place that provides great bang for your buck, with a launderette, onsen-style bathing facilities, a free drinks bar and rooftop dining overlooking the metropolis.

Henn na Hotel Tokyo Akasaka ¥¥

MAP P85

Humanoid-looking robots greet you at the reception for check-in (real humans are a phone call away) here. Rooms come with clothes-deodorising closets, an enormous LCD TV and smartphones.

CAPSULE

9h Nine Hours Akasaka Sleep Lab ¥

MAP P85

Basic but well-designed capsule hotel with floor-to-ceiling windows, that offers check-in from 3pm until 5am. Pyjamas, bath set and basic toiletries provided. Showers can get busy.

First Cabin Akasaka ¥

MAP P85

One step up from the capsule format is First Cabins'. Each one-person cabin fits a semi-double bed, TV and safe box, with shared space including a cafe–guest lounge, and a large bathing area.

BOUTIQUE

Hotel and Residence Roppongi ¥¥

MAP P81

An excellent-value oasis in the heart of town. Ample facilities, such as a gym, free lounge, a cafe and a restaurant-bar. Each room has amenities including a microwave, sofa and even bedtime chocolate.

CASH TO SPLASH

Okura Tokyo ¥¥¥

MAP P85

A rare, Japanese-owned luxury hotel brand that oozes tradition, from its design and facilities to its courteous customer service. Free tea and beer after a hotel swim too.

Ebisu, Meguro & Around

CHIC

Ebisuholic ¥¥¥
MAP P94

Boutique business choice for a stylish stay on the south side of Ebisu Station. Go for the funky bathrooms with tiled floors and transparent walls.

TRENDY

Hotel Graphy ¥¥
MAP P94

Cool rooftop terrace overlooking the Shibuya Botanical Center, plus casual gourmet food with fresh ingredients and original cocktails. Various room types available, from ensuite bathrooms to dorm beds.

NO FRILLS

°C ¥
MAP P94

Pronounced 'Do-C', this Ebisu hotel features comfortable capsules with a twist: a Finnish-style sauna.

Prince Smart Inn ¥¥
MAP P94

Modern business hotel with simple rooms, big bright windows and toast breakfasts, located on the quieter west side of Ebisu Station.

Shibuya & Setagaya

GREAT VIEWS

Sequence Miyashita Park ¥¥¥
MAP P105

With a prime location, exceptional park views, late breakfast and even later check-out (2pm), you'll never want to leave the window bench. Dorm rooms are also available.

Hotel Indigo ¥¥¥
MAP P105

Luxury high-rise in the beating red heart of Dōgenzaka has

---

colourful rooms with towering views and a hand-picked collection of vinyl records for in-room listening on request.

GOOD VIBES

Mustard Hotel ¥¥
MAP P106

Low-rise digs at the eastern end of Shimokita Senrogai, where a record player spices up otherwise austere rooms. Stay for the on-site California coffee and bagels.

Trunk Hotel Cat Street ¥¥¥
MAP P105

Chic, eco-friendly, hyperlocal hotel featuring plentiful art and luxurious rooms, gourmet restaurants and a lively lounge-bar with outdoor terrace.

Harajuku & Aoyama

DEPENDABLE CHAIN HOTELS

Tokyu Stay Aoyama Premier ¥¥
MAP P120

As well as a great location near Gaienmae Station, this business hotel offers smartly designed singles, twins and doubles.

Dormy Inn Premium Shibuya Jingumae ¥¥
MAP P120

Branch of a reliable business chain, with compact doubles

---

and twins, and relaxing extras like a sauna and indoor onsen bath.

TRENDY DIGS

Trunk Hotel Cat Street ¥¥¥
MAP P120

Fashionable boutique option with sleekly modern rooms, cool bar and restaurant, and a well-heeled hipster crowd.

West Tokyo & Around

BUDGET

Toyoko Inn Tokyo Akishima-eki Minami-guchi ¥
MAP P131

This business hotel by Akishima Station is a solid choice for exploring the Okutama region. A free buffet breakfast and on-site laundry facilities add to the appeal.

GLAMPING

Woodland Bothy Glamping Auberge ¥¥¥
MAP P131

If you love the outdoors but are a bit squeamish about camping, this secluded facility offers a comfortable stay along the Yozawa River, complete with delicious meals.

RYOKAN

Kamenoi Hotel Ōme ¥¥
MAP P131

A newly renovated family-friendly ryokan by the Tama River, combining the comfort of Western-style beds with hot-spring baths and Japanese course meals. Ten minutes by free shuttle from Ōme Station.

BOUTIQUE

Satologue ¥¥¥
MAP P131

Immerse yourself in nature at this new accommodation in Nishitama, which features local cuisine married with French techniques and locally brewed sake. Guests enjoy curated activities and a private sauna.

Shinjuku & Northwest Tokyo

STATION-SIDE STAYS

Hotel Gracery Shinjuku ¥¥

MAP P147

This modern place offers a convenient base in the heart of Kabukichō. Book the Godzilla Floor for views of the iconic Godzilla Head outside your window.

Shinjuku Granbell Hotel ¥¥

MAP P147

Choose from stylish rooms, some with lofts or full tubs, and visit the rooftop bar. Close to Higashi-Shinjuku and Shinjuku-Sanchōme Metro; 15 minutes from Shinjuku Station.

Vessel Inn Takadanobaba ¥¥

MAP P150

Sleek, family-friendly accommodation with direct access to Takadanobaba Station via lifts. The extensive breakfast buffet includes fresh seafood daily.

Hotel Metropolitan Ikebukuro ¥¥

MAP P150

A local stalwart with comfortable rooms and multiple restaurants, including Italian dining on the 25th floor and made-to-order omelettes for breakfast. One-minute walk from Ikebukuro Station.

Kōrakuen & Akihabara

NOVELTY

Book Hotel Jimbocho ¥¥

MAP P161

A hostel in Jimbocho book district with a formidable library of curated titles.

Under Railway Hotel ¥

MAP P162

A feature of Tokyo urbanism is the interesting use of the space under the rail tracks. This hotel has small but affordable rooms beneath the JR line in between Akihabara and Ueno.

VIEWS

Tokyo Dome Hotel ¥¥

MAP P161

A generic hotel but the views are simply stunning (check out those views from Bar 2000 on the 6th floor). Well located next to Tokyo Dome.

DESIGNER

BnA STUDIO Akihabara ¥¥

MAP P162

This option in Akihabara uses the played-out idea of having a different artist design each room, but the results are truly unique.

Toggle Hotel ¥¥

MAP P161

Hotel with unique, monochromatic colour schemes that extend even into guest rooms. Near Suidobashi Station.

Ueno & Yanesen

CONVENIENT BASES

Hotel Resol Ueno ¥¥

MAP P174

Smart, modern lodgings by Ueno Station with singles, doubles and twin rooms.

LUGGAGE STORAGE

Check-in at most hotels is from 3pm, but if you turn up earlier, they will typically store your luggage until check-in time, which can cut costs on storage lockers.

Modern art in common areas adds a nice touch, especially as some is by young, local artists.

Nohga Hotel ¥¥¥

MAP P174

Spacious and tastefully decorated rooms, plus plenty of cool common spaces to hang out in. A handy location several blocks from Ueno Station.

LOCAL VIBES

Sawanoya Ryokan ¥¥

MAP P174

A traditional ryokan with tatami mat rooms tucked in the backstreets of Yanesen. English-speaking staff.

Asakusa & Sumida River

NOVELTY

Asakusa Saunaland ¥¥

MAP P191

Each room in this designer choice comes with a state-of-the-art sauna.

VIEWS

Asakusa View Hotel ¥¥

MAP P191

Standard, modern hotel but the views of SkyTree at night are spectacular.

TRADITIONAL RETROFITS

Sumida Nagaya ¥

MAP P187

Small hostel inside a *nagaya* wooden tenement house, with an excellent lasagna cafe.

Cyashitsu Ryokan Asakusa ¥¥

MAP P187

Modern ryokan behind Sensō-ji; nice rooms and a half-outdoor private onsen bath.

OKURA TOKYO

Okura Tokyo (p220)

Odaiba & Tokyo Bay

BAYSIDE BATHING

Mitsui Garden Hotel Premier Toyosu ¥¥

MAP P201

Located atop a skyscraper connected to Toyosu Station. Features plush Western-style guestrooms, including well-priced standard rooms, plus a 36th-floor onsen bath with extensive views.

Villa Fontaine Grand Tokyo Ariake ¥¥

MAP P201

A step above a business hotel, this property near Tokyo Big Sight is connected to an onsen facility (extra fee) with multiple baths and saunas.

Around Tokyo

FUJI FIVE LAKES

Glamping Villa Hanz ¥¥

Choose from villas, guesthouses or glamping tents (with a private shower and bathroom) all nestled in a lush forested area near Kawaguchi-ko. There is a public bath, too.

La Vista Fuji Kawaguchiko ¥¥

Provence-style hotel with rooms that look out towards Mt Fuji. There are private baths available to use for no additional fee – great for those with tattoos.

Ubuya ¥¥¥

Longstanding ryokan that is a traditional-modern architectural masterpiece with a vision of Mt Fuji across the lake from cinema-like windows.

Hitsuki Guesthouse ¥

Stay with multigenerational descendants of Fuji pilgrims and sleep on tatami in a rare surviving *oshi-no-ie* (pilgrim's house).

HAKONE

Nagomi no yado Hanagokoro ¥¥¥

A small ryokan in Gōra with private onsen cabins offering wonderful views of the nearby forests and mountains.

Tensei-en ¥¥

Ryokan with private and public baths in Hakone-Yumoto. The baths are available for day use if you just want a soak, but not stay the night.

K's House Hakone ¥

Choose Japanese-style futon dorms, capsules, bunks or neat tatami doubles. It has indoor and outdoor onsen.

KAMAKURA

Guesthouse Kamakura Zen-ji ¥

Beachside traditional Japanese house near the Great Buddha. Spotless private tatami rooms with bathroom.

TOOLKIT

The chapters in this section cover the most important topics you'll need to know about in Tokyo. They're full of nuts-and-bolts information and valuable insights to help you understand and navigate Tokyo and get the most out of your trip.

Money
p224

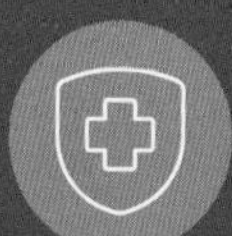

Health & Safe Travel
p225

Family Travel
p226

LGBTIQ+ Travellers
p227

Food, Drink & Nightlife
p228

Responsible Travel
p230

Accessible Travel
p232

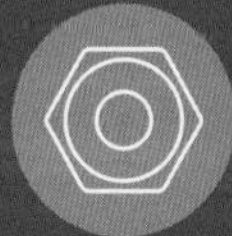

Nuts & Bolts
p233

Language
p234

Sensō-ji (p192)

Money

CURRENCY: YEN (¥ OR 円)

ATMs

Banks, convenience stores, department stores and post offices have ATMs, although not all accept overseas cards. Japan Post machines and Seven Bank machines in 7-Eleven stores are the most reliable, usually accepting Amex, Cirrus, Diner's Club, Maestro, Mastercard, Plus and Visa cards. Seven Bank ATMs operate 24 hours a day, 365 days a year.

Credit Cards

Credit cards are widely accepted in Tokyo, but it's still worth checking in bars, restaurants, stores and taxis before ordering anything. Visa, Mastercard and JCB are the most commonly accepted cards. If you go outside of Tokyo, make sure you carry some cash – ideally smaller denominations included.

Digital Payments

Smartphone payment apps like PayPay and Rakuten Pay are becoming increasingly common, with the shops that use them displaying signs by the cashier. IC travel cards Pasmo and Suica, initially designed for trains, subways and buses, can also be used for purchasing items in convenience stores, supermarkets and newer vending machines.

HOW MUCH FOR A...

museum ticket
¥1000

Tokyo Metro ride
from ¥180

cinema ticket
¥2000

Disney 1-day Passport
from ¥8400

HOW TO... Save on Admissions

If you are planning on visiting multiple museums, galleries, gardens and other cultural facilities, get the **Tokyo Pass** app. Valid for one, two, three or five consecutive days (*¥5600 to ¥10,300*), it gives unlimited Tokyo Metro subway usage and admission to roughly 50 facilities, including Tokyo National Museum, Mori Art Museum, Hama-rikyū Garden and other top attractions. The app also lists lots of stores and cafes where travellers can mingle with locals.

ON A BUDGET

Tokyo is expensive, but there are ways to cut costs. You can save on rail and subway fares by picking up a transport pass, such as a 24-, 48- or 72-hour **Tokyo Subway Ticket** (*¥800 to ¥1500*).

If your budget is really tight, visit the *bentō* (boxed meals) section of supermarkets near closing time, when ready-to-eat meals tend to be half price. Eating at local lunch spots is cheaper than tourist traps.

Head to free attractions like Sensō-ji, Meiji-jingū and the Imperial Palace's East Gardens, or go for a walk through Shibuya and Harajuku.

LOCAL TIP

Don't tip. It's not part of Japanese culture, and you only risk embarrassing someone by offering them a tip. Simply saying 'Thank you' for good service or great food goes a long way.

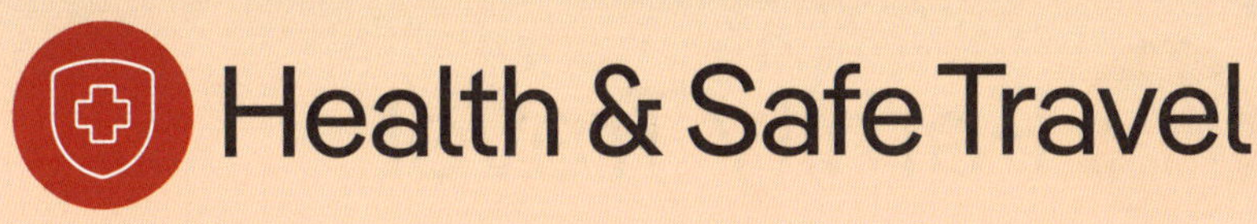

Health & Safe Travel

EARTHQUAKES

Thousands of small earthquakes are felt in Japan on an annual basis, with occasional major tremors like the 9.0 magnitude Tohoku Earthquake in 2011. For emergency alerts and information on what to do in the event of an earthquake and other disasters, download the free, multilingual Safety Tips app. It also features useful language information and guidance for getting medical care.

Emergency Help

The Japan National Tourism Organization's (JNTO) visitor hotline *(050 3816 2787)* provides 24-hour emergency consultation in English in the event of illness or disaster. The JNTO's online **'Guide for when you are feeling ill'** *(jnto.go.jp/ emergency/eng/mi_guide.html)* lists medical institutions in Tokyo that can treat patients in English. It also has information on how to buy insurance once you are in Japan

Summer Heat

Roughly 50,000 people are hospitalised with heatstroke every summer in Japan. In July and August, high temperatures in Tokyo typically remain above 30°C, with frequent spells in the mid- to high 30s, coupled with very high humidity. Avoid going outside in the hottest hours, use hats and parasols, and hydrate frequently. When indoors, make sure to use air-conditioning and fans.

INSURANCE

Travel insurance isn't mandatory for travel to Japan, but it is advisable to purchase insurance (pre-trip) that covers medical care.

THE SHINDO EARTHQUAKE SCALE

Rather than the Richter scale, Japan measures earthquakes with the Shindo Intensity Scale, ranging from 0 (weakest) to 7 (strongest). If you turn on the TV immediately after a tremor, these are the numbers you'll see.

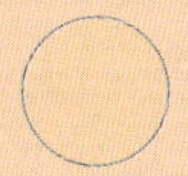

Shindo 3
Noticed by people in buildings and some who are walking.

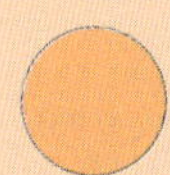

Shindo 4
Startling.
Can wake you.
Felt by most.

Shindo 5
Difficult to walk.

Shindo 6–7
Can't stand.
Substantial damage.

Typhoons

May to October is typhoon season in Japan, with most arriving from August onwards. While Tokyo doesn't get hit as badly as the south and west of Japan, typhoons still bring heavy rain and strong winds that disrupt transportation and business operations. The worst tends to pass in a day, so wait it out inside and follow updates on NHK TV.

WOMEN-ONLY CARRIAGES

For much of the morning commute (from 6am to 9.30am), most JR trains and Tokyo Metro subways have women-only carriages, clearly marked by signs on the floor of the platform and in the carriage windows. This is in response to the sexual harassment and sexual abuse of women on public transport in Japan, especially with regard to groping. Children can also use these carriages.

Family Travel

Exploring Tokyo with kids can be an unforgettably brilliant experience. Despite the crowds, the city is well geared to families and children of all ages, with theme parks, high-tech arcades, kid-friendly restaurants and cultural differences to enjoy. Add to that plenty of parks where small kids can run wild (for free) and excellent concessions, and it doesn't have to cost a fortune once you're here.

Facilities

Changing Multipurpose toilets in department stores, malls, stations and other places have well-maintained changing beds.

Seating Family-friendly restaurants often have high-chairs available.

Medical For doctors, dentists and other medical assistance, try the 24-hour **Japan Visitor Hotline** *(050 3816 2787).*

Drugstores Japanese pharmacists like Matsumoto Kiyoshi and Tomods stock nappies/diapers and other essentials, but brands are often local and ingredients/instructions in Japanese.

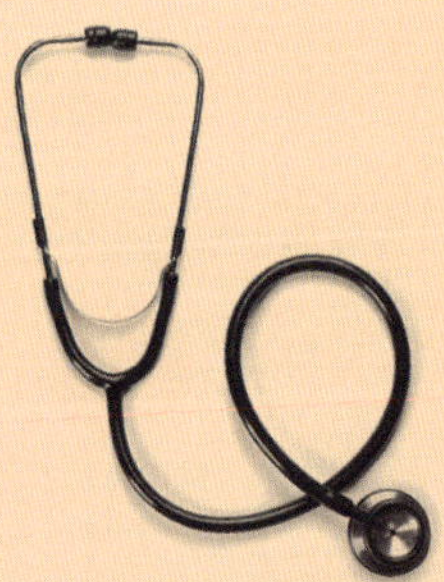

Eating Out

If you want to experience sushi with kids, hit a *kaiten-zushi* (conveyor-belt sushi) chain restaurant. Young ones can make a noise here, everything is cheap yet good quality, and there's plenty of non-sushi items on the menu for picky eaters. Family restaurants are another reasonably priced option, serving familiar foods and smaller portions. Also look out for fun themed cafes and restaurants.

Concessions

Those aged 12 and up typically pay adult rates for attractions and transportation, including rail and bus passes. Kids 11 and under usually pay 50% of the adult price, with those 5 and under often going for free.

Tokyo Disney Resort

Mickey and friends deliver classic Disney thrills and entertainment at the neighbouring Tokyo Disneyland and Tokyo DisneySea theme parks.

Sanrio Puroland (p136)

This theme park aimed at younger kids is home to Japan's favourite feline, Hello Kitty.

Odaiba (p198)

Bayside district full of family-friendly attractions, including the interactive Miraikan museum and indoor Joypolis theme park.

The Making of Harry Potter

Opened in 2023, this Harry Potter theme park features movie sets, props and other Hogwarts-related fun.

INDEPENDENT KIDS

One thing that can be quite striking when visiting Japan is just how independent children are. In residential areas and even on trains, it's normal to see elementary and middle school kids travelling to and from school without adult supervision.

Likewise, small children are allowed to go to the park to play without their parents. One reason for this is that Japan has a relatively low crime rate – it's ranked among the safest countries on the planet, according to the Global Peace Index.

In schools, kids are also given the responsibility of cleaning their own classrooms and taking turns with chores such as lunch service.

LGBTIQ+ Travellers

Like many things in Japan, sexual and gender diversity is full of contrasts. LGBTIQ+ travellers are unlikely to run into overt discrimination and, beyond age restrictions, there are no laws against same-sex sexual activities, but same-sex marriage is still to be recognised legally. Tokyo has a vibrant LGBTIQ+ community, with Shinjuku's Nichōme area a main hub, but many in the community are still hesitant to live openly.

Resources & Networks

Opened in 2021, Pride House Tokyo in Shinjuku is Japan's first permanent LGBTIQ+ centre, offering a safe space for all members of the community. For insider information on LGBTIQ+ life and travel in Japan, **Utopia Asia** (*utopia-asia.com*) is a handy resource. Or there's tour operator **Out Asia Travel** (*outasiatravel. com*), if a package trip is your thing. Finally, consider a side trip to Japan's second city, Osaka, the first municipality in Japan to launch a travel website aimed at the LGBTIQ+ community (*visitgayosaka.com*).

NICHŌME NIGHTLIFE

Tokyo's largest concentration of LGBTIQ+ bars, clubs and restaurants is in Shinjuku's Nichōme neighbourhood. While some of the several hundred venues here aren't open to non-Japanese travellers, many are extremely welcoming. Among the bars particularly open to newcomers from out of town is Campy, run by a celebrity drag queen. Clubbing options include **Aisotope Lounge** (p149) and **Arty Farty** (p149).

RAINBOW REEL TOKYO

Held since 1992, this international film festival is run by volunteers who select films from Japan and overseas for an LGBTIQ+ audience. It's held over two weekends in mid-June and mid-July at various venues.

Tokyo Pride

Over a weekend in early June, Japan's biggest Pride event unleashes a burst of colour on Tokyo. With parades, parties and more in Yoyogi Park, LGBTIQ+ individuals and their allies celebrate and advocate for diversity and inclusion.

Public Affection

Regardless of sexuality or gender, the Japanese tend to avoid public displays of affection, even holding hands. While doing so is very unlikely to trigger abuse or hate speech, it can attract a few odd looks.

WOMEN-ONLY VENUES

Nichōme has a collection of bars, clubs and restaurants aimed at women and non-male-identifying clientele. The most famous is Goldfinger, a lively bar with regular themed nights that becomes women-only on Saturdays. **Adezakura** (p149) is a female-identifying-only bar with karaoke that opens till 6am on weekends. Quieter is Dorobune, a laidback hangout for sake and *okonomiyaki* (savoury pancakes).

Food, Drink & Nightlife

When to Eat

Chōshoku (7am to 10am) Except for cafes and family restaurants, not many places are open for breakfast.

Chūshoku (11am to 2pm) Typically features set meals or single-dish meals. This is also the best time to try out those less expensive sampler set menus at high-end restaurants

Yūshoku (5pm to 11pm) Often features numerous dishes for sharing and/or enjoyed across multiple courses.

Where to Eat

Family Restaurant AKA *famiresu*, these diner-like chain restaurants have affordable mixed menus.

Izakaya Lively pubs with bites like *yakitori* (chicken skewers) and sashimi to pair with a night of drinking.

Kaiten-zushi Low-cost sushi restaurants with conveyor-belt service.

Kaiseki-ryōri Japanese haute cuisine.

Kissaten Old-fashioned cafes/coffee shops.

Tachinomiya No-frills standing bars.

Teishokuya Budget-friendly spots that focus on *teishoku* (set meals).

Yatai Street stalls that often have just a few seats and specialise in just one type of food.

MENU DECODER

Ippin (一品) Appetisers/single dishes

Teishoku (定食) Set meal

Meibutsu (名物) Speciality

Chūmon (注文) Order

Tabemono (食べ物) Food

Sushi (寿司) Sushi

Sakana (魚) Fish

Niku (肉) Meat

Yasai (野菜) Vegetables

Dezāto (デザート) Dessert

Nomimono (飲み物) Drinks

Sake (酒) Alcohol

Nihonshu (日本酒) Sake

Bīru (ビール) Beer

O-cha (お茶) Tea

Aka wain (赤ワイン) Red wine

Shiro wain (白ワイン) White wine

En (円) Yen

Genkin nomi (現金のみ) Cash only

Zeikomi (税込) Tax included

Kaikei (会計) Bill/Amount due

Otsuri (お釣り) Change

Muryō (無料) Free

Amakuchi (甘口) Slightly spicy

Chukara (中辛) Medium spicy

Karakuchi (辛口) Spicy

Gekikara (激辛) Extremely spicy

Seriakku-byō (セリアック病) Coeliac

Arerugī (アレルギー) Allergy

Bīgan (ビーガン) Vegan

Bejitarian (ベジタリアン) Vegetarian

Okosama Setto (お子様セット) Kids' meal

Gurutenfurī (グルテンフリー) Gluten free

HOW TO… Pay the Bill

It depends. In some low-cost restaurants, like a *ramen-ya* (ramen restaurant), you often choose your food and pay upfront at a vending machine that issues a meal ticket, which you then hand to staff. In most places, however, you pay after the meal. In places such as a *teishoku* restaurant, where the meal is quick and you aren't making repeated orders, you might receive the bill (to pay later) just after the food arrives. Elsewhere, staff will bring the bill when they know you've finished or once you've asked for it. To do that, say *kaikei* (bill) or just make an 'X' with your index fingers. In more expensive restaurants, you can pay at your table, but it's more common to take the bill to the cashier by the exit. It's important to check beforehand whether the restaurant takes credit cards or other forms of cashless payment. Some smaller or older places are still cash only.

HOW MUCH FOR A...

kaiten-zushi
¥2000

ramen
¥700-900

izakaya
¥4000

kaiseki
¥20,000

teishoku
¥1000-1200

draft beer
¥500-700

coffee
¥500

HOW TO... **Order**

Like paying the bill, ordering varies with the type of restaurant and meal. If you go for *kaiten-zushi*, you can either grab items off the conveyor belt or use the touch-screen panel to order directly from the kitchen – the latter is fresher. At midrange sushi, à la carte and sets are usually available, but pointing to a picture of a set on the menu is the easiest option. At exclusive sushi restaurants, the service is *omakase* – the chef chooses what you'll be eating.

Restaurants serving quick, cheap meals – such as ramen, *gyūdon* (simmered slices of beef and onion on rice) and curry rice – often use a system where you select and pay for your food via a vending machine, which in turn issues a ticket that you hand to staff.

Chain *izakaya* and family restaurants often have touch-screen panels at the table or picture menus, both frequently with English. Independent *izakaya* can be much harder – they might only have the menu written in Japanese on strips of paper hanging on the wall. In that case, ask the staff what they recommend (*o-susume wa nan desu ka*). Many lunchtime or *teishoku* places have replicas of their dishes in the window display, so if there's no English menu or picture menu, you can always go out and point. To grab the attention of staff at any restaurant, raise your hand and say *sumimasen* (excuse me).

Ordering Sake

Ordering sake brings many challenges, from choosing the grade to a variety of serving temperatures, be that *hiya* (chilled) or *atsukan* (warmed). A good starting point is choosing whether you want it *karakuchi* (dry) or *amakuchi* (sweet).

CULINARY SPECIALISATION

Specialisation is a major theme in Japan's culinary scene. While there are jack-of-all-trade restaurants like budget *famiresu* and *izakaya* with a broad menu, plus restaurants that focus on the food of a single country or region, Tokyo (and the rest of Japan) has many restaurants with a hyper-specific focus on a single dish or culinary style. One thing that unites many of these is the use of *-ya* (屋). Literally meaning 'house', *-ya* as a suffix also signifies 'a shop that sells', so a sushi restaurant is a *sushi-ya* (寿司屋) and a ramen joint is a *ramen-ya* (ラーメン屋).

Beyond those well-known Japanese foods, there are plenty of other *-ya* to look out for. Head to a *yakitori-ya* (焼き鳥屋) for a few drinks and skewers of chargrilled chicken, or pay a visit to an *okonomiyaki-ya* (お好み焼き屋) to try the pan-fried mix of batter, cabbage and other ingredients that make up these savoury pancakes. A *tendon-ya* (天丼屋) offers an affordable way to try tempura, serving it atop a bowl of hot rice.

Other restaurants without the *-ya* might specialise in gyōza dumplings or, at the high-end of the culinary spectrum, *kaiseki-ryōri* (懐石料理), Japanese haute cuisine. To all this you can add places that might focus only on the Buddhist, plant-based *shojin-ryōri* (精進料理) or spots where the menus are centred on tofu. And that is just the tip of Tokyo's culinary iceberg.

Responsible Travel

Climate Change & Travel

It's impossible to ignore the impact we have when travelling; Lonely Planet urges all travellers to engage with their travel carbon footprint, which will mainly come from air travel. While there often isn't an alternative, travellers can look to minimise the number of flights they take, opt for newer aircrafts and use cleaner ground transport, such as trains. One proposed solution — purchasing carbon offsets — unfortunately does not cancel out the impact of individual flights. While most destinations will depend on air travel for the foreseeable future, for now, pursuing ground-based options where possible is the best course of action.

The **UN carbon footprint calculator** shows how flying impacts a household's emissions

The **ICAO's carbon emissions calculator** allows visitors to analyse the CO2 generated by point-to-point journeys

Sustainable Sushi

Remember the four 'Ss' when it comes to ordering sushi: eating small, silver, seasonal and shellfish tends to be more sustainable. Also, skip the worst offenders: *unagi* (freshwater eel), shrimp and bluefin tuna.

Animal Cafes

Cuddling a dog while sipping on a coffee might sound appealing, but before going to an animal cafe, consider the stress the animals are under, and the poor reputation these animal cafes have when it comes to animal care.

Save money and cut waste with end-of-day bargains on *bentō* and deli food at supermarkets and department stores. The discounts often start by mid-afternoon but will reach half price or better as closing time nears.

Crowd shots aside, it's bad manners to take photos of people in public spaces without asking. Snapping photos of children could even land you in trouble with the police. Also keep an eye out for no-photo signs in shops, temples and other attractions.

SUSTAINABLE DEVELOPMENT GOALS

More Japanese businesses are promoting their efforts in achieving the UN's Sustainable Development Goals. In some cases, it's a greenwashing exercise. Look out for businesses that specify which of the 17 specific SDGs they are focusing on.

FARM TO TABLE

Look out for restaurants supporting rural areas by sourcing directly from producers. Happo-en is one example – it collaborates with an agricultural high school in Fukushima, an area badly affected by the earthquake, tsunami and nuclear disaster of 2011.

Go Independent

There are chain cafes all over Tokyo, but maybe try out some independent places instead. You're not only supporting the local economy, the vibe and coffee is better, and they also tend to source their beans more ethically.

Walk or Cycle

While using public transportation in Tokyo is low impact, it's such a great city to stroll or cycle in that you could reduce your carbon footprint even more by exploring it on foot or by bike.

Circular Economy Initiatives

Though not yet widespread, circular-economy-related initiatives, such as Bunji and Peace Coin, are starting to take root in parts of Tokyo. The aim is to promote spending within local communities and the exchange of services between community members.

Pre-loved Souvenirs

Hunt for bargains at the city's flea markets and antiques fairs. Several hundred vendors gather a couple of weekends a month at Ōi Racecourse, while Oedo Antique Market, held two Sundays a month at Tokyo International Forum, is great for art and vintage items.

Carry your Rubbish

Beyond convenience stores and the recycle bins by vending machines, public rubbish bins aren't common in Tokyo. While littering happens – especially away from busy streets – be like most locals and carry your trash with you.

Vending machines are everywhere, but skip them. Running 24/7, they eat up energy.

For water on the go, pack a refillable bottle and find refill spots with the MyMizu app.

20 billion

That's roughly how many pairs of disposable chopsticks (called *waribashi*) are used in Japan annually. In other words, almost 160 pairs per person. Pack your own reusable chopsticks.

RESOURCES

theinvisibletourist.com
Do's and don'ts in Tokyo; responsible travel ideas.

happycow.net
Vegan and vegetarian restaurant listings.

japan.travel/en/uk
Travel info and also covers manners, laws and sustainability.

Accessible Travel

Tokyo still has multiple accessibility issues, but it truly has come on in leaps and bounds in recent years, with more and more business and municipalities offering a wider range of accessible facilities such as multipurpose toilets, wheelchair ramps and lifts.

Buses

Buses in the city require an access ramp for wheelchair users. The driver will get off and set this up, then rearrange seats to create a spot for the wheelchair.

Airport

Both Narita and Haneda airports have staff ready to assist passengers. Visit an information counter for help and information. Narita Airport also details its accessibility services online, with information on quiet rooms, barrier-free access, staff assistance and more (*narita-airport.jp/en/bf*).

Accommodation

From budget business hotels to luxury property, most modern hotels increasingly have between one and a few barrier-free rooms, but older hotels and traditional ryokan typically don't. Large, higher range hotels typically offer better accessibility service.

TAXIS

Most taxis don't have space for wheelchairs. If you have a small manual wheelchair, the taxis that look like London black cabs are an option. If not, you'll need to book an accessible taxi.

WHEELCHAIR SIZE

Barrier-free facilities are designed for compact Japanese wheelchairs, which tend to be a manual–electric hybrid. Overseas wheelchairs might be too wide for some ramps and elevators. Local rentals are possible through Accessible Japan with two weeks notice.

Multipurpose Toilets

At stations, airports, malls, departments stores, museums and some other public areas, there are spacious multipurpose toilets. They have emergency call buttons, handrails, a sink/shower for ostomate bag users and a multipurpose bed/mat.

Stations

Most stations are fully accessible, but trains require a staff member to manually place a ramp. Tell staff at the gate where you're going, and they'll help you to the train and arrange for staff to meet you at your destination.

RESOURCES

Accessible Japan (accessible-japan.com)
An excellent English-language resource, especially for getting around Japan in a wheelchair.

Japan Accessible Tourism Centre (japan-accessible.com)
Info on destinations, tours, taxis and more in Tokyo and around the country.

Tokyo Sightseeing Accessibility Guide (sangyo-rodo1.metro.tokyo.lg.jp/tourism/accessible/en)
Tourism website run by Tokyo Metropolitan Government, offering 35 accessible model courses for travellers.

Tactile Paving

Through stations and along pavements across Tokyo, tactile paving is designed to aid people with visual impairments. Called Tenji Blocks, they are coloured bright yellow so those with partial vision can see them more easily and are textured to indicate direction of travel and hazards.

Nuts & Bolts

OPENING HOURS

Banks 9am–3pm Monday to Friday

Bars 5pm–midnight

Clubs 10pm–4am

Museums 10am–5pm

Restaurants 11am–2pm and 5–11pm

Shops 10am–8pm

Internet Access

Airports, stations, cafes, hotels and busy tourist areas often have free wi-fi, but it can be unreliable. Consider renting a mobile wi-fi router, getting an e-SIM, or buying a SIM card at the airport when you arrive.

Smoking

Smoking is prohibited in many public areas, with some cafes and bars being the main exception. Hotels typically have smoking and nonsmoking rooms.

Tap Water

Tap water is safe to drink in Tokyo. You can find public refill points with the MyMizu app.

Weights & Measures

Japan uses a mix of metric and traditional measures. Distances are kilometres. Sake is often served per *-go* (180ml).

GOOD TO KNOW

Time Zone
GMT+9

Country Calling Code
+81

Emergency Number
119

Population
14.2 million

PUBLIC HOLIDAYS

Some businesses and nonessential services may be closed on public holidays and during the Obon (13–15 August) and year-end periods.

New Year's Day 1 January

Coming of Age Day 2nd Monday in January

National Foundation Day 11 February

Emperor's Birthday 23 February

Vernal Equinox Day 20 March

Shōwa Day 29 April

Constitution Memorial Day 3 May

Greenery Day 4 May

Children's Day 5 May

Marine Day 3rd Monday in July

Mountain Day 11 August

Respect for the Aged Day 3rd Monday in September

Autumnal Equinox Day 23 September

Sports Day 2nd Monday in October

Culture Day 3 November

Labour Thanksgiving Day 23 November

Electricity 100V/50Hz

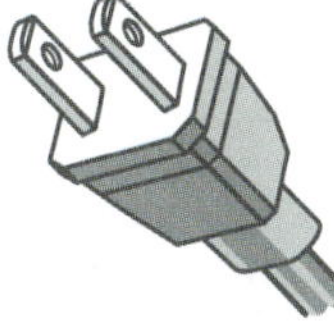

Type A

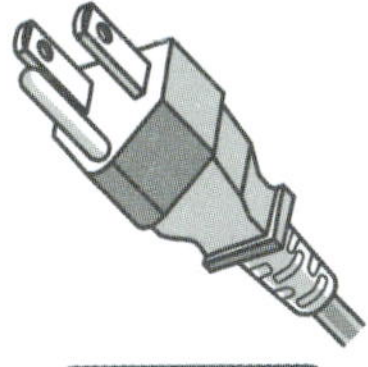

Type B

Language

You can have a fantastic time in Tokyo without speaking Japanese, but even just a few phrases will help you make friends, attract smiles and advice from locals, and ensure you have a rich and rewarding travel experience.

Basics

Hello こんにちは
kon·ni·chi·wa

Goodbye さようなら *sa·you·na·ra*

Yes はい *hai*

No いいえ *ee·ay*

Please (when asking) ください
ku·da·sai

Please (when offering) どうぞ
dō·zo

Thank you ありがとう *a·ri·ga·tō*

Excuse me (to get attention)
すみません *su·mi·ma·sen*

Sorry ごめんなさい
go·men·na·sai

What's your name?
お名前は何ですか?
o·na·ma·e wa nan desu ka

My name is ...
私の名前は … です
wa·ta·shi no na·ma·e wa ... desu

How are you?
お元気ですか?
o·gen·ki desu ka

Fine. And you?
はい、元気です。 あなたは?
hai, gen·ki desu. a·na·ta wa

Do you speak English?
英語が話せますか?
eigo ga ha·na·se·masu ka

I don't understand.
わかりません
wa·ka·ri·ma·sen

Does anyone speak English?
どなたか英語を 話せますか?
do·na·ta ka eigo o ha·na·se·masu ka

Directions

Where's the ... ?
…はどこですか?
... wa do·ko desu ka

What's the address?
住所は何ですか?
jū·sho wa nan desu ka

Could you please write it down?
書いてくれませんか?
kai·te ku·re·ma·sen ka

Can you show me (on the map)?
(地図で)教えて くれませんか?
(chi·zu de) o·shi·e·te ku·re·ma·sen ka

Signs

Entrance 入口

Exit 出口

Open 営業中/開館

Closed 閉店/閉館

Information インフォメーショ
ン

Danger 危険

Toilets トイレ

Women 女

Men 男

Emergencies

Help! たすけて!
tasukete

Go away! 離れろ!
ha·na·re·ro

Call the police! 警察を呼んで!
kē·sa·tsu o yon·de

Call a doctor! 医者を呼んで!
i·sha o yon·de

I'm ill. 私は病気です
wa·ta·shi wa byō·ki desu

NUMBERS

1 一 *i·chi*

2 二 *ni*

3 三 *san*

4 四 *shi/yon*

5 五 *go*

6 六 *ro·ku*

7 七 *shi·chi/ na·na*

8 八 *ha·chi*

9 九 *ku/kyū*

10 十 *jū*

DONATIONS TO ENGLISH

There are several – you may recognise futon, karaoke, tsunami, bentō box, skosh, rickshaw, head honcho and manga, to name a few.

PRONUNCIATION TIPS

Japanese pronunciation is not considered difficult for English speakers. Unlike some other Asian languages, it has no tones and most of its sounds are also found in English.

Vowels

Vowels in Japanese can be either short or long. The long ones should be held twice as long as the short ones and are represented with a macron (horizontal line) on top of them.

Consonants

Most consonant sounds are pretty close to their English counterparts. Pronounce the double consonants with a slight pause between them, as this can change the meaning.

Phrases to Sound Like a Local

How are you? Genki? – *gen-key*

I'm fine – Genki – *gen-key*

Delicious – Umai – *ooh-my*

That looks delicious – Oishisō – *o-ee-she-so*

You're kidding!? – Uso – *ooh-so*

See you later – Jyaa-ne – *ja-nay*

Wow! – Sugoi – *su-goy-ee*

Excuse me – Sumimasen – *su-mee-ma-sen*

Good luck/Do your best – Ganbare – *gan-ba-ray*

That's funny – Omoshiroi – *omo-shi-roy*

All good? – Daijōbu? – *dai-jo-bu*

Really? – Maji? – *ma-jee*

Awesome! – Sugoi! – *su-goy-ee*

Uncool! – Dasai! – *da-sa-ee*

Cute! – Kawaii! – *ka-wa-ee*

Ridiculous! – Yabai! – *ya-ba-ee*

The worst! – Saitei! – *sa-ee-tay-ee*

Sneaky! – Zurui! – *zu-ru-ee*

WHO SPEAKS JAPANESE?

Japanese is spoken by more than 125 million people. While it bears some resemblance to Altaic languages such as Mongolian and Turkish, and has grammatical similarities to Korean, its origins are unclear.

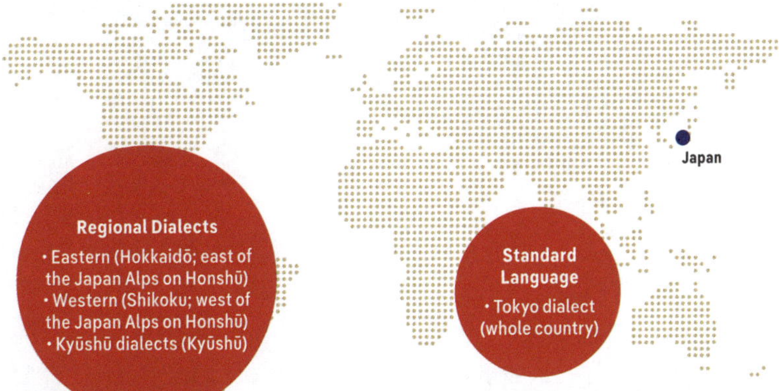

STORYBOOK

STORYBOOK

Our writers delve deep into different aspects of Tokyo life

Sengaku-ji (p247)

A HISTORY OF TOKYO IN
15 PLACES

The story of Tokyo is punctuated by repeated bouts of destruction and recovery. Most recently, disasters like the Great Kantō Earthquake of 1923 and the bombing of WWII claimed most of Tokyo's historic buildings, but within the ever-redeveloping capital remain sights and locations that document the city's journey from wilderness to megacity. By Rob Goss

ACCORDING TO MYTHOLOGY, Japan was created when two gods, Izanagi and Izanami, stirred the ocean with a heavenly jewelled spear from which fell drops of salt that formed the first of Japan's islands. Tokyo's creation story, on the other hand, is far less dramatic. What's now the world's largest metropolitan area was barely more than a collection of villages when the Tokugawa clan repurposed a castle here as their base of power in the late 1500s. At that time, the former capital, Kyoto, had already been a thriving political and cultural centre for 800 years.

But in two and a half centuries of Tokugawa rule, Tokyo (then called Edo) developed into a thriving city, with a population of more than one million by 1800 – the same as London. Post-Tokugawa, with Japan having taken a fast track to industrialisation and modernisation, Tokyo's population had hit 7 million just prior to WWII. All that despite frequent devastation from fire, earthquakes and eventually war. Maybe that's why Tokyoites have such an acceptance of impermanence and rarely seem fazed by the changes that always seem to be unfolding around the capital.

After all, like the cherry blossoms ingrained in Japanese culture, nothing is meant to last.

1. Todoroki Valley

A REMNANT OF ANCIENT TOKYO

Walking around Tokyo's urban sprawl today, it's hard to imagine what life was like here 100 years ago – let alone a thousand years past. But you can get a hint in residential Setagaya. Only 20 minutes from bustling Shibuya, Setagaya's Todoroki Valley is a peaceful ravine with a kilometre-long pathway that leads to small temples, waterfalls and burial mounds that date to the 7th century. These burial mounds most likely belonged to an early clan leader whose name has been lost to history, but who, when alive, might have looked upon the same scenery in Todoroki as visitors do today.

For more on Todoroki, see page 240.

2. Sensō-ji

THE CAPITAL'S OLDEST TEMPLE

Legend has it that in the spring of 628, brothers Hamanari and Takenari caught a Buddhist statue in their net while fishing the Sumida River, in what's now Asakusa. The find inspired their village chief to build a temple, which saw this small settlement in the wilds flourish into a centre of worship. Now called Sensō-ji, the temple has been through multiple incarnations, and although the statue hasn't been seen for more than a thousand years, the site remains a major draw, with 30 million people visiting annually to see the Five-Storeyed Pagoda and numerous towering gateways.

For more on Senso-ji, see page 192.

3. Imperial Palace

SHOGUNS AND EMPERORS

Like so many historical spots in Tokyo, the current Imperial Palace isn't all that old. Except for a few Edo-era turrets that survived repeated fires and Allied bombings, most of the buildings date to the 1960s. The roots, however, go back far longer, to 1497, when a samurai called Ota Dokan built a castle on the site. For centuries thereafter, the castle remained a centre of power, most notably as the headquarters of the ruling Tokugawa clan during the Edo era (1603–1868). After fire destroyed much of the castle in 1873, it was rebuilt as the Imperial Palace, serving as home to the imperial family ever since.

For more on the Imperial Palace, see page 60.

4. Nihonbashi Bridge

THE GATEWAY TO EDO

Originally a wooden bridge built in 1603, but now a steel-on-stone affair dating to 1911, the Nihonbashi bridge traditionally marked the terminus of the Nakasendō and Tōkaidō, the key routes connecting Edo (present-day Tokyo) to Kyoto. Being such a prominent location on trade routes, the wider Nihombashi area flourished as a mercantile centre, with many businesses here today still able to trace their foundations to the early Edo era.

The bridge also still plays a key role for Japan: on the road in the middle of the crossing is a marker signalling the point from where all distances to and from Tokyo are officially measured.

For more on Nihombashi, see page 56.

5. Koishikawa Kōrakuen

EDO-ERA LANDSCAPING

The Edo era saw 260 years of peace and prosperity, albeit with Japan largely self-isolating from the rest of the world and contact restricted to a small number of trading posts. Peace brought with it more funds and more time to spend on traditional refinement, like the magnificent 17th-century garden of Koishikawa Kōrakuen. A classic stroll garden, it features a central pond around which pathways are accented by a succession of scenic points, many of which take inspiration from Ming-dynasty China.

For more on Koishikawa Kōrakuen, see page 160.

6. Ueno Park

THE END OF EDO

In 1868, after 260 years at peace, the Japanese Civil War saw the country thrown into violent turmoil as imperial forces sought to seize power from the Tokugawa shogunate. One of the war's many battles took place in Ueno – now the site of Ueno Park and a collection of magnificent museums – and it proved decisive.

With the shogunate replaced by imperial rule, the emperor moved from Kyoto to Edo, which was renamed Tokyo (meaning 'Eastern Capital'), and oversaw the period known as the Meiji era (1868–1912), when Japan embraced industrialisation and foreign influences, and emerged from isolation to become a world power.

For more on Ueno Park, see page 172.

Sensō-ji (p192)

7. Kabuki-za

BUILD, REBUILD, REPEAT

If any building in Tokyo exemplifies the up-and-down history of the city, it's the Kabuki-za theatre. Built on the outskirts of Ginza in 1889 as a venue for traditional kabuki (a form of stylised Japanese theatre) performances, it then burned down in 1921 and, mid-reconstruction, was flattened (along with most of Tokyo) by the Great Kantō Earthquake of 1923. The next rebuild was destroyed by Allied bombing during the war, before the 1950s' incarnation was replaced by an earthquake-proof version in 2013 – modern behind the scenes, but with a traditional facade that recalls the original theatre.

For more on Kabuki-za, see page 69.

8. Tokyo Station

ADOPTING WESTERN STYLES

As the Meiji era and the subsequent Taishō era (1912–26) progressed, Tokyo continued to modernise. Electric streetlights were installed in Ginza, and varied styles of buildings began to appear around the city as the government invited European architects and engineers to the country. They in turn trained Japanese architects like Tatsuno Kingo, who designed the iconic red-brick facade of Tokyo Station (completed 1914) – now a retro element of a sprawling, modern complex.

For more on Tokyo Station, see page 57.

9. Meiji-jingū

A MEIJI MEMORIAL

After Emperor Meiji and his wife, Empress Shōken, passed away in 1912 and 1914, respectively, Meiji-jingū was built in central Tokyo in their honour. Completed in 1920, then rebuilt after war damage, it has become the capital's most visited and important shrine. Fittingly for an emperor who wanted East to meet West, it's located in what's now the cosmopolitan heart of the city, a short walk from the street fashions of Harajuku and the contemporary architecture of Omotesandō. Unlike Harajuku and Omotesandō, however, the shrine is an oasis of tranquillity.

For more on Meiji-jingū, see page 126.

10. Hachikō Statue

JAPAN'S MOST LOYAL CANINE

Japanese history is full of tales of loyal samurai avenging wronged masters and choosing death over dishonour. But the loyalty of a dog called Hachikō, remembered by a bronze statue beside Shibuya Station, eclipses them all. An Akita breed, Hachikō would wait by the station to meet his owner off the train as he returned from work. Until one day in 1925, when the owner never came. Unaware his owner had passed away, Hachikō kept returning to the station, day after day, for nine years. Once his story made the news, he became a canine celebrity and won a place in the hearts of the nation.

For more on Hachikō (and Shibuya), see page 102.

11. Tokyo Tower

THE POST-WAR REBUILD

An iconic sight, with its Eiffel-esque lattice design, Tokyo Tower was built in 1958 to function as a broadcasting tower and tourist attraction. At the time, it was the tallest structure in the land, at 333m, with its vivid white and orange framework visible from all corners of the city. As Tokyo began to rebuild from the ashes of WWII, having lost an estimated 100,000 lives and 250,000 buildings in firebombing raids, the tower also served as a statement that the capital was back on its feet.

For more on Tokyo Tower, see page 87.

12. Odaiba

A BUBBLE-ERA LEGACY

Tokyo was revelling in the excesses of an economic boom in the 1980s. Flushed with cash, anything seemed possible. That included a vast landfill project that saw a collection of small manufactured islands (originally built as forts in the Edo era) in Tokyo Bay joined together to create Odaiba.

With Japan's economic bubble bursting spectacularly in 1992, and development all but grinding to a halt, it wasn't until the late 1990s that Odaiba's transformation belatedly began to take shape. It was worth the wait. Today, the island is a top destination for family fun, home to the Miraikan museum, the Joypolis theme park and numerous other attractions.

For more on Odaiba, see page 198.

Tokyo Skytree (p186)

13. Roppongi Hills

WELCOME TO THE 2000S

As Japan entered the new millennium, Tokyo started to see the rise of sleek urban complexes. It began with Roppongi Hills, launched in 2003 after a three-year construction project. Centred around the 54-storey Mori Tower, it mixes prestigious office spaces with fashionable shops, restaurants, leading art galleries like Mori Art Museum and a Grand Hyatt. Back then, Roppongi Hills was groundbreaking, as was its neighbour, Tokyo Midtown, in 2007. Today, new urban complexes appear with incredible regularity. Toranomon Hills, Hikarie, Shibuya Scramble Square – the list could go on and on.

For more on Roppongi Hills see page 80.

14. Tokyo Skytree

JAPAN'S TALLEST STRUCTURE

When Tokyo Skytree was completed in 2012, the 634m tower officially became the tallest structure in Japan and the second tallest on the planet, after Dubai's Burj Khalifa. A combination of broadcast tower and multi-use entertainment complex, the Skytree is most notably home to observation decks that offer dizzying views over the urban sprawl.

Upon completion, the tower also represented another in a long line of Tokyo's groundbreaking developments, incorporating cutting-edge anti-seismic technology that was put to the test (successfully) mid-construction, when the city was rattled by the Great East Japan Earthquake of 2011.

For more on Tokyo Skytree, see page 186

15. Japan National Stadium

AN OLYMPIC LEGACY

Built for the Tokyo 2020 Olympic and Paralympic Games, the Kengo Kuma–designed stadium is one of the capital's newest landmarks. While lauded for its sustainable construction and accessibility, it also serves as a reminder of a troubled games. Where the 1964 Tokyo Olympics signalled Japan's return to prominence after the post-war rebuild, Tokyo 2020 didn't quite have the same impact. From the bidding stage and corruption claims to the Olympic Games themselves, there was substantial animosity towards them in Japan – something that was compounded when it was held a year late and closed to the public in the middle of the pandemic.

MEET THE TOKYOITES

Always on the go, and most active at night, Tokyoites are a high-intensity bunch of people. They also know the value of community – finding yours is the key to enjoying this city. Manami Okazaki introduces her people.

ON A MACRO level Tokyo is a case study of sorts, an example that is focused on for its statistical extremities. Population density, isolation and an ageing society are all social trends associated with the city. However, on a micro level, it's a liveable place, and the people are a lot more fun-loving, open and friendly than their overly polite veneer might suggest at first glance. Locals are good at forming communities and enjoy both the minutiae of their interests and each other's company. Fostering a sense of belonging is crucial in order to not get swallowed up by this ginormous megalopolis.

The genesis of Tokyo is recent – the newly formed capital was created in the Edo era, making it a relatively young city. The term *'edokko'* (literally 'child of Edo') sprang up in the 1700s and describes the commoners who were born in the city. They speak their mind, are cheerful, bold and brash, and *edokko* are considered to be the 'real' locals – still abundant in downtown Tokyo.

Over the years, Tokyoites have developed a 'live for the moment' attitude born from the fact that their home was being constantly destroyed. Even now, rather than be overly concerned with heritage, Tokyoites look to the latest and seek new trends. Famed architectural masterpieces are torn down with impunity, the city is constantly changing – embracing that change is a survival mechanism, and either going along with development, or resisting it, is something that Tokyoites are constantly dealing with.

The capital is currently the world's largest city, and houses approximately 37 million inhabitants. In 2024, according to the Ministry of Internal Affairs and Communications, 461,454 people moved to Tokyo. Of the 382,169 who left, the majority were in their 50s and above, so the age of Tokyoites is under the average for the rest of Japan and there are many neighbourhoods that are geared towards a younger demographic. Tokyoites are hyper conscious of youth and make the most of it while it lasts. On the other hand, many couples are childless, so don't expect locals to be too accommodating to younger kids.

One of the biggest differences between Tokyo and other global cities is that its identity is not one of multiculturalism, owing to its strict visa policies. However, the cliché that Japan is homogenous is increasingly obsolete, and aside from the established enclaves such as the Indian community in Kasai and Koreatown in Ōkubo, there are more Tokyoites from abroad adding diversity to the city.

Pet Population

Don't be surprised to see many people pushing pooches in strollers – according to the Bureau of Statistics, there are more cats and dogs than children under 15 in Japan. In 2023, the pet-related economy reached ¥1.86 trillion.

Pictured clockwise from top left: Young woman at Shibuya Crossing; Woman working at a rice cake shop, Yanaka; Chef at a Tokyo sushi restaurant; Night out in an *izakaya* bar in Tokyo

MY LIFE IN TOKYO

Despite being born in Australia, I have lived in Tokyo most of my life, and it's the place I will always call home. My day to day is that of a typical downtown denizen. Without fail, I go to a *sentō* (public bath) every day to catch up with the locals and chit chat. I get all my groceries from an old-school shopping street and I live in a wooden *nagaya* row house. At the same time, Tokyo is a night city. I am also obsessed with everything retro cyberpunk and grew up immersed in the capital's street culture and fashion scenes.

Having lived overseas, I can also recognise things that Tokyoites take for granted, like the beauty of our artisanal traditions.

In Sydney multiculturalism is the established norm; here it feels like Japan is on training wheels. Many Japanese people talk about immigrants in terms of economic benefit, but there are creators in my community who are indulging in fresh perspectives and collaborating.

THE 47 RŌNIN

This gruesome, true story of samurai honour and loyalty has echoed through the centuries – not just in Japan, but around the world. By Rob Goss

IN 1701, A *daimyō* (feudal lord) by the name of Naganori Asano drew his sword on another samurai at court in Edo Castle, setting in motion a chain of events that have since become the classic Japanese tale of loyalty and vengeance. Though Asano was said to have been provoked by an insult, not even a *daimyō* could escape from the rigid rules and protocols of society – by law, anyone drawing a sword in Edo Castle would be punished by death.

A brief account of the long and complex tale that followed, goes like this. Asano was sentenced to death by seppuku (a form of ritual suicide by disembowelment), his lands were confiscated and his retinue of samurai were disbanded – left to live as *rōnin* (lordless samurai). Yet the man he attacked, Yoshinaka Kira, oddly faced no repercussions for his part in the incident. Not immediately anyway.

Under the leadership of a senior samurai called Yoshio Ōishi, Asano's loyal warriors slowly hatched a plan. After two years of waiting for Kira to become complacent, Ōishi and 46 others – the 47 Rōnin – secretly came to Edo (now Tokyo) from around the country to draw up plans for an attack on Kira. On 31 January 1703, they struck, overrunning Kira's mansion, beheading

Pictured clockwise from top left: Sengaku-ji (p99); Naganori Asano's grave; Yoshio Ōishi's grave; Some of the 47 Rōnin graves

him, and then carrying the severed head across Edo to Asano's grave at Sengaku-ji temple. They then turned themselves in to the authorities, knowing that their own punishment would be death. So it was, in March 1703, that 46 of the *rōnin* committed seppuku and were buried alongside Asano at Sengaku-ji.

Sengaku-ji

Located a short walk from Takanawa Gateway Station (near Shinagawa), Sengaku-ji is still home to Asano and 46 of the *rōnin*. It's a modest temple in many ways, with a simple roofed gateway and largely understated graves, but look closely and there are some fascinating features – including a well where Ōishi is said to have washed Kira's head before placing it upon Asano's grave. If you visit, you'll likely see incense sticks that visitors have lit in the *rōnin's* memory. There's a small museum here too, housing artefacts connected to the men. Or time a trip for 14 December, when Sengaku-ji celebrates the 47 Rōnin with a memorial service and a procession of men in samurai attire.

The 47th Rōnin

But what of the 47th *rōnin*? That's where history is a little hazy. Kichiemon Terasaka, a low-ranking foot soldier, was later captured and pardoned, although accounts vary as to why. Was it because he fled before the battle and took no part in the revenge? Was the leniency to appease public opinion? One theory suggests he took part in the raid, but was immediately sent by Ōishi to inform Asano's family of their success. Whatever, upon his death some 40 years later at the ripe of age of 87, Terasaka wasn't reunited with the other *rōnin*. He was instead buried at Sōkei-ji temple, where he had spent his final years as caretaker, in the plush part of Tokyo that's now called Azabu.

On Stage & Screen

The *Chūshingura*, as fictionalised retellings of the 47 *rōnin's* story are commonly known, have spanned generations, from 18th-century *bunraku* puppet plays and kabuki performances through to TV dramas and movies. The latter alone have included silent movies, WWII propaganda films designed to boost public morale and animated features. Even Hollywood has had a go, with a 2013 movie starring Keanu Reeves and a pair of actors who'll be familiar to *Shōgun* fans – Tadanobu Asano and Hiroyuki Sanada. Taking the *rōnin* story into the realm of fantasy, there's also the 2022 sequel, *Blade of the 47 Rōnin*, which picks up the tale hundreds of years in the future with one of the *rōnin's* descendants.

Samurai & Edo Experiences

While Tokyo is a very modern city, there are opportunities to experience culture from the time of the samurai. You could stop by the Sword Museum in Ryōgoku for a look at historic samurai swords and afterwards stroll over to the Hokusai Museum to see *ukiyo-e* (woodblock prints) of the Edo era – it was through *ukiyo-e* that many artists portrayed the 47 Rōnin's story in graphic detail.

In Asakusa, you could dress up in kimono for a traditional tea ceremony at Maikoya or take a ride in a rickshaw. Another option is to take in kabuki at the Kabuki-za theatre in Higashi Ginza – if you are really lucky, you might even get to see a performance of the *Chūshingura*. Or for an all-round look at Japanese history, it's hard to beat a couple of hours at Tokyo National Museum in Ueno – the exhibits there cover everything from samurai attire to traditional arts.

Stories of Loyalty

Why has the tale of the 47 Rōnin had such an impact? It touches upon many qualities that are seen as admirable in Japanese culture – loyalty, perseverance, quiet determination and (harking back to the Edo era) the willingness to sacrifice oneself for honour. The 47 Rōnin is arguably the standout of such tales, but there are others you might encounter on a visit to Japan.

Pop to youthful Shibuya and by the station you'll see a bronze statue of a dog called Hachikō, the loyal dog who, for years, would go to Shibuya Station every day in the hopes of once again meeting its owner off the train – not knowing that he'd died at work.

Head out of Tokyo to Aizu-Wakamatsu – to the north in Fukushima Prefecture – and you'll encounter the heartbreaking tale of the teenage Byakkotai brigade, who died by suicide after mistakenly believing their castle had fallen. They are now honoured by an annual festival.

DOWNTOWN TOKYO'S LEATHER LEGACY

From outcast to aspirational, the changing face of leatherware.
By Manami Okazaki

WALKING AROUND DOWNTOWN Tokyo, particularly the Taitō and Sumida wards around Sumida River, you will notice two things: a lot of cafes in former warehouse-like loft spaces, and stylish leatherware stores, whose products range from wallets to footwear. Leather shops REN, ETiam, Delife in Kuramae, CRAFSTO in Asakusabashi and bespoke handbag store HIS Factory in Azumabashi form part of a new wave of retail shops that are artisanal, but rather than traditional *shokunin* craftspeople, they display their designer wares in sleek, minimalistic concrete showrooms with museum-like lighting.

Even though they might not look it at first glance, their presence harkens back to a wider Edo-era artisanal culture that flourished during a time of exploding urbanism.

Unlike the preceding eras, which were characterised by war and civil unrest, it was a time of stability. Culture – both in terms of creation and consumption – flourished, and along with it, a 'live for the moment' ethos among the commoner class, as well as an appreciation for fashion and flamboyance, with craft trades catering to theatre actors, courtesans and religious institutions alike.

In terms of leatherware, utilitarian items such as tobacco pouches and small bags were popular, examples of which can be seen at the excellent Azumaya atelier in Ryōgoku at its small Fukuromono museum, which is open to the public.

Life on the Rivers

The Sumida River, the largest in Tokyo, houses Sensō-ji temple and a large entertainment district on the west bank, while Honjō and Fukagawa on the east bank were the site of many lumberyards, storehouses and wharves. When Japan opened up to the rest of the world in the Meiji era, the Sumida became the base for industrial production as modernisation advanced, with kilns, glass ateliers and textile mills as well as many leather tanneries on its banks.

These cottage-industry-sized tanners used Western production techniques such as chrome and vegetable leather tanning, and an ecosystem developed where most of the processing took place along the river, while wholesalers and shops set up base in Asakusabashi and Kuramae. Arakawa and Edogawa Rivers were also home to many leather factories because of the basic fact that tanners need a lot of water in the production process.

STORYBOOK

One such factory in Sumida is Ogasawara tannery on the banks of the Arakawa River, which was established in 1903.

'We moved to this land after the Great Kantō Earthquake in Tokyo. Our peak was probably in the 1950s and '60s, when we were six times bigger than now. During wartime, we mainly made gloves – military gloves for soldiers and gloves for workers. Then, around the 1980s, there was a boom in leather products – people wore Japanese-made leather jackets,' explains owner Takayuki Ogasawara.

The factory is impressive, with hides being processed on each floor with giant wooden dye barrels. Owing to the skill of the tanners, they also export to high fashion brands.

From Burakumin to Bourgeois

The recent trend in leatherware is related to a wider interest in artisanal quality riding on the back of a 'craft boom' among urban consumers. However, historically, the leather trade was associated with an untouchable class known as *eta* and *hinin* then, and *burakumin* now, with the largest community around where Imado is now. They are considered to be the descendants of people working in leather and meat slaughterhouses, considered taboo by Buddhist values as they involved in the taking of lives. They were compelled to reside in designated areas as an outcaste minority.

According to scholar John Porter at the Tokyo University of Foreign Studies, the term *'burakumin'* was not a word that was used in premodern Japan, rather, it came into use after the 1868 Meiji Restoration. 'During both the Tokugawa and Meiji periods, most of the people living there performed trades related to the disposal of deceased livestock and production and sale of leather and leather goods.'

Even after the abolishment of the caste system, discrimination persisted, particularly in terms of employment and marriage; as such, it's rare that people identify as *burakumin* themselves, and it's not an ethnic, racial or religious identity. In the '70s, lists used by companies to vet possible employees surfaced.

In 2019, the Ministry of Justice revealed that 15.8% of the people surveyed said they were concerned about having a partner from a district associated with *burakumin* communities. In 2023, the Tokyo High Court banned the publication of geographic locations of *burakumin* communities as they were used to perpetuate discrimination.

Despite this tarnished history, when manufacturing started to shift abroad, artist studios, galleries and cafes sprang up where warehouses once stood. The Sumida River was rejuvenated as a site of recreation as the water quality improved from a state of abysmal pollution during the industrial era.

Particularly post-COVID, an interest in localism and a rejection of the low-cost, mass-production model has meant that being a leatherworker is somewhat aspirational, rather than untouchable. This trend has led to shops such as And-Leather, which has six stores in Asakusabashi, selling single hides and scraps to hobbyists who want to try their hand at being a crafter.

New Generations

Nowadays, rather than leathermakers' public image, the main issue that surrounds the industry is the ageing of the artisans despite rising demand. Asakusa Leather Department has hundreds of rolls of leather, and they wholesale to designers such as Comme des Garçons.

Owner Eiichiro Amano laments that along with a recognition of Japanese craftsmanship abroad, interest is flourishing – but artisans are declining. 'We talk about this issue a lot within the industry – many craftspeople are in their 70s or 80s now.'

Azumaya is a fantastic small atelier that that dates back to 1914 and is where sixth-generation CEO Maki Kido works on vibrant designs such as bright red, dotted patterns that reference the bubbles in the Sumida. While she says that many artisans have retired or died, she remains optimistic. 'Still, we're opening our doors to young artisans and meeting new craftspeople. I always try to focus on the details and meticulousness. I also maintain close communication with them and can see things others might overlook. We treat our self-branded items like children – with love.'

B-GRADE GOURMET'S ENDURING APPEAL

The evolution of Japan's soul food. By Melinda Joe

ON A FRIDAY night, the line outside of Momijiya, a restaurant in Kagurazaka neighbourhood, snakes around the corner. Momijiya specialises in Hiroshima-style *okonomiyaki* – savoury pancakes filled with cabbage and your choice of ingredients. From beyond the sliding wooden doors, the scent of sizzling pork and seafood from the iron griddle floats in the air – both an enticement and a torment to eager diners who can already imagine sinking their teeth into the layers of cabbage and noodles sandwiched between eggy crêpes.

A hearty staple that rose to prominence during rice shortages following WWII, *okonomiyaki* is emblematic of *B-kyu gurume* ('B-grade gourmet cuisine', a play on the English expression 'B-grade movie'), a sprawling category encompassing some of Japan's most soul-satisfying dishes. The term includes both regional specialities like Hiroshima's *okonomiyaki* – and Tokyo's *monjayaki*, a looser, flatter version – as well as certain styles of *yoshoku* (Western-influenced fare originating in the late 1800s and early 1900s), such as curry rice and deep-fried potato croquettes.

Some *B-kyu gurume* dishes have travelled internationally — ramen, gyōza and *gyūdon* (rice topped with beef and onions simmered in a sweetened soy broth). Others, such as spaghetti Napolitan – pasta tossed in a ketchup-based sauce, allegedly created in post-war Yokohama for American servicemen – remain distinctly local. For many Japanese, these meals evoke deep nostalgia, and the best establishments still attract crowds.

Feeding a Nation on the Rise

Long before *B-kyu gurume* had a name, the cuisine sustained a nation rebuilding itself. In the 1970s, Tokyo's landscape still bore traces of its recent past – former black market districts where wooden stalls had given way to cramped restaurants in narrow alleys threading between buildings that rose from the ashes of wartime destruction.

Amid the economic turbulence that followed the 1973 oil shock, working people learned to stretch their yen. Wages rose rapidly – 20%, then 33% – but inflation rose faster still, pushing the cost of living to new heights. A bowl of *gyūdon*, for example, cost ¥280 when part-time work paid ¥250 per hour, making even humble meals a considered purchase. In this environment, corner ramen shops, curry counters and standing noodle bars were lifelines that kept the city fed while it transformed itself into the economic powerhouse it would become.

By the early 1980s, Japan stood on the cusp of unprecedented prosperity. Tokyo's business districts began to glitter with establishments that would define *A-kyu* (A-grade, or first-class) dining: exclusive *kaiseki* restaurants where seasonal multi-course meals could cost ¥40,000 per person, upscale sushi counters and French restaurants serving imported wines to wealthy clientele.

STORYBOOK

The Counterattack of B-Kyu Gourmet

It was into this rapidly stratifying food landscape that freelance writer Ryusji Tazawa introduced a radical concept, coining the term *B-kyu gurume* as a counterpoint to the emerging fine-dining culture. In 1985, Tazawa published *Tokyo Gourmet Tsushin*, a guide to cheap and cheerful eateries in the Japanese capital, with a provocative declaration printed on the book jacket: 'The Counterattack of *B-Kyu* Gourmet'.

Tazawa wasn't simply cataloguing casual restaurants. His statement read like a manifesto: 'Even if all the first-class restaurants, bistros, *kappo* (a less formal version of *kaiseki*) and long-established tempura shops were to disappear today, I could at least survive. But if standing soba shops, *teishoku* (set meal) restaurants, *gyūdon* places, conveyor belt sushi, and dive bars were to vanish from Tokyo, I could not go on living.'

Tazawa understood the reality he was defending, eking out a living on meagre wages in the 1970s. He sought out the best meals he could afford at local noodle shops, *gyōza* joints, and mom-and-pop *izakaya* – and they were indeed delicious.

Even as the capital transformed at breakneck speed – new buildings, new wealth, new social expectations – people still craved the familiar, comforting flavours that anchored them to something recognisable. A typical issue of *Hanako*, the popular women's magazine that helped bring *B-kyu gurume* into the mainstream, might feature both an exclusive French restaurant and a neighbourhood ramen shop, but it was often the latter that resonated most with readers navigating rapid change.

From Survival to Sensational

When Japan's bubble economy burst in the 1990s, *B-kyu* cuisine found itself perfectly positioned for the times. New publications like *Tokyo Walker* magazine systematised the hunt for exceptional cheap eats, while television programmes began featuring no-frills eateries beloved by locals. In the late 1990s, the concept of *B-kyū gurume* evolved with a new regional spin – driven in part by the popularity of local ramen styles – as communities began promoting inexpensive hometown dishes as a way to attract tourists.

By the early 2000s, the *B-kyu* phenomenon had entered a new phase. The food once associated with survival had become a source of pride, curiosity and even adventure. Couples lined up at famous ramen shops, while foodies took multiple trains to reach a recommended curry restaurant hidden in an underground shopping complex. The rise of food blogs and mobile phones with cameras imbued these experiences with social currency.

The economic stagnation that began in the '90s has persisted for decades. But the COVID-19 pandemic gave *B-kyu* another push into the spotlight – this time, as an accessible source of comfort and familiarity. Sales of curry rice soared as people rediscovered the satisfaction of a dish that had sustained the country through times of boom and bust alike. Shops selling *karaage* – deep-fried pieces of marinated chicken – and homemade *onigiri* rice balls proliferated across Tokyo, maintaining their popularity even in the post-pandemic era.

The wars in Ukraine and the Middle East have brought further uncertainty, along with inflation that has led to massive price increases. Against this backdrop, nostalgia for Japan's affluent heyday – and the foods most closely associated with the nation's rise – has emerged. The recent *B-kyu gurume* revival isn't just about economics; it's about identity, longing and connection to a time when life seemed less complicated and simple pleasures felt more meaningful.

From postwar necessity to bubble-era rebellion to pandemic-era solace, *B-kyu gurume* has endured. In Tokyo's side streets and shopping arcades, the best *B-kyu* meals still cost less than a movie ticket – unassuming, but offering a taste of continuity in a city that's constantly reinventing itself.

INDEX

47 Rōnin 99, 246-7
1923 Great Kantō Earthquake 77
1964 Tokyo Olympics 111, 125, 205

A

accessible travel 34, 232
accommodation 216-21
activities 26-7
airports 30-1
Akigawa Valley 135
Akihabara 25, 158-67, **161, 162**
  accommodation 220
  drinking 162
  food 160, 162, 163
  highlights 159, **159**
  travel within Akihabara 159
  walking tour 167, **167**
Akihabara Radio Kaikan 25, 159, 163, 165
Ameya-yokochō 24, 171, 179
Ameyoko 180
anime 25, 130, 157, 202-3
Aoyama 25, 116-17, 120-7, **120-1**
  accommodation 219
  highlights 117, **117**
  travel within Aoyama 117
  walking tour 124, **124**
aquariums 188-9
architecture
  Art Silo 86
  Bank of Japan Head Office 61, 64
  Bottega Veneta 74, 124
  Chigo Daishi-dō 112
  Dior 124
  Ginza Sony Park 75
  Hermès Ginza 74
  Kyū Asakura House 97
  Marunouchi Building 56-7
  National Diet building 89
  Officine Universelle Buly 92
  Old Ministry of Justice Building 89

Map Pages **000**

Omotesandō Hills 118
Takeshita-dōri 118
Tokyo International Forum 64
Tokyo Metropolitan Memorial Hall 194
Tokyo Skytree 186
Tokyo Tower 240
Tokyu Plaza Ginza 75
V88 building 74
walking tour 64, **64**
Wall, The 86
Zakkyō buildings 164
art 10, *see also* museums & galleries
Asakusa 24, 184-91, 197, **187, 191**
  accommodation 220
  food 186, 187, 188, 189
  highlights 185, **185**
  travel within Asakusa 185
ATMs 30, 224
Azabudai Hills 87

B

Banksy 205
baseball 160
bathrooms 92, 98
beer halls, *see also* breweries
  Ginza Lion 76
B-kyu gurum 249-51
boat trips
  Hama-rikyū 68
  Nihonbashi Cruise 65
  Tokyo Bay 202
books 29
Brazilians 125
breweries (beer), *see also* sake
  Toranomon Brewery 88
  Yebisu Brewery Tokyo 93
bridges
  Engetsu-kyo Bridge 163
  Kachidoki-bashi 77
  Nihonbashi bridge 56, 61, 239
  Rainbow Bridge 203
budgeting 18-19
bus travel 31, 33-4
business hours 233

C

car travel 34
caves
  Nippara Limestone Caves 135

cemeteries
  Aoyama Cemetery 82, 86
  Yanaka-reien 180
Cerulean Tower 110
cherry blossoms 61, 110, 145-6
children, travel with 12-13, 226
  Odaiba 203-4
  West Tokyo 135
Chōfu 138-9
churches
  Tsukiji Catholic Church 77
cinemas 113, 115
climate 26-7, 230
clothes 28
country code 233
courses, *see* workshops
credit cards 224
cruises, *see* boat trips
culture 242-3
currency 30, 224

D

Daikanyama 92-4
dangers 225
daruma dolls 136
day trips 206-15
Decks Tokyo Beach 205
desserts 8-9, 41
digital payments 224
dinner cruises 202
disabilities, travellers with 34, 232
distilleries
  Toranomon Distillery 88
domestic flights 31
drinking 228-9, *see also individual locations,* beer halls, breweries, distilleries, teahouses,
drinking water 231, 233
drinks, *see* gin, sake
driving 34

E

earthquakes 225
  1923 Great Kantō Earthquake 77
Ebisu 90-8, **94-5**
  accommodation 220-1
  food 92, 97
  highlights 91, **91**
  shopping 97

  travel within Ebisu 91
  walking tour 98, **98**
electricity 233
emergencies 225, 233
English-language theatre 45
Enoshima 209-10
entertainment 44-6
etiquette 28, 33, 35-6, 39
events, *see* festivals & events

F

family travel, *see* children, travel with
festivals & events 26-7 *see also* food festivals, music festivals
  Awa-Odori Festival 166
  Bon Odori 197
  Botan Matsuri 179
  Design Festa 202-3
  Fukagawa Hachiman Matsuri 45
  Kagurazaka Bakeneko Matsuri 166
  Kanda Matsuri 45
  Kanda Used Book Festival 45
  Kawagoe Festival 212
  Kōenji Awa Odori festival 45, 133
  Nihonbashi-Kyobashi Matsuri Parade 62
  Obon 27
  Reitaisai Festival 115
  Roppongi Art Night 80
  Sanja Matsuri 27, 197
  Sanno Matsuri 62, 88
  Setsubun 27, 197
  Shimo-Kitazawa International Puppet Festival 115
  Shimo-tazawa Film Festival 115
  Shitamachi Tanabata Matsuri 197
  Sumida River Fireworks Festival 45, 197
  Tanabata Matsuri 27, 83
  Tokyo International Film Festival 45
  Tokyo Kimono Show 62
  Tokyo Pride 27, 227
  Tokyo Yosakoi 27
  Tori no Ichi 27
  Tōrō Nagashi 197

Map Pages **000**

"The first time I saw female wrestling at Kōrakuen Hall, I was in equal parts both in shock and in hysterics. I had a total blast."

MANAMI OKAZAKI

"I loved hopping on all the different express trains going out of Tokyo and watching the world go by."

WINNIE TAN

"After exploring Hossawa Falls (pictured) in Hinohara – Tokyo's waterfall central – I couldn't resist chasing other lesser-known cascades hidden nearby."

LOUISE GEORGE KITTAKA

"Buying my first ever piece of gallery ar[t] mid-walking tour. For the price of a ¥¥ meal, it was mine!"

KIM KAHAN

Mapping data sources:

© Lonely Planet

© OpenStreetMap http://openstreetmap.org/copyright

THIS BOOK

Destination Editor
Selena Hoy

Production Editor
Sarah Farrell

Image Researcher
Lyn Horst

Cartographer
Dorothy Davidson

Coordinating Editor
Andrea Dobbin

Assisting Editor
Clifton Wilkinson

Cover Researcher
Sam Ubinas

Thanks
Sofie Foldager Andersen,
Ray Bartlett,
Gwen Cotter,
Kimberly Hughes,
Alison Killilea,
Ailbhe MacMahon,
Yuriko McLachlan,
Phillip Tang

Paper in this book is certified against the Forest Stewardship Council™ standards. FSC™ promotes environmentally responsible, socially beneficial and economically viable management of the world's forests.

Published by Lonely Planet Global Limited
CRN 554153
15th edition – Jul 2026
ISBN 978 1 83869 970 3
© Lonely Planet 2026 Photographs © as indicated 2026
10 9 8 7 6 5 4 3 2 1
Printed in Malaysia